D1710783

WATER BEINGS

WATER BEINGS

From Nature Worship to the Environmental Crisis

Veronica Strang

REAKTION BOOKS

To my father, who always encouraged curiosity, and to the wonderful feminist dragons in my life, all of whom deserve to be venerated.

Published by Reaktion Books Ltd
Unit 32, Waterside
44–48 Wharf Road
London N1 7UX, UK
www.reaktionbooks.co.uk

First published 2023

Printed and bound in India by Replika Press Pvt. Ltd

A catalogue record for this book is available from the British Library
ISBN 978 1 78914 688 2

CONTENTS

Introduction 7

1 Being Ubiquitous 13

2 Original Beings 31

3 Living Beings 49

4 Nature Beings 67

5 Cultivating Beings 85

6 Irrigating Beings 101

7 Travelling Beings 119

8 Supreme Beings 141

9 Demonized Beings 163

10 Reformed Beings 183

11 Transformational Beings 205

Turning the Tide 228

REFERENCES 245

SELECT BIBLIOGRAPHY 269

ACKNOWLEDGEMENTS 271

PHOTO ACKNOWLEDGEMENTS 273

INDEX 275

1 Aztec bicephalous (double-headed) serpent, 1400–1521, turquoise and oyster shell on cedar wood.

Introduction

In the early history of humankind, when all societies worshipped nature, they expressed their relationships with water via beliefs in serpentine water beings. Snake-like dragons and similarly ophidian creatures occupied leading roles in their pantheons of deities. Serpent gods rose up out of primal seas to create worlds. They appeared wherever water flowed, sparkling in the celestial river we now call the Milky Way, emerging out of the clouds, arching over the Earth in rainbows and meandering across the land in shining streams. They roiled the seas, gleamed in the depths of lakes and wells and lay hidden underground. Spiralling in hydro-theological cycles between Earth and sky, they were the bringers of water and life. Reflecting water, manifesting water, composed of water, serpent beings flowed through the world with beautiful and dangerous fluidity (illus. 1).

Represented in multiple cultural forms – as rainbow serpents, celestial boas, ascending and descending dragons, hooded cobras, giant anacondas and feathered or horned serpents – these water deities were creator beings, totemic ancestors, guardian spirits and lawmakers. When people migrated around the world they took their water serpent beings with them, so as populations retreated from ice ages, 'beachcombed' around coasts and launched themselves across the seas in flimsy canoes, dragons and serpentine beings from the most ancient societies wound their sinuous way around the globe. With all the fluidity of their natures, they shapeshifted as they went, acquiring the colours and features of new environments. Travelling through Africa, they took on the diamond patterns of the big pythons that shared their winding, coiling nature. In Central America, Quetzalcoatl, the great plumed serpent, was cloaked in the bright green feathers of the sacred quetzal. In Japan, soft, whiskery cloud dragons curled like smoke from the misty mountains. In Europe and the Americas, winged serpents swooped from thunderclouds, sparking lightning and fire.

Wherever they went, water serpent beings embodied ideas about non-human powers and water's elemental capacities to shape human lives. Celebrated, worshipped and propitiated, they expressed respectful relationships with water and people's appreciation of its essentiality to all living organisms. For millennia human groups around the world both loved and feared serpentine water deities. And some societies still do.

Yet, today, although the notion that 'water is life' is a well-worn mantra, fresh- and saltwater ecosystems and oceans around the world have been critically compromised by human activities. Dammed, over-abstracted, poisoned by industrial detritus and disrupted by anthropogenically created climate change, water is bearing the brunt of many societies' exploitative short-termism. So too are the other species that depend upon it: since 1970, 60 per cent of mammals, fish, birds and amphibians have been lost in the world's largest ever – and still accelerating – mass extinction event; a million more species are critically endangered; and the International Panel on Climate Change (IPCC) has warned that we are within a decade of irretrievably destructive increases in global temperatures.[1]

How did humankind move from worshipping water to wreaking havoc upon it, and upon the ecosystems through which it flows? How did the trajectories of many societies' relationships with the non-human domain take such a turn? The study of water serpent beings, and the examination of what has happened to them over time, offers some answers to these questions.

A Polysemic Family

There is a plethora of images and artefacts depicting water serpent beings in museums, archaeological sites and ancient and modern temples. Hunter-gatherers painted serpentine beings onto cave walls and chiselled them into rock. On clay tablets, parchment and bark, ancient societies recorded water beings' creative world-making and their central importance in their pantheons of gods. Early

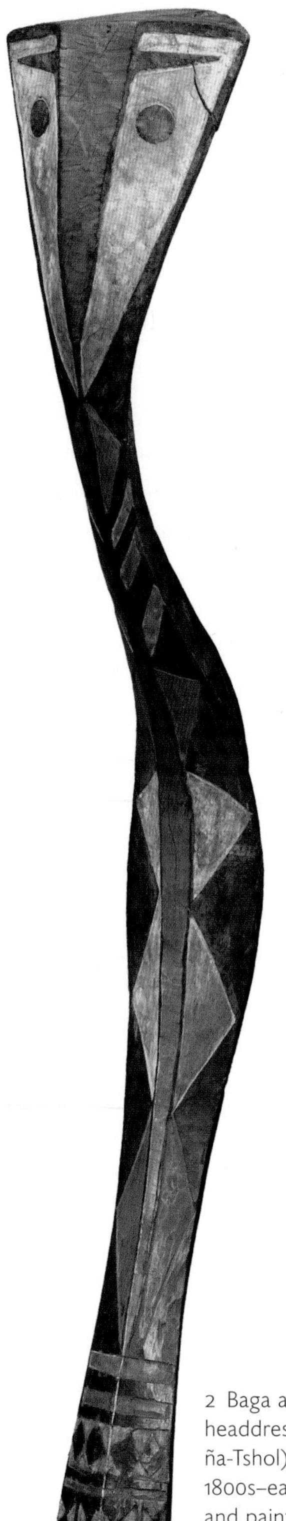

2 Baga aquatic serpent headdress (a-Mantsho-ña-Tshol), Guinea, late 1800s–early 1900s, wood and paint.

agriculturalists and irrigators carved serpentine statues, and built mounds, temples and pyramids to worship them. Rainforest and mountain tribes celebrated ancestral serpent beings with objects made of precious metals, and cast these into sacred lakes to please them (illus. 3).

The result is a vast polysemic family of objects and images containing both historical and cultural diversity as well as consistent 'family resemblances'. Echoing serpents' historical role as sources of wisdom, these representations tell a crucially important story. Understanding how and why water serpent beings were so ubiquitous, and what has happened to them in different cultural contexts, illuminates the critical social, religious and material changes in societies' relationships with their environments, and with water.

Drawing on an extraordinarily beautiful array of objects and artworks representing these beings, this book sets out to tell their story. It follows their serpentine journeys around the world: how they emerged in human history; how they travelled across and connected diverse cultures; how some survived to the present day and why others did not. Through these images and narratives it becomes possible to see how humankind has arrived at a point where the well-being of water, the element on which all organic life depends, has become one of the most urgent issues facing the world today.

Going with the Flow

Water serpent beings swim in a vast aquifer of scholarly material. Reflecting their cross-cultural

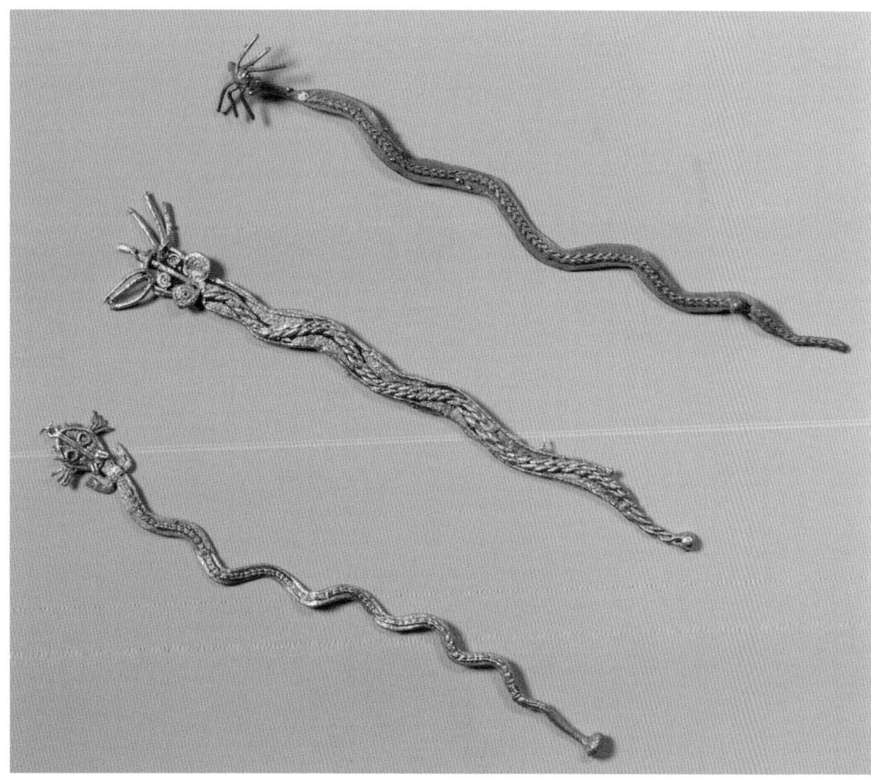

3 Muisca tunjos, votive offerings to ancestral serpents believed to inhabit Lake Guatavita, Colombia, 10th–16th century CE, gold.

ubiquity, they appear in thousands of anthropological and archaeological accounts. They flow through histories of religion, theology, classical studies and philosophical concerns with values and ethics. They carry powerful meanings in art and literature, and in psychological studies of inner lifeworlds. They surface in studies of neurological and cognitive processes. Although environmental studies, hydrology and engineering remain dominated by Western techno-managerial discourses, on-the-ground experience has required many practitioners to engage with belief systems that include water deities and the meanings that they embody.

Following water serpent beings through these braided intellectual streams presents some methodological challenges. Each contains much substantiating material and multiple interpretations, and, as classicist Barry Powell comments on his own discipline, 'Greek myth taken together is too complex . . . to be explained by a single theory . . . To understand it, we must make use of insights offered by different schools of interpretation.'[2] This reality is magnified in a comparative interdisciplinary approach, and it is not possible to do justice to any single disciplinary contribution to the topic. However, pooling knowledge from all of them can reveal underlying patterns of ideas that are otherwise obscured.

Human relationships with water are similarly complex and diverse. Every society has a particular engagement with water and the material environment, but their developmental trajectories cannot be neatly compartmentalized. There is no 'given' linear process of human development through which they evolve. Some choose to make transitions through different socio-political arrangements, to grow their populations and expand their economic activities; others are more conservative in maintaining non-expansive social and economic practices. Changes emerge at different times, at different rates and for different reasons. Ideas, beliefs and practices flow back and forth across cultural and geographic boundaries, and rarely progress in tidy linear form. The big picture is irretrievably messy. Nevertheless, in people's changing relationships with the non-human world there are some discernible patterns that water serpent beings reveal: the kinds of changes that emerge, for example, when societies move from hunting and gathering to agriculture, or when they enlarge and become more politically and socially stratified. As water beings flow through multiple cultures and histories, these patterns are remarkably consistent.

How can the worship – or demonization – of serpentine water deities help us to understand shifting human–environmental relations as well as water's more constant meanings and values? My central hypothesis builds on the sociologist Émile Durkheim's famous dictum, that societies' religious beliefs and practices reflect their particular socio-political arrangements.[3] I suggest that a third factor is needed to triangulate Durkheim's view. People's beliefs and values are co-constituted by how they engage materially with their environments, and by the extent to which human agency supersedes that of the non-human domain. Changes in the levels of technical and instrumental control that societies impose on their surroundings, and how this affects human-non-human relations, are reflected in their religious and political arrangements and therefore in changing representations of water serpent deities and other 'nature beings'.

This text therefore explores the intensely localized water serpent beings of hunter-gatherers, the stronger emphasis on celestial rain-bringing beings in small-scale agricultural societies, and the powerful hydro-cyclical serpent deities of major irrigation societies. It charts how water beings transformed as societies centralized and urbanized, developed hierarchical class systems and further intensified their control over the material world. It looks at what happens to water deities with the emergence of monotheisms, the development of technical and perceptual dominion over the non-human world, and major religious conflicts between 'pagan' and new cosmological beliefs. It considers how scientific ideas changed people's thinking about the material environment and its processes.

In many – particularly Western – societies, as human–environmental relationships changed, water serpent beings underwent key transitions. They ceased to have a central role in stories of cosmogenesis (the creation of the world) or in generating water and life. Losing their former gender complementarity, they became representative of feminized nature and emotion as opposed to (male) culture and reason. They were subsumed by new deities, marginalized and, with increasing frequency, demonized as embodying an adversarial other. Their sentience and wisdom were appropriated by humanized deities or superseded by scientific 'disenchantment'. Yet even in less sympathetic contexts they continued to find expression, reappearing in multiple representational forms.

In other geographical and cultural contexts – particularly in Eastern regions – they retained a central creative role as bringers of water and life, and as the animators of hydrological and spiritual cycles. For indigenous communities around the world, they continued to uphold egalitarian partnerships with the non-human domain.

In recent years, water serpent beings have become an important symbol of protest, a *cri de coeur* against ecological destruction. They represent the core beliefs and values of diverse indigenous communities and enable them to critique the exploitative practices that have been imposed on their homelands. Providing, as they always have, imaginative ways to express non-human agency, and the needs and interests of all species, water serpent beings help to articulate the passionate concerns of indigenous and other environmental activists who argue that all societies must, without delay, re-establish more sustainable lifeways.

In their most important role ever, contemporary water beings give the non-human world, and all of its inhabitants, a voice in the discussions and decisions that will shape the future of all living kinds.[4] At a time when major organizations – the United Nations, the World Bank, NGOs and multiple governments – are being forced to recognize the urgency of these issues, water serpent beings, rising up from deep historical undercurrents, have the capacity to connect a vital global conversation about water.

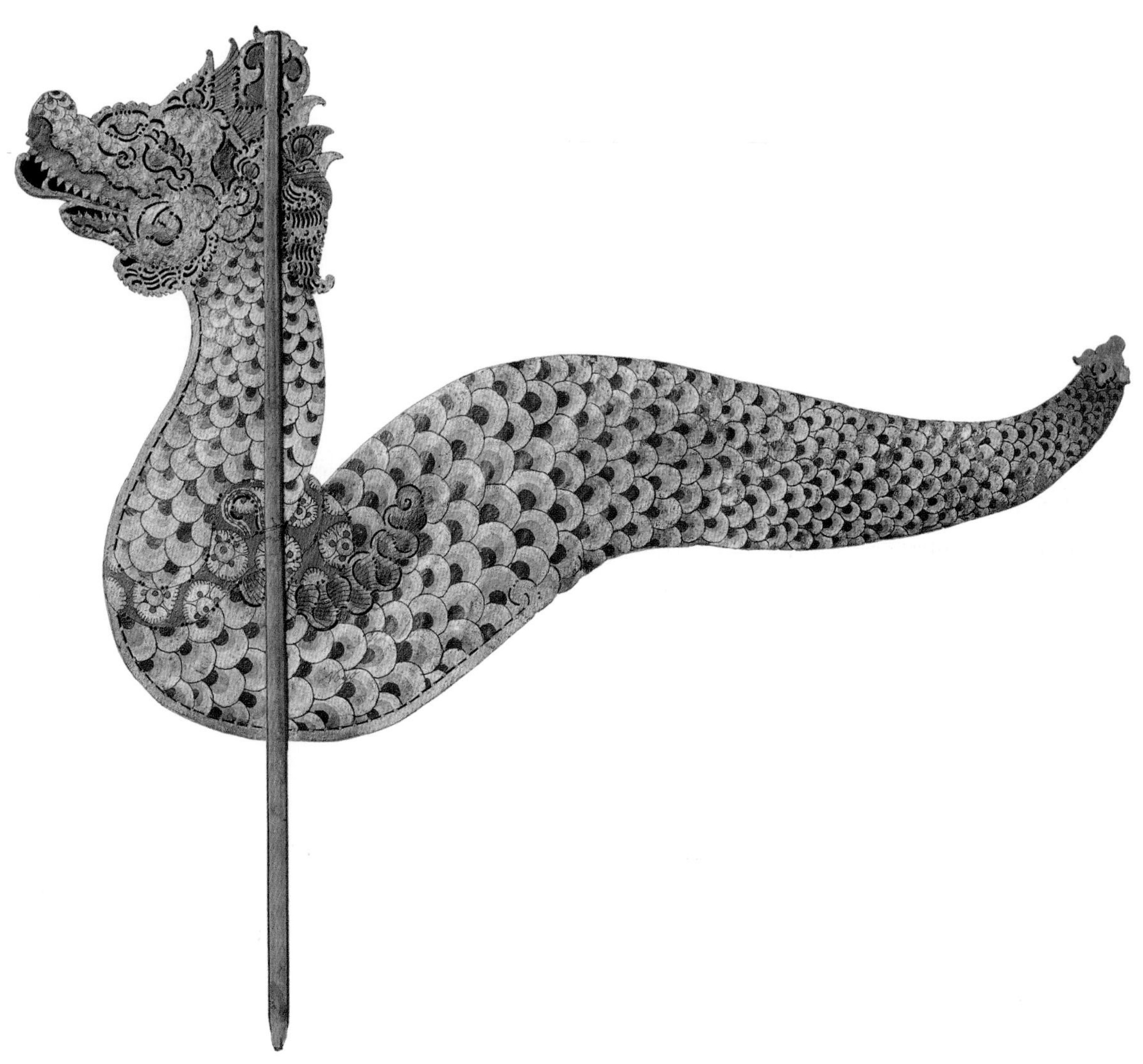

4 Shadow puppet of the character Nagaraja (serpent king), Java, late 1700s–early 1800s, painted hide, bamboo and gold leaf.

1
Being Ubiquitous

Why did water serpent beings appear so ubiquitously in early human history? And why have they resurfaced so persistently over time? Part of the answer, obviously, is that such deities manifested the power of the world's most essential element. But they also travelled well and had ample opportunity to do so. Stephen Oppenheimer's long-term genetic studies show populations moving in concert with ice ages, global warming and rising and falling sea levels.[1] Migrants carried their cultural narratives and practices with them, exchanging them with other groups. Even firmly localized hunting and gathering societies had wider trading networks: stone axes were traded across Australia, and its northern communities were involved in overseas trade with Macassan seafarers.[2] There were lively circulations of shells and beads through the *kula* rings of the Pacific.[3] Ideas and goods flowed from India across Asia.[4] Societies exchanged crops, pottery, cloth, animals and other products along extensive trade routes, and emerging empires expanded and colonized large areas of the globe. Thus, there were multiple social, economic and spatial channels through which ideas, objects and stories could flow.

Along these channels water serpent beings travelled from the ancient world into Africa, and into Europe via ancient Greece and Rome.[5] The slave trade brought 'snake worship' from Africa to the West Indies and parts of Central and South America, and beliefs about serpent beings flowed through the Americas into the continent's most northerly regions.[6] India generated the *nagās* that became Chinese dragons, and Chinese expansion carried serpentine water beings across Southeast Asia (illus. 4).[7]

Such processes are both spatial and temporal. Over time, new narratives and interpretations flow into and transform existing religious beliefs. In being written down, oral traditions sometimes become 'history'. Old Testament writers borrowed from Canaanite narratives describing the storm god Baal and the seven-headed sea serpent Leviathan, and from Mesopotamian flood stories: for example a Babylonian cuneiform tablet dating from about 1850 BCE describes the building of a large boat much like Noah's Ark.[8] New Testament authors reformulated these ideas, as well as drawing on Graeco-Roman religious beliefs and practices.[9] Ideas from the ancient world also influenced Celtic traditions.[10] Scandinavia's Eddic poems preserved much of that region's earliest mythology, and the early Vedic texts influenced the Mahābhārata in India, and the Gāthā, the later Avesta, the Pahlavi treatises and the 'Books of Kings' in Iran.[11]

As this implies, key narrative tropes accompanied water serpent beings in their spatio-temporal travels. Along with recurrent serpent imagery, literature from the ancient world also contained creation stories, the Fall of Man, trees of life and quests for immortality.[12] Critically, in a series of narrative transitions, some ideas about serpentine deities bringing water and life were reconfigured to compose the destructive death-bringing serpent in the Garden of Eden.[13]

Religious ritual practices similarly borrowed from earlier forms. Egyptian rituals propitiating serpent deities were echoed in later Greek ceremonies, and these practices may even have influenced the rituals described in the Last Supper.[14] For example, 'serpent worship' persisted among the Ophites, who kept living snakes in chests and enticed them out to fold themselves around the sacramental bread. The bread was then distributed among the worshippers, who were allowed to kiss the serpent, and this 'Eucharist' concluded with a hymn sung through the serpent to the Supreme Father.[15]

As with other objects, the movement of images and artefacts representing water serpent beings through multiple cultural and historical contexts constituted a fluid 'social life' in which they acquired new forms, meanings and values.[16]

> Certain images and motifs are repeatedly drawn from a pretheological mythology and pool of imagery, and are appropriated to a new but related use. In this way layers of interchangeable or associated meaning accrue to an image. Especially rich in this regard, for example, is the vast symbol language developed over time to express ideas related to water.[17]

In this way, the polysemic family of artefacts and imagery representing water serpent beings around the world appears, appropriately, like a pit of snakes, with ideas and narratives winding around and crossing over and under each other.

Materialities

Although dependence on water and the diffusion and intergenerational transmission of beliefs are important parts of the picture, they are not sufficient to explain the extraordinary ubiquity of water serpent beings and their associated meanings (illus. 5). The human mind reaches out and makes imaginative use of the material world.[18] Recurrent symbolic themes and ideas arise from shared cognitive and sensory processes of engagement, and the reality that elements of the physical world also share common material properties and behaviours.[19] Water, in every context, retains its unique characteristics. This suggests that water serpent beings are generated not only by human phenomenological experience but by water itself.

As rock art sites in Africa, the Americas and Australia demonstrate, serpentine representations of water have been integral to creative expressions throughout human history,[20] with recent uranium–thorium dating techniques suggesting that such artwork may date back to Neanderthal populations. Sometimes abstract and personified forms

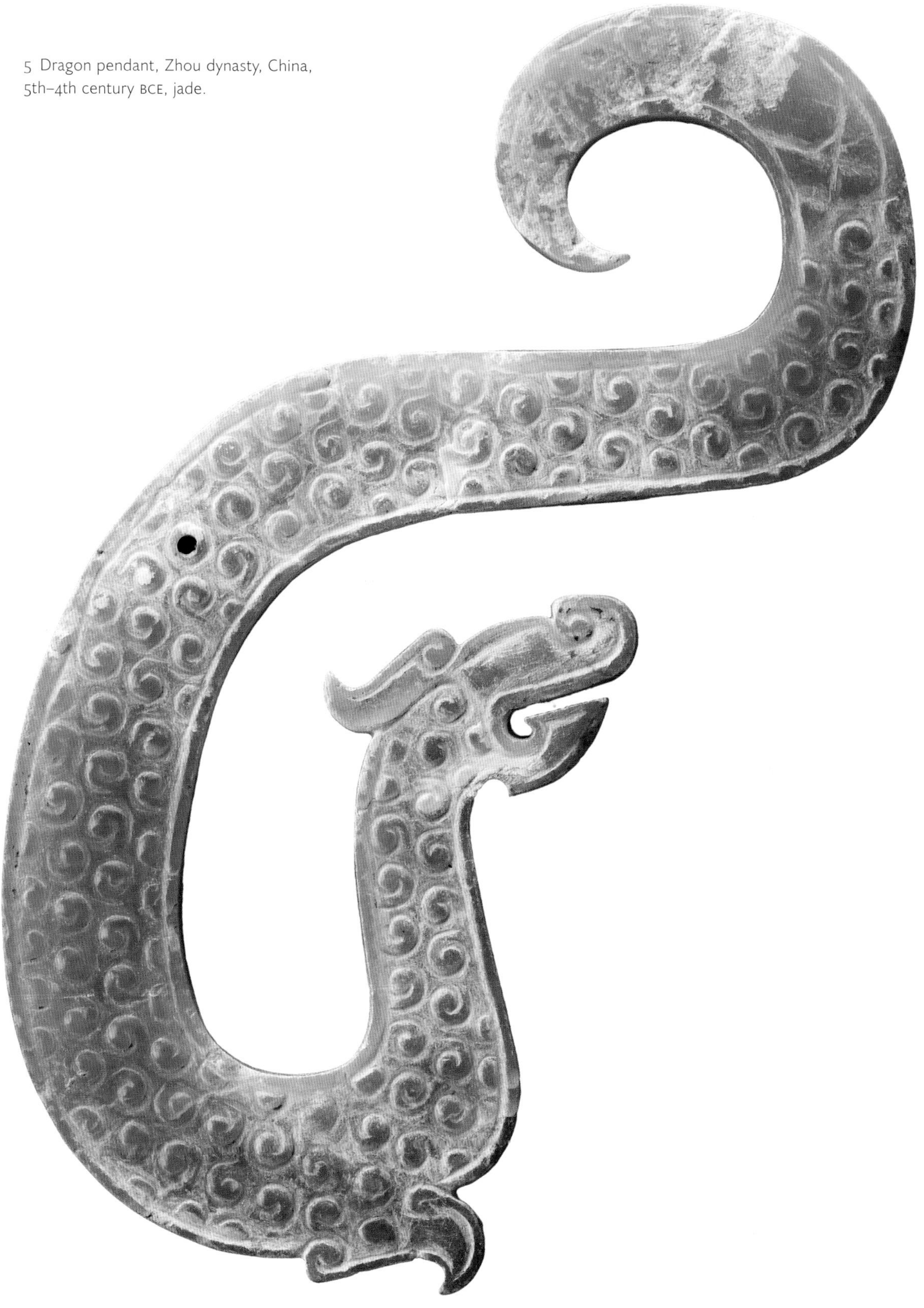

5 Dragon pendant, Zhou dynasty, China, 5th–4th century BCE, jade.

of water imagery are brought together. For example, a horned serpent being at Nine Mile Canyon in Utah has a classic water spiral attached (illus. 6).[21]

More abstract fluid images – zigzags, spirals and concentric circles – also appear in ancient African rock art, in the well-known Egyptian hieroglyph for water and in Neolithic tombs such as those at Gavrinis in Brittany (*c.* 5500 BCE) and Newgrange in Ireland (*c.* 3200 BCE). These are highly condensed symbols: a form of visual shorthand whose meanings would be readily understood by small communities with a shared knowledge base, but whose deeper meanings are not explicit.[22] However, it has been suggested that the serpentine spirals at Newgrange, as well as referring to water, express Celtic ideas about 'the never-ending cycle of infinitude'.[23]

Combinations of highly condensed images and more literal representations are common in hunter-gatherer art traditions. Aboriginal Australian rock art paintings, thought to be at least 30,000 years old, therefore shift between abstract patterns representing ancestral water beings and those depicting them in explicitly figurative form (illus. 7). Demonstrating the extraordinary cultural continuities maintained by indigenous communities in Australia, these kinds of representations pertain in recent and contemporary bark paintings, body art and ritual practices.[24] Similar combinations of abstract water, rainbow patterns and figurative beings appear in late Stone Age African rock art, for example in the cave paintings in the Chongoni sites near Dedza in Malawi.

As more elaborate art-making technologies developed, water serpent beings were represented in multiple objects, appearing in the paraphernalia of priests and shamans and in the magnificent adornments of the kings, pharaohs and emperors

6 Fremont culture spiral-horned serpent petroglyph, Nine Mile Canyon, Utah, *c.* 950–1250 CE.

7 Mawalan Marika, *The Wawilag Sisters and Yulungurr, the Rainbow Serpent*, 1959, bark and ochre.

believed to be descended from the gods and/or to have divine powers (illus. 8). However, key family resemblances link the earliest rock art images with later representational forms. All such images and objects are shaped by water's material properties. Water beings are invariably serpentine. They share the colours of local waters – turquoise and blue, green and brown – or the colours of the rainbow. They are depicted or described as shining and glittering like water, and many emerge from clouds or are surrounded by water.

These formal connections with the fluid materialities of water are a vital clue to water serpent beings' extraordinary ubiquity and persistence. They are not merely 'about' water, they are in essence composed of water, reflecting the way that humans think *with* the material world and make creative use of it in composing ideas. To borrow the essence of Claude Lévi-Strauss's phrase, water is 'good to think'.[25] Its fluid properties enable people to imagine concepts of flow, movement, time, change and transformation, all of which are vital in composing cosmological understandings of dynamic social and material processes, and the capacities of water to generate life.

Following this material logic, it is unsurprising to find that water serpent beings absorb the physical characteristics of local flora and fauna. They embody features from crocodiles, wolves, jaguars, birds, ungulates, elephants, water lilies/lotuses and fish. Archaeologist Paul Taçon suggests, for example, that some images of the Australian Rainbow Serpent suggest a morphological resemblance to a pipefish found in northern Australia.[26] The *makara*, a water serpent being that appears across Asia, typically incorporates features from the Indian crocodile, lotus plants and elephants.[27]

However, snakes, with their serpentine bodies, provide the major formal ingredient in the composition of water beings, demonstrating a further characteristic of human cognition: the propensity to associate things that bear 'likenesses' to each other. Making such connections between things is described as 'apophenia', and while extreme forms represent dysfunctional attempts to connect unrelated phenomena, efforts to discern consistent visual relationships between things are a normal part of human sense-making.[28]

While formal physical likenesses are key, behavioural resonances are equally important. Snakes swim in water and wriggle across the land, mimicking the sinuous meanders of watercourses. They share water's ability to slip down through crevices into hidden watery underworlds. They emerge from hibernation alongside annual floods, and many lay eggs in shallow nests so that their hatchlings

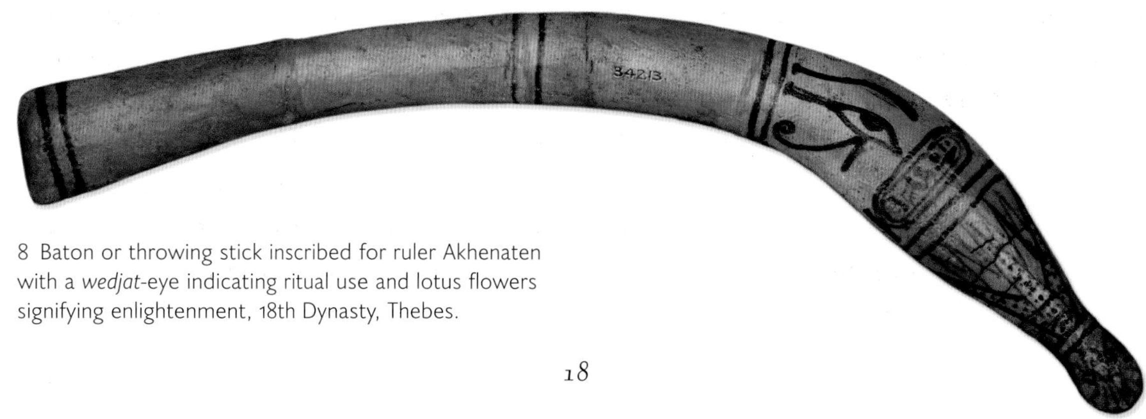

8 Baton or throwing stick inscribed for ruler Akhenaten with a *wedjat*-eye indicating ritual use and lotus flowers signifying enlightenment, 18th Dynasty, Thebes.

9 Chinese dragon with arched back, Summer Palace, Beijing, bronze.

surface from the earth with the rains. In shedding their skin, they appear to 'rejuvenate' themselves, lending intuitive logic to their associations with a (re)generative element and immortality.

These likeness-based connections are readily apparent in the recurrence of rainbow serpents in diverse cosmologies. In Africa and Australia rainbow serpent beings echo the bright colours of local snakes, control the rain and act as guardians of water.[29] The Chinese dragon 'is bent and curved like a bow and, like the sky dome itself, hovers over the aerial hemisphere'.[30] In fact the Chinese term for dragon, *lung* or *luoong*, literally means 'bow', and the arched back commonly seen in objects and images representing Eastern dragons refers directly to their rainbow origins (illus. 9).

Associative thinking also produces homologues, in which the most familiar primary model, the human body, is transposed outwards, to imagine the 'mouths' of caves, the 'bowels' of the earth and the 'eye' of the storm, among others. Especially relevant is a robust association between phallic imagery, the life-generating powers of water and serpent beings. Dennis Slifer observes that 'In mythology worldwide, the serpent is a common metaphor for fertility and sexual activity, including the act of creation,' and 'ritual vessels used in Crete resembled a vagina with a snake crawling inside.'[31] Philip Gardiner and Gary Osborn note a common belief that the ouroboros, with its tail in its mouth, similarly represents the unification of male and female creative powers in an infinite reproductive cycle.[32]

There is also a longstanding representational association between water serpent beings and the lotus (Nelumbo) or water lily (Nymphaea). The cosmic lotus made an early appearance in Egyptian cosmology, when Nefertum, the 'redolent flower', was worshipped in Memphis.[33] Serpent imagery then took centre stage, but the lotus's phallic likeness to the rearing serpent gained a more central place in many Asian narratives of cosmogenesis. 'In Buddhism the flower became the most pervasive symbol of all,'[34] and in Hindu imagery the creative lotus rises up from Vishnu's navel as he dreams:

> The lotus floats upon the water . . . the earth floats upon the waters and thereby the lotus is the symbol of the earth, source of all life and fortune . . . After the devastating flood and between creations (of which there have been many), the first life of a new age arises from the ocean floor in the form of a lotus. In Hinduism, therefore, the lotus is the symbol of creation. In one myth the lotus grows from the navel of Viṣṇu to begin a new creation, as Viṣṇu dreams it while he sleeps floating on the waters. Out of the lotus that grows from his navel as he sleeps, emerges Brahmā, Lord of Creation.[35]

The lotus is also a recurrent motif in Central American water imagery. In Maya iconography its phallic peduncles and rhizomes compose a major ophidian deity, the water lily serpent, which – echoing the hydrological cycle – acts as a conduit between the aquatic underworld of Xibalba, the everyday world of the Maya and the celestial domain (illus. 10).[36] Central American iconography also contains many lightning serpents. Winged 'fire-breathing' dragons represent the airborne aspects of water's hydrological cycle and its capacities to bring both rain and fire.

This capacity is echoed in other traditions: the Eastern dragon, as well as controlling water, is strongly associated with thunder and lightning,[37] and the fiery nature of dragons is often foregrounded in European narratives. For early human societies the lightning zigzagging out of rainclouds offered logical associations between water beings and fire. As the philosopher Ivan Illich reminds us, 'the substance that is considered "water" or "fire" varies with culture and epoch. And water is always dual . . . The border between water and fire can shift.'[38] Hence the beings commonly described as 'dragons' are true water serpent beings, representing water's material characteristics, its movements through the air and its creative and destructive powers.

There are many positive images of fire-bringing serpent beings, representing relationships with the celestial realm, with the Sun, or with light and enlightenment, and these are explored in the next chapter. But human history has also been punctuated by traumatic volcanic eruptions occurring when there was no scientific explanation for such devastating events. Some produced sunless 'mini ice ages', in which crops failed and populations starved. Attempts to explain such outpourings of fire and brimstone from above resonated with other ways of understanding the power of water serpent beings and beliefs that the deities who personified and delivered rain could be punitive as well as beneficent.

Narrative tropes associating water serpent beings with fire are persistent: there are obvious similarities between biblical references to Leviathan's 'breathing out fire and smoke', and reports of medieval dragons exhaling 'pestilence' and poison.[39] In North America, the Cherokee *utkena*, a predatory aquatic serpent, was said to spew forth fire and smoke, and it was believed that anyone who inhaled this poisonous breath would die instantly.[40] In early Indian religious texts, snake venom was described as fire and malaria was called 'snake-wind-disease', and Sanskritist Jean-Philippe Vogel recorded multiple stories in which destruction was brought about by fiery blasts from the nostrils of *nāgas*: 'Hence the snake belongs to those beings which are believed to possess in a high degree that magical energy which is indicated by the Sanscrit word *tejas* ("heat, fire") . . . The Nāga could cause harm by its mere breath or by its sight alone.'[41]

Serpent beings' abilities to bring both water and fire underline the dual nature of each element: the life-bringing powers of water, and its potential to overwhelm and consume; the enlightening and warming vitality of fire, and its potential destruction. But whether positive or negative, what water serpent beings express most of all is the agentive powers of the non-human domain and its material elements to act upon human lives. They underline a reality that – contrary to dominant techno-managerial discourses – land, water, soil, ecosystems and their non-human inhabitants are not the passive subjects of humankind but active co-creators of a shared lifeworld.

Living Water

While water serpent beings personify the powers of water (and fire) in the form of animate and sentient beings, there is considerable variety in what societies consider to be 'living'.[42] Science confines this

10 Aztec Xuihcoatl (lightning/fire serpent), Texcoco, 1300–1521, stone.

category to biological organisms, but throughout human history people have believed that many things, including landscapes and water, can have sentience and agency.

Outward-reaching projections of the mind readily enable beliefs in the presence of ancestors in the landscape, in the notion of watchful and potentially judgemental deities, or the patriarchal gaze of an 'omnipresent' monotheistic god.[43] Water's immanent powers can be expressed through personified water serpent beings, or in more abstract ideas about spiritually infused 'living water'.

Another key criterion for defining life is that of animation: the difference between 'the quick and the dead'.[44] Material environments are alive with movement: wind, water and light all produce an animated world, and at every spatial and temporal scale there is nothing more animated than water. It swirls and pours as mist and rain, rushes down waterfalls and hurls itself onto shores. It zigzags in tiny runnels and meanders in great loops across landscapes. In small pools and vast seas, it glitters restlessly with numinous light. It is inherently animated and 'lively', suggesting a power within nature to be self-moving and therefore divine.[45] Such assumptions benefit from the inherent tendencies of the human mind to assume causality and to personify, which has been said to explain the near universality of religious beliefs.[46]

A nice example of personified causality is provided by a Māori story describing how the breathing in and out of the great sea *taniwha* Parata causes the tides to rise and fall.[47] The idea of a vast water serpent being 'breathing' the tides also points to a larger scale of material inspiration: the celestial bodies whose movements have long been the focus of human efforts to discern orderly patterns in the cosmos. Unhindered by light pollution, many early societies saw the Milky Way as a celestial river or – sometimes simultaneously – as a vast generative serpent being. The Chinese 'sky river' or 'silvery way', Yin He, emerged from 'the dual powers of *Yang* and *Yin*, the male and female principles of nature'.[48] For many North American groups it is 'the liquid, conceptive, serpent energy of the universe,' and for Aboriginal Australians the celestial serpent being, like earthbound rivers, is inhabited and animated by totemic ancestors.[49]

There are more specific celestial serpents: in the second century, the Graeco-Roman astronomer Ptolemy described a constellation known as Draco (Latin, 'dragon') (illus. 11). Its leading star, Thuban, was the northern pole star for about 5,000 years, from 3942 BCE, and Egyptian pyramids were built so that one side faced the 'Head of the Serpent'.[50] The constellation commonly known as Scorpius (or Scorpio) appears as a serpent being in many cosmological schemes. In the Arawak cosmos, for example, it is the Celestial Boa. In traditional Chinese astrology it is called the Azure Dragon, and its tail is hooked into the Milky Way:

> Azure Dragon, who presides over spring and thus the ascendancy of yang . . . retains within itself elements of yin, while White Tiger presiding over autumn and the ascendance of yin . . . contains within itself the seeds of yang. Just as the sexual nature of humans carries within itself elements of the opposite sex, so White Tiger and Azure Dragon balance each other. Their dualism is represented in the heavens by the constellations of Scorpio and Orion.[51]

11 Draco constellation, from Johann Bayer, *Uranometria* (c. 1624 edn).

As well as embodying water's generative powers, water serpent beings articulate understandings of the hydrological cycle. 'Ascending' and 'descending' dragons recur throughout Asia: in Vietnam, for example, Ha Long Bay (*Vịnh Hạ Long*), with its vertical karst mountains spiking out of the water, translates directly as 'Descending Dragon'. Chinese dragons emerge from both celestial and earthly water bodies: 'Dragons and clouds summon each other . . . When the dragon hears the thunder it then rises up . . . When the clouds arrive the dragon rides on them; the clouds and rain are moved by the dragon, the dragon also rises on the clouds and ascends to the sky.'[52] Many cosmological schemes contain celestial 'sky' or 'mountain' serpent beings and those associated with more earthbound springs and lakes. Indeed, it is often the task of water serpent beings to flow between and connect celestial and earthly waters. The historian of religion Mircea Eliade notes the plethora of ancient narratives describing giant serpents, ladders and braided ropes linking Earth with the sky, underlining how this narrative trope is carried forward into the early scriptures, in which Jacob dreams of a staircase reaching up to Heaven, 'with the angels of God ascending or descending on it'.[53] The Old Testament scholar John Day notes that this resonates with Mesopotamian stories in which deities envisaged 'journeying between Heaven and Earth on celestial staircases'.[54] Such a cross-cultural array of serpents and sky ladders raises an entertaining question as to whether the popular board game snakes and ladders, with its ascending ladders and serpentine slides, may contain a deeper reflection of human cosmological beliefs than is immediately obvious.

Another contribution to understanding water serpents' ubiquity, and their regular appearances in dreams and trance states, is provided by recent research on the brain. Neuroscientists have established that a particular part of the posterior cortex is dedicated to the recognition of faces and other simple visual stimuli or 'releasers'. All primates, including human babies and lab-reared monkeys, show fear in response to snakes or snake-like images, even expressing such a reaction to just a few curves or sinuous patterns of movement. Thus the discernment of serpent beings in water may be ubiquitous, in part, because the serpentine characteristics of water trigger the evolved visual circuitry of the human brain.[55]

Cosmological schemes centring on two entwined serpent beings are also common, particularly in South American groups such as the Yagua and the Yaminahua, who make ritual use of hallucinogens such as *ayahuasca* to enter otherworldly dimensions of being.[56] In Colombia, Desana communities

12 Twin *makaras*, Wat Pha That Luang, Vientiane, Laos.

13 Dick Price, Kwakiuti, *Sisiutl*, c. 1927, painted wood.

describe the brain as being divided by the cosmic serpent, a giant anaconda. Within this fissure,

> Two intertwined snakes are lying, a giant anaconda (*Eunectes murinus*) and a rainbow boa (*Epicrates conchria*), a large river snake of dark dull colors and an equally large land snake of spectacular bright colors . . . they represent a concept of binary opposition which has to be overcome in order to achieve individual awareness and integration. The snakes are imagined as spiralling rhythmically in a swaying motion from one side to another.[57]

In Central America, where ancient rituals aimed to conjure up 'vision serpents', the Aztec word *coatl* means both 'serpent' and 'twin'. The name Quetzalcoatl can therefore be interpreted either as 'Plumed Serpent' or 'Magnificent Twin'.[58] The serpentine *makaras* that appear across Asia also appear as twins, or as bicephalous (double-headed) beings (illus. 12). The *makara*,

> like its Chinese counterpart in Han decorative art, appears as a rainbow emblem with a monstrous head at each extremity. The Chinese version, with outward facing heads, even influenced the figures assumed by sea and rain dragons in Javanese and Cambodian sculpture of the ninth century.[59]

Representations of water serpent beings on the northwest coast of the American continent are similarly multi-headed. With a wolf- or bear-like head at each end of its body, the sea serpent Sisiutl is often shown with a human head at its centre, locating binary opposition squarely within the mind (illus. 13).

The Good, the Bad and the Ugly

Duality, or binary opposition, is fundamental to human cognition and, assisted by the capacities of water to be both creative and destructive, water serpent beings express many conceptual dualities. These include foundational polarities of order and disorder, and although each historical and cultural context produces its own visions of what constitutes order, a well-ordered world is generally assumed to possess some degree of material stability. As the anthropologist Mary Douglas observed, 'this implies only two conditions, a set of ordered relations and a contravention of that order.'[60] Ideas about well-being are similarly founded upon notions of material integrity or 'wholeness' (linked etymologically with 'haleness', 'heartiness' and 'health'). Remaining 'whole' is a vision of stability at odds with the fluidities of water. Fluidity is formless and disorderly, readily representing chaos – a term that comes from the Greek *khaos*, meaning 'abyss' – and which resurfaces on the other side of the planet in the Māori *Te Kore*, which similarly describes formlessness and non-being.

The political scientist Hannah Arendt suggests that modernity has replaced *Homo sapiens* (wise humans) aiming to live *in* the world with *Homo faber* (man the maker), who aim to act *upon* it to realize particular visions of order. This shift is amply illustrated in desires to control the material environment by imposing infrastructures to reshape the land and direct water flows to serve human interests.[61] The anthropologist Anna Tsing argues that it is this long march to assert patriarchal notions of order that has led to the current planetary crisis.[62] The stories told by water serpent beings in contemporary political debates challenge this commitment to increasingly coercive instrumentality and suggest that there are other ways to achieve stable and more sustainable lifeways. But for societies that depend heavily upon infrastructural control, extreme variations in water flows (exacerbated by climate change, the same infrastructures and poor land management) are recast as 'volatility'.[63] Water fails to arrive, leaving crops and animals to die of thirst. It arrives in unmanageable floods, sweeping away structural certainties. Volatility threatens to destabilize social and material arrangements, inducing tipping points that can lead to what the geographer Jared Diamond describes as 'collapse'.[64]

Other kinds of flows can be disorderly too: just as water can breach physical boundaries with contaminating matter, populations on the move, or flows of information, can carry people and ideas 'out of place'.[65] The fear of foul flooding that expresses repugnance about sewage flowing into domestic dwellings is echoed in the language of flow and pollution applied to other foreign influxes, such as migrants that threaten to 'swamp' local identities, as well as alternate and therefore 'contaminating' political and religious ideas.[66]

Fluidity readily becomes instability, transgressing the boundaries that maintain form. In societies with high expectations that human agency will impose order, water cannot be trusted. Hence archaeologist Matthew Edgeworth describes it as the 'dark matter' of the landscape.[67] The ambiguous marshes that sit between stable form (dry land) and the absolute fluidity of water are therefore literally and perceptually uneasy. Although resource-rich wetlands were intimately known and valued by hunter-gatherers, agricultural societies seeking safely drained and contained land saw them as dangerous and undesirable.[68] Ideas about swamps as fetid sources of miasma and dangerous 'nether' regions had a particularly powerful effect on the Victorian imagination, being conflated with anxieties about out-of-control feminine sexuality and other Oedipal insecurities.

But anxieties – Freudian or otherwise – about wetlands and water, and the monsters that may lurk within them, run much deeper in human history. Even societies less desirous of exerting instrumental control over the non-human world are afraid of water's darker destructive powers, and this fear is manifested in the capacities of water serpent beings to be 'monstrous'.

The term 'monster' derives from the Latin *mōnstrum* (portent, monstrous creature, wonder), which is the base of *monstrare*, to 'demonstrate' or reveal. Like water serpent beings, monsters lie under the surface in every cultural and historical context, and they similarly move with the times, fulfilling the needs of each generation and adapting to changing social and material environments.[69] Horrifying though they may be, monsters have a vital social role. They serve to articulate anxieties about leaving known and familiar territories and entering strange places. Pliny the Elder describes how ancient Greeks and Romans regularly encountered monstrous beings in their travels across their empires, and, drawing on these accounts, medieval cartographers, indicating the margins of the known world, had no hesitation in suggesting HIC SVNT DRACONES (Here Be Dragons).[70] Science may have challenged medieval certainties about the reality of monsters, shifting them – along with water serpent beings – into the imaginative realm, but whether as folkloric fictions or as metaphorical analogues of horrifying real-world events, monsters continue to personify societal terrors.[71]

In ethnographies, as in classical stories, monsters often lurk on the margins. Anthony Seeger's account of the Suya tribe in central Brazil observes that, in their multi-layered concentric model of the universe, the zones ranging from the village centre to the 'distant forest' are associated with particular kinds of persons or activities ranging 'from men to monsters'.[72] Also working with South American belief systems, Peter Rivière points out that although they may appear in the visible world from time to time, monstrous beings tend to inhabit the invisible domain.[73] Anthropological studies of monsters emphasize their cultural specificities and underline the complexity of their social roles. In Yasmine Musharbash and Geir Presterudstuen's compilation of ethnographic examples, Australian cannibal monsters threaten an indigenous community but also unite it and affirm its cultural heritage. Vampirical monsters in Sarawak terrorize villagers but simultaneously explain disasters and uphold taboos. In Fiji, ghosts emerge in response to fears about climate change and its capacities to disrupt a delicate spirit world. In some cases, monsters are rendered benign: for example with colonial change the terrifying Australian underwater *bunyip* becomes an Antipodean Winnie the Pooh. But for the most part monsters articulate humankind's deepest fears (illus. 14).[74]

There is considerable familial resemblance between monsters and the dark side of water serpent beings. Like monsters, water beings are often able to shape-shift between human and non-human forms. Monsters are commonly connected to water, living in underground lairs, in swamps, or in the depths of rivers, lakes and oceans. Both monsters and water serpent beings are hybrid and therefore ontologically transgressive in form, personifying categorical uncertainties and representing 'all that is beyond human control'.[75] Revealing the potential chaos that threatens the stability of social and material worlds, they bring fire and floods, and often have jaws and teeth reflecting their capacities to swallow and consume.

Water serpent beings' abilities to be monstrous also traverse scales. They can lurk within the individual psyche and represent the seething inner sea of instincts and emotions, or they can reflect tensions and fluid capacities for disorder at a societal level, such as the chaos represented by war or revolution ('Après moi, le déluge').[76] At a cosmic level, they can represent apocalyptic events – the Flood, the volcanic eruption, the earthquake, the tsunami. On every scale they represent the capacities of the non-human domain to overwhelm social and material order with the wild fluidity of chaos.

Human mythologies are full of flood stories, possibly supported by long-term oral histories recalling the rising seas that pushed many coastal communities inland 10,000 years ago, at the end of the last ice age. In northern Australia, for example, ethnographers working with groups around the coastline have recorded multiple flood stories describing the encroaching seas that created the Gulf of Carpentaria. But even without a material foundation, the flood is an archetypal metaphor. Whether caused by punitive deities, or by anthropocentric culpability in creating climate change, floods quintessentially represent water's capacities to reduce form to formlessness and order to chaos.

14 Aztec Xiuhcoatl, Tenochtitlan, 1325 1521, basaltic andesite.

Narratives about water serpent beings therefore represent them as monstrous as well as life-giving. A restless serpent being said to lie beneath Japan causes earthquakes and tsunamis. In Malawi, the underground movements of the serpent being Napolo bring floods and landslides. In Old Norse sagas, the ship-swallowing *kraken* means 'something twisted', and in the thirteenth-century Icelandic saga *Örvar-Oddr*, travellers are lost forever in *hafgufa*, a consuming 'sea mist'.[77]

Cultural underworlds are diverse. Writing about 'underlands' Robert Macfarlane observes that, in the ancient world, the dark underworld became a negative counterpoint to ideas about being spiritually 'uplifted' into the light.[78] The underground is often seen as a source of chaos monsters, but it is also the location of springs, aquifers and multiple forms of mineral 'resources'.[79] These may fuel environmental exploitation, but, at least for the people gaining from extractive activities, the ground's hidden capacities to produce wealth have powerful symbolic resonances with many traditional ideas about generative underworld powers.[80]

Water serpent beings are therefore 'a powerful and compressed symbol of human imaginative and cognitive capacity'.[81] The materialities of the world, and of water itself, have a vital role in their formation. Their monstrous aspects articulate societies' apocalyptic visions of chaos and disorder. Yet, in their wonderful and frightening forms, serpent beings also provide ways to manage such terrors, and to recognize that chaos is also a source of creativity. Their protean fluidity contains the potential for new life. The extent to which their elemental natural power is valorized or feared depends heavily on whether societies see the non-human world as a largely benevolent reciprocal partner in events or as a threatening, oppositional 'wilderness' that must be tamed and made to conform to instrumental concepts of order. Changing views on this question have had major implications for water serpent beings and for human engagements with water.

15 Maya cylinder vessel with water lily serpent, northeast Petén, Guatemala, 650–850 CE, slip-painted ceramic.

2
Original Beings

The existential questions shared by human societies are fundamental. How did this world come into being, and – faced with apocalyptic threats such as floods, droughts, earthquakes and volcanic eruptions – can it be relied upon, or is there some eschatological abyss to be confronted? How do *we* come into being, as material, conscious persons, and, when physical form collapses, where does the evanescent spark of life go? Or, to pose the fourth-century query popular with medieval poets: *Ubi sunt qui ante nos fuerunt?* (Where are those who were before us?).[1] Any cosmological scheme must answer such questions, explaining the creation and loss of material existence, and presenting a model of 'orderly' social and environmental reproduction.

Humans have been wonderfully imaginative in composing such schemes, and because water beings are so perfectly suited to representing flow and movement they feature centrally in multiple visions of cosmogenesis. This chapter therefore explores narrative tropes describing the creative, life-generating powers of the great serpent beings through which whole worlds and their human and non-human living kinds have 'taken form'. As always with water, however, there is also a dark side to this fluidity – a capacity to represent death and destruction.

Many archaeological sites depict serpent beings' creative powers, and in early written accounts, which probably recycle pre-literate Neolithic ideas, the most recurrent image is that of a cosmic serpent emerging to create life out of a primal sea. This image is central to the *Enuma Elish*, the origin story of the Babylonian civilization, which flourished between 1750 and 539 BCE.[2] According to this narrative, probably written in about 1100 BCE, the world was a dark primordial ocean containing neither light nor air, only water extending in all directions.[3] But the waters were also the basic matter of the Universe – the essence of life composed of Apsû, a male spirit of fresh water, and Tiâmat, the female spirit of salt water.[4] This notion of primeval chaos and creative potential is echoed in the Hebrew concept of *tohu wa-bhohu*, which describes the formlessness of primeval matter (Genesis 1:2).[5]

In such visions of creation the sky is a firmament that separates limitless waters, so that when the great serpent emerges the world 'takes form'. Land, and therefore material order, is created between watery celestial worlds and underworlds, in which there may be multiple layers or dimensions. In ancient Egypt, for example, the world arose from the primeval waters of Nun, from which the creator god, Atum, 'took form . . . as a snake or eel', as did his counterpart, the soul-devouring Apophis.[6] Thus, 'the serpent was the symbol for duality . . . simultaneously creative and destructive.'[7]

> The serpent in the Ancient Near East . . . was a symbol of both life and fertility, of chaos and death. Such a synthesis of life and death is summarized in a statement concerning the serpent in the Egyptian Book of the Dead: 'Thou art wavering by turns between loving and hating the gods.'[8]

In the Orphic theology attributed to Hieronymus of Rhodes, Earth (Ge or Gaea) is drawn from the water, Okeanus, and the matter that it contains, via a winged dragon called Khronos (Χρόνος, meaning 'undecaying time'), which, embodying male and female principles, generates all things.[9]

Visions of form literally materializing from primeval waters recur in many cultural and historical contexts. In Māori creation stories the world also emerges from fluid chaos: 'European writers have mostly translated *Te Kore* as "nothingness" or "void", but to the Māori mind *Te Kore* is the source of all things . . . Matter has always existed . . . In the state of *Te Kore* there exists unlimited potential for "being" although it had no organized form.'[10]

The Māori ancestor Maui pulled a great fish out of the creative chaos of the sea forming New Zealand/Aotearoa's North Island.[11] A collective process of creating the world was undertaken by multiple *Atua*. These gods, representing each aspect of the environment, are connected by *mauri*, an animating life force, and empowered by *mana*, which is the 'enduring, indestructible power of the gods . . . the sacred fire that is without beginning and without end'.[12] Gods compose human beings by bringing body and spirit together. Among the supernatural beings there is a primal figure:

> Io formed and shaped every living thing from the elements in *Te Kore* . . . Io is supreme and is known by many names: Io-taketake (from whom all things have sprung); Io-matangaro (of the hidden countenance); Io-te-waiora (giver of life); Io-te-wānanga (all knowing); Io-te-whiwhia (omnipotent, unfathomable); Io-matāho (of the flashing countenance) . . . The power of Io moved upon the elements of chaos, and from chaos came eons of darkness, from which light was emitted. From these forms of energy, light and darkness, evolved Ranginui (Sky Father) and Papatūānuku (Earth Mother).[13]

One of Ranginui and Papatūānuku's major progeny is Tangaroa, god of the sea, lakes and rivers. Like other water deities Tangaroa is both a source of life and a potentially destructive force. Though there is a deeper underworld inhabited by Rūaumoko, the god of earthquakes and volcanoes, the sea provides the major 'otherworld' in the Māori cosmos, as the fluid realm from which the world and humankind first emerged, and in which spiritual being resides:

> According to tradition, when a person dies, the spirit journeys over the hills and mountains until it arrives at Te Reinga. Once there, it dives into

the sea and follows the pathway of the ocean maid, Hinemoana, to various distant homelands until it finally comes to rest in the spirit world. The spirit world is the place where the spirits of humans resided before coming to this life and is known as Hawaiki.[14]

In this story of cosmic origins, water serpent beings, or *taniwha*, have a central role as creators. For example, in attempting to reach the Cook Strait from their nearby lake, two *taniwha*, Whātaitai and Ngake, scooped out the bay of Wellington Harbour. Further north, a female *taniwha*, Āraiteuru, having escorted an ancestral canoe from Hawaiki, gave birth to eleven sons who dug the trenches that compose the branches of Hokianga Harbour. She remains there with her partner, Niua, deep in a cave, as the guardian of the waters.[15]

A similar model characterizes classical Maya creation stories, in which 'serpents or saurian creatures were the forms upon which the world rested, between the underworld and the heavens.'[16] In the Maya cosmos the 'Celestial Iguana', Itzam Na, emerged from the fluidity of primeval chaos to carry the world upon its back.[17] Bicephalous in form, it is often represented with the head of a serpent at one end and that of a humanized god at the other.[18]

The other crucial ingredient for cosmic creation is light, which illuminates the universe to create 'a bubble of clarity and order'. Again, in ancient Egypt, 'light, life, land and consciousness' are brought into being by the rearing up of the great serpent, or by the appearance of its visual analogue, the cosmic lotus. According to early hieroglyphs, it is with the opening of the lotus bud that the light of the world is released (illus. 15).[19]

Following its appearance in Egyptian iconography, lotus imagery became an important analogue for creative water serpent beings across Asia, as well as in Central America.[20] The Maya Water Lily Serpent, linked to the aquatic realm and the sacred underworld, symbolizes the ocean as well as the lakes, swamps and canals in which the water lily grows. It is sometimes represented by a fish (*xoc*), but in essence it is a serpentine creature 'capable of transmuting itself into a dragon'.[21] It is also described as having generated all of the other deities.[22] Maya origin stories describe a water serpent being, Q'uq'umatz, who mirrors the green-plumed Quetzalcoatl of Aztec traditions:

> Before the gods made *kajulew*, the sky-earth, there was nothing . . . There was only the sky above and *chopalo*, the lake-sea, pooled and calm, below. The dark and empty universe pulsated with a silence as profound as infinity. In the lake-sea the quetzal feathers which clothed the gods of the water flashed blue-green, dusting the sea with a sprinkling of light . . . In the sky, Hurricane, Heart of Heaven, gazed about at the void of the universe and fretted. Descending to the lake-sea, Hurricane placed the problem which concerned him before Tepew Qukumatz, the Sovereign Plumed Serpent. 'How shall we sow the seeds of creation so that the dawn of creation may come?' he asked.
>
> Finally it was agreed: the lake-sea would have to part to make way for the earth and then the rest of creation could follow. Such was the power of the god's words that they had only to say 'Earth' and it began to form, like swirling mist, before their eyes. Mountains rose out of the lake-sea, sculpting the earth's surface with their

keen edges, sharp as a sacrificial knife. Forests grew on the land, and the water that had collected in the gulleys and ravines became rivers and streams.[23]

Reflecting an understanding that water and light are the prerequisites for organic life, stories of genesis frequently describe fertile interactions between celestial or solar beings and water deities such as the Maya Hurricane and Q'uq'umatz. Throughout the Americas, snakes are commonly seen as intermediaries between the celestial, earthly and subterranean domains, and as generative beings from which living kinds emerge. In Amazonia, Desana hunter-gatherers describe the great anaconda that once contained all humankind as the 'fermentation-placenta'.[24] For them,

> The same energy that animates life in the cyclical pattern of reproduction moves the stars and sets the seasons in sequence. Nearly everything of consequence follows the celestial cycles – the weather, the growth of plants, the availability of fish, the abundance of game – and so the sky is the key to the state of the world at any given time . . . The center of their homeland was determined, they say, by Sun Father, who, when time began, picked a place where his upright staff could cast no shadow. There, at a whirlpool entrance to the womb of the earth, Sun Father impregnated the earth, and from that spot the Desana and their neighbors emerged, transported by living anaconda canoes to the places they settled along the river. Figuratively, the shaft of light from the zenith sun fertilized the earth with the procreative energy.[25]

Enlightening Beings

As well as creating material order out of fluid chaos, water serpent beings are commonly associated with knowledge and wisdom. In being literally 'enlightening', they also express the emergence of human consciousness through acts of 'speaking', providing 'the word' and naming everything. In the Pyramid Texts, the serpent speaks of its creative role:

> I am the outflow of the Primeval Flood,
> he who emerged from the waters.
> I am the 'Provider of Attributes' serpent with
> its many coils.
> I am the Scribe of the Divine Book
> which says what has been and effects what is
> yet to be.[26]

In the Egyptian cosmos, enlightenment was seen to arise more generally from the fluid realm of Nun, 'a personification of the primeval ocean . . . Since the *nun* also contained the potential to create life, Nun was thought of as a *demiurge*, a kind of instinctive movement towards consciousness.' It was similarly personified in Thoth, the god of wisdom and secret knowledge, and the creator of language. Described as a 'divine physician', he was said to have sprung from the lips of Ra or, underlining the relationship between generative power and consciousness, 'from the forehead of Seth after this god swallowed some of the semen of his rival, Horus'.[27]

In the third century BCE, the Babylonian writer Berossus described Oannes (Ὠάννης), an aquatic being in the Persian Gulf who conveyed wisdom to humankind. British Assyriologist Stephanie Dalley observes that in ancient Mesopotamia, the Seven

Sages emerged from the water in the form of carp, 'bringing the arts and crafts of urban, civilised life to mankind':

> Water had a special association with wisdom. This is illustrated by the opening lines of the great Epic of Gilgamesh 'He who found out (literally "saw") *nagbu* – the depths of all things – gained complete wisdom,' in which *nagbu* can mean either the depths from which springs of water gush; or the totality of knowledge. The god in charge of freshwater, Ea, was also the god of wisdom and craftsmanship.[28]

In Greek stories, Apollo, in slaying Python and seizing the oracle at Delphi, both appropriated and reconfigured the knowledge of the serpent being.[29] Zeus (whose pre-classical form is that of a 'kindly serpent') gave birth to Athena from his head, and Stoic philosophers called creative reason *lógos spermatikós*, underlining the fertile relationship between words, consciousness and creativity.[30]

In western and southern India snakes were regarded as 'tutelary deities', and 'the Buddhistic serpent possessed the treasures of knowledge'.[31] According to anthropologist Francis Huxley, 'many traditions describe an abyss of water stirred by a fiery spirit whose light allows it to see. In this state, say the Hindi Upanishads, it looks about itself hungrily – the very activity (in Greek *derkesthai*, to glance dartingly) that gives the dragon its name.'[32]

Enlightenment is similarly central to the *nāga* worship that recurs across Asia. Indian *nāgas* travelled, via Hinduism, Buddhism and Jainism, into Nepal, Cambodia, Laos, Malaysia, Indonesia and the Philippines to dominate the iconography and literature of these societies. They often combine human and serpent form, and are frequently multicephalous, forming an overarching hood of numerous cobra heads (illus. 16). Historically their veneration sometimes included the use of *soma*. Said to have made its way into early Indic religions from the Bronze Age societies of Central Asia (2300–1700 BCE), *soma* is a plant-based intoxicating or hallucinogenic Vedic ritual drink, believed to confer immortality and enlightenment.[33] The *Rigveda* makes a direct link with serpent wisdom: 'the gushing stream of strained *Soma* is akin to the serpent creeping out of his slough . . . We have drunk *soma* and become immortal; we have attained the light, the Gods discovered.'[34]

Water serpent beings were similarly associated with enlightenment in Africa. In Dahomey 'the python god is the god of wisdom, earthly bliss, and benefaction. The first man and woman were blind, but he opened their eyes.'[35] African beliefs that were carried to the Caribbean and combined with pre-Christian traditions in Haiti describe the creative deities Damballah, the great serpent, whose writhing emergence released Earth and all the celestial bodies, and Ayida Wedo, the Rainbow, with whom he 'gave birth to the spirit that animates blood': 'The Serpent and the Rainbow . . . taught the people to partake of the blood as a sacrament, that they might become the spirit and embrace the wisdom of the Serpent.'[36]

The theme of serpentine wisdom recurs in Central American traditions, too. For the Aztecs:

> When Quetzalcoatl the Plumed Serpent appeared on earth, he brought with him knowledge of many things. He showed the people the

16 Multi-headed serpent being, Ho Chi Minh City, Vietnam, mural.

patterns of time, governed by the Sun, and gave them a sacred calendar whose days and years contained the signs of divination. He gave them maize so that they would never go hungry. He taught them different skills so that they became adept in writing, in gold and silver smithing, in jewel work, in healing.[37]

In the Classic Maya period (third to ninth centuries), visionary states and spiritual wisdom were attained via bloodletting rituals (illus. 17). The famous Yaxchilán lintels show Lady K'ab'al Xook pulling a rope woven with obsidian blades through her tongue to release the blood. The double-headed Vision Serpent that she has conjured emerges from a basket of blood-soaked paper. In the jaws of its upper head sits Yoaat B'alam, the ancestor of the Yaxchilán royal line. In its lower jaw is Chac, the Maya rain god, linking the Vision Serpent to water and to Maya beliefs about *itz*, a generative cosmic fluid signifying multiple substances, including dew, sap, resin, semen and milk. Such fluids, at a cosmic level, represent *ch'ul*, a term still used by Tzotzil Maya (in the form *ch'ulel*) to describe the 'essence' of the soul.[38] It also means 'to dream or envision' and 'holy or sacred'. The links between the Yaxchilán lintel images are underlined by the term *itzam*, meaning 'shaman', or 'one who manipulates *itz*'.[39] In another image the shaman Itzamnaaj B'alam II holds a lamp to illuminate Lady K'ab'al Xook's bloodletting. *Itz* is therefore the source of the spiritual knowledge and consciousness that emerged from the primal ocean with the world-creating serpent being Itzam Na.

The presence of a watery underworld of non-material being, from which consciousness and being emerge, is also expressed in the Maya term for death, *och-ha*, 'to enter the water'.[40] The notion

17 Lady K'ab'al Xook conjuring up a Teotihuacan serpent, Yaxchilán Lintel 25, Chiapas, Mexico, 600–900 CE, carved limestone panel.

of 'entering the world of the gods' or other non-material dimensions is common to many shamanic rituals. Access to the nine-layered Maya underworld, Xibalba, was achieved via sacred *cenotes* (large sinkholes containing water), caves and pools in which the rain god Chac and other water beings were believed to reside:

> [*Cenotes*] served simultaneously as sources of water, sacred and symbolic spaces, magical portals to mythic realms, and centers of religious and ancestral veneration. Offerings deposited in them, together with their accompanying rituals, were believed to facilitate communication between the everyday and sacred worlds, thereby guaranteeing the preservation of the natural cycles of life, death, and rebirth.[41]

The glittering surfaces of water bodies providing access to the underworld were represented by the mirrors used in shamanic rituals.[42] Religious leaders could enter Xibalba via the serpent's swallowing 'maw', which is represented as a zoomorphic cleft or fontanel, associating it with knowledge and consciousness.[43] Temples are therefore portals to Xibalba, and this is expressed with particular clarity by the Serpent's Mouth at Chicanná (illus. 18).[44] As in other cultural and historical contexts, the process of moving between worlds and conjuring vision serpents was probably aided by the use of opiates derived from the water lily.[45]

At Teotihuacan, near Mexico City, the Temple of the Feathered Serpent sits alongside the Sun and Moon pyramids. It is decorated with images of plumed serpents which appear to depict their creative role in cosmogenesis and in the regulation of calendrical time. These carvings and the accompanying structures suggest that it was a centre for political authority. Archaeologists found more than a hundred bodies underneath the pyramid, presumed to be sacrifices made at the dedication of the temple (*c.* 150–200 CE).[46] In 2003, an

18 Chicanná, House of the Serpent's Mouth, Structure II, Campeche, Mexico, c. 600–830 CE.

19 Kukulkan, the feathered serpent at Chichen Itza, Mexico, c. 700–1100 CE. The serpent flowing down the pyramid connects celestial and earthly realms at the spring and autumn solstices.

underground tunnel was discovered. It was full of intricate ritual objects, including a miniature landscape with pools of liquid mercury representing lakes or rivers in the spirit world.[47]

Like the sacred water places joined by avenues to ancient European stone and wooden henges, *cenotes* such as the Well of God at Chichen Itza are often linked to key temples. Chichen Itza translates to 'mouth' (*chichen*) and 'well' (*itza*), and it is etymologically linked with not only the origin serpent Itzam Na but the fluid substance of life, *itz*.

Like the temples in classical Greece, Mesoamerican architecture was aligned with celestial bodies so that, at the equinox, precisely directed shafts of light would open up access to the underworld. The light would also enliven the great stone serpents on the steps of sacred pyramids, causing them to writhe like rivers pouring down a mountain (illus. 19).

In arid landscapes, because water can be found beneath them, anthills also feature as ways of 'entering the serpent'. A Maya initiation ceremony requires the subject 'to sit by an anthill from which a large serpent emerges to swallow him and later to expel him through defecation, in the process imbuing him with supernatural shamanic powers'.[48] In India, traditional stories similarly describe anthills as being 'pregnant of snakes', and as the source of rainbows representing the 'bow of Indra'. They are still used as altars in rituals venerating water serpent beings. In both Hindu and Buddhist stories the anthill provides an access point through which serpent figures flow down into the underworld of the *nāgas*, called Pātāla or Rāsatala, which lies far beneath the human world.[49]

In South America, Desana priests use powerful psychotropic plants such as *Banisteriopsis* to re-enter the body of the cosmic anaconda 'gestation snake' so that they can die and be reborn. At night such rituals enable them to travel beyond the Celestial Anaconda (the Milky Way) to enter alternate landscapes and spatio-temporal dimensions.[50]

As with many Amazonian tribes, this is essentially a transition between coexisting visible and invisible worlds, with shamanic powers conferred by the capacity to enter the world 'on the other side'.[51]

A similarly empowering process of swallowing and regurgitation occurs in Aboriginal Australia, where the life-generating Rainbow Serpent is also the source of all knowledge, or 'the Law'. In one of the indigenous community's most important rituals, the initiate is immersed in the water embodying this most powerful serpent being. By 'passing through the Rainbow' they become a 'clever doctor', with access to secret, sacred knowledge, including that required for rainmaking rituals.

Such journeys to other worlds empower shamans, enabling them to take leading roles as what Edwin Krupp describes as 'ecological brokers' who act as intermediaries with supernatural forces and guide their communities' relationships with the non-human world.[52] In some cultural and historical contexts, resonating with ideas about *itz* in Maya beliefs, there is a focus on fluid substances relating to serpent beings, suggesting that ingesting these provides entry into other worlds:

> *The Saga of the Volsungs* recounts eerie stories whose roots reach back into European prehistory . . . The account of Sigmund and his son Sinfjotli in the forest, and others like it in the saga, reflect the uncertain boundaries between nature and culture and between the world of men and the world of the supernatural. The saga's frequent descriptions of crossings of these borders reveal glimpses not only of fears and dreams but also of long-forgotten beliefs and cultic practices. Not least among these is Sigurd's tasting the blood of the dragon, thereby acquiring the ability to understand the speech of birds.[53]

The Norse Odhrerir cauldron was said to contain, in the form of mead, the blood of the 'wise' Kvasir, who had been created from the spittle of the Aesir and Vanir gods. The *Prose Edda* suggests that the mead turned the person drinking it into a *skald* or scholar. In one story, Odin, the major Aesir god, transforms himself into a serpent in order to swallow the mead from the cauldron and then regurgitates it into a vessel in Asgard, linking the underworld with the celestial domain.[54] The journey between Nordic otherworlds is described in the epic *Draumkvedet*:

> I have travelled over sacred seas
> And over steep valleys,
> I hear the water, and see the unknown,
> Which flows beneath the earth.
> I have travelled in the sky
> And fallen down beneath the black ditch,
> I have seen the hot hell
> And a part of the Celestial Empire.[55]

Celtic societies made similar use of cauldrons, whose function as water vessels sympathetically echoed that of the holy wells believed to provide access to the underworld. Major goddesses such as Ceridwen and Brigid were 'keepers of the cauldron' (later reframed as a chalice or cup), and drinking from the 'cauldron of rebirth' was 'a metaphor for receiving great healing, fertility and sustenance'.[56]

In other contexts, as with the lotus bud emerging from the primal sea, the emphasis was on light, and the 'fiery' serpent beings who brought wisdom

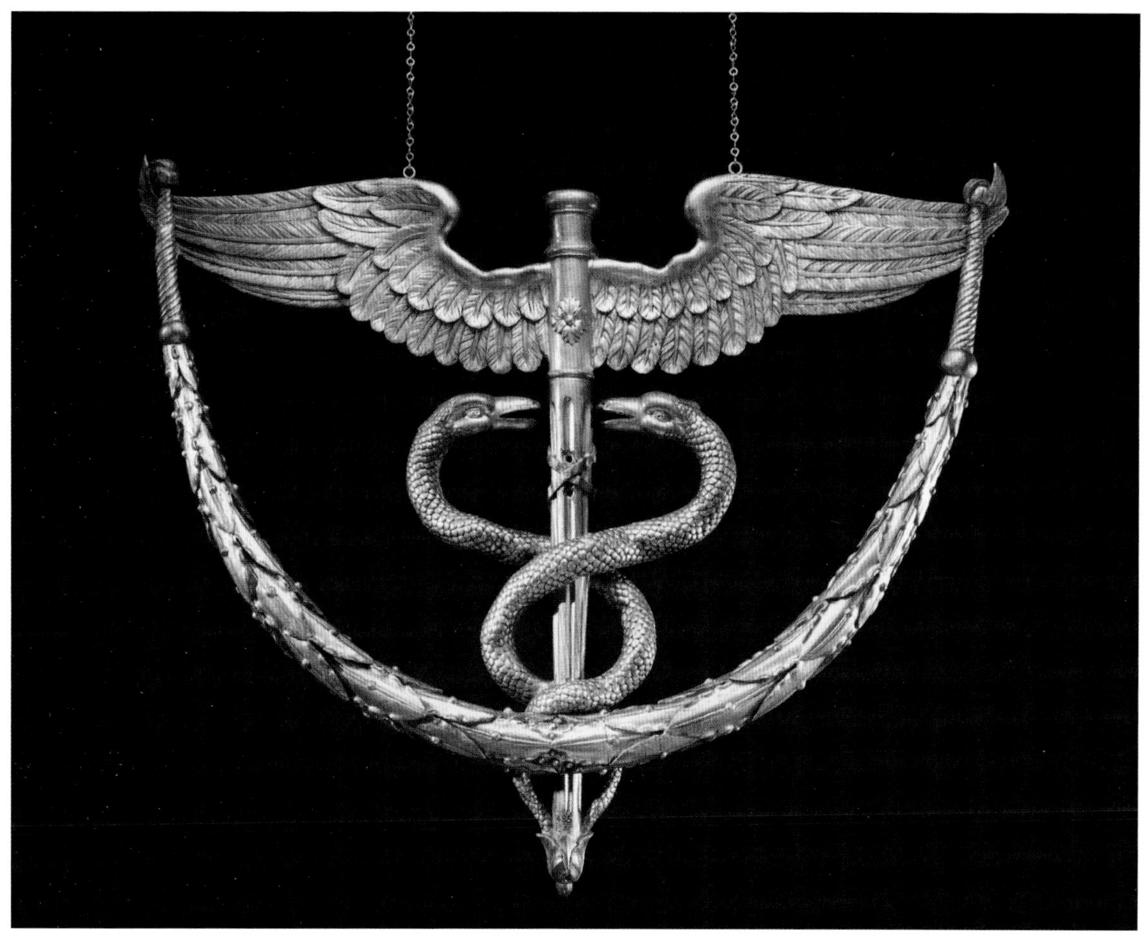

20 Winged caduceus, apothecary's shop sign, France, 1840–1910, gilt wood and plaster.

and enlightenment. As noted in the previous chapter, fire and water have not always been seen as distinct elemental categories. Although fiery serpents, like fire-breathing dragons, may not seem immediately aquatic, they are part of the hydro-theological cycle carrying light and consciousness between celestial and earthly realms. Fiery serpents appeared in Egyptian iconography from the early dynastic period to the Graeco-Roman era. On the tomb of Rameses IV, Nesret, the personification of flame, is represented as a rearing cobra. Her role, like that of similar goddesses such as Isis (also represented in serpentine form), was to assist Osiris in illuminating the darkness of the underworld.[57] Like the celestial Nut, the goddess Hathor, associated with motherhood and fertility, is sometimes represented with bovine characteristics, signifying love and nurturance, but with such generative capacities she is also 'a fiery solar deity ... of many colours', and 'an instrument of divine energy and power'.[58]

Recognition of the vital links between light, water and life itself led naturally to an association between serpent beings and health, and literary historian Karen Joines observes that ancient Egyptian ideas carried over into Greek narratives. 'The Greek goddess of health, Hygieia, could be represented by a serpent', and it was 'probably Egypt who handed down to Greece the serpent-sceptre, or the caduceus, and the staff of Aesculapius, the god of medicine.'[59] Aesculapius' medical knowledge was regarded as the 'the wisdom of the serpent', and the twin snakes of the caduceus are still one of the most prevalent representations of their healing powers (illus. 20).[60]

Visions of 'enlightening' serpents persisted in monotheistic religions. Judean seals from the eighth century BCE depict 'flying asps'.[61] The earlier biblical texts, written between 1200 and 165 BCE, offered positive representations of light-bringing serpent beings in the form of *seraphim* or *saraphs*, the 'burning ones' whose thunderous voices shook the temples (Isaiah 6:2–6). Though recast as angels and 'divine messengers', these celestial beings were initially described as 'fiery serpents' (Numbers 21:6–8).

The second book of Enoch, possibly from the first century BCE,[62] describes celestial serpents that represent both water and 'flying elements of the sun', as implied by their Greek name, *chalkydri*, which combines *khalkós* (copper or brass) and *hýdra* (water serpent).[63] Their enlightening role was well understood by medieval scholars. As the philosopher/theologian Thomas Aquinas put it:

> The name 'Seraphim' does not come from charity only, but from the excess of charity, expressed by the word ardour or fire. Hence Dionysius . . . expounds the name 'Seraphim' according to the properties of fire, containing an excess of heat. Now in fire we may consider three things.
>
> First, the movement which is upwards and continuous. This signifies that they are borne inflexibly towards God.
>
> Secondly, the active force which is 'heat', which is not found in fire simply, but . . . is signified by the action of these angels, exercised powerfully upon those who are subject to them, rousing them to a like fervour, and cleansing them wholly by their heat.
>
> Thirdly, we consider in fire the quality of clarity, or brightness; which signifies that these angels have in themselves an inextinguishable light, and that they also perfectly enlighten others.[64]

One of the most powerful 'brazen' serpent beings appeared when, instructed by Yahweh to make a serpent out of bronze, 'Moses lifted up the serpent in the wilderness' to heal the beleaguered Israelites (Numbers 21: 6–9; John 3:14) (illus. 21). Other images and objects representing knowledgeable serpents included the uraeus raised on a pole that was common in both Upper and Lower Egypt; the serpents twisted around the trident of Jupiter Ammon; the staff of Thoth; and the rod of Hermes Trismegistus.[65] Karen Joines also highlights the politically critical role of Moses' bronze serpent in the power struggles between belief systems:

> Yahweh reveals His power privately to Moses by changing his rod into a serpent (Exodus 4:2–3). Later Aaron casts down Moses' rod before the pharaoh and again it becomes a serpent (Exodus 7:9ff.). To the Egyptians the rod or staff represented power . . . When Moses' serpent-rod devours those of the Egyptian magicians, Moses and his God are proven the mightier.[66]

As well as bringing enlightenment and asserting his religious authority, Moses' rod also conferred vital powers in relation to water. In both Christian and Islamic narratives (in which he appears as Mūsā), Moses uses it to part the Red Sea, enabling the Israelites to escape the Egyptian army (Exodus 14:16). The rod is also used to find water in the desert, creating an archetypal image that recurs in many subsequent stories of Christian saints: 'Moses raised his arm and struck the rock twice with his staff. Water gushed out, and the community and their livestock drank' (Numbers 20:11).

Although the serpent was later demonized in biblical texts, Gnostic Christians persisted in representing it as the 'genius of divine wisdom'.[67] Even in Eden, wickedly giving access to forbidden knowledge, the serpent was still 'more subtil than any beast', 'crafty' and 'cunning' (Genesis 3:1). Joines reminds us that 'The serpent of Genesis 3 represents also supernatural wisdom . . . It knows of God's prohibition before accosting Eve, it pretends to know as much about the tree "to make one wise" as God does (Genesis 3:4–5), it is explicitly described as "subtle" which is generally used to mean wisdom.'[68] In providing Eve and Adam with an awareness of their nakedness, enabling them to 'see themselves', the serpent also brought them reflexive consciousness, leading Matthew to say to Christians 'be ye therefore wise as serpents' (Matthew 10:16).

21 Moses' serpent (Colonna del Serpente), Byzantine, 4th century (placed on column, 11th century), bronze, Basilica of Sant'Ambrogio, Milan.

Taking Form

As well as bringing 'enlightened' consciousness, water serpent beings bring the material form to support it. Whether descending from celestial realms or rising from the chaotic primal sea, they are, in effect, the waters taking form. This Deleuzian notion of emergence is beautifully illustrated by a seventeenth-century painting of a Japanese cloud dragon attributed to Soga Nichokuan (illus. 22).[69] It is composed of clouds and water, and yet it is 'becoming' something more tangible.

In moving from chaos to order, from formlessness to form and back again, water serpent beings have enabled people to imagine the movement of matter and the spirit through time and space. Serpentine transformations that begin with 'becoming' or 'taking form' end in 'un-becoming' or 'loss of form'. Such transitions can be cosmic in scale, with the world emerging from nothingness into being, and dissolving back into apocalyptic chaos, when 'the windows on high are opened, and the foundations of the earth do shake' (Isaiah 24:18). They can also be individual, carrying the human spirit between visible, material dimensions of being and invisible, non-material underworlds or heavenly otherworlds, with an associated creation and dissolution of personhood, memory and consciousness.[70]

Underlining the cognitive logic of thinking with water, serpent beings' capacities to represent transitions between materiality and non-materiality reflect water's physical transformations between tangible and intangible forms.[71] Chinese philosophers assumed that dragons, like water, could be cloaked in invisibility or dissipated like clouds.[72] In the work of early Chinese authors: 'The dragon . . . wields the power of transformation and the gift of rendering itself visible or invisible . . . In the spring it

22 Soga Nichokuan, attrib., *Dragon*, six-panel folding screen of a Japanese cloud dragon representing the elements of wind and water, early to mid-1600s, ink, slight colour, gold and silver on paper.

ascends to the skies, and in the autumn it buries itself in the watery depth.'[73] He Xin defines dragons as the 'living form' of the cloud god, and describes an intricate set of ideas about transformation: 'The "dragon" goes from "hidden" to "seen", and then to "leaping", and then to "flying" . . . this is not simply talking about the travelling state of the dragon, but mainly it is talking about the rules of development and change of everything, from small to big, from weak to strong . . . eventually things will return [to a former state] after reaching their peak.'[74]

This draws attention to the vital role of water serpent beings in providing ways to envisage the cycles of existence of all living kinds. Societies' concepts of temporality are as diverse as their broader cosmological beliefs.[75] They include highly localized hydro-theological cycles, larger visions of reincarnation and the more linear 'time's arrow' of modernity. In all visions of time, however, the material properties of water, manifested in the form of water serpent beings, support concepts of movement and flow.

Temporal change is readily indicated by shifts between light and dark. Just as water serpent beings' swallowing and regurgitation of shamans and 'clever doctors' signify their initiation and rebirth, this process also serves to represent broader temporal movements between genesis, death and revival. A well-known Egyptian example is the sky goddess Nut, whose name 'probably derives from an Ancient Egyptian word for water (*nw*) and her symbol was a water pot'.[76] Sometimes identified with the Milky Way, her titles included 'Mistress of All', 'She Who Holds a Thousand Souls', and 'She Who Protects'. Nut illustrates the upper half of a hydro-theological cycle between worlds. As well as gathering up into her body the souls who become stars, Nut swallows the sun god Atum each day. Engulfed in the watery underworld of Duat, he must fend off the soul-devouring serpent Apep, to be reborn from Nut into the sky each morning, thus regulating diurnal time.[77]

Images of the Sun, personified in the gods Atum/Re-Atum/Ra and Horus, are often encircled by serpent beings (illus. 23). Osiris is sometimes described as Ob-El ('shining serpent') or Pytho-Sol ('serpent sun'). He is also the ruler of the underworld paradise that replicates the above world. His serpentine, encompassing form is described in the Pyramid Texts: 'Thou art great, thou art green, in thy name of Great Green (Sea); lo, thou art round as the great circle (Okeanos); lo, thou art turned about, thou art round as the circle that encircles the Haunebu (Aegeans) . . . Thou includest all things in thy embrace.'[78] Possibly based on older predynastic beliefs in generative beings, Osiris takes many forms, but, along with his female counterpart, Isis, he is invariably associated with annual inundations of floodwater and its life-generating capacities, and with the rebirth represented by the spring.[79] In some narratives this 'green god' is swallowed by his evil twin Seth/Typhon, and must pass through the underworld and escape in order for the cycle of rebirth to be completed. He enters the tail of the serpent and emerges from its mouth, and his reappearance marks the spring solstice. This cyclical renewal is similarly evident in the roles of the Mesopotamian deities Inanna and Dumuzi, and the Phrygian god Attis.

Narratives of swallowing and regurgitation also provide lunar calendars. In the Indian cosmos Indra, the sun, regularly consumes and spits out Vritra,

23 Stela depicting Hotepamun, Thebes, 25th Dynasty, sycamore fig wood. Under a curved sky-sign and a winged sun-disc, the lady of the house, Hotepamun, stands on the right in adoration of a rearing serpent, Ra-Horakhty, and Osiris.

the moon. In Chinese stories the dragon swallows and vomits up the pearl moon to generate rain. Water serpent beings, in various forms, therefore represent cycles of time marking the diurnal, monthly and seasonal cycles that bring the renewal of life.

Being Forever

Nowhere is humankind's hope for renewal more precisely encapsulated than in the image of the ouroboros: the circular serpent that, with its tail in its mouth, represents an eternal flow of death and rebirth in which there is constant renewal – of worlds, seasons, years and lives (illus. 24).

The 'tail devourer' emerges in visual representations in Egypt in about 1600 BCE, 'but is probably much older . . . It carries the simple message that Creation is a cyclical process – creation, destruction, regeneration, or birth, death, rebirth – in which patterns repeat themselves in a series of never-ending cycles.'[80] Major deities are given to making statements about infinite revival. Just as the serpentine Egyptian goddess Isis asserts that 'I am all that has been, that is, and that will be,'[81] the Alchemist's ouroboros announces that 'the all is one' and Jesus states that 'I am the Alpha and the Omega, the first and last, the beginning and the end' (Revelation 22:13).

In representing infinite cycles of life, water serpent beings are linked to ideas about immortality. In 314 CE, the early Christian historian Eusebius wrote that the Phoenicians and the Egyptians believed that the serpent could renew its youth almost indefinitely, and the Egyptian Book of the Dead contains an incantation in which, by transforming into a serpent, a person becomes immortal. 'The cobra, or uraeus, is the Egyptian ideograph for

24 Theodoros Pelecanos' drawing of the ouroboros in an alchemical tract, the *Synosius* (1478), attributed to Synesius.

"immortal", and the immortality of the pharaoh can be described as "the living years of the uraeus". On the coffin of Rameses III is inscribed an enormous serpent, its extremities conjoined to represent the eternal life of the king. The name of the serpent is "millions of years".'[82]

Ancient Mesopotamia provides the story of Gilgamesh, an Akkadian epic in which the hero sets off on a journey to seek out Utnapishtim, the hero of the 'Great Flood' who was granted immortality. Gilgamesh descends to the bottom of the sea seeking the plant that provides eternal life but, when he pauses to rest, a serpent emerges from the water, smells the fragrance of the plant and carries it away, along with the rejuvenating powers that it confers.[83]

In Graeco-Roman traditions the Milky Way gained its name from a narrative about the goddess Hera, wife of Zeus. Her breast milk was believed to confer immortality, and when Hermes and his half-sister Athena placed Heracles on Hera's breast while she was sleeping, in an attempt to gain eternal life for him, she pulled away, spraying the milk into the heavens.

Serpentine water bodies encircling Earth are also signified by the 'world stream' of the Greek Okeanos and by Indian representations of a sky river described as the Path of the Snake, or Bed of the Ganges. In the Norse legends of the *Prose Edda*, the water-dwelling Midgard 'world serpent' Jörmungandr is described in true ouroboros form: 'holding his tail in his mouth, he encircles the whole earth.'[84]

The ouroboros continues to provide a powerful symbol in modern Celtic traditions, in which, cultural historian Samantha Riches points out, 'the long-standing Celtic fondness for dragons has meant that they appear as decorations on many artefacts, especially in the form of the Uroboros, or the tail-swallower, which functions as an evocation of eternity and the ongoing cycle of birth, fertility, death and rebirth.'[85]

It is clear that the water serpent beings, which appear throughout human history, are doing a great deal of imaginative work. They provide ways to describe the creation (and potential destruction) of the cosmos and everything in it; the movement of the human spirit between material and non-material being; the emergence of consciousness; the acquisition of knowledge; and the loss – and potential renewal – of all of these things. Is it any wonder, then, that for millennia they occupied a central place in humans' hearts and minds?

3

Living Beings

The cosmic creativity of water serpent beings in forming the world out of water and light is echoed in representations celebrating their more down-to-earth powers. They embody the most important thing about water: its vital role in the reproduction of all forms of organic life. This is what gives today's water serpent beings a vital contemporary role in debates about sustainability: they are quintessential symbols of the non-human domain's generative capacities.

Some water beings indicate their capacities to produce all living kinds by changing form. Maya *nagual*, for example, are fluid, shape-shifting beings that represent multiple species. *Nagual* translates directly as 'co-essence', and in several Mayan languages 'words for *nagual* . . . have cognates that mean "serpent"', suggesting that all living kinds are produced by generative serpent beings.[1] For this reason *nagual* are often shown emerging from the jaws of the overarching creator serpent.

More typically water serpent beings incorporate aspects of the living kinds that they generate, acquiring features such as animal heads, horns, scales or feathers. This hybridity can be seen in the earliest representations of serpentine beings – generally referred to as dragons – in China, in the Neolithic objects originating along the Yellow River that date from circa 5000–3000 BCE: 'The dragon depicted on a clamshell unearthed at the Yangshao culture site of Puyang Xishuipo already has the composite characteristics of a horse's head, a deer's horn, a snake's body, an eagle's talons, a scaly body, a fish tail, and so on.'[2]

In the later Shang and Zhou dynasties, when domesticated animals became central to economic production, bronzes and jade or bone carvings show water beings with the features of pigs, cows and sheep. With the rise of imperial power in China, representations of dragons began to incorporate more powerful animals, such as lions and horses. By the later Song, Ming and Qing dynasties dragons were highly ornamental, typically featuring the head of a horse and a mane running along the back or tail, the horns of a deer, and bird-like claws (illus. 25).[3]

Gendered Beings

Ideas about the generative capacities of water serpent beings have naturally echoed understandings of human reproduction. Prior to the emergence

25 Dragon screen in Yuantong Temple, Kunming, China.

of the major monotheisms, representations of supernatural beings generally expressed gender complementarity, either through the interaction of female and male deities, or by combining gender in creator beings – such as the ouroboros with its phallic tail and receptive 'womb' – that were androgynous or hermaphroditic, and able to reproduce independently. Such images reflected a belief that androgyny represented a *coincidentia oppositorum*, in which humans and divine beings can only reach their full potential when both genders are combined.[4] Thus the archaeologist and art historian Arthur Frothingham suggested that the paired serpents entwined on Babylonian cylinders in 4000 BCE, which prefigured the familiar caduceus, originally represented a primal god embodying both male and female principles, who propagated life throughout the universe.[5]

Gender balance is often demonstrated in early cosmological ideas about rainbows as generative water beings. In China, the rainbow is a manifestation of male *ghung* and female *ngei* rain deities, and representations sometimes show them in the sky together.[6] Snake queens and dragons similarly provided the complementarity that would later become a more abstract balance of *yin* and *yang*. In ancient China the gender of dragons was ambiguous or variable, but *yin* and female attributes were more dominant. However, medieval literature shows that as patriarchal hierarchies began to prevail, with the rise of imperial power in the eighth century, dragons masculinized and began to represent more *yang* than *yin* attributes.[7]

An example is provided by the serpentine Nüwa, originally a powerful female creator being. The historian Edward Schafer notes, 'A Han source makes her a personification of the abstract creative force . . . "Transformer of the Myriad Creatures". In her cosmic aspect she is also the creator of man.' In later accounts she is linked with a male twin, and 'such divine incestuous pairs are well known among the ethnic minorities of southern China' (illus. 26).[8]

26 Unknown artist, *Fuxi and Nüwa*, 3rd–8th century CE, painting on silk fabric, discovered at the Astana Graves, Xinjiang, China.

27 Mural of Mwali and Thunga at Kungoni Centre, Mua Mission, Malawi.

Eliade maintained that a single androgynous divinity, or original 'oneness of being' (Urmonotheismus), was a common feature of early human societies.[9] As hunter-gatherers tend to have gerontocratic societies, led by both female and male elders, singular androgyny or gender complementarity logically reflects the parity of their social and political arrangements.[10] A similar balance in creator beings characterized the Central and South American societies that flourished in about 1200 BCE: 'The gods of these ancient peoples . . . inhabit primordial waters – Lake Titicaca or the Maya "lake-sea"; they infuse the heavens with their presence; or they are immeasurably ancient and are called Grandfather and Grandmother.'[11] Original oneness is also expressed in the Aztec being Ōmeteōtl, which in Nahuatl translates as *ōme* (dual or two) and *teōtl* (god). Located in what the Florentine Codex defines as a 'place of duality', Ōmeteōtl has been described as an overarching creator deity combining the reproductive capacities of both genders.[12]

Societies maintaining hunting and gathering or small-scale agricultural lifeways still tend to venerate androgynous or complementary water serpent beings. In Australia, the central water being in the indigenous cosmos, the Rainbow Serpent, can be female, male or both. In Africa, for the Chewa community in Malawi, the rainbow is said to be the breath of the python, and their more abstract name for god, or 'the big bow', has both masculine and feminine forms: Chiuta and Chauta.[13] The Chewa people are a matrilineal society that came to Malawi in the nineteenth century, fleeing tribal wars further south. Displacing the local Batwa hunter-gatherers, the Chewa established agricultural practices and made ritual sacrifices of crops (such as sorghum or millet) to multiple nature beings. Their major deity, Thunga, is a male rainbow serpent being, and their sacred ritual dance, *Chinamwali*, centres on his insemination of the Earth Mother, which assures the annual coming of the rains: 'He even makes himself visible in the form of Thunga, the mystical snake as messenger. Mwali and Thunga take great delight in each other's company, and their encounter is thoroughly creative . . . Mwali is our great mother from our distant past, and she cares for us. She teaches us the Mwambo, the wisdom of our people' (illus. 27).[14]

Python worship in the African kingdom of Dahomey (now part of Benin) similarly highlights the role of water serpent beings as primary ancestors and sources of fertility. Male and female powers are called upon to restore order in excessively wet or dry seasons. This involves rituals in which votive offerings to 'my father and my mother' are placed on the banks of rivers or lagoons in which the python god dwells.[15]

The twin serpents in Central and South American cosmologies enjoy similar gender complementarity: 'In Desana shamanism they symbolize a female and male principle, a mother and father image, water and land.'[16] As implied in the previous chapter, Desana narratives are homologous and explicit, describing a 'Sun Father', also known as 'The Progenitor', whose phallic stick rattle or staff (*yeegë*) must stand upright in the 'centre' of a primordial lake/womb called *ahpikon dia*, 'milk-lake' or 'milk-river', and scatter semen into it.[17] In Desana terminology, spit and saliva are categorically equivalent to semen, and 'the act of spitting symbolises ejaculation', while the word for 'vagina', *pero*, also means 'whirlpool'.[18] The multiple origin stories that describe water serpent beings 'spitting out' humankind are therefore readily discernible as analogues for more fundamental processes of reproduction.

'Two-in-one' bicephality, seen in representations of the water serpent beings of the American West Coast tribes as well as in the *makaras* across Asia, is also indicative of gender complementarity. The *makara*'s open jaw, which is often shown generating humans, is typically formed of a lotus plant. The lotus itself, with its 'rearing serpent/phallus' bud and receptive 'vulva' flower, embodies both male and female characteristics.

28 Double-headed water being in the form of a ship, Viking Age plate brooch from a grave in Lillevang, Bornholm.

> Because of the means of reproduction of the lotus plant from a seed that matures within the pod, or calyx, of the plant and then bursts out as a new plant, an analogy to human reproduction is made. Thus the lotus is seen as a plant carrying the potential for future generations and is given meanings of cyclic renewal of life, or regeneration of life, or reincarnations . . . The lotus is associated with the goddess Lajjā Gaurī, [with] a fully mature, open flower as her head and new buds held in her hands as appropriate symbols of generation suggesting adult and child, and womb and phallus, or the potential for new life.[19]

Bicephalism also features in representations of the generative deities of Nordic societies (illus. 28). Influenced by ideas about the 'tree of life', thirteenth-century Scandinavian prose and poetry describe the world tree Yggdrasil, whose branches reach up to Heaven and whose roots reach down into Mimir, the well of wisdom, and Niflheim, a darker underworld where they are gnawed on by the serpent Níðhöggr.[20]

This complementarity is evident in other northern societies. Bringing traditions from Scythia, Greece and Thrace, the Celts dominated much of northern Europe, the Iberian Peninsula and Britain during the Bronze Age, until they were conquered by the Romans in the first century.[21] Although little is recorded about their priestly class – the Druids – it seems that the Celts venerated solar deities, including a gorgon or sun god, and multiple serpentine river beings. According to the nineteenth-century cleric Edward Davies, the priests themselves were described as *gnadrs* (adders), and a poem by Taliesin, a sixth-century Welsh poet, enumerates their titles: 'I am a Druid; I am an architect; I am a prophet; I am a serpent.'[22] Representations of Celtic deities often contain serpentine associations; for example, the Welsh goddess Ceridwen was said to have a cart drawn by serpents and lived by the lake Llyn Tegid, the name of which arises from *lin*, meaning 'snake'.[23]

Like other serpentine deities, Celtic water beings had a central role in generating the 'life of the earth'.[24] The spiral water petroglyphs at Newgrange are part of a structure that, similar to other ancient monuments, aligns with the Sun on the winter solstice. The Celts' most important pan-tribal gods – the celestial deities and the mother-goddesses – provided light, heat and fertility.[25] Miranda Green describes Celtic religion as essentially animistic, founded on the belief that every part of the non-human world was numinous, containing a spiritual presence. Lakes, springs and trees were therefore venerated, and a gendered Celtic cultural landscape of upstanding groves and receptive holy wells was replicated in henges and the avenues linking them with sacred water places (illus. 29).

Evidence of Celtic water worship has been found in temples at the sources of rivers such as the Seine, and in the offerings cast into ancient holy wells. Their river deities are celebrated in many European river names. Dan or Dana is the source of the present-day Danube. Deva ('the divine one') is memorialized in the Dee; the goddess Sequana in the Seine; Clota (the 'divine washer') in the Clyde; Brigid in Dorset's Bride, and Tamesa ('river deity') in the Thames. In Ireland the rivers Liffey and the Shannon derive their names from the goddesses Life and Sinnann. The name of a major Celtic tribe, the Durotriges (who, 'dur' being water, are 'water people'), is recalled in the Duro, in several river Stours and in other nominative relatives.

Celtic serpentine deities are also celebrated in ancient sites, such as the 'hak-pen' (serpent's head) at Avebury, and 'the Lizard', which comprises the southernmost tip of Cornwall. The high political status of these beings is evident in Celtic terms such as *pendragon* ('head of the dragon/chief'). At Llandudno in North Wales, the headlands, Great Orme and Little Orme, from the Norse *orme* meaning 'worm or serpent', indicate some common ground between Viking and Celtic ideas.

The famous Gundestrup Cauldron, found in a Danish peat bog in 1891, provides further insights into pre-Christian worldviews (illus. 30). Made by Celts in the lower Danube region in the second or first century BCE, the ornate silver cauldron is thought to have been a major votive offering. It incorporates

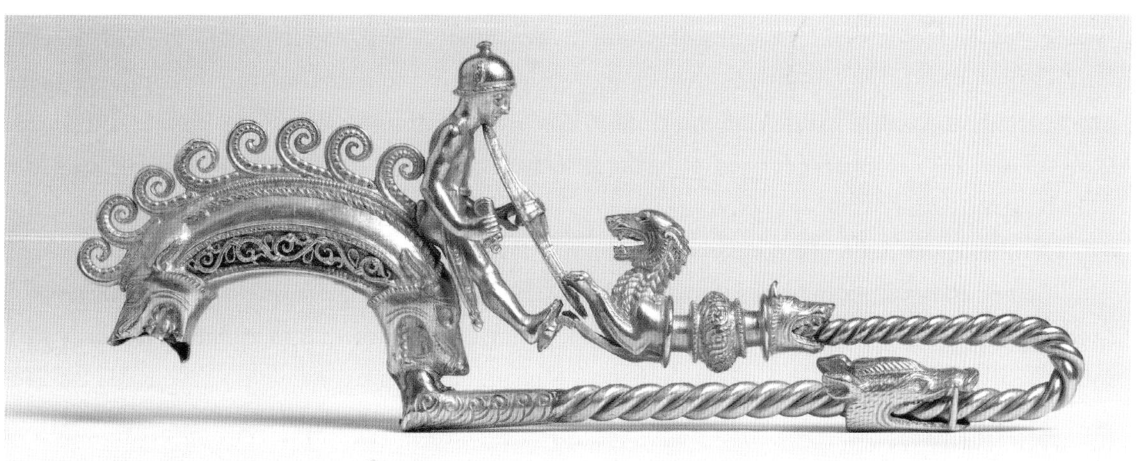

29 Hellenistic/La Tène-style Braganza brooch decorated with a warrior wearing a Celtic helmet, seated upon a serpent figure with watery tendrils, Spain, 250–200 BCE.

30 Inside panel from the Gundestrup cauldron, Celtic/Thracian, *c.* 150 BCE, silver.

imagery from not only Thrace, Greece and Persia, but India too. A prominent image of an antlered being holding a serpent has been interpreted as a depiction of the Celtic God of fertility, flora and fauna, Cernunnos, known variously as 'the Horned God' or Herne and linked with Orion the Hunter, Dionysus and the Greek serpent god of healing, Aesculapius.

In conquering Britain, the Romans adopted Celtic deities and their holy places (illus. 31). At Coventina's Well, an ancient water goddess site beside Hadrian's Wall, they added a mithraeum, a nymphaeum and an altar. Coventina's sacred cult extended across Spain and Portugal, and this Romanized version of her name adapts the Celtic *gover* meaning 'rivulet', and/or possibly *cof* or *cofen*, meaning 'memory' or 'memorial'.[26] When medieval Christian authorities became more punitive about what they regarded as idolatry, Coventina's Well was concealed. On being rediscovered, in 1876, it was found to contain more than 16,000 votive offerings to the goddess: coins, pottery and objects made of bronze, bone, glass, lead, jet, leather and shale (illus. 32).[27]

Though transforming over time into a major Christian saint, Brigid was a powerful pre-Christian goddess, appearing as a serpent being in poems celebrating the arrival of spring: 'Today is the Day of Bride ... The serpent shall come from the hole.'[28] The Romans connected Brigid with their goddess of wisdom, Minerva, often represented by an owl, but also by images of serpents and olive trees. They saw parallels between Isis (borrowed from the Egyptian Osiris myth and responsible for the resurrection of life), Vesta (a deity who cared for the home) and the goddess Sul or Sulis (meaning Eye or Sun), whose temple at the hot springs in Bath contained perpetual fires. The ritual bringing together of fire and water serves as a reminder that water goddesses often had male counterparts – celestial or solar beings – representing the co-creativity of light and water.

In synthesizing multiple influences, Romano-Celtic beliefs therefore maintained gender complementarity in the beings through which they conceptualized human and non-human reproduction. These often retained serpentine forms, which carried forward into later Anglo-Saxon images and artefacts (illus. 33).

The oneness or duality of creative serpent beings, in the form of androgyny, bicephality and twinning, did not vanish when they were superseded by more humanized deities. The Egyptian creator god Atum 'is said to have masturbated and swallowed his own semen in order to reproduce himself', sneezing or spitting out Shu (the god of air) and Tefnut (the god of dew and rain).[29] The more humanized Egyptian Nile god, Hapi, was explicitly hermaphroditic: wearing a crown of lotus plants, s/he was commonly represented with breasts and a beard.[30] Ancient Egyptian imagery also suggests a 'twin' or brother–sister relationship between Osiris and Isis, who appear in both serpent and human form.

As well as appearing as a serpent in earlier imagery, the Graeco-Roman Zeus, in begetting his daughter from his head, contained everything that was needed for creating life. Even the most well-known primogenitor human couple, Adam and Eve, begin as a single male being from which the female is created when Eve is 'made of' Adam's rib.[31] Vestigial traces of original oneness are also implicit in the notion of virgin mothers, able to conceive without a biological counterpart, which the religious historian Claas Bleeker suggests includes (as well as other obvious candidates) the Greek goddess Athene, the Persian goddess Anāhitā and – more tenuously – the Egyptian divinity Hathor.[32] As Alison Roberts observes, Hathor achieved prominence at a time when 'strong women were

31 Roman carving of the goddess Coventina, from the sacred well at Chesters Roman Fort, Hadrian's Wall, 143 CE.

32 Dragonesque brooch, Romano-British, 1st–2nd century CE, copper alloy inlaid with enamel.

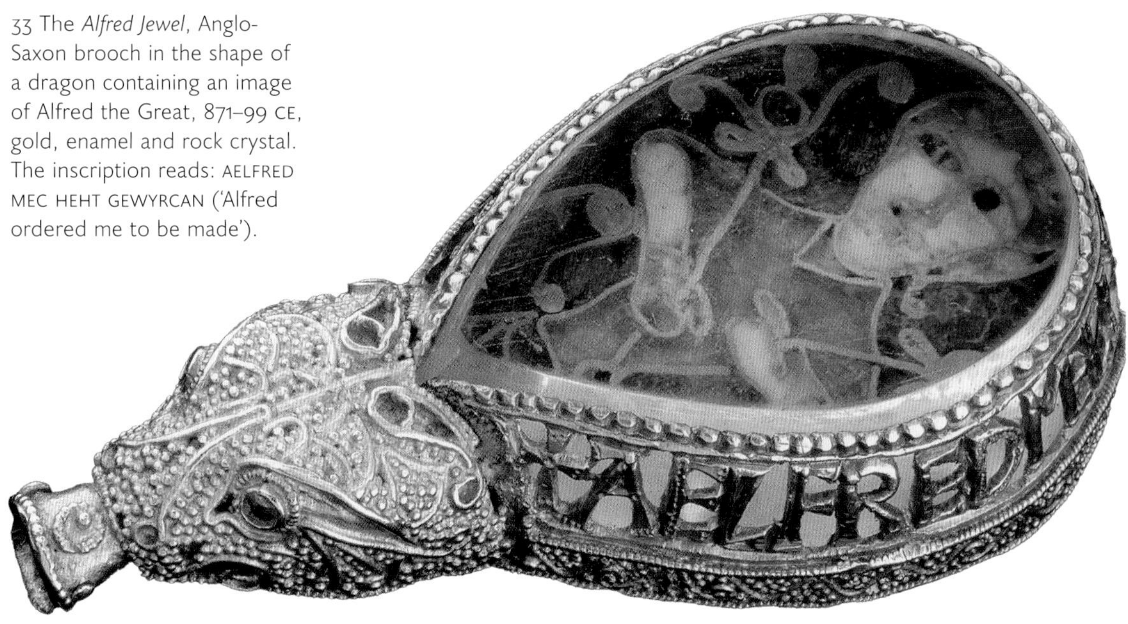

33 The *Alfred Jewel*, Anglo-Saxon brooch in the shape of a dragon containing an image of Alfred the Great, 871–99 CE, gold, enamel and rock crystal. The inscription reads: AELFRED MEC HEHT GEWYRCAN ('Alfred ordered me to be made').

inextricably bound up with the Pharaoh's rule', underlining the relationship between religious and political arrangements.[33]

In later representations of more humanized deities, such relationships tend to segue into conventional coupledom. In Hindu and Buddhist stories, for example, Vishnu, generally associated with the Sun, is associated with Lakshmi, who represents fluid feminine powers. But both are often shown reclining on Shesha, the androgynous creator serpent being.

Matters of Substance

The fertility of water serpent beings draws attention to ideas about the generative and connective fluids of which things and persons are formed. 'Water . . . tends to stand for the original couple – more often than not for the twins who before creation lay in each other's arms . . . Water is the blood that nourishes even before milk can flow.'[34]

Returning to the Celts, there is some evidence that *Imbolc*, their first day of spring, 'which translates variously as ewe-milk, parturition, lustration and purification . . . [and] is associated with breast feeding', was linked with the Druids' wider ritual celebrations of generative substances including amniotic fluid and sacred waters.[35]

The Greek story of the Milky Way described earlier resonates with the connections drawn between Maya *itz* and generative body fluids: semen, milk and blood. Even the fluids of bodily decomposition can be seen as potentially fruitful. In the Egyptian Pyramid Texts the libations necessary to restore life are composed of 'god's fluid' from the body of Osiris, whose 'semen, sweat and pools of putrefaction' formed the waters of the Nile.[36] In irrigation societies, rituals involving libations with water were invariably associated with fertility and revival, and when deified rulers took the place of earlier serpent beings they inherited

34 Horned serpent, Pueblo rock art, Galisteo Basin, New Mexico.

their responsibilities to assure annual inundations of water.[37] Ancient Egyptian and Babylonian royal beneficence is therefore illustrated by images depicting kings ritually initiating irrigation infrastructure. Over time ruling monarchs came to be seen as not only the providers of water but personifications of its powers, which made agricultural fertility and the welfare of the population dependent upon their vitality.[38]

Relationships between religious authority and 'fertilizing fluids' are common. Clifford Bishop maintains that religious rituals sublimate sexual drives, and Dennis Slifer reminds us that, in ancient Germanic languages, the word *lust* meant 'religious joy'.[39] There are other linguistic connections: biblical texts describe the house of Jacob as 'coming forth out of the waters of Judah', and observe that 'Water shall flow from his buckets and his seed shall be in many waters' (Isaiah 14:1, Numbers 24:7).

On examining the rock art of early hunter-gatherers in the American Southwest, Slifer notes, 'The Horned Serpent, or Horned Water Serpent, is described as a gigantic serpent inside the earth presiding over all the waters and nourishing the lifeblood of animals and the sap of vegetation.' In Anasazi and Mogollon rock art, and in contemporary pueblos, the serpent's horn or plume represents its generative powers, and it is invariably associated with water, fertility and health. Its powers may be invoked to overcome sterility or to bring rain, and from its location in springs and aquifers it is said to be able to impregnate bathing women (illus. 34).[40]

Ancestral Serpents

As these examples demonstrate, there are multiple and diverse narratives in which water serpent deities express notions of fertility. The divine protagonists are male and female, or both. They are conceptually linked with the life-bearing fluids that ensure biological and ecological reproduction, and they are the fundamental matter from which all living beings are composed. This draws attention to an important recurring theme: water serpent beings are ancestral. Origin stories often contain powerful homologues about parthenogenesis, in which worlds are literally formed out of the body of primeval parents. In the Mesopotamian *Enuma Elish*, these are Apsû, the male freshwater being, and the female saltwater being Tiâmat ('Sea'). Tiâmat is also called 'Mother

Hubur who forms everything', and descriptions of her note breasts, or udders, and horns, suggesting that she typifies the hybridity of water serpent beings in incorporating the features of species (in this case cows or goats) that are important to their cultural creators.[41] In the *Enuma Elish*, the creative process is then carried forward by Marduk, a 'sun of the heavens' so powerful that 'flame shot forth as he moved his lips.'[42] Marduk gathers up the foam of Tiâmat to form clouds, and with 'the raging of the winds, violent rainstorms, the billowing of mist – the accumulation of her spittle' – makes Heaven and Earth out of the two halves of her body, causing the Tigris and Euphrates to flow from her eyes and mountains to be heaped up on her breasts (illus. 35).[43]

Parthenogenesis is also central to Chinese origin stories, in which a great creator being, Pan Gu, emerges from a giant egg to quell the chaos of the universe by separating Earth and sky:

> He stood there like a tall pillar, supporting the sky and the earth . . . Many years passed this way, but finally exhausted, he felt that his support was no longer necessary, thinking that the sky and the earth were forever separated. Exhausted, he died. His dying breath became the wind and the clouds, his voice the roaring thunder, his left eye the sun, and the right eye the moon. His muscles turned into rich soil and his blood flowed as rivers and lakes. His veins and sinews became roads and his hair became the bright stars in the sky. His skin and fine body hair became beautiful flowers, grass and trees. His teeth and bone became hard stone and glittering metal and his marrow became jade and pearls. Even his sweat became raindrops.[44]

The androgynous Aztec creator Ōmeteōtl is similarly creative. 'In this coming together of opposites He-and-She gave birth to the first race of gods . . . Together they made the world, the creatures on it, the sacred calendar and fire.'[45] In the tumultuous formation of the Aztec cosmos, which passes through lively cycles of creation and destruction, twin serpent beings Tezcatlipoca and Quetzalcoatl create the world out of the body of the sea monster

35 Horned serpent being, possibly Tiâmat in 'dragon' form, impression of a Neo-Assyrian cylinder seal in the linear style, 900–750 BCE.

Tlaltecuhtli, whom they see 'moving about in the primordial sea':

> Tezcatlipoca and Quetzalcoatl seized Tlaltecuhtli ... They pulled her apart, throwing one half up to become the sky and the other half, left floating on the sea, became the earth. She changed, bringing forth everything to sustain humankind ... Her hair became the soughing trees and the sighing grasses, her skin the smaller plants. Her limpid eyes and their sockets became wells and caves, her nose hills and valleys, her shoulders mountains. But old appetites linger and at night, from deep within her carapace of soil and rock, the goddess still howls for blood. To ensure her continuing favour, she is fed the hearts of men.[46]

Parthenogenesis is equally central to Norse descriptions of the hermaphrodite creator being, Ymir, formed from the 'venom' that dripped from the icy rivers of Élivágar.[47] Emerging from the gaping chaotic abyss of Ginnungagap, Ymir begets various progeny and provides the substance of the world:

> There was in times of old, where Ymir dwelt,
> nor sand nor sea, nor gelid waves;
> earth existed not, nor heaven above,
> 'twas a chaotic chasm, and grass nowhere.
>
> Of Ymir's flesh was earth created,
> of his blood the sea,
> of his bones the hills,
> of his hair trees and plants,
> of his skull the heaven;
> and of his brows the gentle powers
> formed Midgard for the sons of men;
> but of his brain
> the heavy clouds are all created.[48]

Such 'creative death' narratives recur in many cultures, relating how the body of the killed and dismembered primordial being forms the cosmos or some important aspects of it. As religious historian Bruce Lincoln observes, the creator's body is therefore an 'alloform' (model) of the cosmos and vice versa.[49] But this is also a classic 'scheme transfer' across scales, containing not only a macrocosm of cosmogony (creation of cosmos), but a mesocosm of sociogony (creation of society) and a microcosm of anthropogony (creation of humankind).[50]

> The general thrust in each instance is to establish a set of homologies between bodily parts and corresponding parts of the cosmos: eyes and sun, flesh and earth, and so forth ... Between the two parts linked in such a homology, there is thus posited a fundamental consubstantiality, whereby one entity may be created out of the material substance of the other.[51]

Such narratives establish a powerful archetype of creator beings as literally substantial ancestors to humankind, and this underpins many belief systems in which water serpent beings are described in precisely this way. In Asia, the term *nāgas* describes not only divine generative beings but the Naga people in northeastern India. Said to inhabit lakes, ponds and the sources of rivers, *nāgas* are beneficent rain bringers, but are believed to be

36 Nāgarāja carving in ceiling, Hindu and Jain, Badami cave temples, Karnataka, India, 6th century.

equally capable of sending punitive hailstorms and floods to devastate agricultural activities (illus. 36).[52]

This last point reminds us that while water serpent beings may be primordial parents, and are therefore assumed to have nurturing responsibilities, they are not invariably benign. They also manifest societies' deeper tensions and terrors, and these include the complex power relations and psychological dangers that can lurk in parent–child relations.[53] The anthropologist David Gilmore provides a Freudian view, noting that throughout the Polynesian islands, and especially in New Zealand, monstrous original twins generate humankind either through direct birth, through totemistic parthenogenesis or by spewing, spitting or defecating protohumans.[54] He suggests that these fearsome progenitors and the young heroes who seek to vanquish them are linked by blood, hatred and violence in a tormented Oedipal relationship. But, as he says, 'men create monsters from nothing, from thought. So who is father to whom?'[55]

Also borrowing from psychoanalysis, Ernest Jones suggests that the anthropophagic monster represents 'the primary sadistic eroticism of the infant. The inevitable cannibalism and fear of being eaten . . . reflect primitive oral aggression, and the monster's fierce, unbridled power mixes erotic and hostile impulses.'[56] As Gilmore puts it, the consuming mouth is a primal image, linked to the earliest stages of infancy (illus. 37):

[It is] this oral primacy that also explains the *form* of aggression associated with monsters: the tearing and rending, the gobbling mouths, the gnashing teeth, the cavernous maws, cannibalism itself, and the overwhelming sense of eating and being eaten as simultaneous experiences – all aspects of oral sadism, of the incorporation and destruction of the ambivalent infantile omnipotence, as well as infantile helplessness.[57]

Jungian analyses provide a more cerebral perspective, in which monstrous beings are archetypal products of an unconscious id, held in check by the rational ego.[58] Arthur Schopenhauer describes this as a contest between the blindly destructive will and the cool logic of the intellect.[59] In Jungian terms the id appears as a chaotic inner sea, seething with the potential to produce an overwhelming tsunami of emotion.

Many societies have envisaged dangerous places populated by demonic beings able to enter and seize control of the individual, but with the scientific disenchantment of the material world this fear required new forms of representation. Writing about monsters in early modern literature, Wes Williams suggests that monsters shifted into internal spaces with the emergence of psychological introspection, so that by the seventeenth century, as with the sea monster in Racine's *Phèdre*, they were 'more likely to denote hidden intensions, unspoken desires'. There was 'a process of increasing internalization: one which follows the migration of monsters from natural history to moral philosophy, their wandering out of the external world and into the drama of human motivation, of sexual and political identity'.[60]

Whether located externally or internalized, water serpent beings in their most monstrous

37 Rainbow serpent, Aboriginal cave painting, Mount Borradaile, Western Arnhem Land, Australia.

38 The damned being cast into Hell in the Last Judgement, stained-glass window, Bourges Cathedral, *c.* 1215–25.

manifestations represent an existential fear of being overwhelmed and consumed. An evolutionary perspective may also have relevance. For prehistoric societies vulnerable to terrestrial and marine predators, this horrendous fate was a real possibility, and Joseph Andriano therefore suggests that images of consuming monsters reflect a primal fear of being eaten.[61] Water serpent beings readily manifest these fears: equipped with great jaws and sharp, serrated teeth, hidden in treacherous depths, and known to have a dark side punitive towards human transgression, they may very well swallow people. Anthropophagic serpents include the Aztec *Hapai-Can*; the Māori *taniwha*; the Algonquin *windigo*; Australian Rainbow Serpents; the Cheroki *utkena*; and the *Kiau* in the seas of northern China.[62] The existential threat of mortality that underlies such imagery is equally recognizable in the maw of the great serpent that comprises the 'mouth of Hell' in Christian iconography, surely one of the most terrifying representations of death imaginable (illus. 38).

Yet, as Gilmore says, 'the mind needs monsters. Monsters embody all that is dangerous and horrible in the human imagination. Since earliest times people have invented fantasy creations on which their fears could safely settle.'[63] Water serpent beings are cyclical in nature: as well as articulating human angst about mortality, they offer the prospect of rebirth.

The traditional serpent's maw is rarely a one-way portal, and movement into formlessness is not necessarily the literal 'end of the matter'. Just as images of consuming monsters represent humankind's deepest existential fears, they also encapsulate its greatest hope: that, like the Sun and the Moon re-emerging from the serpent's body, the human spirit will return from the darkness of the otherworld and be reconstituted in material form.

To be 'spewed out' is therefore to be reborn, providing a metaphor for spiritual and/or material reincarnation, and it is worth noting that the etymology of 'reincarnation' is rooted in Latin, meaning 'again' and *incarnare*, 'to make flesh'. This notion of material 'becoming' and 'unbecoming' is nicely illustrated in anthropologist Gerardo Reichel-Dolmatoff's account of the hydro-theological cycles of the Kogi groups in northern Colombia. These cycles describe how death entails a process of 'forgetting': the soul reaches a stage at which it must try to forget everything the person has learned. It enters a 'cold' state of *seiváke*, in which it is possible to abandon all sensory feeling and emotion. This loss of the individual material self and its memories allows it to return to a state of innocence and perfection (*ishkuéldyi*) from which it can be reborn into the visible, material world.[64] There are many such cyclical visions of spiritual departure and return, and even the most demonized serpent being – whose maw is the mouth of Hell – does not entirely preclude the possibility of redemption.

Thus the consuming water serpent being is concerned with the movement of both spirit and matter through time and space, and with life cycles in which persons lose and regain form and consciousness. They are the darkness into which life is swallowed, and the creative fluid chaos from which it may be regenerated. This cyclical life production is their most fundamental role, and the one that most clearly assures their contemporary relevance. However, as we will see in the next chapter, they also do a great deal of other work to maintain orderly flows in human and non-human lives.

4
Nature Beings

The previous chapters considered the most fundamental roles of water serpent beings in dealing with the 'life and death' matters that confront all human societies: the creation and potential destruction of the cosmos, the production and reproduction of social worlds and the generation and re-generation of all living kinds. But in early societies, and in those retaining hunter-gatherer or small-scale horticultural lifeways, water serpent beings have had much more comprehensive roles in guiding all aspects of human life. This holism has considerable relevance for contemporary efforts to encourage more 'joined-up' thinking in human-non-human relationships. In effect, water serpent beings, embedded in every aspect of indigenous lifeways, provide a model of the kind of social and material coherence that supports sustainable practices.

Prior to the incursion of other societies and their belief systems, hunter-gatherer groups generally practised 'nature religions' venerating non-human deities. However, the nomenclature is misleading: such societies did not categorize nature as something 'other' from themselves, or differentiate nature from culture. Such perceptual dualism and its hierarchical implications emerged later, in very different kinds of societies, and had a profound effect on relations between humans and non-humans. Hunter-gatherers positioned humankind in more equal and reciprocal relations alongside other living kinds, and venerated non-human totemic beings of both genders as their creator beings and ancestors.[1] As *über* totemic beings, often responsible for creating all others, water serpent beings were integral to maintaining an orderly world in every aspect of their lives (illus. 39).

This chapter therefore explores the role of water serpent beings in 'place-based' societies – that is, those in which people have permanent and inalienable relationships with their homelands. Focusing especially on the Australian Rainbow Serpent, with some examples from elsewhere, it considers how water beings mediate social and spatial organization, forms of political governance, economic rights and practices, and, above all, people's relationships with non-human beings and environments.

Since *Homo sapiens* emerged approximately 200,000 years ago, until agriculture was established in the Neolithic period (barely 10,000 years ago), all human societies relied upon hunting and gathering.[2] The persistence of these lifeways for so many millennia makes the obvious point that they were highly sustainable. Albeit with significant cultural variations and adaptations to diverse environments, hunting and gathering societies shared some important commonalities. They generally maintained small populations, and had low-key forms of land and water management, modest levels of resource use and commensurately limited impacts on material environments and their non-human inhabitants. That is not to suggest that their practices had no long-term effects: in Australia, for example, hunting led to the disappearance of some mega-fauna, and practices such as burning scrub, to encourage new grass and support game, opened up forests and encouraged the flourishing of fire-resistant plant species. But such changes were slow and subtle, permitting non-human co-evolution and allowing ecosystems to maintain robust levels of health.

Based on studies in Australia and Africa, anthropologist Marshall Sahlins argued that, as the 'original affluent societies', hunter-gatherers could collect sufficient food and resources in about three to five hours a day.[3] This did not constitute a life of Arcadian bliss: pre-modern technologies had severe limitations in terms of material comfort and health (particularly in relation to infant mortality), and there is evidence of some feuding and warfare.[4]

39 Yuwunyuwun Marruwarr, *Rainbow Serpent Wrapped around Tree*, Gunbalanya, 1974, painting, ochre on bark.

However, it remains that these lifeways were demonstrably sustainable over very long periods of time.

Hunting and gathering depend on high levels of ecological expertise, requiring people to know precisely what resources will be available, where and when. Although colonial imagery presented hunter-gatherers as 'nomadic' wanderers, their travels were anything but aimless. Carefully calibrated annual patterns of movement accommodated changing seasons and water flows, the availability of food and water, and social and religious needs. In northern Australia, for example, groups would camp up on sand ridges in the Wet, when many kinds of food were abundant and movement was more difficult; then, in the Dry, they would go further afield to seek other resources, to exchange people and goods, and to conduct social and religious events.

Hunter-gatherer societies were typically organized into small clans and/or language groups. Their political structures were flat, with all of the elders collectively responsible for decisions and for the intergenerational transmission of the knowledge required to maintain social and ecological order. Though far from static, such lifeways tended to be conservative, and hunter-gatherer societies often maintained greater long-term continuities than those that shifted into agriculture. Further stability was maintained by particular relations to place. Communal and inalienable ownership of estates, and a worldview that assumed that local clans had lived there 'forever', supported (and still support) a deep attachment to homelands that is barely imaginable to people living in more mobile societies.

Coming from the Rainbow

Aboriginal Australian societies exemplify this kind of long-term engagement. Establishing homelands across the continent at least 40,000 years ago, hundreds of small language groups clustered densely in rich tropical wetlands and around major river estuaries and scattered their populations more thinly in the arid interior.[5]

Each language group in Australia has its own set of stories and songlines relating to their 'country', but all describe a creative Dreaming or Story Time in which the Rainbow Serpent, sometimes simply called 'the Rainbow', personifies water. Held in the land, this recurrent central figure is the primary ancestor and the source of all the other totemic ancestral beings who, representing all living kinds, emerged from the rainbow to act upon a flat, empty landscape. Having formed its features and demonstrated how human and non-human beings should live, the ancestors then 'sat down' back into the land, where they remained as a sentient and nurturing presence and as a wellspring of ancestral power.

The Rainbow Serpent therefore features across Australia as a world-creating being and an ongoing source of life. Having spat or spewed out all living kinds in the Dreaming, it continues to generate them in perpetuity. It is a classically hybrid water serpent being, composed of aspects of its local environment. As well as sharing the features of the marine pipefish noted earlier, it often appears with a kangaroo- or crocodile-like head and patterned crocodile skin or claws, and may be shown trailing water lilies or other plants, such as yam leaves. In Arnhem Land, traditional bark paintings are frequently infilled with cross-hatching intended to

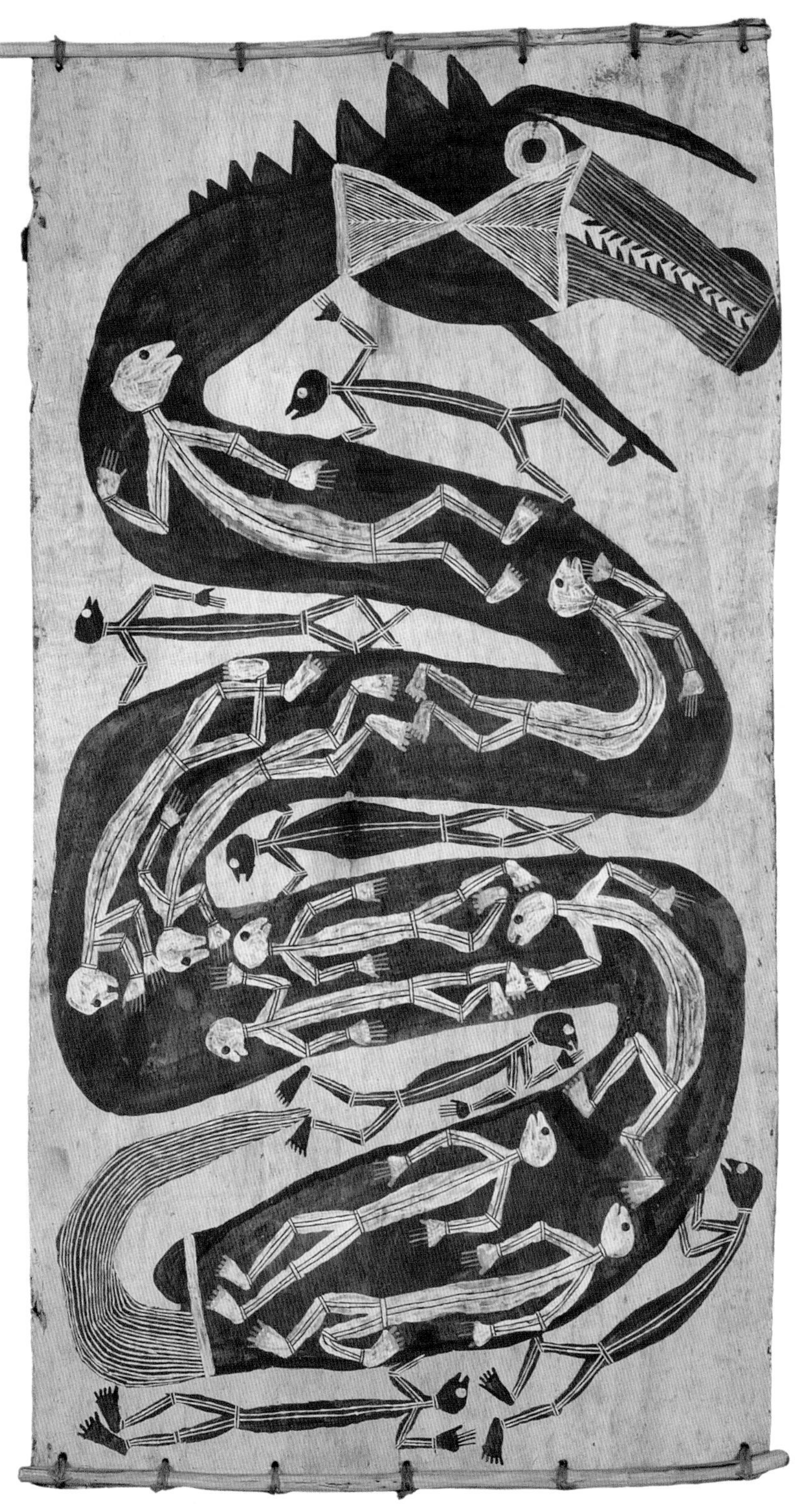

40 Bilinyara Nabegeyo, *Yingarna, the Rainbow Serpent*, Western Arnhem Land, Australia, 1960s–early 1970s, natural pigment on bark.

depict the shimmering of sun on water, and the rainbow colours and iridescence that indicate the emanation of life-generating ancestral powers.[6]

In an Aboriginal cosmos the Rainbow flows between a non-material domain held within the land; the material world above its surface; and a celestial sky river and constellations forming serpentine ancestors and other totemic beings, such as the Emu. The Rainbow Serpent therefore represents a classic hydro-theological cycle: it generates life out into the world to be manifested in material form, and at the end of life carries it back into a deep pool of creative ancestral power.

This orderly cyclical movement reflects the purpose of human life. An individual is meant to relive the lives of the ancestors, over time growing closer to them and becoming an elder by acquiring secret, sacred knowledge. Upon death, relatives sing the person's spirit back to its home place, to be reunited with its totemic 'mate'. As the elders say: 'we all come from the Rainbow,' and, at the end of their lives, 'they will send my spirit back here, the same place where my other brothers [came from]. We all go back in.'[7] The Rainbow Serpent therefore performs an archetypal process of swallowing and regurgitation (illus. 40). The regenerative potential held in Aboriginal cultural landscapes is equally clear in kin terminology, in which grandchildren are often called 'little grandmother' and 'little grandfather'.

Like the spatio-temporal models of South American tribes, the Aboriginal Australian cosmos conflates space and time and offers multiple dimensions, so that it has more in common with contemporary quantum physics than with historically linear concepts of time.[8] Aboriginal time is dominated not by calendars, but by close observation of interrelated seasonal events. Elders in Cape York know that the tea trees coming into blossom signals the laying of crocodile eggs and that the flowering of cotton trees means 'fat wallaby time'. These productive processes are driven by ancestral powers, in particular by the water brought by serpent beings.[9] For example, in Arnhem Land, lightning snakes are believed to initiate the wet season and to cause the floodwaters to rise.[10]

The Dreaming is therefore 'where' rather than 'when', and the ancestral domain is an alternate dimension from which things and persons emerge, coalescing only temporarily in material and conscious form.[11] This bodily incarnation is often translated as 'becoming visible' or 'becoming material'.[12] As the being that 'holds the Law' the Rainbow is a wise and enlightening serpent, containing all of the knowledge, beliefs and values on which Aboriginal society depends. The process of becoming material also brings consciousness, and Warlpiri people describe this as movement between the unconscious disorder of a creative ancestral time/place, *tjukurrpa*, and the conscious order of a material 'time of awakeness', *yitjara*.[13] Coming into being begins with the person's arrival in the material world, so in Arnhem Land, the Yolngu term *liya gapu-mirr* (*gapu-mirr* meaning 'water-having') describes an infant whose fontanelle is still open and pulsing, and therefore ready to be permeated by the ancestral knowledge held in the waters of sacred sites.[14]

In addition to providing a cycle of death and rebirth, swallowing and regurgitation stories describe the Rainbow Serpent's role in enabling rites of passage and individual transformations. Initiation ceremonies perform a process of separation that

41 Waterhole near Kowanyama, Mitchell River, Cape York, Australia.

hides boys from female kin inside the serpent and allows them to be reborn as men, sometimes from a male being.[15] The secret, sacred knowledge held within the Rainbow Serpent is revealed to people at key life stages. Becoming a person is therefore a process of gaining knowledge over time.

The deepest secret knowledge, conferring healing and other shamanic powers, can only be gained by immersive 'passing through the rainbow' and gaining access to the hidden domain of the Rainbow Serpent. Like other shamanic visits to invisible otherworlds, the journey into the fluid creative chaos of the Rainbow Serpent is dangerous, risking a premature dissolution of the self. The ethnographer John Taylor describes how this ritual was traditionally conducted in Cape York (illus. 41):

> A would-be *wangath* [doctor] went off to one of the lagoons that the mythic creature was known to haunt and, after rubbing himself with native honey and sweet fruit, began swimming in the water. Attracted by the smell of the honey and fruit the Rainbow Serpent/Cyclone would swim up and swallow the neophyte whole. It would then swim up to another place carrying the neophyte in its stomach. Ghosts of the neophyte's ancestors, especially the poison [magically powerful] grandfathers, *kaman*, would sing out to the creature warning it not to keep their kinsman too long in its stomach. Later the man would be regurgitated on the bank of a lagoon. As he lay there, recovering from the experience, red ants would come and clean the new doctor of the coating he had acquired in the belly of the creature.[16]

As in other belief systems, such as those of the Kogi, Aboriginal Australians believe that a return to the ancestral domain at the end of life entails a loss of material form and consciousness, and a process of forgetting. For the Yolngu in Arnhem Land, the forehead, *buku*, represents intent or will, or 'intentionally acquired knowledge', while *buku-y-moma* describes a process of 'forgetting' or 'leaving knowledge behind at death'. The term *buku buṯ-marama*, 'forehead, fly away cause', therefore describes the mortuary rituals through which the human spirit, freed from its material form, is returned to the ancestral domain.[17] A part of it will 'fly away, out West' towards the Sun, acknowledging that the non-material domain also has a celestial dimension. But for the most part the spirit returns 'down under' to its original home, and in losing material form may regain the non-human totemic identity from which it arose:

> *After when we die, that spirit go back to errk elampungk . . . Go back to what he really came from, like brolga – from the beginning. Because he was a catfish, or a goanna, like that, wallaby: he form back to these animals.* (Alma Wason)[18]

Being in Place

In generating each person, the Rainbow Serpent locates them both socially and spatially. An individual emerges from a 'home' place in the clan land, usually a water body of some kind, associated with a particular ancestral being and their stories. In Cape York the Kunjen term for this spiritual home, *errk elampungk*, translates as 'place' (*errk*), 'eye' (*el*) and 'home' (*ampungk*). This means 'the home place of your image', signifying that until a person emerges from the land, they have no material form. Their arrival, animating the foetus in a woman's womb, is usually signalled to the father by an odd event: a strange birdcall, an inexplicable instance of animal behaviour or the discovery of an unusually marked animal or fish.

> *Might be baby here, in this* [water] *here, old Dad might see him 'Oh! My baby here!' Because that Rainbow* [is] *here . . . Baby come from water, you see . . . Might be mother over there, sitting down, cooking away, she don't know baby come . . . He look, his wife, then say 'I got a baby now' . . . He go tell his grandmother, his mother. They wait now. Then her belly growing big. Well they better call this place . . . 'errk elampungk.'* (Lefty Yam and Victor Highbury)

The way that the Rainbow Serpent generates spirit children highlights the broader sentience of a cultural landscape responsive to its inhabitants. For example, a waterhole might dry up with grief when the 'boss' for that place dies. It will offer resources to those who belong there, while withholding them from strangers.

> *When people go to a place where those old people* [ancestors] *used to be, in that home, before we catch anything we have to call out to them, to give us some food, you know, and fish or turtle to catch, and then people start catching something. If you are a stranger and go fishing, you catch nothing, because you don't know how to talk to them, and they don't know you.* (Alma Wason)

Traditionally, elders would conduct 'increase rituals' encouraging the land and its waters to provide particular resources. In rainmaking ceremonies, directed particularly at the great serpent, there are predictable homologues with human reproduction. The spitting or scattering of white quartz stones is common, as these are said to resemble semen, and anthropologist Francesca Merlan describes secret–sacred associations between semen and gleaming or luminous ritual objects, such as pearlshell.[19] Other ethnographers have recorded similar associations: Erich Kolig reports the ritual use of stone rods carved as penises, and John Morton describes a traditional ceremony in which an actor representing a phallic ancestral being, having covered his body with down, dances vigorously to scatter it onto the ground. The ritual is called *alkngantama*, meaning 'to throw out seed': 'The down . . . will turn into animals and plants of the totem . . . after the next summer rains.'[20]

At a place called Darkness Story, in the Errk Oykangand National Park, taboos forbid the killing of snakes, and a rainmaking ritual involves a gleaming shell that controls light and dark:

> *They make the rain here . . . They get the leaf and put 'em in the water down here. Big rain come, and strong wind, big strong wind, just like cyclone, he lift everybody up. If you walking about out here . . . lift you, carry you down to that main place over there.* (Victor Highbury)

As these accounts imply, though connected by visible and invisible water flows and by the powers of the Rainbow Serpent, every place in an Aboriginal cultural landscape is unique. A person emerges into a specific place, and is co-substantially composed of that place, 'grown up' by its foods and, above all, by the waters from which they were generated. Place therefore forms individual identity, socially and materially situating individuals within both a kin group and its country (illus. 42).

Having a spiritual 'home' in clan land comes with rights and obligations. Every clan member shares collective ownership of its common estate, which is defined by the sacred sites at which ancestral power is concentrated, and by the stories that connect these. Flowing down the generations from the Rainbow, via songs, storytelling, dance and artworks, these stories – the Law – are a holistic template for life. They contain maps of the land and waterscapes, accounts of its features, its sacred sites and the associated clans, descriptions of flora and fauna, and how to make use of and take care of these. They contain social rules: who should marry whom (cross-cousin marriage being common) and prohibitions against incest or 'wrong-way' marriage, how descent should be traced (this might be matrilineal or patrilineal), who can be joked with (often an uncle), and who should be ritually avoided (usually the mother-in-law). There is information about how to conduct ceremonies, who should do so, where and when. Many sacred sites require careful rituals to pay respects to their ancestral beings and ensure that they continue to provide resources.

The Rainbow Serpent also enforces the Law: along with the other ancestral beings, it is always present and watching. Moving about in a sentient cultural landscape requires care. When I undertook some cultural mapping to record details about sacred sites with the Kunjen community, elders would often call out to the ancestral beings, explaining what we were doing there and asking permission for photographs to be taken.[21] Small children and visitors to Aboriginal land must be baptized so that the resident beings will recognize them, keep them safe and provide them with resources. Illustrating the co-substantiality implicit in many baptism rituals, this entails being splashed

42 Kunjen elder Alma Wason at sacred site on the Mitchell River, Cape York.

with water from a sacred site. The notion of fluid co-substantiality is further underlined by an earlier form of this ritual, in which sweat from local clan members was rubbed onto a newcomer, so that the ancestral beings could 'smell' and recognize them as being literally familiar.

Individuals failing to undergo such rituals or trespassing without permission into sacred sites might be afflicted with an injury or illness. For example, at Poison Snake Story Place, a local station owner ('some silly feller') decided to build a cattle yard, against the elders' advice. This resulted in stock workers being injured:

> *Young fellers might get hurt, bull might hit him, might be kicked, yeah, all like that . . . I fall* [off my horse] *over there . . . just across here, at the water crossing. I was dead! I was there, conked out . . . My eldest brother was here, he just come over, looked at me, 'You all right?'* (Paddy Yam)

A serious transgression might result in a person being swallowed by the Rainbow Serpent. At a place called Og Ewarr (Water Rainbow Story Place),[22] Kunjen elders Lefty Yam and Charlie Pindi related how a 'jealous' or 'cheeky' (dangerous) rainbow swallowed a fisherman who came to its sacred waterhole after attending a *bora* (ceremony) and failed to conduct the necessary baptism ritual.

Like the Maya *nagual*, the Australian Rainbow Serpent sometimes brings about morphological transformations, in its own form and that of other beings. At Molorr Ampungk (Two Girl Story Place), a couple of ancestral women attempting to catch a manifestation of the Rainbow Serpent in the form of a giant catfish are pulled downstream, swallowed and turned into cabbage palm trees. These trees are readily distinguishable because, filled with ancestral power, they grow especially high.[23] It is forbidden to disturb the soil around the lagoon where the two girls tried to net the catfish, or at the waterhole where it was revealed as a Rainbow:

> *He* [the rainbow] *stay – still there. That's the story them two girls there, that cabbage tree here. That's where they finished up . . . We don't touch this place . . .* [If] *we stir 'em up, bad for everybody.* (Lefty Yam and Victor Highbury)

While contact with the Rainbow Serpent is inherently dangerous, a story about Inh-elar, the ancestral Night Pigeon (an owlet or nightjar), illustrates that 'passing through the rainbow' confers considerable powers. In this story, told by Lefty Yam – himself a 'clever doctor' – the Rainbow, Ewarr, comes from the Gulf of Carpentaria, surging under the land and leaving a great river in its wake. Following the ancestral Green Frog, Elbmelbmal, it travels eastwards across the peninsula, carrying a dilly (string) bag full of flying foxes:

> *We call him Ewarr . . . that's the Rainbow,* [or] *An-ganb. He bring flying fox, many, maybe 4,000 of them, carry him in a big dilly bag.*

The Night Pigeon followed its track. Though the rainbow was travelling underground he could hear the tree roots breaking and see water bubbling up in its wake.

> *Follow the same creek, you know the watercourse here, that old feller, they call Night Pigeon, Inh-elar . . .*

'Hey! What's this track here?' He look, the root and all, he [the Rainbow] *pulled 'em out . . . Water followed that Rainbow, all the way.*

Inh-elar flew ahead to a waterhole and waited.

That little pigeon, night pigeon, he go round that side. 'I'll try waiting.' He wait here, right here with a spear, you know.

The Night Pigeon heard Elbmelbmal calling back to the Rainbow, and the Rainbow coming along, singing out behind.

'Olp!' Old Green Frog, Green Frog, he sing out. 'Ewp!' He sing out, Rainbow sing out. 'Ewp!'

'Olp!' Green Frog, he walking on front see, he walk along, little short feller. He still following him, Rainbow still following him, all the way.

Inh-elar let the Green Frog go by, but when he saw the Rainbow, he speared him through the chest.

He had a good spear too . . . He spear him right here . . . Ooooh!' He is coil up now; for he long eh, Rainbow, he long!

The Rainbow wrapped its coils over Inh-elar, trapping him so that he couldn't get away.

Chuck that coil riiight over him, cover him all that coil, gone! He couldn't get away; tried to run away. No, he couldn't go that way, no. 'Which way I gonna come out? This way?' He go this way – no. He [the Rainbow] *all round him, you know . . .*

The Rainbow tightened its coils:

He coming close la him. 'Oh!' He going swallow him, you know, he going swallow him you see! He look around . . .

Inh-elar saw the hole where he had speared the Rainbow clean through the chest. He dived through the hole.

Yeah! That boy bin spear him, that mark, cut here with a spear. He get in that hole see . . . That minya [being], *Night Pigeon . . . him bin get in that same mark, get in, come out other side, gone!*

The Rainbow coiled up, but Inh-elar had escaped. In 'passing through the Rainbow', he gained special knowledge and became the first 'clever doctor', able to do *puri* (sorcery).

He coil up, no, nothing – he over there! Rainbow he think, 'where he gone now?' . . . That's why him today, he clever doctor now, Inh-elar.

The Green Frog, meanwhile, had run away, leaving all of the flying foxes with the Rainbow.

Old Frog, he took off, he took off with a fright! He took off that way now . . . He [the Rainbow] *still have 'em there. Oh big bag . . . thousands of flying fox.*

The Rainbow cried out: '*he bin say "Sooooooh!"*' He let all the flying foxes go, and they flew all over Australia.

He left that dilly bag there . . . Flying fox, they come out of there, they go up that tree, you know, where that

> *big swamp* [is]. *They still there today, still going, flying fox, they go everywhere, you know.*

The Rainbow stayed at the waterhole:

> *Ewarr, they call him, that bush name this waterhole now, Ewarr. Today call him Rainbow Story. That Story finish here.*

Inh-elar gave the Rainbow the sacred name An-ganb, to demonstrate its power. He was relieved to have escaped.

> *Him look, eh, he think about it now, Inh-elar: 'Hmm, An-ganb'. He call him An-ganb, that Rainbow now . . . 'Good job he not be swallowing me. Good job I bin get away.'*

Because of its connection with this important ritual, Rainbow Story Place is a particularly powerful site. If someone is sick, they can go there and call out to the Rainbow, and sometimes rain will come to heal them.

> *They go there, bogey* [wash or swim in water], *call him name, call out that Rainbow. He speak* [to] *that fellow. He might be sick, that fellow. He'll fix him up . . . might be little rain come, get over that sick.*

As these stories illustrate, sacred sites command deep respect, in particular those so powerful as to be defined as 'poison places'. Hunting or fishing is often prohibited at them, and it has been posited that they therefore functioned traditionally as 'game reserves', ensuring the replenishment of resources in what is, even in Australia's rich wetland areas, a delicate ecosystem with fragile, friable soils and variable water flows.[24]

In a cultural context in which relations with place are inalienable, it is unsurprising that Aboriginal law contains a major subtext underlining a responsibility to act sustainably. 'Taking care of country' includes keeping it 'clean' (that is, orderly) through careful fire management. Rights to clan land come with obligations not to overuse resources: as the above stories illustrate, a frequent cause of retribution by the Rainbow Serpent is people fishing without permission, or taking too many fish. Ancestral stories describe conservative practices, for example how to cut spears so that the trees providing these will regenerate, or describing when and how to harvest yams so that new tubers will grow:

> *Time for yam would be when first rain come, because new shoots coming up. That time for digging eh, and that time end. Then after the wet when them yam leaf go yellow . . . that's the time for digging again. They can't dig it when they green.* (Alma Wason)

There is also a recurrent theme regarding the need not to disturb things, as this will affect not only the well-being of the landscape but that of its Aboriginal inhabitants. At Poison Snake Story Place, the Kokobera elder Winston Gilbert described how he had to tell a European fencing contractor not to cut the sacred tree at the site, as this would cause him, as the primary 'boss' of the place, to get sick and die. The increasing numbers of tourists visiting Cape York in the 1990s were seen as potentially harmful, and a Kunjen elder, Nelson Brumby, wanted to prohibit access to his 'home' place:

> *I got to put Law against this place* [to prevent] *too many people come here. They make me go down too – make me sick . . . because this place I got story. Too much footprint on me . . .* (Nelson Brumby)

There are multiple references to the resistance of the Rainbow Serpent to the polluting incursions of newcomers into clan country. Merlan describes it as an autochthonous force that, having an aversion to the foreign sweat or smell of strangers, assaults the unfamiliar.[25]

Understanding the close connections that the Rainbow Serpent maintains between people and place also illuminates Aboriginal responses to European economic practices. Settlers introduced mining to Australia, hard on the heels of the violence that accompanied the colonial invasion. Strangers gouging into the ancestral domain was a terrible trauma; a penetrative assault on the landscape and its people. The use of dynamite in a development in Katherine was said to have killed the local manifestations of the Rainbow Serpent.

It is no wonder, then, that mines and quarries have sparked some of Australia's most anguished indigenous protests. On the Gove Peninsula in Arnhem Land, the distribution of mining rights to Nabalco provoked Australia's first formal assertion of Native Title. The Yolngu community sent a bark petition to the government in 1963 (see illus. 126), stating that 'the land in question has been hunting and food gathering land for the Yirrkala tribes from time immemorial,' and seeking protection for 'places sacred to the Yirrkala people, as well as vital to their livelihood'. The petition called on the House of Representatives to intercede and ensure that 'no arrangements be entered into with any company which will destroy the livelihood and independence of the Yirrkala people'.[26] Strenuous legal efforts followed that, although they did not prevent the mining, began the long progress towards the national acceptance of Native Title which finally came in 1993.[27]

These efforts also laid the foundations for contemporary indigenous critiques of European modes of engagement with their homelands, which are often directed towards the impacts of mine pollution on rivers and aquifers. Cape York was the site of a major gold rush in the late 1800s. As well as increasing the turbidity of waterways, mining uses cyanide to extract gold from ore, creating – on larger sites – massive tailing dams, putatively containing the wastewater but often allowing it to leach into the surrounding landscape. The results can be severe: in the 1990s, the edge of the tailings dam at Red Dome gold mine was littered with the decaying bodies or faint outlines of dead animals. The downstream indigenous community is keenly aware of the problem:

> *We worry about that mining company too, 'cause, see the mining, you know, they can really muck 'em up the river . . . Up this end here, you know, because we know we got a big river, comes up this way, and we worry about that thing . . . We want to keep that river clean.* (Colin Lawrence)

Keeping the river 'clean' also means not disrupting or impeding it. Traditional material culture included fish weirs or, occasionally, small channels directing water towards edible plants; however, large interventions, such as the enormous dams and irrigation channels imposed by European settlers, are considered to prevent proper flows and are at odds with indigenous respect and care for country.

There is thus a crucial historical and contemporary relationship between the veneration of a major water serpent being, its practical and conceptual integration into all domains of life, and the maintenance of highly respectful and reciprocal relationships with water. Through the Law that it continuously regenerates, the Rainbow Serpent is a guiding presence that promotes orderly human-non-human relations designed to be sustained, as the elders put it, 'for future generations'.

> *Trees and animals – they are like our brothers and sisters. We got to care for them, they are part of us too. When you grow up you got to think about this, how to care for the land, for your children.* (Colin Lawrence)

Sustaining Lifeways

Ethnographic and archaeological studies of other hunter-gatherer societies have not generally focused on how their water serpent beings enable sustainable ideas and practices, but many accounts suggest that similar beliefs and values, and an ethos of reciprocity vis-a-vis the non-human world, pertain in other place-based groups.

In the far north of Canada and in Alaska, hunter-gatherers variously called Eskimos, Inuit, Yup'ik and First Nation peoples have maintained social continuities and ecological equilibrium since prehistoric times.[28] While having their own origin stories, communities across the region share recurrent cosmological themes. Creation is initiated by an incestuous relationship between the Sun and the Moon. Following a violent and chaotic era of floods and darkness, light emerges, and four worlds form: a sky world; a world of earth, ice and water inhabited by living kinds; an undersea world; and beneath that a deeper underworld.[29] All are inhabited by powerful supernatural beings, including deities such as the 'Great Serpent' discernible in the constellation of stars known as Scorpius, and connected narratively with serpentine beings in the 'Beneath World'.

In these northern cosmological schemes, there is little differentiation between human and non-human beings. All are persons who can shift between human and animal form, and movement between human and non-human societies is common in stories such as 'The Boy Who Went to Live with the Seals'.[30]

> Many elders view the world as inhabited by a variety of persons, including human persons, non-human persons (animals) and extraordinary or other-than-human persons . . . Appearances are often deceiving. A man encountered on the tundra might be an *incenrraat* [shape-shifting persons who live in the wilderness]. Wolves running in the grass might be beluga whales in mammal incarnation.[31]

All living kinds, and sometimes inanimate objects, have immortal souls that return after death to the undersea fluid domain from which they emerged. Inuit people in the western Arctic describe this as the home of Sedna. Called the 'Spirit of the Sea Depths' (*Saituma Uva*) in Greenland, Sedna is a powerful sea goddess who rules the spirit world of the deep (illus. 43).[32] She is often depicted in

43 Pitseolak Niviaqsi,
Sedna, 1991, soapstone.

semi-human or mermaid form and, in a classic creation story of parthenogenesis, Sedna's severed fingers become the whales, walruses and seals hunted by the Inuit. She is widely regarded as the 'mother of all' from whose body all living beings were made and who continues to generate them into the material world in 'a continuous collective cycle of incarnation'.[33] Mediating interactions between human and animals, Sedna demands mutual respect. Ethnographers George and Deborah Sabo, working with indigenous communities on Baffin Island, suggest,

> We may interpret sea mammal hunting as a sort of social transaction between humans, the souls of sea mammals and Sedna . . . A cyclical flow characterises this transaction in which the Inuit receive the bodies of sea mammals whose souls then return to Sedna to be regenerated or reproduced. Humans may negatively affect this cycle by breaking certain taboos, in which case Sedna responds by cutting off the food supply or otherwise causing trouble.[34]

Transgressions might include hunting land and sea animals at the same time, instead of maintaining orderly seasonal activities; treating animals with cruelty or disrespect; or failing to conduct propitiatory ceremonies in relation to hunting.[35] Remedial action requires a shaman (*angakok*) to intercede with Sedna by using magical powers to transport his or her soul to her watery abode: 'Only the greatest shamans can survive a direct and intimate encounter with Sedna. In a trance and in the presence of the gathered community, the shaman must leave his or her body, headfirst, and travel across a great abyss to the bottom of the sea. "The way is made ready for me, the way is opening before me"'.[36] On meeting Sedna, the *angakok* performs cleansing rituals to remove the human sins that pollute her and her home. This purifies and restores order to the relationship, reviving the flows of spirits and resources between human and non-human domains. Multiple rules and taboos provide a strong imperative to demonstrate respect for the non-human world, and for the animals who have offered themselves to the hunter. As one Igulik man put it:

> The greatest peril in life lies in the fact that human food consists entirely of souls. All the creatures that we have to kill and eat, all those that we have to strike down and destroy to make clothes for ourselves, have souls, like we have, souls that do not perish with the body, and which must therefore be propitiated lest they should revenge themselves on us for taking away their bodies.[37]

Just as all animals have souls, all things in the environment have sentience, which Yup'ik describe as *ella*. This can be translated as 'awareness' or 'sense', but also as 'world', 'outdoors' and 'universe'. Even the ocean 'has eyes' and 'knows everything that is going on': 'Our ancestors took great care of everything around them as they lived their lives because they fully understood that everything had awareness.'[38] Taking care of everything includes a moral obligation to look after other human beings, and to be generous and compassionate. Yup'ik view the human mind as having agency that can push events towards negative or positive consequences. A person's gratitude is powerful, as are hurt feelings, creating a causal relationship between good behaviour and good weather, or good hunting.

Order is similarly maintained by the elders teaching younger generations sustainable ways of collecting resources, which means harvesting things in season, and never wasting resources or being careless with them.

> When they took care of food, they did not leave any behind, not throwing them away in any manner; not letting them become messy. They watched over them closely, and they admonished us never to step on food scraps or scatter the bones . . . those who improperly handled things became less and less capable of obtaining food . . . We were taught about everything having to do with the area around our village. They let us know about the deep lakes and the small rivers. They let us learn about spring hunting routes, currents, places where ice forms and the dangerous places we should avoid.[39]

Synchronicity with seasonal cycles is underpinned by a cyclical view of spiritual regeneration that (as in Aboriginal Australia) is emphasized by the bestowal of deceased persons' names on new generations, and the use of kin terms that reflect earlier relationships.[40] In these ways, guided by supernatural beings and powers, orderly lifeways were sustained for millennia in the Arctic region (illus. 44).

Similar precepts are discernible in the cosmology and philosophy of other First Nation groups. While Sedna and other water beings in the Arctic are often represented in seal- or whale-like bodies, demonstrating the fluid capacities of aquatic deities

44 Lucy Qinnuayuak, *Sedna with Spotted Bird*, 1982, stonecut and stencil.

to adopt local forms, the water beings of the Great Lakes, in the traditional lands of the Iroquois, have more serpentine manifestations. Archaeologists have found underwater sites with artefacts suggesting long-term practices (of more than 2,000 years) of offering ceramic vessels and their contents to 'Grandfather Long-Tail', described as a 'panther or dragon being'.[41] Rock art imagery in the region suggests that this may have been connected to a ceremony of 'calling the salmon back to the river' and ensuring fish regeneration: 'The Iroquoian belief in this supernatural being parallels that of the neighbouring Algonquin-speaking people. There were a number of Grandfather Long-Tail beings that controlled the waters and could bestow benefits upon deserving humans. They were believed to reside in deep bodies of water in the realm of the Underwater World.'[42]

There are obvious resonances in this antipodean comparison, between the water serpent beings of Native Canadian, American and Australian hunter-gatherers. In many of the place-based communities that lie between them, water serpent beings have similarly comprehensive roles. Linked with life and death processes, and with cycles of spiritual and material flows, they are invariably powerful and dangerous, but they are also essential guardians, healers and suppliers of water and resources. They contain secret, sacred knowledge which confers special powers upon those willing to engage directly with them and which is central to the authority of community elders. They are deeply venerated in songs, dances, artworks and ritual ceremonies. They enforce strict rules and moral codes that maintain social order and reciprocal relations with non-human worlds. They are integral to lifeways that have been maintained sustainably for millennia and are central to an ethos that locates humankind indivisibly among all living kinds. They tell us loudly and clearly, with obvious relevance to the current environmental crisis, that sustainable values and practices are not a luxury 'add-on' to societies' choices but rather must be embedded in all human activities. And what happens to these wise serpents in developmental trajectories elsewhere tells us how we lost sight of this reality.

5
Cultivating Beings

This chapter considers how the role and form of water serpent beings began to change as some societies adopted new social and economic practices, seeking to act more instrumentally on their environments and to direct water and resources towards human needs and interests. A new pathway opened, leading to less equal human-non-human relations. The first steps in this direction were small and tentative to begin with, but technological advancements seeming to offer abundance and security are always 'enchanting'.[1]

While hunting and gathering predominated for many millennia, other modes of environmental engagement had also demonstrated long-term sustainability. In some tropical forest areas, for example in Africa, South America and parts of Oceania, place-based communities practised small-scale shifting cultivation. This did not differ radically from the lifeways described in the previous chapter. Hunter-gatherers often practised 'domiculture', planting food or medicine trees around campsites, and quite a few societies employed both forms of production.

Horticultural communities created temporary 'forest gardens' of fruit trees and crops such as cassava, corn, plantain and sweet potatoes. When soils became tired, plots would be moved, and the surrounding forest would reclaim the area. These pockets of instrumental activity had limited effects upon human population levels or the local environment.[2] The necessary investment of labour introduced some new ideas about the ownership of land and resources, as well as gender roles, and encouraged small village settlements. However, such societies maintained relatively egalitarian social and political structures and close attachments to place, and they still required comprehensive ecological knowledge. In cosmological terms, beliefs about the supernatural remained focused on multiple and largely non-human deities.

Water serpent beings retained their primary generative and authoritative role, but this altered slightly as societies dependent upon crops naturally paid closer attention to the timing of annual rains and to the ecological and celestial indicators heralding their arrival. An example is provided by the Arawak-speaking groups who originated in northwest Venezuela and, circa 3000 BCE, spread to the Amazon basin and the Caribbean. Traditionally, they combined hunting and gathering with growing manioc, and their seasonal cycles of activity shifted in emphasis between these modes of production.

Arawak origin stories, like those of the contiguous Desana groups, centre upon ancestral serpent beings (giant anacondas and boas) whose creative activities locate their human progeny in a sentient land and waterscape. There is a strong focus on celestial beings, with the constellations of the night sky providing a map of totemic ancestors, clans and their social and spatial relationships with each other. The celestial Boa, identified with Scorpius, has a central role in mediating social and economic relationships, creating 'moieties', in which groups divide into halves for the purpose of exchanging people and goods. This mediatory role is supported by the Boa's relationship with the Pleiades, whose helical setting and rising at dawn and dusk represent both opposite and complementary relationships.[3]

As well as providing social order, the major role of Arawak celestial water serpent beings is to coordinate annual productive and ritual activities with wet and dry seasons and the two inter-seasons, signalling, for example, when it is time to clear a space in the forest and open a new agricultural cycle.[4]

> Scorpius bears the name of the water boa (*Eunectes murinus*) in most Arawak groups, and 'announces the December rains' . . . At the end of the season, according to the Wapisian group, it swallows the red macaw, which represents Antares. For the Paicur, Antares appears as an agouti in the belly of the snake which is known as the 'father of the rains'.[5]

Many South American tribes retained these lifeways and reciprocal human-non-human relationships for millennia and have persevered in trying to do so, despite a familiar story of colonization, genocide and the imposition of colonizing settlers' beliefs and values. For many decades it was possible for them to retreat deeper into the continent's vast rainforests, but from the 1950s onwards it became more difficult to avoid increasing exploitative economic incursions into their homelands, righteously determined Christian missionaries and decimating European diseases.

Agricultural Beings

Although small-scale shifting cultivation initiated only minor changes in human–environmental relationships, when societies settled more firmly and gave precedence to agriculture the rain-bringing role of water serpent beings became more critical. However, as long as agricultural activities remained small in scale the concomitant social and religious changes expressed through water serpent beings were relatively subtle.

For example, in the American pueblos, where maize production became central to local tribal economies between circa 500 BCE and the 1400s, horned water serpent beings performed similar roles to the freshwater and marine beings of the hunter-gatherer societies explored previously, and the celestial boas of shifting cultivators. They were equally associated with water and fertility.[6] They shared linkages to Scorpius and the 'eye star', and images representing these serpents echo the shape of this constellation. In the Ohio Valley, an ancient serpent mound more than 400 metres (1,300 ft) in length, seemingly aligned to annual

45 Winged and plumed rattlesnakes on engraved shell cup fragment, Spiro Mounds, Oklahoma, 1200–1500 CE, after drawing by Henry W. Hamilton.

solstices and equinoxes, suggests that the early Mississippian agriculturalists paid close attention to celestial events.[7] The annual appearances of the Great Serpent, Scorpius, with its red jewel or eye (Antares), signified a shift in focus from the Beneath World to the Sky World.[8] The horned serpents from this region sometimes have wings that, like the feathers of serpents in Central America, indicate their association with wind and water, and their hydrological capacities to connect heavenly and earthly domains (illus. 45).

Cultural narratives about horned water serpent beings in the region resonate with those further afield. They often feature a hero who, having been swallowed by the serpent, finds a weapon and cuts his way out.[9] Sacred knowledge and shamanistic powers are gained via dangerous journeys to the underwater 'lodge' of the serpent.[10] Most importantly, water serpent beings such as Avanyu, the horned serpent of the Tewa pueblos around Santa Fe, mediate both hydrological and spiritual cycles (illus. 47).

Inhabiting springs, ponds, rivers and ultimately the oceans, all of which are believed to connect under the earth's surface, Avanyu may bring orderly and vital annual rains, or express displeasure about human transgressions by inflicting floods.[11] First represented in classic Mimbres pottery (1000–1150),

46 Hopi snake (rain) dance, Tusayan Pueblo, Arizona, *c.* 1902, photomechanical print.

47 Maria Martinez and Julian Martinez, *Bowl with Avanyu*, San Ildefonso Pueblo, New Mexico, 1925–35, earthenware with slip.

and still a key icon in contemporary pueblo artefacts, Avanyu is most commonly depicted with clouds around its tail and lightning spitting from its mouth. As well as representing the fire believed to be found in 'below and above worlds', this refers to the serpent's major role. Lightning is believed to be the trigger that persuades celestial guardians to release the rain, and in ancient petroglyphs the serpent itself is sometimes depicted in a sharply zigzag form. The vital importance of this rain-bringing role is illustrated in other visual details: the crops crucial to pueblo communities' subsistence are represented in a maize collar or in corncobs sprouting from the serpent's mouth (illus. 48).[12]

For small-scale agricultural communities such as the Tewa, rainmaking rituals are central and elaborate, particularly during periods of drought. The ceremonies also manage the social tensions arising from competition for the best agricultural land around settlements, facilitating the redistribution of food to farmers with less productive land.[13] In an account of a contemporary Pueblo rain dance, writer Rosemary Diaz describes a long line of dancers emerging from the *kiva* (a sunken ceremonial lodge). The men's kilts are inscribed with serpentine figures. Moving in snaking patterns to the accompaniment of drums and songs, the dancers perform a dance asking for the annual rains that will allow their crops to grow (illus. 46).[14]

Other small-scale agricultural societies around the world also prioritize rainmaking rituals. The anthropologist Camille Tounouga observes that for diverse communities across Africa water places are invested with meaning and constitute the 'realm of the spirits'.[15] Rain shrines, at which offerings are made to propitiate local water deities,

48 Horned serpents with maize collars at Tenabo, New Mexico.

can be found alongside many small agricultural holdings. Ethnographer Luc de Heusch describes a Zulu ceremony performed in times of persistent drought, in which a *calao*, or hornbill, associated with the celestial rainbow, is sacrificed to persuade the divinity to provide rain:

> Under its black plumage, coloured feathers are hidden. During serious droughts, the Zulu go off to a well-watered region to capture a hornbill alive. At early dawn they take it to a river where they break its neck or suffocate it, taking care to

avoid any spilling of blood. When the body is cold, they attach a stone to its feet and throw it into deep water in order to bring on the rain. The sky will 'weep' over the death of its favourite animal.[16]

In the Zulu cosmos, alongside the Master of the Sky whose presence is revealed through thunder, the co-sovereignty of the universe is held by a black python deity. As the terrestrial counterpart to the female rainbow, the python's role is to control rainfall, and in times of severe drought ritual offerings to him are meant to elicit 'soft and penetrating rain'.

> The procedure calls for the participation of a qualified rainmaker ... The emissaries from the drought-stricken area undertake the sacrifice of an absolutely black sheep (sometimes a goat) ... When it has been carved, the rainmaker, unaccompanied, carries the skin off to a stream. He settles down, on a black rock, in midstream, laying down beside him the horns containing magic medicine, and puts on the animal skin. He remains motionless for a long time. In the dead of night a python emerges from depths of the water and comes to lick off the fat that clings to the goatskin. The python genie then lies down on the magic horns in order to communicate his own coolness to them. He disappears, suddenly, silently.[17]

Like other such deities, African water serpent beings uphold the law and can bring punitive floods and landslides if angered by immoral behaviour, in which case animal sacrifices may be required to appease them.[18] Even where local societies have added monotheistic concepts of God to their traditional beliefs, water beings still regulate aquatic flows. Maintaining the gendered duality of early nature religions, they observe that God made two rainbows – a narrower male one and a wider female one – who can only stop excessive rains from falling by working together.[19]

It seems that the water serpent beings of small-scale agriculturalists are not fundamentally different from those of hunter-gatherers. They retain their gender complementarity and their responsibility for orderly flows in all domains of life, but they have a more critical role in providing sufficient rain to produce annual crops, and in preventing excessive rain that would destroy these. They also demonstrate that such societies maintain a highly respectful view of non-human powers, appealing to their major water beings as potentially beneficent or punitive authorities.

However, between 10,000 and 15,000 years ago, following a major ice age, there was an important turning point that directed many societies towards more instrumental and expansive trajectories of human development. Neolithic farmers began to establish substantial villages and to rely on more intensive crop production and animal husbandry.[20] This supported larger and more hierarchical societies but also introduced new uncertainties. Despite some initial flourishing, people did not always benefit from narrower diets and greater vulnerability to sudden variations in environmental conditions, such as lengthy droughts.[21] After millennia of sustainable 'steady-state' small-scale economies, some societies experienced forms of 'collapse'.[22] Higher levels of risk also drove people to seek more control over the non-human domain. A greater dependence upon agriculture led – seemingly inexorably – to population growth, increased resource use, negative impacts on non-human species and ecosystems, and ever more instrumental direction of the material world. This vital shift in direction was reflected in people's relationships with water and with water serpent beings.

Oceanic Beings

In larger, more hierarchical societies, water serpent beings began to change form. An example is provided by the Māori people who migrated from the Taiwan region across Oceania, arriving in New Zealand/Aotearoa between the late thirteenth and mid-fourteenth centuries.[23] Though initially focused on hunting, gathering and fishing, communities in the North Island turned to kumara cultivation and developed a horticultural economy. This supported sizeable populations, organized in kin groups (*whenua*) according to their descent from an ancestral 'canoe' (*whakapapa*). Sometimes numbering several thousand people, such sub-tribes or clans (*hapū*) are generally part of a larger tribe (*iwi*). These kinship arrangements flow from the primal ancestral beings, the female, male or androgynous deities who created the world, and their progeny, who remain present as 'living ancestors' in rivers, forests and water bodies.

Guardian water serpent beings called *taniwha* protect sacred sites and water places (*waahi tapu*). As well as providing vital sustenance, *taniwha* punish individuals who fail to respect sacred places and the *tapu* (power) of the gods or those, such as adulterers, who transgress social laws. Punitive action by a *taniwha* may involve swallowing people or causing floods or landslides that subsume them, and their dual nature is plainly expressed in the term for the Great White Shark, Mangō Taniwha.

Like other water serpent beings, *taniwha* incorporate the features of local species, especially aquatic creatures, and are often represented with fish scales and the sinuous bodies of the freshwater eels that are a popular food source. They sometimes have wings, or are bicephalous, and their heads are either 'dragon-like' or have highly stylized human faces (illus. 49).

This shift towards a more humanized form is important. Although representing many non-human species, Māori ancestral beings are often depicted in human or semi-human form, or with human faces. This constitutes a key visual deviation from the serpentine/non-human representations of the water beings created by hunter-gatherer and small-scale cultivation societies. I would suggest that this reflects the more hierarchical organization of Māori and Polynesian societies, in which major chiefs or 'big men' occupy positions of leadership and there is a 'royal' elite or *kingitanga*. In effect, the elevation of individuals to positions of greater power not only distinguishes them from lower classes but differentiates human and non-human beings. It is worth noting that this apparent increase in social hierarchy came with higher levels of material instrumentality. In intensifying their farming activities, and to assist hunting, Māori communities burned and cleared large areas of ancient forest, shaping a new kind of cultural landscape.

A shift in human-non-human relations is also suggested by Māori stories valorizing dragon-slaying culture heroes such as Tamure. Such stories are so recurrent across New Zealand that, when Europeans arrived with gold coins depicting St

49 Māori *taniwha* 'Ureia' from Tikapa, the Firth of Thames, on carved poupou (house post) from marae of Ngati Maru people, built in 1878 by Ngati Awa carvers from Whakatane.

George and the Dragon, this image was readily recognized as a battle between a culture hero and a *taniwha*. A Māori story about Tamure describes a classic defeat of a 'chaos monster':

> Not so long ago . . . there lived in an underwater cave at Piha, north of the Manukau Heads, a dreaded taniwha named Kai-whare. He was a monstrous cross between man and reptiles and was feared as a voracious man-eater. He was more clever than most taniwhas: he hunted with cunning, not just brute force. On quiet nights he would lie patiently just beneath the waves outside the harbour bar until he saw the glow of the torches of the fishermen wading in the shallow waters trying to spear fish; or until the canoes drifted down with the tide as the fishermen tossed their nets overboard to catch the plentiful snapper and flounder. The monster would then swim swiftly but stealthily into the harbour and seize a man or woman preoccupied with spearing fish or pull an unwary fisherman from a canoe. He would sink his awesome teeth into the victim and drag him away to his water lair for a leisurely meal. Such predation went on for a long time; the people were unable to do anything about it . . .
>
> So they turned to Tamure who was a giant of a man in Hauraki. He said he would deal with the taniwha and told them to go fishing as usual . . . The following day, as planned, the hero strode resolutely out to the bay and waited for the creature to make his appearance . . . The beast smelled prey and came crashing out of his underwater cave. Tamure heard a rumbling on the seabed as rocks were thrown aside and giant waves dashed upon the shore. The taniwha's hideous head rose above the water. As the beast was preoccupied looking for victims, Tamure unleashed a powerful blow of his mighty club upon its head, so violent a blow that the waters flew upward into the sky and the earth shook. Mortally wounded, Kai-whare thrashed about in agony, and the waves pounded against the cliffs, sending pillars of foam and water. The tail of the huge taniwha flung rocks and cliffs into the sea, leaving a clear-swept area of smooth rock that can be seen to this day.[24]

Though adversarial, stories about the hero Tamure are also creative, describing how the battle formed features of the coastline. Some are explicit in describing the *taniwha* as the kin of its victims, referring to it as the 'ancestor of the tribe'. These ancestral connections are explained by Chief Te Anaua: 'A *taniwha* is one of the very great chiefs who after death becomes a spirit within a fish. Tutae-poroporo was one of the greatest of this kind of fish and lived at Poutou . . . He destroyed a canoe, men and all, and everything that came in his way, until he himself was destroyed by Aokehu, the progenitor of the Whanganui tribes.'[25] Māori narratives therefore suggest a somewhat more contested relationship with the non-human forces represented by water serpent beings, in which veneration and ancestral ties coexist with some tensions about where power and authority lie.

Hydro-Agricultural Beings

A further influential change in human–environmental interactions came when people began to grow crops requiring irrigation. Approximately 9,000 years ago, Neolithic farmers in Southeast

50 Balinese rice terraces.

Asia started to modify swamps to grow taro. Like societies' broader shifts into agriculture, moves into hydro-agriculture were initially subtle, merely involving the construction of low bunds to retain annual floods. Similar techniques enabled rice cultivation to flourish from the upper Brahmaputra valley in northeastern India to central China. One of the oldest sites bearing traces of intensive rice cultivation is at Memudu, on the edge of Lake Taihu close to the Yangtze River delta. At least 8,000 years ago the Neolithic inhabitants made use of receding floods to cultivate rice, using only digging sticks and stone tools.[26] These low-key methods were quite sustainable, as were other small-scale, carefully managed forms of irrigation.

A useful example is provided by Stephen Lansing's well-known study of rice growing in Bali (illus. 50), enabled by hydrological schemes that, until the late twentieth century, were managed by local religious leaders via a form of Hinduism that blended not only Buddhist and Shiva ideas but an earlier nature religion called Agama Tirtha, the 'religion of water'.[27] The rice terraces belonging to village-based farmer associations (*subaks*) were irrigated from mountain lakes via an intricate network of channels and water temples. Local priests provided three key things: interlocution with the water goddesses to whom the temples are dedicated, hydrological and ecological expertise, and leadership and authority to ensure that all farmers received sufficient water flows. In this way religious rituals venerating local water beings simultaneously provided social, economic and hydrological management for each community and upheld sustainable human–environmental relationships.

An Early Collapse

Not all forays into irrigation were so successful. The rise and fall of Classic Maya societies in Central America, between circa 750 BCE and 900 CE, illustrate how reliance upon irrigation could be both empowering and risky. Early Maya societies had much in common with the American pueblo agriculturalists. They shifted from hunting and gathering to agriculture in approximately 5000 BCE. Building small thatch and pole houses, they established settlements alongside agricultural land, on which they grew maize.

Maya imagery reveals a lifeworld of intricate interdependency with non-human beings which ethnographer Lisa Lucero describes as a cosmocentric (rather than anthropocentric) worldview, in which all things played a role in maintaining an orderly social and ecological environment.[28] The sacred *cenotes* that defined local community identities provided not only water supplies but portals to the mythical underworld of Xibalba. Offerings to the deities inhabiting these water bodies, and related rituals connecting sacred and everyday worlds, were believed to uphold cycles of life, death and rebirth.[29]

But shifting into more intensive agriculture transformed Maya relationships with the non-human world, creating some important changes in perception. Instead of wild game and edible wild plants being provided by higher powers, societies had to 'bargain with' forces such as weather, rainfall, soil erosion and soil quality. New meanings were attached to wild animals such as large cats, predatory birds and poisonous snakes. Instead of being enemies and competitors for food, their dangerous characteristics provided inspiration for more assertive ideas about superior human power.[30]

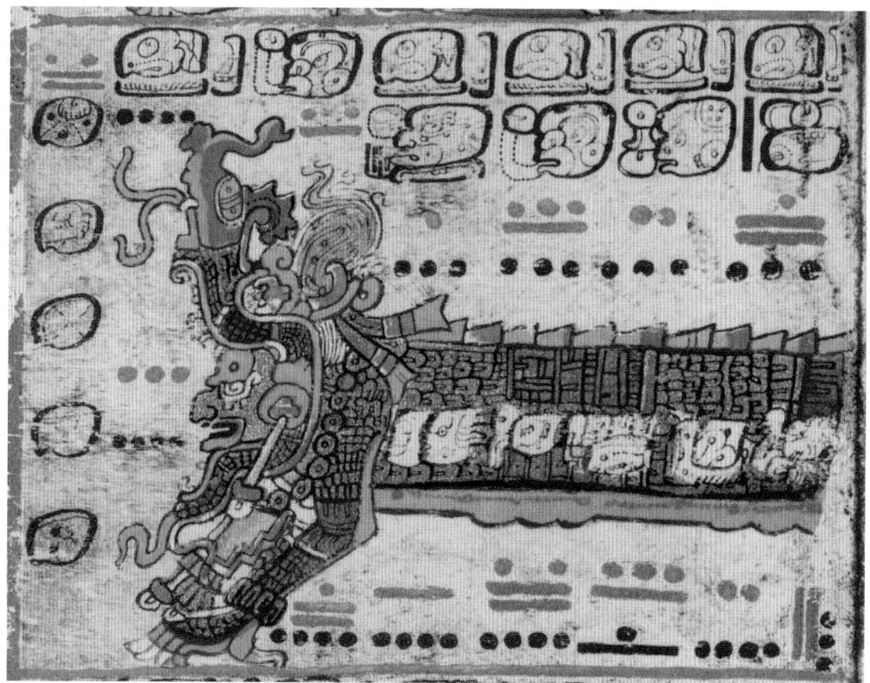

51 Itzam Na emerging in human form from the original world-creating serpent, *Dresden Codex*, 11th or 12th century, amate (bark) paper; this version is the Ernst Förstemann facsimile.

Maya agriculturalists acquired new maize gods, although, as in the pueblos, many were still depicted as water serpent beings representing the creative powers of the universe.[31] Seasonal cycles and the hydrological movements of water were represented by a range of serpentine beings, including the major creator being Itzam Na; the feathered serpent Kulkulkán/Q'uq'umatz; the rain-sparking lightning serpents; and the Water Lily Serpent, which communicated the relationship between water and fecundity through elaborate lotus imagery (illus. 51).

The iconographic evolution of Maya deities suggests a particular societal trajectory. Maya groups inhabited a lowland environment that, though disadvantaged by thin soils, contained rich wetland areas which they modified intensively with ditches and raised fields in order to grow crops such as avocados and maize. In the Classic period their irrigation technologies developed to include substantial water collection and storage (including sizeable dams, for example at Tikal). They built channels between wetland areas, used sand filtration and had switching stations to guide the seasonal movements of water. This sophisticated hydraulic instrumentality supported considerable population growth, to the extent that population estimates from 700 BCE suggest that there were 5 million people in the region – a much greater number than it supports today.[32]

Sophisticated irrigation also enabled the growth of urban centres and, from about 250 BCE onwards, Maya political structures began to exhibit the characteristics of a nascent state. Archaeologist Vernon Scarborough notes that

> As a critical and scarce resource during the lengthy dry season, water was politically manipulated by a Maya elite to centralize and control power during the Classic period . . . The fundamental need for water and the food that it allows – preparing and maintaining the earth for planting or the daily requirements for drinking water – made water management in a fragile, water-stressed environment another powerful organizing force. The construction and maintenance of water systems in the towns and cities of the ancient Maya concentrated water in a quantity and quality unavailable naturally. By placing water and its management apparatus in the center of their elevated Classic-period communities, the Maya permitted a controlling elite to manipulate the resource.[33]

With reservoirs and crops heavily dependent on seasonal rainfall, predicting the onset of the rainy season became a crucial challenge requiring intercession with the gods.[34] Religious leaders appropriated earlier household and ancestor-orientated rituals seeking rain and annual renewal, and turned them into ceremonies that gave increasing power to emergent rulers. The sacred land and waterscape reflected these changes. Ambitious religious monuments, pyramids or 'water mountains' represented the sacred *witz* mountains from which water flows, and 'Mayan temples became ancestral shrines writ large, highlighting the ruler's lineage and ties to the divine realm.'[35]

These sacred temple complexes enlarged and formalized religious ritual practices, including those engaging with water serpent beings. The ability to enter and return from the serpent's domain gave authority not just to priests but to political rulers, creating a governing elite associated with immortal deities and the creative powers of water. The political control of this elite also relied upon warfare, wealth, strong leadership and more centralized water management.[36] However, even as Maya society flourished, there were tensions between groups and anxieties about a challenging environment that, despite sophisticated water infrastructures, depended heavily upon seasonal rain and the deities responsible for its delivery. Pilgrimages to sacred sites and rituals propitiating ancestral beings were vital.[37] In times of drought, the sacred pools and temples became the focus of extreme rituals, sometimes involving multiple human sacrifices.

As in other enlarging societies, representations of Classic Maya gods became an elaborate mix of human and zoomorphic iconography, in which images of humanized deities suggest increasingly competitive relations with non-human powers. Towards the end of the Classic period, despite strenuous efforts to maintain stability, Maya society experienced severe problems relating to deforestation, soil erosion and overuse of resources. The precarity of dependence upon irrigation was fully revealed when, in the Late Classic period (*c.* 550–850), prolonged droughts triggered a major collapse.[38]

This early collapse illustrates the higher risks of a societal trajectory supporting growing populations with intensive irrigation. It also illuminates some key changes in how societies positioned themselves in relation to non-human worlds, shifting from reciprocal partnerships with non-human kin towards more hierarchical and adversarial relations in which human or semi-human deities competed with or tried to supersede non-human beings.

Flowing Out of Control

The 'collapse' experienced by Maya society was a salutary warning that highly instrumental crop irrigation represented a new and increasingly problematic developmental trajectory. Even more than agricultural expansion, technologies systematically diverting water into human activities permitted rapid growth in populations and economies, and greatly intensified people's use of land and resources. Today, with the imposition of major infrastructures, nearly 75 per cent of the world's fresh water is used to irrigate crops, supplying 40 per cent of global food production, and there are more than 1 million irrigation schemes ranging from small communal systems to vast state-led enterprises.[39] The World Bank predicts that irrigation to feed a growing human population will soon require the diversion of a further 15 per cent of Earth's fresh water.[40] How did this massive shift towards more instrumental lifeways come about?

It would appear that instrumental capacities to control water – that magical, elemental essence of life, health and wealth – are indeed 'enchanting'.[41] With no 20/20 hindsight regarding the social inequalities and conflicts that would ensue, or the ecological costs that would devastate environments and drive many non-human species to extinction, what could be more appealing than to direct water into the service of humankind? The ability to do so must have seemed wholly beneficial. Irrigation supported major increases in food production and wealth, and it conferred significant social and political power.[42] That this potential is intensely alluring remains evident today in contemporary desires for the giant dams that are still seen, by some, to represent successful leadership, nationhood and societal wealth and well-being.[43] It is therefore unsurprising that many societies were seduced into abandoning ecologically conservative lifeways and developing more and more sophisticated methods of directing water flows.

Even when modest in scale, new irrigation technologies had significant effects. *Qanats* (from the Akkadian terms for 'reed' or 'pipe') reflected a growing interest in water infrastructure (illus. 52). With vertical shafts down to the water table linking underground channels, *qanats* directed water to local fields. Becoming increasingly sophisticated over time (permitting ice storage and cooling shafts to houses), this technology spread to other arid regions in Asia and North Africa, creating distinctive patterns of settlement. The waterwheel, or *noria*, appearing in Egypt in the fourth century BCE, lifted water from its natural courses into irrigation channels or aqueducts that could irrigate extensive areas. Waterwheels also provided power – initially for milling, but later for multiple purposes

52 *Qanat* well of Tehrani Ha House, Yazd, Iran.

53 Historical *norias* at Hama on the Orontes River, Syria.

– eventually driving the Industrial Revolution (illus. 53).

One of the major effects of irrigated farming was that although small-scale practices could be sustained, larger-scale endeavours pushed societies onto more expansive developmental trajectories. Revisiting the Balinese rice growers described previously, Stephen Lansing found that although traditional hydrological practices, in which water temples mediated water flows, had proved stable and effective management of people and ecosystems, the more ambitious 'development' schemes subsequently imposed by rather volatile state governments were more problematic and unstable.[44] Lansing was prescient in anticipating the problems that would arise with a drive towards growth and development in the region. As well as imposing less sustainable land and water management, state aspirations have encouraged a tourism industry that now uses more than 60 per cent of Bali's freshwater. The result is an ongoing water crisis.

These examples therefore reveal an important tension between conservative and expansive beliefs and practices in relation to water and the non-human domain. Sustainable lifeways require a modest and respectful stance, one that limits economic growth and the extent to which human agency is imposed on local ecosystems. Greater technical instrumentality in directing water flows appears to encourage more authoritative modes of human–environmental engagement and aspirations for growth and expansion.[45] Introducing structural inequalities and exploitative practices, this is a trajectory that necessarily alienates humankind from the non-human beings that co-create our shared ecosystems. It is therefore revealing to consider what happened to water serpent beings in larger irrigation societies.

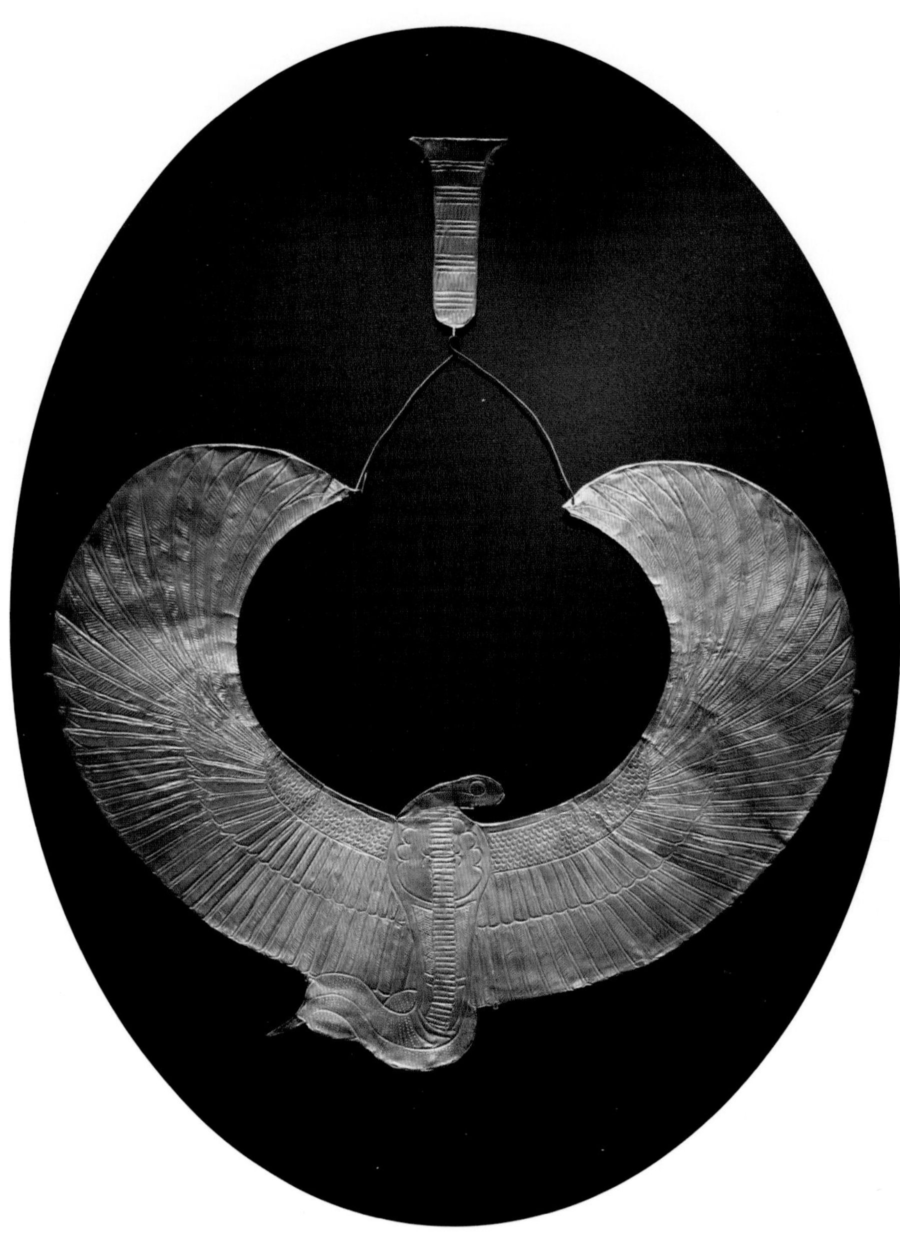

54 Winged uraeus, depicting the serpent goddess Wadjet, found in Tutankhamun's tomb, Egypt, 18th Dynasty, 1332–1323 BCE, gold.

6
Irrigating Beings

The religious and social changes that emerged in societies adopting more instrumental practices, replacing serpentine water beings with semi-human gods, or giving higher status to supernatural beings in human form, was carried further in societies that irrigated on a grand scale. Major water management schemes supported larger populations and demanded a considerable investment of communal labour in building water-retaining terraces, storage tanks, canals, dams and reservoirs. They required citizens to accept obligations to provide skills and labour or to pay taxes to support infrastructural development and maintenance. They needed specialist hydrological and technical expertise, regulation and new forms of property and rights.[1] These changes widened social inequalities based on class and gender and supported more patriarchal political arrangements.[2] By encouraging centralized governance, irrigation enabled the emergence of the state and created bureaucratic structures that alienated it from its subjects.[3]

As political and religious elites were empowered, authority was increasingly invested in dynastic kings and emperors. These anointed leaders became earthly representatives of the gods or were deified as gods or demi-gods themselves. The religious and socio-political arrangements of large irrigation societies therefore differed radically from those maintaining smaller-scale conservative lifeways. As ever, water was a perfect mirror, reflecting social fission and changing relations of power not only between people but between human and non-human beings.[4]

The societies explored in this chapter are commonly described as 'hydraulic civilizations'. The Latin *civilis* refers to 'citizens' and 'the city', highlighting tendencies, in dominant discourses, to equate technological advances and urbanization with social progress. Such assumptions about what constitutes civilization still underpin societies' efforts to reshape their surroundings and redirect water flows on a grand scale.

Ancient Egypt provides one of the earliest examples of such progressive aspirations. With verdant savannahs and wetlands, the region was inhabited by hunter-gatherers for many millennia.[5] Little is known about their beliefs, but it is likely that, along with other foraging societies, they worshipped deities manifesting the powers of the non-human world. As elsewhere, there was a transition to agriculture in the Neolithic period. Climate change and desertification pushed the population towards the Nile, and it coalesced into a unified state in circa 3100 BCE.[6] Successive dynasties, conventionally described as the Old, Middle and New Kingdoms, coincided with key stages of the Bronze Age. Egypt's citizens domesticated plants, ducks, geese and local ungulates, as well as importing cattle from Asia. They produced elaborate material culture (including gold jewellery, pottery and glass objects), developed a sophisticated system of hieroglyphs and established trading relationships across the region.[7] With the transition to agriculture and the emergence of cities the material record suggests a religious shift towards more humanized (or semi-human) deities, though many retained non-human features or continued to shift between multiple human and non-human forms.

Adaption to environmental pressures led to collaborative efforts to enhance natural drainage channels and build small bunds to retain floodwaters, and these soon succumbed to the allure of more substantial irrigation infrastructures. Their fortunes suggest an ongoing struggle: periods of stability alternated with semi-collapses in which severe droughts, combined with excessive government demands, caused famine and political strife.[8] However, there was no retrenchment to more conservative lifeways: historical accounts of the development of the Faiyum under the early Ptolemies suggest that strong governments responded to the vagaries of the Nile by instigating ever more elaborate systems of artificial irrigation.[9]

Substantial dykes were constructed to capture the Nile's annual flood and irrigate agricultural land. This vital inundation was celebrated with major ritual practices that continued until the nineteenth century. Along the river, annual flood levels were marked on Nilometers. As well as helping communities to manage the annual inundations and maintain their livelihoods, these measuring devices enabled them to anticipate excessive floods, such as the one in 638 BCE that turned the valley of the Nile into 'a primordial ocean and inert expanse'.[10] A system was established based on readings of the Nilometers and sightings from a watchtower built in Memphis, which enabled fast rowers to race down the river with flood warnings.

The first pharaoh, Menes (*c.* 3110–2884 BCE), built one of the world's earliest major dams 20 kilometres (12½ mi.) south of Memphis. It was about 450 metres (1,475 ft) long and 15 metres (50 ft) high. The Nile's waters were diverted into an artificial lake and channel, simultaneously providing the city with a defensive moat that, 2,500 years later, Herodotus noted was still guarded with care: 'to this day the Persians keep careful watch on this bend of the river, strengthening its dam every year to keep the current in; for were the Nile to burst its dikes and overflow here, all Memphis would be in danger of flooding.'[11] As well as providing flood control, the dam directed water through a series of basins that distributed the annual inundations. Between Aswan and the Mediterranean coast terraces were built ranging from a few hundred feddans (about half a hectare) to more than 60,000 feddans, and this system still supports much of Egypt's cultivation.[12]

The construction of major water infrastructures and the concurrent emergence of Egyptian dynasties illustrate the relationships between social, political and technological changes. The coalescence of smaller groups into a hydraulic state brought key shifts in how people understood the world, reflecting a movement from prehistoric nature worship to new ways of conceptualizing human–environmental relationships.

The early Egyptian cosmos shared with other nature religions beliefs in which multiple deities representing non-human powers were responsible for the direction of events. As noted previously, primeval water serpent beings were central to stories of cosmogenesis: indeed, it was from this region that much ophiolatry (snake worship) flowed around the world. It provided the seminal images of the creator serpent rearing up out of Nun, the watery chaos, to 'speak' the world into being, as well as those of the analogous lotus flower, rising from the waters as a symbol of 'life arising from the darkness of death'.[13]

A pantheon of gods was generated by these original water beings. Emerging from the lotus, the sun god Atum ('the all') formed the primeval mound and produced two 'fledglings', Shu (air) and Tefnut (moisture).[14] They in turn created the celestial goddess Nut (sky), arching protectively over her brother/consort, the green-hued god Geb (earth). A world-ordering principle, *maat*, personified as a winged goddess Ma'at, was countered by an apocalyptic prophecy about a disorderly 'end of time' when, according to the Egyptian Book of the Dead, 'the world will revert to the primary state of undifferentiated chaos and Atum will become a serpent once more.'[15] Egypt's water serpent beings therefore fulfilled their quintessential role in creating the world and mediating spatio-temporal flows of spirit and matter. Osiris and Isis, the next generation of deities responsible for maintaining these life flows, were also represented in serpentine form (illus. 55).

As well as producing the earliest representations of the ouroboros as a symbol of infinite time, one of the region's most abiding serpent images is that of the immortal uraeus, a tutelary deity. 'Incarnated in a serpent', the goddess 'rests in a shrine or sits upon a throne to receive the worship of her votary'.[16] In the Lower Egyptian town of Buto, a cult dating back to the pre-dynastic period worshipped Wadjet, a powerful serpent goddess whose name means 'the green one' or 'she of the papyrus'. Papyrus is made from the pith of a wetland sedge (*Cyperus papyrus*), and the first papyrus plant is said to have come from Wadjet's body.[17] Often depicted as a snake twined around a papyrus reed, Wadjet offers one of the very first images of the snake and the staff.[18] Spiralling around a reed, she was associated with earthly waters, but she was also sometimes depicted with wings, indicating a relationship with air and the celestial domain, and she was said to be able to spit fire (see illus. 54). Serpent beings were thus both protective and dangerous, and the sacred groves of the Egyptian otherworld were similarly guarded by a fire-breathing uraeus, who would 'destroy any invading or unjustified soul'.[19]

As a distillation of multiple religious traditions, the images and texts of ancient Egypt are fragmentary, presenting diverse and sometimes only loosely related narratives. Still, there are consistent patterns: serpent beings were cosmologically creative, representing water and its generative capacities, and infinite cycles of death and rebirth. They were tutelary and authoritative, with capacities to be punitive if necessary, and they were worshipped with great respect.

However, as religious leaders gained political ascendence, ideas and practices began to change.

Ceremonies were adapted to reflect the increasing power of the priests of Heliopolis and Memphis, whose influence spread to the rest of the country, upholding the king's religious authority and strengthening a process of centralization.[20] As cosmological beliefs began to favour more humanized deities, the multiple beings of earlier religions merged and transformed, acquiring new names and attributes. A process of humanization can be seen in images of Osiris, previously referred to as the world-encompassing 'round one' or 'green one'. On the sarcophagus of Seti I, he appears as a human figure engulfed in water and lying coiled, with head and heels meeting, around a space

55 Stela showing Isis and Osiris in serpent form, with the griffin of the goddess Nemesis.

containing the inscription: 'It is Osiris, encircling the Nether-World.'[21] So a classic water serpent being is humanized but retains key elements of its serpentine form and its association with deeper domains. His earthly counterpart, Isis, appears in serpent form on the same sarcophagus.

In later imagery, Osiris is represented in wholly human form. Narratives relate how he was murdered by Seth, and his 'wife' Isis – similarly humanized – mourns and holds a vigil over his body. Horus, the sun god, visits him in the underworld, liberates his soul and begets a lineage of earthly (that is, human) monarchs.[22] Critically, this narrative established the pharaoh as the scion of the sun god, and as an immortal representative of the gods. At the same time, at a human level, he was required to be a moral leader and a source of collective vitality and power, most obviously through ensuring reliable supplies of water.[23]

Reflecting the pharaohs' displacement of earlier serpent gods, portraits of them also slip between human and serpentine form. A serpent hieroglyph marks the tomb of Djet, the ruler of the First Dynasty, whose name means 'Horus cobra' or 'serpent of Horus'.[24] As noted previously, on the coffin of Rameses III, an ouroboros indicates the eternal life of the king.[25] The authority of the uraeus is transferred to the pharoah, and it becomes an accessory: 'an archetypal serpent image of kingship, which protruded just above the forehead in most royal crowns and headdresses'.[26] These changes in cultural imagery illustrate the process through which divine power and authority shifted away from serpentine gods into deified human hands.

By the Rivers of Babylon

The ideas that characterized the Egyptian cosmos resonated with those in Mesopotamia. While Egypt was developing large-scale water infrastructures the Sumerians had begun to irrigate the floodplain between the Rivers Tigris and Euphrates. They inhabited the area from about 3000 BCE to 1800 BCE, after which it came under the control of Akkadian, Hittite, Assyrian and Babylonian societies. The incomers made good use of Sumerian innovations, which included a written language that, inscribed on clay tablets, provided a detailed record of changing beliefs and practices, including transitions from theocratic forms of government to monarchies and a semi-democratic state. Their dependence on agriculture, as elsewhere, led to a close interest in the celestial domain and the development of annual calendars, which proved influential throughout the ancient world.[27]

Mesopotamian irrigation schemes were even more ambitious than those in Egypt, as the Tigris and Euphrates were more volatile than the Nile. There was no reliable annual flood, but rather unpredictable flows that led to Sumer offering the first 'great flood' story. Water storage and flood mitigation demanded major engineering works, such as the Nahrawān Canal, which absorbed much of the summer flow of the Tigris and its tributaries. Large canals, containing multiple sluices to control the water, were built on a scale similar to modern works.[28]

With a fast-growing urban population, there was considerable pressure to intensify agriculture. Babylonian cuneiform tablets from about 1800 BCE describe a range of water management problems and solutions, such as water clocks, wells and dams. Greater competition for water led to 'more intricate division of labor, social stratification, and, ultimately, state superstructures'.[29] Babylon also generated one of the earliest systems of law focusing on water rights, providing a model for many subsequent regulatory regimes. Initiated by King Hammurapi (often written as Hammurabi), who reigned from circa 1792 to 1750 BCE, the Hammurapi Code, inscribed on a stone stele just over 2 metres (7½ ft) tall, defined people's responsibilities to maintain irrigation schemes. 'Section 53. If anyone be too lazy to keep his dam in proper condition, and does not keep it so; if then the dam breaks and all the fields are flooded, then shall he in whose dam the break occurred be sold for money and the money shall replace the corn which he has caused to be ruined.'[30] Hammurapi's determination to impose authority, and to extend his rule across Mesopotamia, was made clear in a hymn in which he states: 'I am the king, the brace that grasps wrongdoers, that makes people of one mind. I am the great dragon among kings.'[31]

Mesopotamia therefore illustrates the social and material changes wrought by highly instrumental irrigation schemes, and the vulnerabilities introduced by dependence on them. Competition for water led to conflicts, for example King Sennacherib (705–681 BCE) dammed the Euphrates in order to release a punitive flood to drown his enemies. Sennacherib was a leading water engineer. He invented water-lifting screws cast in bronze and used these and aqueducts to irrigate the Hanging Gardens of Babylon at his palace in Nineveh. Centuries later these gardens were still described by Hellenic writers as one of the Wonders of the World. They presented in microcosm a vision of the world in which humankind enjoyed complete instrumental control of water.[32]

> The monarch played a vital role in assuring the fruitfulness of his own land and indeed all his empire, so fertility in its many aspects was symbolized in the garden . . . A freshwater lake . . . replicated the Apsû, which was the name for the water beneath the earth that supplies rivers and wells, and its personification as a force in nature . . . Just as chaos was represented by water in the Babylonian Epic of Creation – Tiâmat and Apsû, brought under control by Marduk – so Sennacherib's redirection of mountain streams demonstrated his ability to bring chaotic turbulence under control. But more than that, in raising water with screws, the natural chaotic tendency of water to flow downhill is reversed, and seasonal aridity is banished. Normally a garden in the latitude of Nineveh would lose its greenery during the fierce heat of high summer . . . The palace garden overrode these natural changes due to the abundance of water supplied throughout the months of summer heat, and kept its greenness as if in perpetual springtime while all around became desiccated, brown and dusty . . . Sennacherib's power over nature was apparent in all those ways.[33]

Sennacherib also introduced cotton to Assyria, and as large-scale irrigation schemes became the responsibility of all-powerful monarchs, representations of the deities responsible for water and life altered accordingly. Early Sumerian and Akkadian images show a tree or pole as a world axis, with two great serpents twined around it. But, as in Egypt, later humanized deities are shown carrying such images as accessories to signify their divine/human authority. Thus the Sumerian goddess Inanna, worshipped from circa 4000 BCE, 'carries the caduceus in her hand, two serpents twining about a staff'.[34]

While the worship of serpentine beings persisted throughout the dynastic period in both Egypt and Mesopotamia, this region also provided the first images of the serpent as an embodiment of evil who must be slain by a male culture hero. In Egypt, Apophis, 'the destroyer', was outwitted and defeated by the sun god, and Seth, who murdered Osiris, became a dragon or evil serpent, offering a nominative precedent and template for images of Set/Satan.

These stories may stem, in part, from an inherent psychological need for humans to slay 'the chaos monster' (see Chapter Three).[35] But set alongside a process in which humans themselves achieved divinity and appropriated the material, social and spiritual powers of nature beings, the emergent imagery of conflict also points to some important changes in human-non-human relations.

Flows from the Indus Valley

A broad pattern of deity humanization also emerged in the Indus Valley belief systems that spread across the Indian continent and into Asia. As in Egypt and Mesopotamia, increasing regional aridity drew tribal Neolithic farmers together into a larger irrigation society supporting about 5 million people.[36] The 'Harappan civilization', as it became known, enjoyed strong trading relationships with Sumer, enabling a flow of ideas between these areas.

Like other early irrigators, farmers in the Indus Valley relied on annual inundations from the Indus River and its tributaries. In addition to constructing bunds, they were expert builders of storage tanks, canals and reservoirs, for example constructing a series of major reservoirs at Girnar in 3000 BCE.[37] Indian texts from the fourth century BCE describe *cakkavattaka* (water-lifting devices, or 'turning wheels').[38] Cities benefited from urban sanitation schemes, which included household rooms set aside for bathing and wastewater flowing into covered drains adjoining the city streets.

The Harappans also invented a form of writing (which has yet to be deciphered) and sophisticated systems of measurement, including some of the world's first rain gauges. Their society depended upon centralized urban administration, and wider bureaucratic coordination is revealed in the seals used to identify property and shipments of goods. In the later Harappan period, between the tenth and sixth centuries BCE, powerful kingdoms emerged. A priestly class gained power and entrenched its authority by formalizing the Vedic religious scripts.

These developments established a hierarchy of castes that, even now, structures relations with water throughout India.[39] However, neither elaborate governance nor technical sophistication renders an irrigation-dependent society immune to vagaries in water flows. Having merged smaller groups to deal with increasing regional aridity in the first place, Harappan society found that, after a period of flourishing and rapid population growth, intensive irrigation was not enough to counter climate change and a two-hundred-year drought.[40] The historian Upinder Singh describes 'a breakdown of urban networks' in the late Harappan period.[41] Cities were abandoned and the population dispersed, returning to scattered rural communities or migrating into other regions.

With the Indus Valley 'collapse' Harappan ideas and practices were carried to the Ganges and Yamuna River basins, and further across the Indian subcontinent. The Mahabharata texts, written between 400 BCE and 400 CE, refer to multiple canals (the word *kanwa* coming from the ancient Persian word *kan*, 'to dig'), and the early Bengal kings directed overflows from the Ganges by cutting temporary channels across the system during floods.[42] Their water management enabled the region's economies to expand to the extent that Bengal traded with the Romans, and this prosperity continued under Mughal rule throughout the pre-colonial period. Sultan Ghias-al-Din Iwad Khalji (r. 1213–27), who rose from being a governor to ruling Bengal, built massive embankments and bridges to protect the capital, Lakhnawati, from flooding. He also constructed a high trunk road about 240 kilometres (150 mi.) long, intending not only to control floods and facilitate irrigation but to enable communication and military manoeuvres.[43] Travelling by boat from Sylhet to Sonargaon in the 1300s, the Moroccan explorer Ibn Battūta recorded a high level of prosperity in the area, with flourishing village gardens on both sides of the river.[44]

Such stability relied upon strict state control and hierarchies of responsibility. Public works departments devolved funds to local *zamindars* (landlords) responsible for digging canals and drains and repairing roads and embankments. They were authorized to tax local communities to pay for this infrastructural maintenance and to ensure that the work was done by village officials and volunteers (*gramsaranjami*). In these ways, the kingdom maintained control over both people and water.

Indian Water Beings

The flow of irrigation practices across the Indian subcontinent, and the coalescence of tribal societies into larger groups, led to some changes in religious beliefs. Prehistoric rock art, such as the animal paintings at the Bhimbetka Rock Shelters in Madhya Pradesh, suggests the veneration of non-human beings by early hunter-gatherers in the region. In the Indus Valley, archaeologists have surmised, from seals and carvings depicting horned figures surrounded by animals as well as phallus and vulva images, that its post-Neolithic inhabitants worshipped complementary male and female gods and their cosmic reproductive capacities, as well as deifying animals and plants.[45] Migrating into northern India in the late Harappan

56 Tibetan Buddhist dragon/sea serpent *makara* horn, 20th century, brass.

57 *Makaras* at Kidal Temple, Malang, East Java, c. 1248.

period (1600–1500 BCE), Indo-Aryan Vedic tribes of pastoralists brought *devas*: gods personifying aspects of the non-human world, including the weather (Indra) and the waters (Apas). The various strands of Hinduism that subsequently emerged from the region placed a major emphasis on female mother goddesses, embodied, for example, in the Mother Ganges.

Throughout the religious changes in the region, water remained spiritually central. There was widespread use of sacred baths, such as the ancient stepwell found at Dholavira, one of the major cities in the Indus Valley.[46] Built more than 5,000 years ago, this is one of the oldest and largest stepwells on the subcontinent. But there are thousands of sacred wells in India, attesting to a long cultural history of venerating water and its generative powers, and this persisted as Hinduism and Buddhism synthesized earlier religious ideas (illus. 56).

Representations of water beings in Indian art and architecture share a family resemblance with those of the place-based 'nature religions' described earlier in this volume. The *makara* introduced in Chapter One, which recurs in Hindu and Buddhist iconography throughout India and Asia, has all of the formal characteristics of early water beings, manifesting the life-giving powers of water through a hybrid mix of powerful local species, such as crocodiles, elephants, fish and snakes (illus. 57). The term *makara* itself derives from the Sanskrit word meaning 'sea dragon' or 'water monster', and forms the base for the word *magar*, meaning 'crocodile' (as well as generating the English word 'mugger'). *Makaras* are often shown swallowing or spitting out human figures or other species, suggesting a key creative (or destructive) role in enabling movement through different domains of spiritual and material existence. They are usually bicephalous, or appear as twins, typically as the guardians of portals into temples, either curving around doorways or sitting either side of them. They appear similarly at the entrance points to Buddhist stupas, or royal thrones.

58 *Vishnu on Ananta, the Endless Serpent*, with Brahma emerging on lotus flower, India, *c.* 1700, gum tempera and gold on paper.

There is an important difference, however. With the emergence of Hinduism, *makaras* ceased to be primary deities manifesting the generative powers of water and instead became the vehicles (*vahana*) of humanized water deities, such as the goddess Ganga, or the sea deity Varuna, who were depicted riding on their backs. Other serpent beings also took on supporting rather than leading roles. As mentioned previously, humanized images of Vishnu and his consort Lakshmi, and the Buddha, are often shown reclining on the body of the Great Serpent, afloat on the cosmic ocean (illus. 58).

Lajjā Gaurī

Similarly humanizing shifts in form are evident in the representations of the goddess Lajjā Gaurī, a major fertility deity who first appeared in the Indus Valley as part of a popular pre-Vedic cult that was then absorbed into mainstream Hinduism: 'descending from a group of ancient popular symbols . . . [c]onceptually Lajjā Gaurī has antecedents which may be, and in fact have been, traced back to the Indus Valley art of about 2500–1500 BC.'[47]

The art historian Carol Bolon describes the earlier images of Lajjā Gaurī as aniconic, representing a concept of creativity by depicting the lotus plant and the ways in which its various parts offer visual analogues of human reproductive organs. But over time the lotus plant form of the goddess changed and humanized.[48] First she acquired a human body, though she retained a lotus as a head (illus. 59); however, by the sixth century the lotus embodying the goddess was gone. Lajjā Gaurī appeared with a human head and in fully human form, albeit still holding the phallic lotus buds and serpent armlets signifying her longstanding role as a symbol of fertility and regenerative powers.[49]

Bolon suggests that the earlier non-human representations, both of the Buddha and of Lajjā Gaurī, expressed their true essence as 'something beyond the natural, beyond the human, which can most effectively be expressed by use of powerful macrocosmic and primordial symbols'.[50] This may indeed be the case, but I would argue that the progressive humanization of deities in Indian iconography also reflects changing human-non-human relationships, and shifts from low-key hunting and gathering, pastoralism and small-scale agriculture, towards the greater instrumentality and control over water that came with larger-scale endeavours and major irrigation technologies.

59 Sculpture of the fertility goddess Lajjā Gaurī with head of lotus, Madhya Pradesh, India, c. 6th century, sandstone.

The *Nāgas*

The most well-known water serpent beings in India (and in the many regions to which its belief systems spread) are the *nāgas*. As with the *makaras*, *nāgas* can be found across India and the East, linked to ideas about water and fertility in Hinduism, Buddhism and Jainism. Representations of these deities span at least three millennia, and, as Jean-Philippe Vogel says: 'even more astonishing is the endless variety of aspect under which the Nāgas appear in Indian art and literature.'[51] They appear as major figures in the earliest Vedic scripts, dating from circa 1500 BCE, which recorded much older oral narratives,[52] and they feature centrally in major religious texts such as the Mahabharata and the *Puranas*, which continued to recompose this material until circa 800–900 CE.

The *nāgas* described in the Mahabharata, the Puranas and the Rigveda are consistently serpentine in form (illus. 60). Their bodies are often covered in scales, and, like the Egyptian uraeus, they borrow formal characteristics from cobras, having – often multiple – hooded heads. They bring rain, fertility and enlightenment.[53] When they appear as celestial beings, their venom represents lightning and a fiery heat, or *tejas*, that indicates supernatural energy, but they are primarily located in water bodies and a fluid underworld called the Nāgaloka. This domain is believed to be accessible via anthills, which feature as altars in village shrines venerating

60 *Nāgas*,
stone carving,
Hoysala Empire,
10th–14th century,
Chennakeshava
Temple, Belur,
Karnataka, India.

nāgas and are used for the propitiatory rituals that these deities require.[54]

Serpent shrines and rituals venerating snakes remain common in agricultural communities in India and form the basis of several major annual festivals, such as Naga Panchami and Anant Chaturdashi. Celebrations involve offerings of milk (also used for serpent worship in ancient Greece), rice and turmeric; the burning of incense and camphor; and the strewing of flower petals.[55] Historically, they may also have included the consumption of hallucinogenic soma, typically offered to deities in rituals celebrating the 'fiery' and enlightening energies of *nāgas*.[56]

The image of the snake sloughing off its skin recurs powerfully in Indian texts, indicating the liberation of the person from mundane (material) existence, or from the weight of their sins and impurities. Sloughed snake skins were traditionally believed to have magical powers, and the *Tāṇḍya-Mahābrāhmaṇa* (*c.* 1400 BCE) refers to their use, and to 'serpent sacrifices' believed to confer immortality.[57] The hydro-theological movement of *nāgas* as water and fire serpent beings is illustrated by a passage from the *Yajurveda* (*c.* 1200–800 BCE).

> Homage be to the snakes whichsoever move along the earth. Which are in the sky and Heaven, homage to these snakes. Which are the arrows of sorcerers and . . . which lie in holes, homage be to those snakes. Which are in the brightness of heaven, and which are in the rays of the sun, which have made their abodes in the water, homage be to those snakes.[58]

Foundational Buddhist literature describes four ancestral tribes of serpent kings.[59] The *Puranas* offer eight major creator serpents, the Ashta Nāgas.[60] In the *Bhagavata Purana*, the major serpent deity Sankarshana has lived deep within the otherworld Patala since long before the world was created, and is said to be able to destroy and recreate the universe. Over time, Sankarshana became Ananta, the cosmic serpent. This name derives from the Sanskrit term *anant*, interpreted as 'infinite', 'endless' and 'limitless', and as signifying 'the remainder: that which remains when everything else is gone. He is sometimes known as Shesha, too, because he is the *shesha-nāga*, the multi-cobra-headed king of all the *nāgas*. Like other major creative water serpent beings, he is a source of knowledge and enlightenment. The *Puranas* therefore describe him as 'speaking' the *Bhagavata*, and bringing the world and consciousness into existence.

Written narratives about *nāgas* coincide with the synthesis of earlier belief systems into Hinduism. They suggest movement from the veneration of the localized water beings of small-scale, place-based communities, to religious ideas expressing more abstract worldviews. In the Vedic texts, the Waters (*Apah*) are regarded as purifying and, as the first residence of Nara the Eternal Being, they comprise *prahtisha*, the foundational principle of the universe. The early texts also define water as a manifestation of Sakti, the feminine principle.[61]

In later Hindu and Buddhist narratives and images the serpent Ananta exists contemporaneously with humanized gods. As Vishnu and his consort Lakshmi (the goddess of wealth and prosperity) recline on Ananta/Shesha's body, floating on the cosmic ocean, Brahma emerges from the lotus plant growing from Vishnu's belly, and it is he – not the great serpent – that forms Earth and

61 Vishnu incarnated as Matsya (fish) to save humankind and the sacred texts from a deluge, 19th century, gouache painting on mica by an Indian artist.

the Heavens.[62] The Mahabharata describes Shesha being directed by Brahma to inhabit the underworld, Patala, in order to support the unstable Earth upon his hood.

However, in a religious tradition founded on ideas about reincarnation, form and identity are fluid. Hindu deities shift between embodiments and lives, and serpentine and human form. The familiar humanized figure of Kali is also the Mother Goddess, 'the deep blue one' representing the dark fluidity from which everything is born.[63] A 'force of time' associated with seasons and cycles, she has powers to bring life or death.[64] In some stories, the great serpent Ananta is an earlier manifestation of Vishnu (or his avatar Krishna), and the *Puranas* state that 'The foremost manifestation of Lord Vishnu is Sankarṣana, who is known as Ananta. He is the origin of all incarnations within this material world' (illus. 61).[65]

As these stories developed over time, images of Vishnu/Krishna not only tended to take human form but were historicized, highlighting an important narrative movement from religious mythology to human history: 'In Brahminical legend he [Krishna] may become a pious ascetic, in Buddhist lore he may even develop into a self-denying saint. Very often these various types appear strangely blended.'[66] In one popular story, Vishnu is caught eavesdropping on the secret teaching imparted to the goddess Parvati by Lord Shiva and is required, ever after, to impart this knowledge in human form, as Patanjali.[67] Similar humanization is evident in Buddhism when, after centuries of non-figurative 'aniconic' imagery, Greek influence in the first century BCE led to Buddha being depicted in human form, like Vishnu, supported by a great serpent (illus. 62). Thus creative water serpent being narratives in India contain a series of transitions in which originally serpentine beings settle into human form, and those previously represented in abstract form (such as the Buddha) are more explicitly humanized and accompanied by subservient serpent beings.

Shifts in human-non-human relationships are revealed not only by the increasingly servile position into which Ananta and other serpent beings

62 Statue of Buddha and the serpent Mucilinda, Angkor, Cambodia, 12th century, bronze.

63 *Aghasura the Serpent Demon Swallows Krishna, the Gopas and Their Herd*, Madya Pradesh, India, 1700–1875, watercolour on paper.

are placed in relation to humanized deities but also in stories describing tensions between them. Some reflect conflicts between groups wanting to retain their religious veneration of *nāgas* and those committed to worshipping a more humanized vision of Krishna. There are several accounts of humans or humanized deities imposing authority and dominance over *nāgas*. Male culture heroes do so in ways suggestive of sexual violation. For example, in a story from Tiruvārūr: 'The village goddess Mātangī was discovered when a king pierced her anthill home with his lance: Mātangī rose from the anthill bleeding, with the heavens in her left hand and the cosmic serpent Ādiśesa in her right.'[68] The Vedas describe how control over primordial waters was wrested from Vritra, a major water serpent being: 'Vṛtṛa was a snake who encircled the primordial waters and kept them from flowing. His name means "The Suppressor". He is described in the Vedic tradition as tricky, insulting and godless . . . Indra, wielding thunderbolts as Zeus does in his battle with Typhon, slays the dragon and thus frees the waters that were in confinement.'[69] Indra's appropriation of the serpent's power over water is echoed in a well-known story from the *Bhagavata Purana*. Entitled 'Krishna Chastises the Serpent Kâliya', it describes how Krishna subdued the poisonous *nāga* Kâliya, who was polluting the Yamuna River in Vrindavan.[70] 'There was a certain pool where Kâliya . . . resided and its water boiled because of the fire of his poison. Birds flying over it would fall [dead] into its waters. All plant and animal life on the shore died because

64 Krishna dancing on the hood of the serpent Kâliya in the Yamuna River, with two of the serpent's consorts pleading for him. The river is portrayed as circular lotus-filled reservoir. Gouache painting, Thanjavur, Tamil Nadu, India, late 18th–early 19th century.

it came into contact with the poisonous vapor that by the wind was carried from the waves.' Krishna leapt from a Kadamba tree into the poisonous water, which flew into turmoil as Kâliya vomited. As the serpent tried to crush him in its coils, Krishna made himself vast and, with the weight of the universe held in his abdomen, danced on the *nāga*'s multiple heads (illus. 64).

> The Lord who with His kicking feet punishes the evil ones, made the serpent . . . spit horrible [poisonous] blood from its mouth and nostrils while it experienced the greatest anguish . . . The serpent got tired of the heavy weight of the heels of Lord Krishna . . . his umbrella-like hoods were shattered by His trampling . . . His wives in distress approached the Original Lord with their clothing, ornaments and locks of hair in disarray . . . They laid their bodies and children on the ground before Him . . . They bowed down, saintly joined their hands and solicited the liberation of their sinful husband.[71]

Through this dramatic defeat Krishna asserts his authority over the serpent. In some versions of the story Kâliya's submission releases the *nāga* from the 'curse' of its serpentine embodiment, presenting the non-human water serpent being as a yet-to-be-'civilized' manifestation of water's powers. In a similar story Krishna enters the body of a serpent demon to rescue some cow herders (*gopas*) and their cattle. The god's body expands and the serpent bursts, allowing the cow herders to emerge unharmed and praise Krishna for saving them from being consumed (illus. 63).

What emerges is a consistent narrative pattern in which India's water serpent beings (and their lotus analogues) were either humanized themselves or subdued by humanized deities who appropriated their power and control over water. These patterns were repeated in other 'hydraulic civilizations' that, matching religious with material control over water, developed more centralized and hierarchical political arrangements governed by theocratic elites. As well as introducing widening social inequalities, this carried these societies further along a trajectory which enlarged expectations about human instrumentality and overrode the interests of the non-human beings whose habitats and well-being were subsumed by irrigated agriculture.

7
Travelling Beings

The prosperity and power of the great irrigation societies reached across continents and oceans, enabling the spread of Hindu and Buddhist beliefs across Southeast Asia. By the beginning of the Common Era there were trading relationships between the Roman Empire, India and many parts of Asia, and within a couple of centuries Fu-Nan, in the lower Mekong delta, had become a vital commercial centre.[1] Via these trade routes the water serpent beings originating in the Indus Valley flowed across India, Tibet and Nepal and into China. Mingling with Chinese ideas they travelled on into Cambodia, Vietnam, Korea, Burma, Laos, Thailand, Malaysia and Indonesia, and along the way they encountered diverse cultural contexts, each of which brought particular belief systems and cultural traditions to the interactions.[2]

The ideas carried by Indian water serpent beings did not invariably supersede indigenous beliefs. Meeting the 'nature religions' and deities of place-based hunter-gatherer communities, they sometimes regained a more localized role, permeating sentient landscapes, providing rain and resources in return for propitiation and adherence to societal mores and underpinning ideas about cycles of life and death.

> Beliefs among 'tribal' groups in Borneo . . . partially derive from both the Chinese *lung* and the Indian *nāga* deity. This makes sense in the context of the significant relationships which have existed for millennia between SE Asia, including Borneo, and both India and China . . . Among the [Kelabit] terms used for these beings are . . . *menegeg*, which appears to derive from the term *naga* . . . The *menegeg* originates as a python (*menelen*) within the earth, high up on a mountain or hill. When it becomes very big and strong the python is said to transform into a *menegeg* and to break out of the earth, creating a landslide. It makes its way down to the river, and then into a deep pool. Some informants said that *menegeg* can also develop from eels (*delo*) . . . [and] eventually transforms into a *lalau*, which is bigger and more powerful and has horns like a Chinese dragon. When there is heavy rain and high water, the *menegeg* or *lalau* travels downriver, as far as the sea, but it returns eventually to the pool from which it came.[3]

65 Dragon, Haedong Yonggungsa Temple, Busan, South Korea, 1376.

Similarly localized belief systems can be found in many rural areas in Southeast Asia, where – echoing earlier religious traditions – water serpent beings are often described as ancestors. In Vietnam, some of the region's oldest artefacts, Dong Son bronze objects from between 400 BCE and 200 CE, carry engravings of the Giao Long dragon, a pair of ancestral serpent beings. Local stories of cosmogenesis, including popular contemporary narratives, explain that the Vietnamese people are descended from a union between a dragon king and a 'fairy' (spirit being).

Regional transitions from hunting and gathering to Neolithic farming also followed a familiar pattern. In South Korea, a display tellingly entitled 'From Nature to Human Beings' at the National Folk Museum describes how, in the Palaeolithic and Neolithic periods, 'people learned to cultivate and utilize nature rather than merely adapting to their surroundings.' Increased agricultural production led to the emergence of social classes, conflicts over land and resources and the founding of the first state, Gojoseon.[4]

Korean agricultural villages were organized according to ideas about wind and water, and an ideal settlement (*baesanimsu*) had a river at the front and a mountain behind. However, marine resources remained important, and the water deities who provided these were highly valorized, for example in the form of a 'Seawater Great Goddess Buddha' (illus. 65).

In Korea, as in other parts of Asia, ideas about movement and material transformation were expressed in the notion of the 'hidden dragon'. A dragon could hide in the clouds or water, or take the form of a fish and then transform itself into a dragon. For example, Beomeosa Temple near Busan was built in 678 by a monk, Uisang. Its name means 'fish from Heaven', or 'Temple of the Nirvana Fish'. This refers to a story in which a divine fish rides to Earth on a rainbow-coloured cloud to play in a hilltop well, making the water shimmer with its golden hue. The 'golden fountain' (Geumsaem) never runs dry and is said to have magical properties. Such stories, in which a supernatural fish is actually a hidden dragon, are common in the region, and temples often contain representations of both dragons/water serpent beings and those 'hiding' in the form of fish.

While remote rural populations tended to retain traditional worldviews, the urban centres linked by trade were more fluid in their ideas. There was widespread adoption of Indian religious beliefs by Southeast Asian elites. Historical records are patchy prior to the third century BCE, but the extent to which Indian water serpent beings permeated the entire region is readily apparent in the ubiquity of *makara* and *nāga* carvings in temple architecture. *Makaras* in Korean temples are often shown carrying lotus flowers, and their serpentine forms 'combine the traditional Chinese appearance with the Buddhist meaning and character of the nāga imported, along with Buddhism, from India'.[5] The writer Heo Gyun (1569–1618) suggested that in Korean temple motifs, 'The countless dragon's scales are a metaphor for infinity, and the dragon's power is said to be unfathomable . . . It is attributed with an ability to control the weather, causing clouds, fog or dew to form, as well as starting or stopping rainfall.'[6]

In Japan, ancient texts such as the Nihongi (790 BCE) and Kojiki (680 BCE) describe dragons as classic water serpent beings: composite hybrids of local fauna manifesting the generative powers of water (illus. 66).[7] The Japanese rain god Zennyo Ryūō (dragon king) is represented either as a dragon or as a human with a snake's tail; and a shape-shifting god of fertility and agriculture, Inari, is depicted variously as a dragon, a snake and a fox.

Buddhist Indo-Chinese water serpent beings travelling into Japan in the Yayoi period (*c.* 300 BCE to 300 CE) also encountered the deities of early forms of Shintoism, in which non-human beings, *kami*, located in mountain peaks, valleys, rocks and trees, manifested the powers of nature and the spirits of clan ancestors.[8] Religious syncretism followed: the kami were absorbed into Buddhist cosmology and increasingly anthropomorphized. Thus modern Japanese makes use of the ancient Japanese term for dragon (*tatsu*), but also the Sino-Japanese term *ryū*, from the Chinese *lóng*, and the Sanscrit term *nāga*.[9]

As irrigated agricultural practices took hold, rice became Southeast Asia's major subsistence crop, and narratives about water serpent beings suggest some movement from propitiation to dominion.[10] In a Japanese story recognizing the hubris of human instrumentality, Mizuchi, a powerful river being, is offered human sacrifices by Emperor Nintoku to appease its displeasure regarding his

66 Katsushika Hokusai, dragon painting from the ceiling of the Higashimachi Festival Float, 1844.

river engineering projects. A more assertive relationship is implicit in one of Japan's oldest legends, which describes attempts to control the Hii-kawa River. In the story – still popular in theatrical performances – Yamata no Orochi, an eight-headed, eight-tailed giant snake, is slain by Susano, the human 'Son of the Creator'.[11] In other stories, sea serpents (*kuma-wani*) are co-opted to serve as pilots for the ships of Emperor Chūai and Empress Jingū, and several water serpent beings, Toyotama-hime ('luminous pearl princess') and Kotoshiro-nushi-no-kami – a sea serpent 8 fathoms (nearly 15 metres) in length – are described as the ancestors of Japan's first emperors, underlining both their ancestral role and the transferral of their powers to deified human rulers (illus. 67).[12] These changes laid the foundations for a series of transitions towards more instrumental engagements with the non-human domain that, in the mid-twentieth century, culminated in a period of rapid industrialization.

Imperial Beings

Serpent beings from India also met and mingled with ancient Chinese water deities.[13] A character for 'dragon' appears in the Jiaguwen scripts inscribed on the tortoise-shell and bone objects used for divination in the Shang dynasty (*c.* 1556–1046 BCE),[14] and early pottery and jade artefacts show dragons with fish scales and eagle talons.[15] Suggesting some gender parity in religious authority, Edward Schafer notes that female 'shamankas' or 'water women' in Bronze Age China led rituals concerned with fertility, including those hoping to persuade ancestral deities to bring rain to parched farmlands.[16]

Further glimpses of early Chinese water serpent beings are found in the *Yih King*, the divination text that first appeared circa 1000 BCE. Better known subsequently as the *I Ching*, or *Book of Changes*, this describes the dragon as 'a water animal akin the snake which [goes] to sleep in pools during winter and arises in the spring . . . It is the god of thunder, who brings good crops when he appears in the rice fields (as rain) or in the sky (as dark and yellow clouds); in other words when he makes the rain fertilize the ground.'[17]

Writing in the first century CE, Wang Chong states that 'the place where dragons live is often in water pools, not in trees or houses . . . Actual dragon-snakes live among remote mountains and great waters.' Later additions to his text observe that 'Clouds and rains appear on certain high mountains; flood dragons live in certain deep waters.'[18] Other ancient manuscripts describe how 'dragons and clouds summon each other . . . the dragon is the same species as clouds';[19] and 'those of the same ether join together . . . hence rain is brought by dragons.'[20]

Jean-Philippe Vogel observes that 'it cannot be doubted that the character of the dragon, as it appears in the folklore and literature of China, is partly derived from the Indian conception of the *nāgas* as important deities with power over water'.[21] Undertaking pilgrimages to India in the fifth to seventh centuries CE, early Chinese Buddhists such as Fa-hien and Hiuen Tsiang used the term *nāgas*

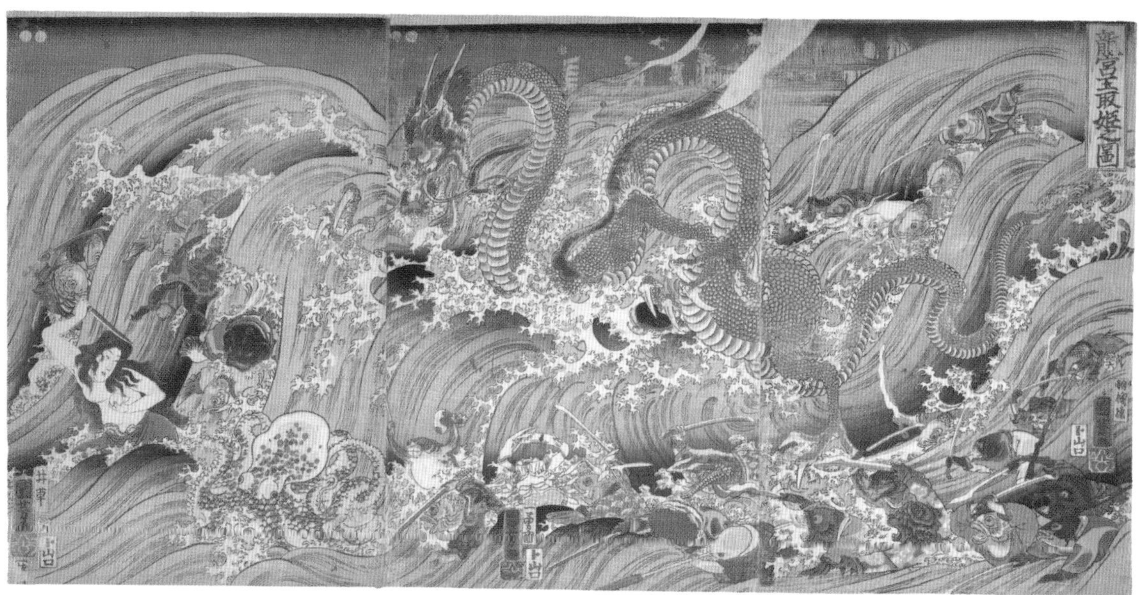

67 Utagawa Kuniyoshi, *Recovering the Stolen Jewel from the Palace of the Dragon King*, 1853, triptych of woodblock prints, ink and colour on paper.

68 Yashima Gakutei, *Chinese Sage Evoking a Dragon*, *c.* 1825, woodblock print (*surimono*), ink and colour on paper.

and 'dragons' interchangeably, and regularly alluded to dragons' capacities to control the elements. Fa-Hien observed that the dragons of the Tsung-ling mountains caused wind, snow and rain, and that, in Sankisa, Buddhist priests worshipped in the temple of a benevolent rain-bringing dragon. Another pilgrim, Sung-Yun, described the Buddha's attempts to convert a *nāga* king whose anger had caused a violent storm.[22]

Chinese scholars have given close attention to the origins and evolution of the dragon (illus. 68). Xin He suggested that the dragon represented 'the living form of the cloud god'. The god of clouds, rain and thunder is called *fenglong* ('abundant and magnificent'), and the same ancient characters are used for *long* (隆, 'magnificent') and *long* (龙, 'dragon').[23] He also proposed that it was based on a now extinct 'snake crocodile' (*Crocodylus porosus*).[24] Anthropologist Bingxiang Zhu notes that Chinese history has long searched for the 'true image' of the dragon but contends that this cannot be found because, in accord with historical and cultural changes, such symbols are bound to undergo regular reinterpretation and changes in form.[25]

However, there are some important consistencies. Chinese dragons are typically shown amid waves and clouds, with the 'precious pearl' or moon that – in a classic 'swallowing and regurgitation' trope – they consume cyclically to create rain (illus. 69).[26] In the Chinese cosmos the 'precious pearl'

69 Imperial dragons, Beihai Park, Beijing, 1756, ceramic tile screen.

70 Descending dragon, Quán Thánh Temple, Hanoi, Vietnam.

was an important symbol representing the relationship between women, the Moon, rain and fertility. In art and literature women represented the moist and receptive principle in nature and the water cycle that enables dry soil to respond to the impregnating masculine sun. The pearls appearing alongside water beings were comprised of lunar and female essence, waxing and waning in foetal form within the oyster in concert with menstrual cycles. Their form represented miniature moons: the Moon itself was a celestial version of feminine water and ice, and 'a woman's tears were both moons and pearls . . . an important link, both ontological and symbolic, between the worlds of women and dragons, and tidal flows'.[27]

As well as aligning the role of water serpent beings with fertility and annual crop production, Chinese worldviews placed a strong emphasis on the hydrological movements of water, describing celestial and earthly elements ruled by different deities. The Taoist cosmos was a world of waters: under the starlight of the heavenly river Tian He (also known as Yin He, the Silvery Way), land was surrounded by a roaring sea, and the celestial sphere was divided into seasonal quarters.[28] As noted previously, Taoist lore describes an Azure Dragon presiding over the spring and the ascendency of the masculine principle *yang* while, in the opposing quarter, the White Tiger provides a counterbalance of *yin*.[29] This vision of finely balanced creative energies throughout the cosmos, conceptualizing order as 'harmony', generated ideas about geomancy or *feng shui*. Composed of the terms for 'wind' (White Tiger) and 'water' (Azure Dragon), *feng shui* was primarily concerned with establishing orderly flows of water, air, energy and the spirit (illus. 70).

As elsewhere, however, there were shifts in ideas about what constituted orderly and desirable social and political arrangements. As imperial dynasties imposed greater authority over diverse cultural regions, their stories of cosmogenesis sought to present a more coherent 'Chinese' (Great Xia) identity, in which all of its peoples were described as the 'children of the River of Heaven' (Tian He/the Milky Way) and as descendants of the primary ancestral serpent twins, Fuxi (male) and Nüwa (female), described in Chapter Three.[30] This collectivized ancestral connection empowered the emperors who ruled China from the 1300s BCE to the early twentieth century.

Like the Egyptian pharaohs, Chinese emperors acquired a divine mandate to impose order on the region's unruly waters. The first major imperial dynasty (the Xia dynasty, *c.* 2070–1600 BCE) was founded by a hydrological engineer, Yü the Great, who is said to have brought civilization to China. As with other figures in antiquity, he sits ambiguously between being a legendary culture hero and a historical figure. His major achievement was to redirect the Yellow River, and then to extend this control over other Chinese rivers, establishing from the beginning a vital relationship between political governance and the control of waterways.[31] David Pietz makes the point more directly:

> Yü the Great is reputed to have dug the channels for the Huai, Yellow and Yangtze Rivers in the prehistoric era. In what had been a massive marshy swamp, these new channels allowed the reclamation of land and provided the agricultural conditions to sustain the development of the Chinese state and empire. As

the legend goes, 'but for Yü we would all have been fishes'.[32]

Dams were built in 598 BCE in Anhui province, and the precursor of a series of Jinjiang levees on the Yangtze in 356 CE.[33] Large infrastructural developments, in particular China's vast canal network, enabled a process through which both people and water were increasingly subject to imperial authority.[34] Power was centralized in patrilineal royal dynasties and more hierarchical social arrangements, and this was reflected in transformations in the character and role of its water serpent beings. By the time of the Han dynasty (206–220 BCE) there were anxieties about *yin* dominating *yang*, and efforts to disempower female water deities:

> The great water deities of Chinese antiquity were . . . snake queens and dragon ladies: they were the avatars of dragons precisely because they were equally spirits of the meres and mists and nimbus clouds . . . In early antiquity, the sex of dragons was ambiguous and variable, with the yin and female attributes dominant. In medieval literature, the yang and masculine attributes come somewhat to the fore, although they never quite submerge the ancient core of yin.[35]

Artists increasingly employed imagery of non-human deities to express the power and status of the Chinese emperors. The imperial dragon's five claws differentiated it from the three-clawed water serpent being of everyday life. As dragons acquired militant and masculinized forms, their role in expressing non-human generative powers segued into the emperor's capacities to deliver wealth and prosperity. Chinese rulers' authority was compared to the dragon's power over water: just as the chief celestial dragon controlled all forms of water, and the rainfall on which life depended, the emperor was believed to watch over his people and provide for their spiritual, social and material well-being.[36]

While empowering the ruling dynasties, China's extensive canal network required constant management, encouraging an instrumental relationship with water that is encapsulated in the term *shuili*, or 'taking advantage of water'. Still in use today, this term first appears in the *Guanzi*, a text dating from the third or second century BCE. In the same era, a Ministry of Water was established and has remained responsible for water management, delivering one of the 'first duties of the State'.[37]

Nearly 1,800 kilometres (1,120 mi.) in length, and still the longest in the world, China's Grand Canal was built between the late 500s and early 600s to carry the emperor Yang Guang between Beijing and Hangzhou. Canal networks expanded agricultural trade, carrying grain tribute to the capital and encouraging a flow of people and goods between regions. However, such ambitious water infrastructures were also extremely labour-intensive and left populations vulnerable to engineering failures, or to the use of water as a flood weapon. In a familiar pattern, imperial dynasties were marked by a series of crises and rehabilitations, and the system finally collapsed beyond redemption in the 1800s.

Despite these setbacks, such determined efforts to control and direct water brought some important changes in ideas. Chinese water beings had long expressed people's understandings of hydrological cycles. Dragons were traditionally shown 'ascending to' or 'descending from' the celestial realm via waves and clouds; emerging from 'dragon springs'; or winding down mountains. Their colours reflected different kinds and qualities of water.

Chinese science and engineering brought new ways to think about hydrology and about water itself. The theory of the Five Elements (*Wu Xing*) presented systemic ideas about materials and energetic forces on all scales, linking non-human elements, weather and seasons with bodily organs, physical well-being, knowledge, emotions, colours and tastes. It encouraged more secular philosophical worldviews and a departure from religious beliefs in supernatural beings. While dragons retained a place as important water deities in rural areas, in the cities, among educated classes, the emergence of science relegated them to a folkloric role. A late nineteenth-century European missionary, whose fourteen-year-long efforts to sow Christian beliefs in China had fallen on stony ground, concluded, 'There is not a religion on the face of the globe where the followers have less religion than in the Church of the learned. The men of China! The prevailing malady is irreligion; happily the disease is not so widespread among the peasantry.'[38]

Scientific Beings

The effects of scientific thinking on human relationships with water were also becoming apparent in other parts of the world. A comparison is provided by classical Greece and Rome, where transformations in the form and meaning of water serpent beings reveal the shifts in cosmological understandings wrought by emergent technological and scientific knowledge. Here too there was a discernible pattern of change in which religious beliefs shifted from the worship of localized ancestral water beings to the serpent deities of larger and more hierarchical societies, and from these to more humanized deities (illus. 71).

Most analyses of Greek cosmology focus on the texts provided by Homer and Hesiod and the largely humanized gods residing on Olympus, but there was an important foundational stratum of pre-Hellenic nature religions.[39] Classical Greek beliefs and practices contain 'an older Bronze Age pattern' that is in part the legacy of the Pelasgians, the earlier inhabitants of the region, whose beliefs were influenced by interactions with the Levant and its religious focus on creative water serpent beings.[40] Minoan 'snake goddesses', faience figures depicting goddesses or priestesses dating from circa 1700 to 1450 BCE, have been linked directly with the Egyptian serpent goddess Wadjet.[41] In a Greek origin story, which the poet and classical scholar Robert Graves suggests is based on an earlier Pelasgian narrative, the great Ophion (serpent/snake) is created by Eurynome, a supreme mother goddess who rises up out of primeval fluid chaos.[42] Finding no *terra firma*, she dances on the waves and, catching the wind (*pneuma*) in her hands, forms Ophion, who then wraps himself around her body and impregnates her.

> Next, she assumed the form of a dove, brooding on the waves and, in due process of time, laid the Universal Egg. At her bidding, Ophion coiled seven times about this egg, until it hatched and split in two. Out tumbled all things that exist, her children: sun, moon, planets, stars, the earth with its mountains and rivers, its trees, herbs, and living creatures.[43]

Multiple stories describing powerful creator goddesses have led some scholars to argue that the religious beliefs of early agricultural societies across Europe and the East contained considerable gender equality. There are accounts of matriarchal Neolithic societies, and cultural historian Charlene Spretnak suggests that pre-classical Graeco-Roman beliefs were more localized and matri-focal than the patriarchal Olympian religious beliefs that followed.[44]

Hesiod, writing in circa 800–700 BCE, refers to Gaea, who emerges from watery chaos to give birth

71 Greek, Attic hippocamp (sea horse-serpent) on a terracotta bell-krater (mixing bowl) with lid, late 5th century BCE.

to the sky, sea and mountains and to be 'a firm seat of things for ever'.[45] Also known as Ge or Gaia (and by the Romans as Terra Mater, or 'the Great Mother'),[46] she was venerated with many altars and sanctuaries. There were other powerful goddess figures. Artemis, associated with the wilderness, the Moon and hunting, was a 'principal deity for many Greeks in Asia Minor'. A major temple at Ephesus was dedicated to her in the mid-500s BCE, and writer David Sacks suggests that, like Hera and Athena, she represents a 'religious survival' from earlier Aegean beliefs.[47] The Mesopotamian

72 Greek, Attic terracotta hydria (water jar) showing the sacred snake guardian in the Garden of Hesperides, with the presence of Pan and a satyr suggesting that it has become a shrine to Dionysus, early 4th century BCE.

goddess Ishtar, drawn from the Sumerian Inanna, had a similar role as goddess of nature and productivity. Generative powers were also personified by the goddess Astarte, who was worshipped across the Levant, and by the Greek goddess Aphrodite who, like her Roman counterpart, Venus, was associated with the ocean and fertility.[48]

Pre-Hellenic ideas were therefore formative of classical Greek narratives about cosmogenesis.[49] These describe a watery void of unformed creative chaos that generates a series of Titanic beings. The primordial serpent Ophion is described as the first ruler of Olympus, and the world-encircling Okeanus is identified in the *Iliad* as the father of all deities.[50] His wife Tethys, the Titaness (otherwise known as 'the nurse'), provides fresh water at an earthly level, via aquifers and springs, and their offspring include the Potomai (river gods) and the Okeanides (the nymphs of springs and fountains).[51]

In some narratives the role of primogeniture is assigned to the sky god Uranus and the earth goddess Gaia, but this union is also concerned with the generative powers of water. 'Uranus' derives, etymologically, from the Proto-Greek term **worsanós* (ϝορσανός),[52] expanded from **u̯orsó-*, and is related to the Greek *ouréō* (to urinate); the Sanskrit *varṣá* (rain) and the Hittite *u̯arša-* (fog, mist). The basic Indo-European root is **u̯érs-* (to rain, moisten), which is also found in Greek *eérsē* (dew). In a complementary role to that of the Earth Mother Gaia, Uranus is the 'rainmaker', and it is this that drew Georges Dumézil to posit a connection with Varuna, the Vedic god of the sky and water.[53]

In other Greek stories, Typhon, son of the goddess Gaia, is described as having been fathered by the great watery void Tartarus.[54] Apollonius of Rhodes, in his epic poem the *Argonautica*, offers the following image of cosmic creativity, sung by Orpheus, the god of the underworld:

> He sang how the earth, the heaven and the sea, once mingled together in one form, after deadly strife were separated each from other; and how the stars and the moon and the paths of the sun ever keep their fixed place in the sky; and how the mountains rose, and how the resounding rivers with their nymphs came into being.[55]

Greek celestial beings also include Drakon (the Roman 'Draco'/dragon), visible in a constellation recorded by Ptolemy, a Graeco-Roman astronomer who lived in Egypt in the second century.[56] Drakon is linked with Ladon, the serpent who guards the tree bearing the golden apples of wisdom in the Hesperides (illus. 72).[57]

Many serpentine deities underwent processes of humanization but retained their capacities for creativity, wisdom and healing.[58] Emphasizing the longstanding associations between serpent beings and enlightenment, the physician and Neoplatonist scholar Alex Wilder noted that the healing deity Aesculapius was both a fire god and a serpent, and his medical knowledge was seen as the wisdom of the serpent.[59] Babylonian and Egyptian use of the serpent and staff also carried over into images of the Greek god Hermes who, as the herald or divine messenger of the gods, was often depicted carrying a 'serpent sceptre' or caduceus.

Several notable Olympian gods were initially represented as serpent beings. This was the case with Hygieia, the goddess of health, although later

73 Votive relief of figures worshipping the great serpent Zeus Meilichios, Pangrati, Athens, 350–300 BCE.

statues and images show her in human form holding a serpent. Often she is offering it a bowl, referencing a well-known domestic ritual in which milk, eggs, fruit, honey and sometimes pine cones were offered to snakes, seen as the *agathodaemones* (bringers of happiness/serpent demons).[60]

The god Okeanus appears in classical representations as a semi-humanized being, with a bull's head, crab-claw horns, a human torso and arms (with hands holding a serpent and a fish) and a serpent body. A humanized Tethys retained wings, suggestive of rain-bringing wind and clouds. And, echoing the ways in which Indian serpent beings were pressed into service by emergent deities, Graeco-Roman water serpent beings were increasingly depicted being ridden by cherubs or other divine figures in fully human form.

Zeus, the Olympian sky god, makes an important early appearance as a 'kindly serpent' (illus. 73).[61] The classicist Jane Harrison described him as a revisioning of a previous serpent deity, Meilichios, and suggests that the Athenian Diasia festival echoed the rituals venerating this 'easy to be entreated', 'gracious and accessible one'.[62] Zeus appears in ophidian form in another important story too. Though supposedly the son of Philip II of Macedonia, Alexander the Great was said to have been conceived by Zeus in the form of a serpent/dragon. According to Plutarch, when Alexander was about to set out to conquer Asia his mother, Olympias, told him that, on the night before her marriage to Philip was consummated, a lightning bolt (Zeus) hit her in the stomach. There was a flash of light, and it was revealed to her that her son had been conceived in this way. Related stories describe Philip as having suspicions that his wife was practising magic and spying on her as she consorted with the serpent god (illus. 74).[63]

At any rate, Alexander departed for Asia confident in his divine powers and, as his empire grew, he sought and received confirmation from the Zeus-Ammon oracle at Siwa (between Egypt and Libya) that he was indeed a living god. In this sense, he exemplifies a pattern in which non-human deities were transformed into humanized ancestral beings and moved from legend into history. Such transitions were not regarded as unusual at the time: the

74 The conception of Alexander the Great, miniature from *Les faize d'Alexandre*, Bruges, *c*. 1468–75.

philosopher Pythagoras, a firmly historicized figure, was said to have been begotten by the Python, the great serpent god descended from Gaea.

Olympian Beings

Greek and Roman worldviews were influenced by multiple factors. Between 2500 and 1000 BCE more patriarchal religious and social practices came with waves of invasion by Ionians, Achaeans and Dorians, and the centuries leading up to the first millennium were characterized by increasingly instrumental technological developments. Drawing upon Etruscan experiments with water channels, engineers constructed sophisticated aqueducts and sewers. One of the first aqueducts was built in Athens in the sixth century BCE, and other cities followed suit. Typically, such channels terminated in central fountains such as the Enneacrounos, provided for Athens's main square by the ruler Peisistratos. Reliant upon terracotta pipes invented for this purpose, the Enneacrounos had nine large 'cannons' supplying drinking water to local residents. It was gravity-fed, but Greek engineers also learned how to siphon water, enabling the vigorously spouting fountains often depicted in traditional imagery.[64]

The Romans were even more ambitious in imposing control over water flows. They brought water mills and related technologies for controlling water to many parts of their vast empire.[65] Efforts to drain the marshes around Rome were made from circa 800 BCE, and the major sewer and drainage system, the Cloaca Maxima, the 'great bowel' of the city, was probably constructed in the 600s BCE. In response to drought and continuing problems with sanitation (probably not improved by emptying the Cloaca Maxima into the Tiber), the first major Roman aqueduct was built in 312 BCE by Appius Claudius Caesus. More than 16 kilometres (10 mi.) in length, this carried 73,000 cubic metres of clean water to the city every day.

In both Greece and Rome, such infrastructures enabled extensive urbanization. By the time of Christ's birth, between 10 and 20 per cent of the population in the Mediterranean region lived in cities. As elsewhere, this diversified economic practices and social arrangements, with the seemingly inevitable emergence of hierarchies and ruling elites.

For the Romans, this meant military imperialism and empire-building, and, as with the Egyptian pharaohs, an increasing tendency to regard their emperor as having divine powers.[66] In their pre-Christian hegemonic forays they readily adopted diverse religious ideas and images from conquered foes, and this religious liberalism, drawing parallels between deities with similar roles and characteristics, enabled extensive syncretism (illus. 75).[67] The Roman veneration of snakes echoed that of the Greeks, and the dragon – as in China – became an important symbol of imperial power, echoing the 'great red dragon' or 'fiery serpent' on the standards of the ancient kings of Assyria, and the dragons depicted on the shields and banners of Teutonic tribes.[68] The conquered Dacians, located to the west of the Black Sea, provided the 'draco', a windsock-shaped dragon ensign that shrieked terrifyingly when held aloft.[69]

For the Greeks, urbanization and centralization resulted in efforts to introduce democratic governance, although this egalitarian impulse did not enfranchise women or slaves. It also provided an educated male elite with time and resources to study the physical world and ask deconstructive questions about water. Where did water come from? How did springs and rivers arise? And what was water itself?

Thales (624–546 BCE) suggested that, as water came in various material forms (rain, hail and dew), it might also turn into earth. Anaximander (610–546 BCE) envisioned a primary form of matter called *apeiron* (infinite, undetermined), and thought that life came from an all-engulfing sea. He also recognized that precipitation came from water drawn upwards by the Sun. There was speculation about fire and water, and whether heavenly fires were fed by moisture rising into the clouds. The notion of a primary substance or *archē* inspired much interest.

75 Fresco from Pompeii showing Bacchus, Mount Vesuvius and Agathodaemon, a god of wisdom and good fortune generally represented as a serpent. His name was widely used to describe guardian or companion spirits, House of the Centenary, *c.* 55–79 CE.

Heraclitus (535–475 BCE) thought that this was fire. Others argued that it was water *and* fire. Empedocles (490–430 BCE) proposed four basic elements: fire, air, water and earth. Hippocrates (*c.* 400 BCE) suggested that water had two parts, one thin and clear and the other thick, dark and turbid, and that the Sun attracted only the lighter kind. Establishing a foundational scientific method, he made experiments demonstrating evaporation.

Anaxagoras (500–428 BCE) almost articulated the hydrological cycle, observing that rivers depended on rain and that Earth was hollow and had water in its cavities. But his suggestion that the Sun and other celestial bodies were just fiery rocks was a heretical step too far: he was sentenced to death, and had to flee from Athens. Entering the debate a little later, Aristotle (384–322 BCE) noted that cold temperatures changed air into water above the earth, and that rivers and streams arose from Tartarus, a huge subterranean reservoir. A complete vision of the hydrological cycle was finally provided by Theophrastus (*c.* 371–288 BCE).

Scholars also sought to understand the powers of water. Aristotle described terrible sea serpents causing shipwrecks: 'As the ships passed on, the serpents attacked the triremes, and some of them threw themselves upon one of the triremes and overturned it.'[70] Much thought was given to the properties of water: Alcmaeon (*c.* fifth century BCE) first pointed to the relationship between water quality and human health, and Hippocrates (460–370 BCE) wrote several treatises regarding different sources of water and their health implications.[71]

Deconstructive thinking also led to consideration of the nature of consciousness, which had significant implications for human-non-human relations. Anaxagoras proposed a theory of Mind (*nous*) as the governing principle of the cosmos, which questioned assumptions about divine powers. Socrates, Plato and Aristotle sought unified scientific explanations for cosmic events. Although religious beliefs pertained, there was a repositioning of humankind in relation to the non-human domain. While pre-Hellenic societies had worshipped deities that were highly localized and enmeshed in people's daily lives, and mother goddesses that were compassionate and nurturing, Hellenic Greece humanized its gods and promoted them to the distant heights of Olympus to survey the world and rule more judgementally upon the fate of its inhabitants.

Although the pantheon of Olympian deities contained both male and female gods, Charlene Spretnak observes that this 'civilization' brought some negative revisioning of formerly revered female goddesses. Hera came to be represented as an angry, jealous wife, Athena as a masculine and uncaring daughter. Aphrodite became a lightweight, frivolous character; Artemis had only a minor role as Apollo's sister; and Pandora became the irresponsible source of all human miseries. As Spretnak says, such changes in gender representation were to have long-term effects: 'these prototypes later evolved into the wicked witch, the cruel stepmother and the passive princess etc. of our fairytales.'[72]

Transforming nature beings into humanized Olympians also led to the demonization of 'snake goddesses' and other serpentine figures. The 'witch' Medea, having slain her own children, flew to Athens 'cleaving the air and dripping with murder'[73] in a chariot drawn by winged *drakones* (dragon-serpents).[74] Medusa, an important figure in ancient Southwest Asia, and said to be the progeny of

76 Benvenuto Cellini, *Perseus with the Head of Medusa*, 1545–54, bronze sculpture in Loggia dei Lanzi, Florence.

77 Etruscan (Caeretan) hydria featuring Hercules slaying the Lernaean Hydra, 520–510 BCE, terracotta.

marine deities, appears in Graeco-Roman narratives as a monstrous 'Gorgon' with hair composed of writhing venomous snakes. A mere glimpse of her turned living beings to stone, and she was beheaded by the culture hero Perseus who, appropriating her powers, used her severed head to petrify opponents (illus. 76). Describing her as the 'mother of all serpents', Ovid suggested that poisonous vipers sprang up from her blood and were scattered by Perseus as he flew over the land.[75] This powerful fluid also spawned the Amphisbaena, a venomous serpent said to have feasted on the corpses left behind after Cato the Younger's army crossed the Libyan Desert. This serpent had a head at each end, 'as though', said Pliny the Elder, 'it were not enough for poison to be poured out of one mouth'.[76]

There were multiple serpent slayings. Hercules defeated the Lernaean Hydra (illus. 77), despite its powers of regeneration, as well as Ladon, the multi-headed serpent guarding the tree of knowledge. Jason slew a guardian dragon to capture the Golden Fleece. Cadmus slaughtered a troublesome dragon in Thebes, from whose scattered teeth arose an army of Spartoi (a story sometimes assigned to Jason). Phorbas dispatched the *drakones* ravaging the island of Rhodes, and warriors killed the dragon guarding the sacred groves of Zeus in Nemea. The serpent was therefore recast as the chaos monster who must be slain so that rationality, morality and (male) human powers over nature could prevail. Affirming the patterns apparent in other historical and cultural contexts, the classicist Norman Austin suggests that this was because Hellenic notions of consciousness and sophisticated technologies made humans feel more godlike, removing the authority of non-human deities and alienating humankind from nature.[77]

> The transformation of the serpent from venerated god to loathsome demon marks the shift from a matriarchal to a patriarchal consciousness . . . The ancient goddess, when not erased from the scriptures altogether, was transformed into the daughter obedient to the father . . . The dragon, conceived of Earth, or nurtured in the dark recesses of earth, is the consort and champion of Earth, symbol of Earth's prodigious vitality . . . In marking the serpent with the sign of all that is irrational and evil, the new gods passed judgement on Nature herself. Hesiod's cosmogonic vision is coloured throughout by the belief that Nature is devious, capricious and lawless. Nature must be brought under the rational, hierarchical control of the new sky gods . . . The higher Olympus reaches into the Heavens, the more monstrous its serpent enemy grows . . . The greater the desire of the Olympians for rational control, the more irrational grows the adversary . . . The combat between the Olympians and the serpent is the ego's own, inner cosmology . . . The loathsome features of the serpent express the ego's fears of the impulses and desires lurking within the human soul . . . The serpent is both the polymorphous libido and the tabu imposed by the superego against the libido's entrance into consciousness. To look upon Medusa is to be turned to stone.[78]

In these ways, in Graeco-Roman history and in other parts of the world, urbanization and 'civilization', and ever-steeper patriarchal hierarchies, led to water serpent beings being transformed from creative and nurturing ancestral beings into life-threatening chaos monsters. These transitions also demonstrate the influence of high levels of technical instrumentality and scholarly efforts to unravel the mysteries of the world. Science and engineering opened a Pandora's box of ideas that would reshape human–environmental relations forever.

8

Supreme Beings

At this stage in the story carried by water serpent beings, we can begin to see the broad patterns of change that their fortunes reveal. They were centrally important to small-scale societies who venerated localized 'nature beings', maintained intimate and permanent relationships with their homelands and saw a sentient non-human world as an active reciprocal partner in their lives. The larger societies that emerged from agriculture and irrigation, having developed increasingly instrumental engagements with water, expressed their greater – more godlike – sense of control over the world by semi-humanizing their supernatural beings and devolving much of their power to intermediary religious elites.

As societies urbanized, became more hierarchical and acquired sophisticated technologies, water serpent beings were either wholly humanized or made subservient to humanized deities, and their powers to provide and direct water were appropriated by 'divine' pharaohs, kings and emperors. Pantheons of gods in largely human form demonstrated widening gender inequalities, with formerly powerful water goddesses being downgraded or demonized. Reflecting the shape of centralized and disembedded national governments, major deities also moved upwards and outwards, to loftier and more distant Olympic or heavenly domains.[1] This chapter considers the next twist in the serpents' tale: how emerging monotheisms entrenched patriarchal dominion in socio-political arrangements and in relation to the non-human world, and created an alienating division between culture and nature.

The major monotheistic religions arose in the kingdoms occupying the Fertile Crescent and Arabia. The religion of Israel (later called Judaism) was the first to locate all supernatural power in a single male God who, its adherents believed, chose the 'children of Abraham' as His people, a term indicative of the region's earlier ancestral religions.[2] This nascent monotheism flourished under successive kings – Saul, David and Solomon – but their kingdoms disintegrated in circa 920 BCE, scattering the followers of monotheism into various diasporas. Led by prophets, they regrouped to some degree, albeit under foreign rule. A rebellion against the Seleucid king of Syria's attempts to impose the Grecian worship of Zeus from 167 to 164 BCE briefly re-established a Jewish kingdom, but this was conquered by the Romans in 63 BCE. These pressures were divisive and, believing that their priests, the Sadducees, had become too closely aligned with the region's new rulers, some groups chose to follow the Pharisees or Scribes. When Jesus emerged as a teacher, those convinced that he was the Messiah made a further departure from Judaism to establish Christianity.

As this suggests, there was considerable ebb and flow as kingdoms expanded or retrenched. The Egyptian Empire, from circa 1550 to 1069 BCE, encompassed Canaan, Sinai and Syria, holding sway when Moses led the Exodus in circa 1250–1200 BCE. The Assyrians retained power in Mesopotamia until conquered by the Babylonians under King Hammurapi in circa 1761 BCE. Babylonian rule was overset in turn by King Cyrus II in circa 539 BCE, but the Persian empire that he established was short-lived. In the late 300s BCE, Alexander the Great conquered much of the region, extending Greek influence across Persia, Syria, Judea and Egypt, and into the Indian Punjab.

The developing monotheisms were therefore surrounded and sometimes subsumed by other belief systems. The competitive push and shove between them generated a need for powerful culture heroes who would defeat or resist 'the other'. Further challenges were posed by the introduction of democratic ideals in ancient Greece, which threatened to replace royal divinity and priestly authority with secular political leadership. This was aided, in part, by emergent scientific thinking, which similarly undermined religious beliefs.

To some extent, therefore, the new monotheisms were reactive reassertions of religious authority. In a region so continuously in flux, such efforts relied heavily upon portable scriptures as the authoritative 'word of God', and these became the guiding template for believers. All of these texts were highly reductive, of course, representing the idealized narratives and visions of their male authors, and excluding other voices and the real complexities of interhuman and human-non-human relations. However, as with other forms of 'law', they distilled the beliefs and tenets prevailing at the time and, like other religious texts, they encouraged the humanization and historicization of earlier 'legendary' beings.

Monotheisms borrowed from a rich palimpsest of existing ideas and images.[3] Much has been written about how narratives and visual representations undergo transformations in form and meaning as belief systems adapt to new social and political realities. Bernard Batto points to the Mesopotamian and Canaanite roots of biblical stories, observing that 'myth permeates virtually every layer of biblical tradition . . . biblical writers borrowed old myths and extended their meanings in novel ways for the purpose of expressing new theological insights.'[4] Of particular relevance here is that this process also enabled deities to undergo multiple reincarnations and take on new and increasingly unified human forms.[5]

The most critical shift from worshipping the non-human world to seeking human control over it can be seen in the transference of divine powers to humanized monotheistic deities. In a transformational narrative the Hebrew Yahweh and the Christian God take over all of the responsibilities of earlier religions' water serpent beings: for cosmogenesis, for generating all living kinds, for providing rain and orderly flows of water, for upholding societal norms and for the gift of knowledge and wisdom.

The description of the serpent god in the Pyramid Texts 'speaking things into being' is echoed in Judeo-Christian descriptions of God making the world by bringing light to the darkness of the primeval ocean, and by providing 'The Word':[6]

78 Bishop's crozier, Armenian, 17th century.

> The earth was without form, and void; and darkness was upon the face of the deep. And the Spirit of God moved upon the face of the waters.
> And God said, 'Let there be light,' and there was light.
> And God divided the light from the darkness.
> And God said, 'Let there be a firmament in the midst of the waters, and let it divide the waters from the waters.'
> And God made the firmament, and divided the waters which were under the firmament from the waters which were above the firmament.
> And God called the firmament Heaven.
> And God said, 'Let the waters under the heaven be gathered together unto one place, and let the dry land appear,' and it was so.
> And God called the dry land Earth; and the gathering together of the waters He called Seas.
> (Genesis 1:2, 6–10)

Still, there were many traces of the new gods' serpentine antecedents (illus. 78). According to Eusebius of Caeserea, the 'Father of Church History' in the first century CE, the Zoroastrians named their expansive heaven after the serpent. The Canaanite god Baal is best known for conquering Yam, the serpentine god of the sea, but this dragon-slaying role came later.[7] As Robert Miller points out, he was first and foremost a storm god, the source of rain and fertility, and in this sense connects conceptually with other 'green' fertility figures, such as Al-Khiḍr and St George.[8] An early manifestation as a rain-bringing storm god also applies to Yahweh, who came to be seen as a primary deity.[9] The name of Nahash, king of the Ammonites, is the ancient Hebrew term for serpent.[10] And among the Gnostic sects, who were particularly resistant to abandoning serpent worship, 'Mani, the Gnostic teacher, declared that Christ was the incarnation of the Great Serpent that glided over the cradle of the infant Mary.'[11]

The goddess Ashtoreth appears in the Hebrew Bible as a symbol of the fertile powers of water and nature, and has sometimes been cast as the original consort of Yahweh, implying a joint parental role. Both were worshipped at sites similar to those at which celebrations of the annual floodwater bringers Osiris and Isis took place:

> Old Testament writings commonly refer to *maṣṣeboth*, or sacred pillars, erected either in honour of dead ancestors or to particular deities. The ancient Israelites, prior to the monotheistic period, worshipped not only Yahweh but also a female consort called Ashtoreth, also known as Astarte, the ancient goddess. So far 14 such sites have been found in the southern Negev and eastern Sinai deserts dating back to 11,000 BCE.[12]

Ancestral gender complementarity was also maintained when creative figures humanized, most obviously in the figures of Adam and Eve, although, as Joseph Campbell observes, 'the legend of the rib is clearly a patriarchal inversion' reversing the biologically rational process of begetting described in earlier stories.[13] But all such original couples, like their serpentine predecessors, fulfil the role of 'primal parents'. Although representations of Adam and Eve in human form rapidly subsumed earlier images of ancestral serpent beings, the theologian Mary Condren points to 'weighty evidence that the figure of Eve is based on much older stories in Near Eastern mythology and that the original Eve appeared in the form of a Serpent. The name Eve, *hawwah*, means "mother of all the living", but *hawwah* also means "serpent" in many Semitic languages.'[14] This view is supported by Arvid Kapelrud, who notes that the name *ādhām* is associated with earth while *chavvāh*, meaning 'serpent', may connect Eve as 'life' or 'mother of the living' with an earlier Phoenician goddess, Havat, a serpent goddess of the underworld.[15] Dennis Slifer further suggests that 'according to early rabbinical tradition Eve's menstruation began after copulating with the serpent in the Garden of Eden, and her firstborn son, Cain, was begotten by the serpent, not Adam'.[16] Although the serpentine connections of Eve are controversial, these linguistic connections do suggest some reformations of earlier deities and their generative powers.[17]

Innovative use was also made of other key symbols. Scholars have noted the visual similarities between the Egyptian *ankh* (the sacred symbol for life), Eastern gods sheltered by hooded cobras or multicephalous serpent beings and images of haloed Christian figures.[18] And the earlier 'fiery' celestial serpents bringing lightning and wisdom surely provided potential models for Moses' brazen serpent and staff and their powers relating to water (illus. 79).[19]

79 William Blake, *Moses Erecting the Brazen Serpent* (Nehushtan), *c.* 1800–1803, pen and watercolour on paper.

Resonating with many cosmological efforts to conceptualize flows between celestial and earthly domains, Sumerian and Akkadian artefacts depict an arboreal *axis mundi* guarded by twin serpents.[20] Mircea Eliade points to multiple associations between the serpent, the tree of knowledge and the cross (illus. 80), noting

> the assimilation, by Christian imagery, liturgy and theology, of the symbolism of the World Tree

80 George Caleb Hedgeland, stained-glass window, serpent and cross, Norwich Cathedral, 1854.

81 Jason being regurgitated by the Colchian dragon after it was drugged by Athena, Attic Greek red-figure cup, attributed to Douris, c. 480–470 BCE, Cerveteri (Etruria). The dragon was the guardian of the Golden Fleece (centre, hanging on the tree), and Athena stands to the right.

> . . . The Cross, made from the wood of the Tree of Good and Evil, is identified with, or replaces, the Cosmic Tree; it is described as a tree that 'rises from earth to heaven,' an immortal plant 'that stands at the center of heaven and earth, firm support of the universe.'[21]

Some images suggest preceding stories of temptation concerned with human desires to appropriate divine knowledge. Paintings on an Egyptian mummy case held in the Louvre show a woman in the form of a serpent, offering fruit to a man. Temptation is illustrated by his visually explicit desire.[22] The British Museum holds a Mesopotamian cylinder seal dating from circa 2200–2100 BCE depicting two gods, male and female, beside a tree bearing fruits, accompanied by two serpents. This is known, controversially, as the 'Adam and Eve' seal, because George Smith, an Assyriologist working at the British Museum between 1840 and 1876, bravely suggested that it was a template for the Old Testament story. Though other scholars have rejected this direct connection, the material record demonstrates that there were, at least, representations that provided imaginative fodder for new religious narratives.[23] Further images connecting wise serpents, holy trees and forbidden fruits or sought-after treasures are provided by objects such as the Etruscan drinking cup depicted here (illus. 81), illustrating the story in which Jason seeks to steal the Golden Fleece. According to the third-century scholar Apollonius Rhodius, the fleece was located at 'the shady grove of Ares, where a dragon, a monster terrible to behold, ever glares around, keeping watch over the fleece that is spread upon the top of an oak; neither by day nor by night does sweet sleep subdue his restless eyes.'[24]

Many ritual practices were also carried forward, with baptismal rituals typically involving immersion in (or sprinkling with) water to signify spiritual 'rebirth'. One of Christianity's most central rituals, that of communion, replicates earlier ceremonies venerating Dionysus (a Greek deity born as a serpent, and often linked with the figure of Osiris), which similarly involved the ritual ingestion of wine and bread symbolizing body and blood.[25]

Regenerative Beings

Water serpent beings' most crucial traditional role was to generate and regenerate life, representing a hydro-theological cycle of spiritual movement between material and non-material worlds and between underworld, earthly and celestial domains. As religions increasingly represented gods in semi-human and human form, it was vital for this regenerative role to be retained. Two major – sometimes overlapping – narrative tropes emerged to meet this need. The first described deities' journeys to dark and fluid underworlds and their return to the visible material world.

The Egyptian 'green god' Osiris' passage through the netherworld provides an early example, as does the sun god Atum's daily circulation. A foundational Zoroastrian text, the Book of Ardā Wīrāz, describes how, with the help of a hallucinogenic drink, *mang*, the 'righteous' Viraz journeys through Heaven and Hell.[26] One of the most famous stories about the Mesopotamian goddess Inanna concerns her journey into the underworld Kur. Although she returns, her husband, Dumuzi, is forced to replace her for half the year, while his sister Geshtinanna, the goddess of fertility and agriculture, remains in the underworld for the other half, resulting in the cycle of the seasons.[27] In early Hebrew versions of this story Dumuzi becomes Tammuz, with a similar 'dying and rising' role and responsibility for fertility, although biblical references express disapproval of these beliefs, and the sin of 'weeping for the pagan god Tammuz' (Ezekiel 8:14).

Further examples come from Greek narratives, in which seasonal cycles of death and rebirth were

82 Bas-relief of Ceres, 50 BCE–50 CE.

represented by the goddess Demeter and her daughter Persephone. Demeter, or Ceres as the Romans called her (illus. 82), was celebrated as a mother goddess of fertility, harvests and agriculture, and as the bringer of sacred law.[28] Stories about her go back to the later stages of the Bronze Age, and tablets from Pylos from circa 1400 to 1200 BCE link her with the ocean god Poseidon.

Demeter was the focus of the Eleusinian Mysteries, and she was worshipped via annual initiation ceremonies at Eleusis. These aimed to conjure visions of the afterlife and are thought to have made use of a psychoactive drink, *kykeon*.[29] The ritual was directly concerned with cyclical movements between life and death, taking the initiates down into an underground cave (descent and loss) and then back up into the light of rebirth (ascent and joy).

A related narrative describes the abduction of Persephone by Hades, the god of the dead and king of the underworld that carries his name. Distraught, Demeter appeals to Zeus for assistance and eventually, using her power over water, causes a drought, depriving the gods of their anticipated sacrifices and forcing Zeus to intercede. Hades is persuaded to send Persephone back to Demeter, and spring and fertility revive the Earth. However, because Hades has tricked Persephone into eating pomegranate seeds from the underworld she is condemned to return to it for part of each year, thus creating winter, during which Demeter's grief over her absence causes the earth to cease providing sustenance. Elements of this narrative trope can also be seen in the story of Orpheus and Eurydice. When Eurydice is bitten by a snake and dies, Orpheus journeys to the underworld to try to bring her back, but his quest fails when he is unable to allow her 'shade' to reach the light unseen, and so to regain material form.[30]

Possibly the most important Greek analogue is the story of Dionysus (known to the Romans as Bacchus), who, having been killed as an infant, is regenerated by Zeus, and therefore 'twice born'. Though this category is theologically contended, this makes him an archetypal 'dying and rising' god.[31] As with Demeter, the worship of Dionysus dates back to Mycenaean Greece. Diodorus Siculus, writing between 60 and 30 BCE, presents him as her son, and he is similarly associated with fertility, although in his case this is a wilder form of generative power involving orgiastic rituals in which wine, dance and music produce religious ecstasy and epiphany.[32]

In visual and narrative representations Dionysus is described as somewhat womanly or androgynous, and the encompassment of both genders is further expressed in his entourage, which includes uninhibited women (*maenads*) as well as satyrs with erect penises. Phallic associations are underlined by images in which he is shown holding a *thyrsus*, a fennel staff twined with (symbolically serpentine) ivy and dripping with honey. This potent object could be used as a magical wand to confer favours, or – like other serpent and staff objects – as a weapon against opponents. Trees, especially fig trees, feature centrally in his cult, and his alternate names, Endendros (he in the tree) or Dendritēs (he of the tree) may indicate earlier links with other trees of life.[33]

It was believed that Dionysus could communicate with the living and the dead, bridging their worlds, and that he was able to descend to the underworld to rescue the dead and restore them to life.[34] Aristophanes' comedy *The Frogs*, written for a festival celebrating Dionysus in Athens in 405 BCE, provides an entertaining account of his trials and tribulations during a journey into Hades. Intending to revive the playwright Euripides, Dionysus chooses, in the end, to revive Aeschylus instead.[35]

Dionysus reportedly entered the underworld via a bottomless lake in Lerna, whose name comes from a Hattic word meaning 'spring', 'well' or 'pool'. Situated at the foot of Mount Ponticos, Lerna's multiple water sources supported a series of Neolithic and early Bronze Age settlements. In the classical era there was still a substantial lake, of which the waters were believed to have powerful healing properties. The lake was the focus of rituals celebrating the Lernaean Mysteries, which were sacred to Demeter, and it was most notably the home of the Lernaean Hydra, known throughout the region as an ancient and powerful water serpent being. Dionysus' journeys down through the lake into the underworld of Hades therefore resonate with many serpent swallowing and regurgitation stories in which the hero 'passes through' the serpent/the rainbow to gain sacred knowledge and power in an otherworldly domain.

This trope also recurs in the legend of Jason's search for the Golden Fleece which, as well as

83 Folio of Jonah and the Whale, from *Jami al-Tavarikh* (Compendium of Chronicles), Iran, c. 1400, ink, opaque watercolour, gold and silver on paper.

offering images of a sacred tree of knowledge and forbidden treasure, describes Jason being regurgitated by the guardian serpent, which had been hypnotized by Medea or (as in illus. 81) drugged by Athena.

Instances of serpentine swallowing and regurgitation resurface in stories of Jonah, in which the whale 'swallowed him . . . and then vomited him out onto dry land'.[36] John Day suggests that the 'great fish' which swallows Jonah is a version of the Canaanite sea serpent of Baal narratives.[37] Pointing to visual echoes between images of encircling serpents and the mandorla (an oval aureole surrounding Christian religious figures), Philip Gardiner and Gary Osborn note that in the ancient city of Nineveh, which has been associated with Jonah, plaster bosses show a man emerging from the mouth of an aquatic creature.[38] Jonah also appears as Yunus in parallel Islamic stories, in which he is similarly swallowed and regurgitated by a giant water being (illus. 83).

Swallowing and regurgitation stories are primarily concerned with movements between material and non-material domains, and in this sense figures such as Dionysus, Persephone and Orpheus replicate the cyclical and regenerative flows of earlier water serpent beings. They carry persons between the visible worlds of the living and the netherworlds of the dead, providing a psychologically imperative prospect of revival and return. Rather than classifying Dionysus and others as 'dying and rising' gods, it may therefore be more useful to consider how such figures appropriated previously serpentine hydro-theological cycles of life, death and renewal.

Rising Beings

Major deities not only entered the underworld or the body of water beings and returned but ascended to heavenly celestial realms – as described in the Pyramid Texts, for example, when the dead kings 'fly up to the Heavens on the wings of Thoth'.[39] The concept of ascension, like that of journeys to fluid worlds below, entails movement between material and non-material domains. In this sense, it is the 'upper half' of the hydro-theological cycle of many water serpent beings, and therefore offers us a new way to consider both the symbolic meanings of Jacob's ladder and the circular nature of ascension and descension.

In the scriptures of monotheism, an early version of empowering movement between celestial and earthly domains is encapsulated in the story of Daniel's vision, that 'one like a son of man' would come from the 'clouds of Heaven' to be given glory and a kingdom over which he would have 'everlasting dominion' (Daniel 7:13–14). The prophet Elijah was said to have been carried to Heaven by 'a whirlwind' in 'chariots of fire and horses of fire' (2 Kings 2:11). The Assumption of the Virgin Mary, according to Catholic and Eastern Orthodox narratives, involved her being taken up into Heaven 'body and soul': 'the Immaculate Mother of God, the ever Virgin Mary, having completed the course of her earthly life, was assumed body and soul into heavenly glory.'[40] Being 'swallowed up' into Heaven avoided the 'corruption' of mortality and dissolution into non-being: 'When this corruptible shall have put on incorruption, and this mortal shall have put on immortality . . . Death is swallowed up in victory.' (1 Corinthians 15:54)

84 Detail of Daniel Gran, *Glory of the Newborn Christ in Presence of God the Father and the Holy Spirit*, 1751, ceiling fresco, Annakirche, Vienna.

Movements to and from celestial realms are often accompanied by angels equipped with the feathered and multicoloured wings common to water beings. Their voices are 'like thunder', and biblical descriptions hint at their associations with rainbows and water: 'And I saw another mighty angel come down from heaven, clothed with a cloud: and a rainbow *was* upon his head, and his face *was* as it were the sun, and his feet as pillars of fire' (Revelation 10:1).

Jesus performs an entire hydro-theological cycle (1 Corinthians 15:45). He descends to the earthly realm from Heaven accompanied by angels, with his incarnation into material form heralded by a celestial omen (illus. 84). At his death he is entombed in a dark cave. Raised from this grave by God, he continues to ascend, through the light to Heaven. His religious legacy, the Holy Trinity, represents each part of this journey: there is a celestial Heavenly Father; an incarnated Son; and, permeating the earthly domain, an invisible, omnipresent Holy Spirit.

There are also narrative resonances in ideas about Hell. Recounted earlier in this volume are multiple origin stories describing fluid underworlds from which humankind and other living kinds emerge. In localized 'nature religions', returning to these domains represents loss and descent into non-being, but they are simultaneously pools of regenerative power. However, in larger societies seeking control over the material world and locating spiritual agency in lofty Olympian or heavenly deities, non-human land- and waterscapes – and their inner/underworlds – ceased to be seen as trusted sources of regeneration.

Classical Greek visions of Hades therefore present the underworld as a grim domain from which it is virtually impossible to return without divine intervention. Its rivers are dark and gloomy, their names representing hatred (the encircling Styx), pain (the Acheron), oblivion (the Lethe), fire (the Phlegethon) and grief and wailing (the Cocytus). Christianity offers even more polarized otherworlds. A glorious light-filled Heaven is countered by a terrifying 'below' world of eternal damnation. The motif of the swallowing serpent acquires an altogether darker role, as the soul-consuming mouth of Hell, wholly recasting the being previously

85 'The Harrowing of Hell', miniature from an illustrated *Vita Christi*, York, 1190–1200, tempera colours and gold leaf.

representing creative non-human powers as the ultimate chaos-monster from which souls can only be saved by God (illus. 85).

Judeo-Christian Transformations

There is a key difference between biblical stories of Genesis and the Mesopotamian narrative of the great water beings Tiâmat and Apsû as the primal creative deities:

> There are some general similarities between the two stories which include the creation of the universe by a god, and an original watery state for the universe. However, the Mesopotamian account gives the Sea and the Abyss of Fresh Water as primeval parents who give birth to several pairs of deities before the creator god is born, whereas in Genesis the creator god alone exists from the very beginning.[41]

In Genesis, God quells the primal waters, imposes order and forms the world and all of its living kinds. In this way a recurrent origin story is reconfigured, establishing patriarchal dominance and claiming human creative control over the world and its generative processes. Yet this appropriation could not shake off an underlying fear that human powers are tenuous in their hold over the great watery 'deep' – a fear that the theologian Catherine Keller describes as *tehomophobia*.[42] As she observes, the author of Genesis assumed that the universe was created from some 'other' form of prevenient primal chaos, called into order by the creator. But the theological ideas that became predominant rejected the power of a disorderly 'other', aiming instead to promote a 'logos of lordship' of Christian mastery.[43]

In the early scriptures, this lordship was achieved by transferring the elemental powers of water to patriarchal deities. The storm god Baal was not the only such figure. The Mesopotamian water deity Enlil, associated with the city of Nippur, is similarly described as 'a rushing deluge that brings woe to mankind, a torrent sweeping away buttresses and dikes, an onrushing storm which none can oppose'.[44] Early narratives about Yahweh also present him as a manifestation of the powers of water. It is only in later re-imaginings that he is 'magnified':

> Among the ancient Hebrews we have a parallel development where Jahweh, originally a god of storms, perhaps also of earthquakes, who manifests himself in the lightning, and whose voice is heard in the thunder, is magnified into the creator of the universe, the producer of vegetation, and the protector of harvests and crops. Like Enlil, Jahweh comes from the mountains. His seat is on the top of Mt Sinai . . . Traces of this early conception of Jahweh as a storm-god still linger in the metaphors of late Psalms, where the power of the god of the universe is described:
>
> The voice of Jahweh is upon the waters,
> The god of glory thundereth,
> Jahweh is upon the great waters.
> The voice of Jahweh is full of power,
> The voice of Jahweh is full of might,
> The voice of Jahweh breaketh cedars,
> Jahweh breaks the cedars of Lebanon and makes them skip like a calf.[45]

A further shift from manifesting the powers of water to ruling over them can be seen in biblical references to God: 'When he thunders, the waters in the heavens roar; he makes clouds rise from the ends of the earth. He sends lightning with the rain and brings out the wind from his storehouses' (Jeremiah 10:13). The scriptures are similarly concerned with God's capacities to control water and provide sufficient rain for irrigation.

> I will give you your rains in their season, and the land shall yield its increase, and the trees of the field shall yield their fruit. (Leviticus 26:4)
> Ask rain from the Lord in the season of the spring rain, from the Lord who makes the storm clouds, and he will give them showers of rain, to everyone the vegetation in the field. (Zechariah 10:1)
> Be glad, O children of Zion, and rejoice in the Lord your God, for he has given the early rain for your vindication; he has poured down for you abundant rain, the early and the latter rain. (Joel 2:23)
> He will give the rain for your land in its season, the early rain and the later rain, that you may gather in your grain and your wine and your oil. (Deuteronomy 11:14)

Only the 'true' God can provide water, and the bringing of rain is simultaneously the bringing of spiritual well-being and enlightenment:

> Are there any among the false gods of the nations that can bring rain? Or can the heavens give showers? Are you not he, O Lord our God? We set our hope on you, for you do all these things. (Jeremiah 14:22.)
> Shower, O heavens, from above, and let the clouds rain down righteousness; let the earth open, that salvation and righteousness may bear fruit; let the earth cause them both to sprout; I the Lord have created it. (Isaiah 45:8)
> I will pour out my Spirit on the house of Israel, declares the Sovereign Lord. (Ezekiel 39:29)

God also echoes the traditional capacities of water serpent beings to punish transgressions of the law. In extreme cases, droughts or floods are visited upon the ungodly:

> And if any of the families of the earth do not go up to Jerusalem to worship the King, the Lord of hosts, there will be no rain on them. (Zechariah 14:17)
> In seven days I will send rain on the earth forty days and forty nights, and every living thing that I have made I will blot out from the face of the ground. (Genesis 7:4)

The biblical flood cleanses the world of the pollution of sin and re-establishes moral order. It is a regenerative baptism, or swallowing and regurgitation on a grand scale, immersing humankind in a process of death and rebirth.[46] But although, like baptism, the waters of the flood wash away sin (1 Peter 3:21), they represent the power and authority of God, not the agency of the non-human 'other'.[47]

Islamic Transformations

Many of the patterns evident in Judeo-Christian narratives recur in Islamic scriptures, similarly regarded as the word of God, and taught by prophets including Noah, Abraham, Moses, Jesus and Muhammad.[48] Like the other monotheisms arising in the region, the religious traditions from which

Islam emerged contained many non-human deities. Some were contemporaneous with the early prophets. For example, a moon god, Wadd, whose symbol was a serpent, was worshipped by the Minaeans inhabiting what is now Yemen in southern Arabia (650–150 BCE). A temple was dedicated to him in Dedan (contemporary Al-'Ula) and the king of Awsān was venerated as a deified 'son of Wadd'.[49] The Qur'an describes Wadd as a deity when Noah was a prophet, and adds 'By no means leave your gods, nor leave Wadd, nor Suwa.'[50] Though Suwa was represented as a woman, other deities appeared in non-human forms as lions, horses and eagles, yet, according to Abd Allah ibn Abbas, a seventh-century Islamic scholar, they were worshipped by 'Noah's people'.[51]

Another important deity, Hubal, believed to have powers of divination, appeared as an idol in the Ka'bah at the Sacred Mosque in Mecca.[52] He was described as a warrior and as a rain god, and sometimes as a moon god.[53] The latter explication became controversial because some Christian scholars suggested that he was a precursor to Allah himself, or that Allah was worshipped formerly as a moon god.[54] Pre-Islamic inscriptions employed the name Allah, but Nabataean inscriptions suggest that it was a general term for 'the god', applied to any divinity.[55]

Just as Christian scholars have rejected accounts of goddess worship, the roles of female deities in the ancient world have been much debated by Islamic theologians. However, the archaeological record indicates some gender complementarity, with multiple representations of female figures including Al-Lāt or Allat (illus. 86). She is generally described as a celestial deity, although occasionally as a goddess of the underworld, suggesting some possible movement between domains.[56] Al-Lāt was particularly important to the Banu Thaqif tribe, and was venerated with a shrine in Ta'if decorated with gold and onyx, but she was also worshipped more widely, as the consort or daughter of major male deities.[57] Graeco-Roman influence in the region caused her to be aligned with the goddess Athena and the Roman Minerva, and she

86 Goddess Al-Lāt with a lion, Temple of Ba'alshamîn, Palmyra, Syria, 2nd century, marble bas-relief altar.

is referred to in Greek inscriptions as 'the Great Goddess'. However, it is now broadly maintained that her name was applied more generally to female deities, in the way that the name Allah signified male deities.[58]

Islamic scriptures also include the story of Adam and Eve, and Muslim iconography depicts their expulsion from the Garden of Paradise, although, as exemplified in the image overleaf, the non-human beings in the narrative – a serpent and multi-hued bird – carry them from the garden, surrounded by colourful angels (illus. 87).

Without trying to resolve their points of contention, several things can be gleaned from these scholarly debates. It appears that pre-Islamic societies did venerate multiple, non-human, male and female and sometimes water-related serpent deities. However, when Islam coalesced under the leadership of the sixth prophet, Muhammad (born *c.* 570 CE), there seems to have been less room for religious plurality. Muhammad ordered idols and temples dedicated to these earlier deities to be destroyed, including the shrine to Al-Lāt in Ta'if, stating that:

> Allāh is Unique, the Creator, Sovereign, and Judge of humankind. It is Allāh who directs the universe through his direct action on nature and who has guided human history through his prophets, Abraham, with whom he made his covenant, Moses, Jesus, and Muḥammad, through all of whom he founded his chosen communities, the 'Peoples of the Book'.[59]

Like other monotheistic gods, the Islamic creator separated the Heavens and the Earth, formed the world out of water, made the mountains to provide *terra firma*, and generated all life. 'God preferred water over any other created thing and made it the basis of creation, as He said: and He made every living thing of water' (Qur'an 31:30). Divine authority over primal chaos is asserted in a Qur'anic verse in which God 'places his throne upon the water' (Qur'an 11:7). As the twelfth-century scholar Al-Kisa'i put it: 'Then the water was told, "Be still." And it was still, awaiting God's command. This is limpid water, which contains neither impurity nor foam.'[60]

These religious developments reflected changing lifeways: major water infrastructures had been constructed in the seventh century; states were emerging; and 'throughout the pre-modern Islamic world, the provision of water was one of the government's essential tasks.' Hydraulic expertise was required in government functionaries:

> The Persians used to say: 'He who does not know the art of making the waters flow; the digging of gaps in the banks of the rivers and their ends, and the blocking of the ravines and the daily increase and decrease of the water courses; the perception of the new moon and the doings connected with it; the weighing of the scales, the measuring of the triangle and the quadrangle and the trapezoid, and the setting up of vaulted bridges and embankments and waterwheels and buckets for raising water; and the state of the instruments for the workmen and the niceties of arithmetic is wanting.'[61]

By the end of the tenth century, Islamic water management had become highly sophisticated. Cities such as Cordoba had approximately six

87 Folio of the *Expulsion of Adam and Eve from Eden*, from a *Falnama* (Book of Omens), Iran, Qazvin, Iran, *c*. 1550, opaque watercolour, ink and gold on paper.

hundred public and private bathhouses, all requiring continuous water flows, as well as many ablution fountains outside its mosques.

The central place of water in Islam highlights ideas shared across the monotheistic religions. In the Great Mosque of Mecca, the well of Zamzam now lies underneath the Ka'bah at which pilgrims congregate annually for the Hajj. Stories about the well pre-date Islam: it is said to have erupted for the benefit of Hagar and her infant son Ishmael, and then to have been rediscovered by the grandfather of the Prophet Muhammad (480–578 CE). Both stories connect Islam with Abraham, 'whom Muslims regard as the founder of monotheism on the Arabian Peninsula'.[62]

Islamic prayers (*hadiths*) underline angels' resemblance to other ascending and descending water beings. The religious scholar Al- Suyūṭī (d. 1505) collected more than seven hundred *hadiths*, in which angels are consistently associated with rain. One states, 'Every day Gabriel is immersed in al-Kawthar [abundance, paradise], and then he shakes himself; every raindrop is created from an angel.'[63]

A long-term interest in astronomy shaped Islamic ideas about Heaven, and its purpose became 'to prepare pure souls and make them desirous of celestial ascent'.[64] Later writing about the Islamic cosmos describes angels inhabiting the heavens and representing aspects of the Universal Soul that, in uniting with 'prime matter', enabled bodies to 'pass from potentiality to actuality'.[65] In this way Islamic thinking resonated with other monotheistic religions in finding new ways to describe the movements between material and non-material domains previously facilitated by the hydro-theological efforts of water serpent beings. Ascension also figures in Islamic scriptures (illus. 88). Awoken from his sleep at the Ka'bah in Mecca by the angel Gabriel, Muhammad embarks upon a Night Journey (*Isrā*). Carried on an angelic winged being, Buraq, he travels in a classic hydro-theological cycle through multiple regions of Heaven meeting former prophets (Moses, Adam and Jesus) along the way, and venturing into the depths of Hell. In Heaven (reached via the ascension, or *Mi'rāj*), he is shown the pool of Paradise, al-Kawthar, whose waters were 'whiter than snow and sweeter than honey' (Qur'an 17:1).

Unsurprisingly in an arid region, water dominates Qur'anic visions of Paradise, a blissful 'otherworld' containing endless rivers, soft rains, fruits, flowers and trees laden with pearls and sapphires. These elements are often referenced in traditional 'garden carpets', and – aided by expertise in hydraulic management – they formed the basis of Islamic garden design in which water fountains, pools and wells feature centrally. These ideas are exemplified in the garden attached to Cordoba's great mosque, built in 785–6 CE.

Like biblical texts, Islamic scriptures present their God as the provider of water. He gives it in abundance to the virtuous pre-Islamic prophet Hud, but also uses it punitively (Qur'an 11:50).

> Muslims are reminded that it is God who created the heavens and the oceans from rain. He can, if He wills, use the rain to inflict a deadly punishment and destroy mankind in a cataclysmic inundation. For example, when Noah's people reject his message, God's reaction is swift: 'We opened the gates of heaven with a flood of water' (Qur'an 54:11). The sea as portrayed in the Qur'an can also be a terrifying symbol of

88 The Prophet Muhammad's ascension to Heaven on his angelic steed, Buraq, guided by angels, from an Islamic manuscript, 1539–43, painting attributed to Sultan Muhammad, gouache and ink on paper.

89 Pendant icon depicting *St George and the Virgin and Child Enthroned*, Ethiopia, 18th century, wood and pigment.

God's retribution on those who disbelieve. Their deeds are like 'Darknesses in an open sea covered in waves upon which are waves upon which are clouds – darknesses piled one upon the other' (Qur'an 24:40). It is important for the faithful to recall that it is God who gives, and it is He who can take away. 'Consider the water which you drink. Was it you that brought it down from the rain cloud or We? If We had pleased, We could make it bitter' (Qur'an 56:68–70).[66]

Noah sailed 'amid waves like mountains', but God made them abate. 'And it was said: O earth! Swallow your water and, O sky! Be cleared of clouds! And the water was made to subside.' (Qur'an 11:44). In these ways God exercised control over the non-human world and, rather than representing non-human powers, its myriad wonders were seen as proof of his existence:

> When Meccan pagans demanded proofs, signs, or miracles for the existence of God, the Qur'ān's response was to direct their gaze at nature's complexity, regularity, and order. The early verses of the Qur'ān, therefore, reveal an invitation to examine and investigate the heavens and the earth, and everything that can be seen in the environment . . . The Qur'ān thus makes it clear that

everything in Creation is a miraculous sign of God (*āyah*).[67]

Over time the monotheisms expanded across contiguous regions, with Muslim influence spreading into North Africa and Spain, and Christianity replacing earlier religions across Europe and Scandinavia (illus. 89). There were important differences in these journeys, but all sought to replace the veneration of multiple non-human powers with the authority of male prophets and a humanized, all-powerful male God. They were competitive, not only with each other but in pushing 'pagan' or 'infidel' societies to conform to their beliefs. Thus Jeremiah rails against Babylonian power: 'Nebuchadnezzar the king of Babylon has devoured me and discomfited me; he has made me an empty vessel, he has swallowed me like a dragon; he has filled his belly with my delicacies, he has spewed me out' (Jeremiah 51:34). Ezekiel promotes resistance towards the 'great Dragon' of Egypt:

> Son of man, set thy face against Pharaoh, king of Egypt, and prophesy against him, and against all Egypt. Speak, and say 'Thus saith the Lord God: Behold, I am against thee, Pharaoh, King of Egypt, the great dragon that lieth in the midst of his rivers . . . My river is mine own, and I have made it for myself . . . I will have thee thrown into the wilderness . . . and all the inhabitants of Egypt shall know that I am the Lord'. (Ezekiel 29:3–6)

Critically, the monotheisms promoted an anthropocentric view, giving humankind dominion 'over the fish of the sea, and over the fowl of the air, and over the cattle, and over all the earth and over every creeping thing that creepeth upon the earth' (Genesis 1:26). The non-human world (and especially water) was defined as an 'other' that must be tamed and controlled, as were women and the diverse cultural groups and belief systems over which monotheisms sought to prevail. However, achieving these goals was a far from easy task.

9
Demonized Beings

This chapter explores how the major monotheistic religions reconfigured human-non-human relations, conceptually dividing culture and nature and asserting the patriarchal dominion that represented their vision of an orderly world.[1] In carrying societies further along trajectories towards anthropocentric and instrumental lifeways, they also established unsustainable patterns of exploitation. This was encouraged, particularly in Europe, by greater urbanization and the development of the technologies that would lead eventually to the Industrial Revolution.

The separation of culture and nature could only be achieved via a process of alienation. Rather than being reciprocal co-creators of events, non-human beings and the material world were recast as an adversarial 'other'. Situating (female) nature and emotion oppositionally to (male) culture and reason, monotheistic religions positioned the non-human domain as potentially 'out-of-control' chaos, or at least as 'wild' and requiring social and technological domestication through the imposition of male authority. Inevitably, these changes were reflected in water.

Monotheistic scriptures contained a critical transition from positive representations of serpent beings to representations depicting them as embodiments of evil. This required an inversion of earlier narratives: 'In the context of the patriarchy of the Iron Age Hebrews of the first millennium BC . . . the mythology adopted from the earlier Neolithic and Bronze Age civilizations . . . became inverted, to render an argument just the opposite to that of its origin.'[2]

This shift is discernible between early and later scriptures. Originally the 'fiery' seraphim, 'winged serpents drawn from Egyptian royal and sacral symbolism', appeared as celestial beings bearing sacred figures between earth and heaven and bringing consciousness and wisdom to humankind (illus. 90).[3] They conveyed enlightenment to Isaiah with a 'burning ember', and he had a vision in which the Supreme Being was seated on a throne and 'around him were seraphs, each with six wings' (Isaiah 6:1). This directly mirrored pre-Christian Assyrian images of enthroned gods surrounded by serpent beings. For example, a carving on the tomb of Rameses V describes a winged serpent as 'the leader', and an inscription states that 'It is She Who Leads the Great God.'[4] But other biblical texts presented a more oppositional view of water and its personifications:

90 God borne by seraphim: Giovanni di Paolo, *The Creation of the World and the Expulsion from Paradise*, 1445, tempera and gold on wood.

Thou didst divide the sea by thy strength: thou brakest the heads of the dragons in the waters. Thou brakest the heads of leviathan in pieces, and gavest him to be meat to the people inhabiting the wilderness. Thou didst cleave the fountain and the flood: thou driedst up mighty rivers. (Psalm 74:13–15)

Further serpent slaying occurred in St John the Divine's revelations about the Apocalypse:

> A red dragon with seven crowned heads and ten horns appears in the sky and sweeps a third of the stars from the sky with his tail. A war breaks out between the dragon and St Michael, both supported by angels, the good and the fallen; the

heavenly army eventually vanquishes the dragon's legions and cast the monster down upon the earth. The dragon who is then named as Satan, causes a huge flood, whereupon the beast of the Apocalypse arises from the sea. The dragon gives this monster his power and authority, but is himself chained up by an angel and sealed into an abyss for a thousand years. (Revelations 12:3)

The most obvious inversion of the meaning of the serpent was in the Garden of Eden. Serpentine water and fertility deities had a positive role in pre-Christian paradisiacal gardens, such as the reed fields of Aaru where Osiris 'the green one' dwelt, or the Sumerian land of Dilmun in which the water god Enki and the mother goddess Ninhursag created humankind. In the original Nasorean Garden, sexual reproduction was indicated by a palm tree called Tamar, the goddess of childbirth, entwined by a vine and overlooking a well. This image was transplanted to Delos by the Greeks, so that Leto could give birth to Apollo there under its shade. There are clear traces of these pre-Christian ideas about water beings as the source of all life in biblical texts. As noted above, 'Eve' is a version of *hawwah*, meaning 'life', or 'serpent', and in Genesis 3:20 we are told that 'Adam named his wife Eve because she would become the mother of all the living'.

While pre-Christian serpent beings conveyed female and male complementarity in generating life, Eve was formed from Adam's rib in a patriarchal appropriation of birth-giving powers. Her fall from grace cursed women with the pains of childbirth and punished humankind with mortality. She was told that the serpent will be forever her enemy and that of her descendants, who would crush its head underfoot (Genesis 3:15). The serpent's wisdom became 'cunning': contradicting God's wishes, 'it dismisses the prohibition and disputes the divine claim that death will follow eating from the tree.'[5]

Eve was the weak link, tempted by the serpent in Adam's absence. This suggests another narrative inversion: where only a few hundred years previously the serpent Zeus had appeared as a powerful procreative being in the story of Alexander the Great, the serpent in Eden is an evil seducer, and this motif was echoed in Joseph's discovery of Mary's pregnancy, recounted in Matthew's gospel: 'Who hath done this evil in my house and defiled the virgin? . . . For just as Adam was at the hour of his thanksgiving, and the serpent came and found Eve alone and deceived her, so also hath it befallen me' (Matthew 1:18–21). The coming of the Messiah further embedded the notion of the evil serpent. Though cognizant of the 'wisdom of serpents', Jesus exhorted his disciples to 'subjugate serpentine creatures' (Matthew 10:16; Luke 10:19).

Despite these narrative inversions the new monotheisms did not achieve religious supremacy readily. James Fergusson observed that tree and serpent worship recurred for centuries, 'bursting forth again with wonderful exuberance in the sects of the Nicolaitans, the Gnostics, and more especially that called the Ophites' (illus. 91). He notes Tertullian's comment:

> They even prefer the Serpent to Christ, because the former brought the knowledge of good and evil into the world . . . They also point to his majesty and power, and the importance of Moses raising the serpent in the wilderness . . . they even quote the Gospels to prove that Christ was an

> imitation of the serpent, because it is said, 'As Moses lifted up the serpent in the wilderness, so must the Son of Man be lifted up.'[6]

For six centuries following Christ's birth, Moses' bronze serpent was preserved in the temple and 'the children of Israel did burn incense to it (2 Kings 18:4). Subsequently such practices and the worship of the sacred groves were deemed idolatrous. But in many parts of Europe and Scandinavia tree and serpent worship continued for much longer, despite the adoption of Christian beliefs and practices by royal leaders and political elites. Olaus Magnus records that in Poland such practices continued into the mid-1500s, while Fergusson notes that household serpent gods were venerated in Sweden until the 1600s, and that serpent worshipping 'by the peasantry' continued in remote parts of Norway, Estonia and Finland into the 1800s.[7]

91 Gnostic gem with a lion-headed serpent, 2nd–3rd century CE, carnelian intaglio.

The Church's primacy could only be achieved by transferring the supernatural powers of other deities to God, and by giving his priests exclusive mediatory authority in relation to the scriptures. As serpent and nature worship persisted, the Church went to ever greater lengths to demonize non-human deities and their acolytes, seeking to slay the serpent in all of its manifestations (illus. 92).

Slaying the Dragon

As the previous chapters have illustrated, while 'nature religions' venerated water serpent beings, they also respected their potential to be punitive. Christian evangelists could draw on a plentiful supply of earlier serpent-slaying narratives addressing these fears, and biblical triumphs over Leviathan, the Red Dragon or Satan himself are readily discernible as analogues. They echo Ugaritic stories of the vanquishing of the serpent Lotan; Egyptian images representing Seth's triumph over the serpent Apep; Hittite accounts of Hupasiyas despatching Illuyankas; and Greek and Roman tales of male heroes slaying the Lernaean Hydra, Medusa, the Sea Serpent, Typhon, Python and the fiery Chimera.[8]

By the first century Alexandria was declining as a seat of learning and science, and there was fertile ground for assertions that knowledge could only be gained from the scriptures. Nevertheless, Christians endured considerable persecution until the emperor Constantine's conversion to Christianity enabled the papacy to establish an administrative base and proselytize across the region. What followed was an increasingly aggressive takeover, with

92 Bernt Notkes, *St George and the Dragon*, 1489, paint on wood sculpture, Church of St Nicholas (Storkyrkan), Stockholm.

the destruction of pre-Christian temples, statues and learned texts that effectively ended the classical era.[9]

Rising opposition to alternate religions also reached more northerly regions. With the Roman invasion of Britain in 55 BCE, Roman observers such as the historian Livy had described Celtic ceremonial practices as barbaric. Their religious leaders, the Druids, were vilified as witches or sorcerers because of their reported capacities to transform themselves into animal form and direct the elements.[10] It became policy to destroy all learned orders, and many of the Druids in Britain were massacred in circa 60 CE at Anglesey.[11] However, once under Roman rule, the Celtic tribes remained relatively free to practise their own religion and early Romano-Christian iconography absorbed many pagan images, including figures 'encircled by a great snake . . . clearly being envisaged as operating in the universe of the pagan World-Serpent'.[12]

But as Christianity gained ground across the Roman Empire, it became more assertive in Britain. Water worship was forbidden, and in 452 a religious canon stated: 'If in the territory of a bishop infidels light torches or venerate trees, fountains or stones, and he neglects to abolish this usage, he must know that he is guilty of sacrilege.'[13] Churches were built over or alongside Celtic sacred wells and Christian saints appropriated their miraculous powers of healing and divination. Christian outposts were established: in 563 St Colmcille (Columba) built a monastery on the Scottish island of Iona, and in 635 this was followed by St Aiden's foundation of a holy order on the island of Lindisfarne.[14] St Augustine arrived in Kent in 597 on a mission to convert the pagan King Egbert and his people. When he reached Dorset and was confronted by the hillside carving of the famously potent Cerne Abbas Giant, he thrust his staff vigorously into the ground, as Moses had, causing a spring to flow and asserting the Christian God's power over water.

In the medieval Church the immanent powers of the natural world that had been venerated through the worship of trees, wells and stones were transferred to Christian religious objects, such as the paraphernalia of the sacrament. The water from church fonts (*fons sapientiae*) supplanted holy wells as the source of knowledge and enlightenment.[15] This addressed an anxiety not wholly assuaged by the conversion of Celtic holy wells. For early medieval Christians water could be holy, if blessed by God, but it could also be inhabited by demons. This belief drew on a long history of fears about malignant waters, in which old Church fathers such as Origen, Jerome and Chrysostom saw the non-human domain as a diabolic 'beast' that had to be subdued by 'banishing the flood of unworthy passions'.[16]

Beliefs in demonic water aligned with ideas about corrupting nature and femininity as a threat to spiritual purity. An ascetic of masculine chastity rejected the 'fleshly pleasures' signified by sensory engagements with water, fluid substances and sexual union. This combined the 'tehomophobic' fear of the deep with a gynophobic revulsion about female bodies that pervaded ideas about gender and sexuality for centuries, and gained new expression in Freudian anxieties about sexuality.[17]

Christian dominion over nature beings was also elaborated in the many hagiographic texts composed in Britain and Europe between the fourth and sixteenth centuries. Recurrent images of saints trampling a serpent are epitomized in a ninth-century image from St Matthew's Gospel (illus. 93). In fact, Christian religious texts contained an orgy of serpent slaying by saints, bishops, priests, popes and virgin martyrs. The narrative tropes were consistent: the serpent or (as the beast was increasingly described) 'the dragon' lurked in wild watery places such as underground caves, marshes or lakes. It emerged to terrorize the local population or harm them with 'poisonous exhalations', a notion that – with descriptions of dragons urinating poison from above – may have referred to polluting knowledge, or (in the 1300s) to the very real pestilence of the Black Death.

Ideas about malevolent fire-breathing dragons, inverting the positive images of the 'fiery' seraphim, may have gained impetus from the volcanic eruptions that darkened the skies and caused catastrophic crop failures during the medieval period. Throughout Christendom the dragon or serpent was recast as an image of chaos and death. Rather than signifying cyclical regenerative transitions between material and non-material domains, the anthropophagic dragon/monster merely consumed life.

Only Christ could offer salvation. In exchange for a promise that the local populace would convert to Christianity, the dragon-slaying saint would visit the beast's lair and call it forth 'in the name of Our Lord Christ'. Sometimes performing a ritual of exorcism, he or she would command it to drown in a nearby river, render it compliant or simply dispatch it.[18] An example is provided by La Tarasque, a serpent being that inhabited the river near Tarascon, and constituted a key symbol of pagan resistance to the Christian message. In a story still celebrated on Christian feast days, St Martha poured holy water upon the serpent as it was devouring a man, rendering it sufficiently helpless that it could be killed.[19] In a similarly 'cleansing' narrative, 'St Romanus is

93 Saint trampling a serpent, miniature from St Matthew's Gospel, in the *Bible of William of St Calais*, 1080–96.

said to have slain a dragon in Rouen in the reign of King Dagobert by miraculously inducing it to enter a specially prepared fire in which it was consumed.'[20]

Across the channel, St Patrick put a stop to serpent worship in Ireland by banishing all of its snakes (illus. 94). A local story describes how he also trapped the soul of King Loeghaire of Tara in Dubh-Loch, a water source known as 'the short road to hell', containing a 'horrible serpent'.[21]

Medieval bestiaries suggest that people believed such creatures to be real. Bartholomew Angelicus, the author of one such text, defined dragons as a form of snake, the 'greatest of all serpents'.[22] Indeed there were times when the skies seemed to be full of malignant serpents. Anglo-Saxon chronicles record many dragon sightings, particularly in the northeast of England, possibly reflecting the fear inspired by the Vikings, who raided the coast in dragon-headed boats in the late 700s with such violence that the monks fled from the Holy Island of Lindisfarne:

> In 793 dire forewarnings came over the land of the Northumbrians, and miserably terrified the people; there were excessive whirlwinds and lightnings; and fiery dragons were seen flying in the air. A great famine soon destroyed these tokens; and a little after that, on the 6th day before

the Ides of January, the ravaging of heathen men lamentably destroyed God's Church, at Lindesfarne, through rapine and slaughter.[23]

A Viking leader who terrorized the northeast was called the Dragon, and the Norse *ormr* or *orme*, meaning 'serpent', was anglicized as 'worm' or 'wyrm' and became a common term for a serpent or dragon. Bearing the brunt of the Viking invasions, Northumbria is particularly rich in tales about monstrous 'worms'. A ballad about *The Laidly Worm of Spindleston Heugh* (hill), describing a worm/princess, appears to be based on an older Nordic saga, *Hjálmþés saga ok Ölvis*, and relates how 'Hunger led the serpent to devastate an area seven miles square, its fierce fumes blighting the crops.'[24]

Near the Scottish Borders, 'the Worm's Den' contained the Wode Worm of Linton, also described as a wyvern, a serpent with two legs and a barbed or fish-like tail. When a local hero, the Laird of Lariston, killed the worm, its dying throes formed a range of hills that are still called Wormington.[25] Like the

94 Lilian Lancaster, map of Ireland representing St Patrick driving out the snakes, 19th century.

Romans before him, and like many emperors and pharoahs, the laird adopted the image of the dragon as a heraldic device, and this subjugation of the serpent as a symbol of its conqueror's powers became a common European practice (illus. 95).

A story in Percy's *Reliques* highlights another belief, that – even when hacked to pieces – a serpent could reconstitute itself in water:

> A huge dragon which could make itself invisible formerly guarded three wells near Longwitton Hall, Northumberland. Guy, Earl of Warwick, was the famous hero responsible for slaying it. 'Wandering in pursuit of chivalrous employment', he commanded the winged serpent to emerge from its den and keep its visible form. This it did, but as quickly as Sir Guy wounded the beast, and his strength from loss of his own blood began to fail, the monster would glide back to one of the wells and dip its tail in and return healed and with renewed vigour. The earl, realizing the cause of the long resistance, placed himself between the dragon and the wells, and with one furious onslaught, stabbed it in the heart, killing it.

Sir Guy describes his feat:

> A dragon in Northumberland
> I alsoe did in fight destroy,
> Which did bothe man and beast oprese,
> And all the countrye sore annoye.[26]

Also in the northeast, the Sockburn Worm (near a major Viking settlement) was slain by Sir John Conyers. In an ancient manuscript now in the British Library the story 'is writ as followeth':

95 The *biscione* (big serpent) or *vipera* of the Visconti of Milan, swallowing (or generating) a person. The image has been used as a heraldic device since the 11th century and still appears in the logo of Alfa Romeo cars.

> Sir John Conyers Kt., slew that monstrous and poisonous vermin . . . or werme, wh. had overthrown and devoured so many people in fight; for that the scent of the poison was so strong that no person might abyde it. And by the providence of Almighty God, the said John Conyers, Kt., overthrew the sd. Monster and slew it. But before he made this enterprise, haing but one sonne, he went to the church in Sockburne in compleat armour and offered up his only son to the Holy Ghost. That place where this great serpent lay was called Graystone, and this John lyeth buried

> in Sockburne Church in compleat armour of the time before the Conquest.[27]

One of the most notable features of the later medieval stories is that their heroic dragon slayers were not saints but knights, underlining the military nature of the Christian mission. 'Brave Sir John', who slaughtered the troublesome Lambton Worm in Durham, came back from Palestine to perform this feat. Dieudonné de Gozon, nicknamed Extinctor Draconis (Dragon Slayer) due to his exploits in killing a dragon that lurked in a swamp and preyed on farmers' cattle, was also the Grand Master of the Knights of Rhodes.[28]

The Crusades

In 1096, Pope Urban II initiated a crusade, seeking to unite the divided areas of Christendom and regain the holy sites under Muslim control. Volunteers to the cause became 'warriors of the cross', hoping to gain forgiveness for their sins or assurance of a place in Heaven. The Knights Templar established military and economic bases in Rhodes and Malta. Papal bulls endorsed their activities, forbidding water worship, condemning paganism and – in 1252 – advocating the burning of 'heretics'. Their efforts to dominate the region failed, but excursions into northern Europe, particularly in Baltic and Prussian areas, were more successful and, to the west, a *reconquista* in 1491 wrested the Iberian Peninsula from the Moors.

All forms of heresy against the Church were violently repressed, including reformist efforts such as those of Jan Hus, burned at the stake in Konstanz in 1415. In the late 1400s the Spanish Inquisition brutally enforced religious orthodoxy. The growing antipathy between Protestants and Catholics was neatly expressed in a 1552 engraving by Peter Gottland, in which the infant Christ takes the place of the classic dragon slayer and is shown in combat with a multi-headed serpent, one of whose heads is wearing the Papal crown.

However, medieval dragon-slaying iconography generally relied on images of a mounted knight spearing the beast, and this visual trope pertained whether the enemy was a serpentine 'embodiment of evil', or recalcitrant 'infidels' (illus. 96). Conflict with non-believers popularized the most heroic Christian figures, St Michael and, in particular, St George, whom Samantha Riches describes as 'the ancient symbol of light and power engaged in perpetual struggle with the forces of darkness and chaos'.[29]

St George was a crusading superhero, a Christian Roman soldier who, despite being cruelly tortured, converted many onlookers by refusing to renounce his beliefs. Iconic images of George slaying the dragon spread rapidly throughout Christendom, and he was adopted as a patron saint in Lithuania, Portugal, Germany, Greece and Britain (illus. 97). His story was retold in multiple popular narratives, including *The Golden Legend*, which was recorded by Jacobus de Voragine circa 1260, but more widely disseminated following the invention of the printing press in the mid-1400s.[30] In later versions of the story, as well as slaying a dragon (most often found lurking in a river), he rescues a virtuous maiden:

> A water-dwelling dragon has been threatening a town in Libya, usually called Silene, with its pestilential breath and, in order to keep it away, the people have been giving it sheep. When the supply of sheep begins to fail the people agree

> to sacrifice one child and one sheep every day. Lots are drawn, and eventually the king's only daughter is chosen . . . The princess is sent out with her sheep. She is wearing her best clothes, but sometimes is explicitly said to be dressed as a bride. St George, the knight-errant, then arrives and offers to kill the dragon. The princess protests but the saint insists on fighting the monster, and succeeds in wounding it with his lance or spear. He then instructs the princess to fasten her girdle around the dragon's neck, and she leads it back to the city as if it were a dog. Everyone is very frightened, but St George says that he will kill the dragon if all the people will convert to Christianity . . . He then baptises the king and many thousands of his subjects, and asks for a church to be built.[31]

As medieval societies embraced Christianity many composed analogues of St George, building on their own cultural traditions and interpretations of the Bible and other texts, including Ovid's *Metamorphosis*, Statius' *Thebaid* and the Homeric epics. Virgil's *Aeneid*, in particular, has been linked with the story of Beowulf and his battle with the dragon who terrorized the Danes.[32]

Celtic and Anglo-Saxon stories were also influenced by Teutonic and Scandinavian sagas. These carried forward imagery of pre-Christian deities such as Thor, the Nordic god of thunder and lightning, whose role was to defeat the world-surrounding Midgard Serpent, Jörmungandr, when, releasing its tail from its mouth, it brought about the apocalypse, Ragnarök (illus. 98).[33]

The thirteenth-century Icelandic *Saga of the Volsungs* has roots both in the Germanic and Asian invasions of Europe in the fourth and fifth centuries and in older, prehistoric tales. The shape-shifting Odinic hero Sigurd has been linked to the phallic Old Norse fertility god Volsi. The saga describes

96 Crusaders spearing serpent and infidels, carving above doorway of St Jawarjius Church and Monastery, Acre, Israel.

97 Unknown artist, Russia, *The Miracle of St George*, c. 1525–50, tempera on wood.

98 Illumination depicting Jörmungandr, the Norse serpent believed to encircle the world, Iceland, 1680. The god Thor is attempting to fish for the serpent using an ox's head.

how he hid in a pit to ambush the serpent Fafnir as it tried to return to the water:

> When the worm crawled to the water the earth quaked mightily, so that all the ground nearby shook. He blew poison over all the path before him, but Sigurd was neither afraid nor concerned by the din. And when the serpent crawled over the pit, Sigurd plunged the sword up under the left shoulder, so that it sank to the hilt. Then Sigurd leapt up out of the ditch and drew the sword out of the serpent. His arms were all bloody to the shoulder. And when the huge worm felt his mortal wound he thrashed his head and his tail, destroying everything that got in his way.[34]

99 Carving of Sigurd slaying Fafnir, Hylestad stave church, Setesdal, Norway, 12th century.

Having tasted the serpent's blood, Sigurd was able to understand the speech of birds and, advised by them that this will make him 'wiser than any man', he ate the dragon's heart. This Eucharistic parallel, resonating with older serpent worship rituals, was celebrated in many carved images of Sigurd across Britain and Norway (illus. 99).[35] In the Middle High German poem *Nibelungenlied* (*c.* 1200), which has similarly ancient roots, bathing in the blood of the slain dragon gave Siegfried magical powers, so that he became (like Achilles) invulnerable to weapons. A Danish thirteenth-century chronicle, the *Gesta Danorum*, relates how the hero, Frotho, hunted down and killed a poisonous dragon, seizing the treasure that it was guarding.[36]

These narratives and images depicting culture heroes triumphing over unruly nature and claiming its wisdom and its treasures were carried by hegemonic crusades, Christian missionization and cultural and economic exchanges to multiple geographic regions. Dragon slaying 'went viral' in diverse cultural contexts, resonating with local stories about gods and warriors subduing chaos monsters. There are obvious similarities with some of the eastern stories related earlier: Indra hurled a thunderbolt at the great cloud serpent, Vritra, who represented the waters of primordial chaos. In a classic 'trampling the serpent' image, Vishnu danced on the head of the poisonous river-dwelling serpent Kâliya; and in a story central to Iranian identity a fearsome dragon was killed by a tenth-century Persian hero, Bharam Gur (illus. 100).[37]

In Vietnam the Dragon King, Lac Long, tackled a giant 'demon-fish' in a deep-sea cavern: thrusting a white-hot iron spear into its mouth, he sliced it into three pieces with his sword. In twelfth-century China a water monster known as the Kiau, said to be able to change colour and camouflage itself in order to attack boats, was slain by a local hero in the mouth of the Qiantang River.[38] In Central America, the Maya Codex shows the god Chac trampling a serpent.[39] In New Zealand, the hero Pitaka lured a voracious *taniwha* from its cave, and he and his warriors, like Fafnir, literally incorporated its powers: 'after a bloody battle lasting days, killed him by inflicting thousands of wounds on his tough hide . . . Taking revenge for the monster's devastation, the heroes quickly dismembered the dead taniwha, rendered the fat from its vast body, and cooked and ate the rest.'[40]

Human triumphs over nature typically appropriated its life-giving capacities, and some key dragon-slaying heroes were identified with earlier 'green gods'. This included St George, whose name means 'tiller of soil'. The leafy visage of the Green Man, sometimes also called Green George, has also been identified as a pre-Christian form of St George, highlighting his role as 'an icon of fertility' who brings forth the spring after the bleakness of the winter.[41] His early encounters with the dragon merely involved him subduing it with the sign of the cross. The dragon slaying and damsel rescuing came later: 'The earliest picture of St George killing the dragon is from the early

100 *Bahram Gur Killing the Dragon*, from a *khamseh* of Nizami, Mughal India, c. 1610, opaque watercolour on paper.

eleventh-century church of St Barbara in Soğanlı, Cappadocia.'[42]

As well as demonstrating 'cultic continuity' with the Canaanite storm god Baal,[43] the Christian St George (or Mar Jirjis) is known throughout the Islamic world as El Khader or Al-Khiḍr. The two figures share a feast day, 23 April, and Robert Miller observes that this was also the date on which sacrifices were offered to Zeus on Kasios Mons, otherwise known as Mount Zaphon, the home of Baal.[44] Miller further links Al-Khiḍr with Elijah, noting that they share a shrine on Mount Carmel.

> Khidr also appears in India, as Khwajah Khizr, patron of sailors . . . His principal shrine is on the Indus River Island of Bukkur, now in Pakistan. Khwajah Khizr is clothed in green, travels on water, and is guardian of springs . . . He provides inexhaustible bread and water like Elijah, and he is immortal. At least some of the Khwajah Khizr stories derive from the Vedic conflict of Indra and Vritra, which is itself genealogically related to the Hittite storm god dragon-slaying myths (and thus, likely, to Baal).[45]

Travelling with Alexander the Great, Al-Khiḍr was said to have discovered the Fountain of Youth, or the Well of Life. When he bathed in it his skin and clothing turned green and he left green footprints wherever he went. There are further resonances with stories of Osiris ('the Green One'); the Greek sea god Glaucos ('the Blue or Green One'), who gained immortality by eating a seaside herb; and the story of Gilgamesh, who journeyed under the ocean to seek immortality. All of these figures were strongly associated with the sea: both Baal and St George were described as striking the sea to send up water and make rain; Al-Khiḍr was said to have lived underwater, and in some Indian images he is shown riding a fish like Matsya, Vishnu's fish avatar.[46] But the most important link between these green gods is a core narrative trope concerned with water, fertility, regeneration and eternal life.

Feminized Beings

The dominance of religions celebrating God the Father effected another critical shift in which water was increasingly feminized, and the sea, and waves in particular, were recast as female.[47] The concomitant feminization of water serpent beings is readily visible in late medieval and early modern Christian iconography, in which the serpent in Eden is represented with a snake's body and a female head and breasts, placing the responsibility for sin and disorder squarely with women and nature (illus. 101).

The biblical figure of Lilith received similar treatment. Her name derives from the Sumerian *lilītu*, meaning 'female demon', and she first appears in a Sumerian epic poem and in Zoroastrian ideas about a seductive serpent-woman, Jahi. But Jewish rabbinical literature describes her as Adam's first wife, who 'refused to lie beneath him' or obey his commands. Lilith was 'a woman who was created equal with her husband rather than fashioned on a rib taken from his side. She . . . is sometimes directly identified as the creature who gave Eve forbidden knowledge and thereby gained revenge on both her husband and God himself.'[48]

Nature was similarly portrayed as potentially corrupting and seductive. Like classical Graeco-Roman sirens, many rivers and lakes across Europe were believed to entice people to their doom:

101 Stone carving of feminized serpent with Adam and Eve, Notre Dame Cathedral, 13th century.

102 Leonhard Beck, *St George Fighting the Dragon*, *c.* 1515, oil on panel. As well as an obvious vulva, the dragon has a baby, which has also been slain.

> Salzungen in Germany has a lake which is known to boil with rage until someone drowns in it. The voice of the water at Madüe can be heard crying 'Now, come! Now is the time!' while the river Lahne shouts 'The time is here, the hour is here, where is the man?' and the spring at Eldberg, 'Come down! Come down!' and those who hear obey.[49]

Stories persisting into the nineteenth century claimed that particular rivers demanded an annual human sacrifice. The River Dee, bordering Wales and England, was said to consume three people a year, and a traditional Devonshire ditty claims that 'Dart, Dart, cruel Dart, Every year thou claim'st a heart.'[50] River confluences – where the waters run wild – were seen as particularly dangerous, with the monstrous Tarasque located at the meeting of the Rhône and the Durance at Tarascon.

In the eleventh and twelfth centuries, a variation of the serpent/dragon figure appeared in Europe in the form of the two-legged wyvern. The name connects the Middle English *wyver*, the old French *guivre* and the Latin *vipera*. The wyvern was said to be able to hypnotize its victims, luring them into its mouth. The story *La Vouivre* describes it as a woman with a wyvern body, wearing a ruby between her eyes to guide her through the underworld. Similar imagery attended multiple versions of the legend of Melusine, a Celtic water being well known in northwest France, Luxembourg and the Netherlands. In 1382 Jean D'Arras collated and popularized these stories, and, with translations into German and English, this resulted in widespread dissemination of images of this half-serpent, half-woman figure.[51]

The dragons slain by saintly heroes also came to be depicted in artworks with vulvas, breasts and sometimes baby dragons (illus. 102). Samantha Riches observes that

> Infants were thought to ingest spiritual values along with physical nutrition when they were suckled . . . the breasts or dugs of a female dragon can thus be interpreted as the evil traits that she will inevitably pass on to her brood . . . We should not overlook the phallic nature of the weaponry St George uses, particularly the way that it often functions as a pointer to the orifice itself . . . The presence of female genitalia in these images defines the dragon in a quite specific way . . . A complex paradigm is set up of an act of penetration by the aggressive male which overthrows the sexuality of the female (he refuses to have actual coition with her) and at the same time sublimates his own sexual desires. This reading is entirely congruent with our understanding of St George . . . St George is presented as the antithesis of the dragon: human to beast, good to bad, male to female . . . chaste in opposition to the dragon's obvious sexuality . . . The dragon and the Virgin seem to be intended to embody the polar opposites inherent in late medieval attitudes to women, the nadir and the epitome; the evil, sexual, bestial creatures and the good, virginal, saintly creature.[52]

Religious narratives represented virtuous femininity as a pure and compliant 'maiden' (virgin), needing to be rescued by a male culture hero, or as a saintly figure 'saved' by commitment to Christ. Identified with the temptress Eve, and always potentially corrupting to men, women could only attain sanctity through a rejection of their sexuality. Most female Christian saints were therefore virgins, martyrs or married women who had taken a vow of chastity.[53] And yet, as Riches says, the most recurrent motif in the imagery of dragon slaying is sexual, entailing the aggressive penetrative stabbing of the non-human serpent being. This can be interpreted as promoting both misogynistic violence towards 'unruly' femininity, and an adversarial engagement aiming to conquer the powers of nature, represented by water serpent beings.

Religious fundamentalism also incited a determination to stamp out witchcraft and sorcery. This called upon the authority of the scriptures: Chronicles relates how Manasseh, the king of Judah, angered God by indulging in pagan practices:

> He did evil in the eyes of the Lord, following the detestable practices of the nations the Lord had driven out before the Israelites. He rebuilt the high places his father Hezekiah had demolished; he also erected altars to the Baals and made Asherah poles . . . He bowed down to the starry hosts and worshiped them. He sacrificed his children in the fire in the Valley of Ben Hinnom, practised divination and witchcraft, sought omens, and consulted mediums and spiritists. (2 Chronicles 33:6)

Leviticus contains a direct warning from God: 'Do not turn to mediums or seek out spiritists, for you will be defiled by them. I am the Lord your God' (Leviticus 19:31). In Galatians believers are told that 'the acts of the flesh are obvious: sexual immorality, impurity and debauchery; idolatry and witchcraft' (Galatians 5:19–20). These texts authorized large-scale witch hunts, particularly during the Counter-Reformation between 1580 and 1630, but continuing to the mid-1700s. More than 50,000 people, 80 per cent of whom were older women, were found guilty of witchcraft and burned at the stake.[54]

Throughout the medieval and early modern period, monotheistic religions therefore demonized and slayed the serpentine water beings of earlier religions and the people who persisted in worshipping them. This enabled them to overcome – or at least to repress – the 'heresy' of paganism, and to entrench patriarchal control over society and nature. And all the while, in material terms, this authority was manifested in new instrumental technologies: dams, mills, canals and drainage systems that reshaped the landscape, imposed control over water and directed its flows to support human needs and interests.

10
Reformed Beings

Medieval Europe was dominated by Christian beliefs that God's plan was inexplicable, and that the scriptures, mediated by priests, provided an exclusively authoritative guide. However, the persistence of indigenous nature religions and competition from other monotheisms were not the only challenges to the Church: human curiosity also proved hard to suppress. Scholars such as the Anglo-Saxon polymath the Venerable Bede (673–735) were inspired by the Greek natural philosophers. St Isidore of Seville (560–636) rescued many ancient texts.[1] There were ongoing exchanges with Islamic science, which had flourished between the eighth and fourteenth centuries, producing ideas about astronomy, mathematics, zoology, chemistry, physics and medicine.[2] In the tenth century, Hildegard of Bingen, a German Benedictine abbess, laid the foundations of natural history.[3] In England the Bishop of Lincoln, Robert Grosseteste (1179–1253), wrote treatises about the physical laws governing the material world. Leonardo da Vinci (1452–1519) sought to understand water's material properties and behaviours, and how it flowed through bodies and environments. Understandings of the hydrological cycle were further advanced by the Huguenot Bernard Palissy in the early 1500s. Scientific ideas might have been regarded as heretical, as Galileo (1564–1642) discovered to his cost, but they were also unstoppable.[4]

Water serpent beings were therefore affected not only by efforts to assert the supremacy of Christianity but by the 'disenchantment' of scientific thinking.[5] Just as their role in carrying the human spirit through material and non-material domains had been usurped by the patriarchal gods of monotheistic religions, new concepts of hydrology replaced their function in providing the flows of water through the world. It became difficult to see the arching bow of the rainbow as a beneficent water serpent being when, through work such as Grosseteste's treatise *De iride* (The Rainbow), it became explicable as a spectrum of light.[6]

Intellectual endeavours to demystify the physical world were matched by intensifying human control over it. Some of this was administrative, supporting new and more elaborate forms of governance. In Britain, following the Norman Conquest, William the Conqueror commissioned a 'Great Survey' of England and Wales. Designed to enable taxation, the Domesday Book (1086) recorded 'hides' of land, stock and other productive aspects of the landscape in more than 3,000 locations. It also documented the increasing physical regulation of water, listing thousands of watermills (for example, finding 66 of them along the 112-kilometre (70 mi.) River Stour in Dorset).[7] As in other parts of the world, harnessing water power was transformational. Mills performed multiple tasks, milling grain, fulling cloth, working iron, breaking ore and making paper. They represented a major step towards the industrial exploitation of water.[8]

Many important springs and wells were taken over by monasteries and abbeys, whose monks were adept hydrological managers. Their control of water upheld the authority of the Church and facilitated the building of the soaring cathedrals that comprised medieval monuments to power. Building these massive edifices required large quantities of stone, transforming the canals begun by the Romans into a vital system of transport that, along with mechanization in rural economies, fuelled economic growth and urbanization. London's population doubled in the thirteenth century to about 50,000 people, and many Continental cities were larger, although the Black Death reduced their populations radically in the mid-1300s.

Pressing needs for urban sanitation required coordinated water and waste management.[9] Older fears about 'demonic' water or 'pestilential' serpents gave way to ideas about material pollution and a belief that disease was caused by 'miasmas' or 'putrid exhalations' from watercourses.[10] Just as the Romans had constructed aqueducts to bring cleaner water into cities, municipalities began to install piped water supplies from springs. The construction of the Great Conduit in London in the 1400s encouraged further development, and water infrastructure became a focus for public philanthropy and Christian charity.

Technical progress also provided similar control over water in other parts of Europe. The Netherlands struggled with flooding for centuries (notably in 1362, when the St Marcellus flood claimed more than 40,000 lives), until the Dutch developed dykes and windmills to defeat 'the waterwolf', as they called the consuming seas: a triumph still celebrated in contemporary festivals.[11]

Reformation

In the 1500s, scientific and technological advances, widening public literacy and new economic practices culminated in the Reformation. Rejecting the cult of saints and the rituals absorbed from earlier religions, this had significant impacts on societal relations with water: 'Puritanism encouraged work rather than works, meaning magic, and this has a particular relevance to the idea of holy water as a sacrament.'[12] Calvinism dismissed beliefs in holy water's miraculous powers as 'popish magic and superstition'.[13] An injunction in 1547 forbade exorcism and, in 1565, Bishop Bentham of Lichfield and Coventry 'commanded the clergy to abolish all monuments of idolatry and superstition'.[14] Priests used former holy water stoups for feeding or watering pigs, or as wash-troughs.

Despite this discouragement, people remained convinced that holy water could protect them from demons and witchcraft, and that ancient wells could assist fertility and healing. Even the royal family visited holy wells, and some sites, such as Lourdes in France, continued to attract religious pilgrims. But theological ideas were changing, reconciling new material understandings with beliefs in divine creativity. Building on Thomas Aquinas's notion of God as 'first cause', Natural Theology proposed that an ordered universe manifested God's plan. Islamic beliefs similarly suggested that Revelation revealed the divine unity of nature and the cosmos. Both incorporated Graeco-Roman philosophy, for example Aristotelian concepts of *nous*, which envisaged a divine mind in a cosmic realm.

Such visions of supernatural 'presence' contained a faint echo of earlier beliefs in which water serpent beings generated life and consciousness, created sentient landscapes inhabited by ancestral beings, and articulated and enforced the law. But Natural Theology did not acknowledge non-human powers: in its terms, the universe was wholly the creation of a humanized God, and its aberrations, such as floods, drought and pestilence, expressed his judgement.[15]

Rather than being seen as primal sources of creativity, the unruly seas represented humankind's Fall. The theologian Thomas Burnet described them as 'the most frightful sights that nature could offer . . . an abyss of debris'.[16] Beneficent waters were the life-giving (domesticated and orderly) flows of fresh water demonstrating God's love, and the reliable hydro-theological cycle reflected his wisdom.[17] Gilbert Lascault suggests that the late seventeenth- and early eighteenth-century Enlightenment was an age 'without monsters',[18] and representations of serpent beings were discouraged in religious iconography: 'Perhaps alarmed by all the attention given to monstrous things, real and imaginary, by the late seventeenth century the European churches began to crack down on such imagery in ecclesiastical art and architecture, leading to a kind of temporary suppression.'[19]

The Protestant work ethic re-imagined Eden as a productive agricultural paradise. The instrumental aim of human dominion over nature, propounded by Aquinas, was to restore the world to a state of prelapsarian perfection.[20] Capacities to reshape the material environment came to represent a moral good, and irrigation in particular enacted God's will, embedding in water infrastructures a religious zeal still evident today.[21]

Such thinking is readily visible in the landscape design of the Renaissance. With elaborate lakes and fountains, social elites expressed water's core meanings as a symbol of wealth, health and potency (illus. 103).[22] In Rome, the restoration of ancient aqueducts and the creation of classical gardens celebrated the power of the papacy. In Britain, wealthy landowners built Palladian mansions surrounded by meticulously designed landscapes. For example, the famous garden at Stourhead in Wiltshire takes the visitor on a spiritual 'journey' around a large artificial lake, through an arboretum and back to St Peter's Church. Yet it contains a sacred pool in a tufa grotto, inhabited not by saints but by Graeco-Roman river gods and water nymphs. Its major features are classical temples, such as the Temple of Apollo, sacred groves, wells and fountains, including St Peter's Pump, which brings together the six wellsprings that originally formed the source of the River Stour. In many such gardens, and in urban water features that are so often central to civic identity, water serpent beings continued to spout water or twine around fountains. In this way – diverted 'harmlessly' into the arts – images and objects celebrating the

103 Water beings in the gardens of Versailles, France.

pre-Christian veneration of nature beings found new forms of expression.

Ideas about 'living water' also persisted. Holy wells and springs were revived as health spas and it became fashionable to imbibe their waters, whose healing powers could now be medically explained with lists of the beneficial minerals that they contained.[23] Effervescent thermal springs were especially popular, such as that in Karlovy Vary (Carlsbad), reportedly named for Charles IV after he bathed a wounded foot there in the 1400s. In these contexts too the 'healing serpent' was a recurrent motif (illus. 104).

104 Bronze serpent at Karlovy Vary health spa, Czechia.

Water serpent beings lived on in many folk tales. There was the Earth-shaking Russian Indrik; water monsters in Estonian lakes; and the Swedish 'lindorn', described by cultural historian Gunnar Olof Hyltén-Cavallius in 1883 as a hissing, venomous creature with a scaly black-and-yellow body and a forked tongue. Sailors – particularly those venturing into unfamiliar seas – returned with stories of sea serpents, and the bishop of Bergen, Erich Pontoppidan, writing *The Natural History of Norway* in 1755, reported hundreds of such sightings.[24] In a comprehensive study of such beings in 1892, the Dutch zoologist Antoon Cornelis Oudemans recorded Olaus Magnus's description (illus. 105):

> There is a Serpent there which is of a vast magnitude, namely 200 foot long, and more – over 20 feet thick; and is wont to live in Rocks and Caves toward the Sea-coast about Berge: which will go alone from his holes in a clear night, in Summer, and devour Calves, Lambs, and Hogs, or else he goes into the Sea to feed on Polypus [octopus], Locusts [lobsters], and all sorts of Sea-Crabs. He hath commonly hair hanging from his neck a Cubit long, and sharp Scales, and is black, and he hath flaming shining eyes. This Snake disquiets the Shippers, and he puts up his head on high like a pillar, and catcheth away men, and he devours them.[25]

Sightings of dragons and serpents also continued in Britain. In Essex in 1668, 'The Henham dragon made its appearance about a quarter of a mile away from the village in 1668, eating cattle and attacking people before it was finally killed by a concerted

105 Detail of the monstrous sea *orm* (worm) and the *maelström* off the coast of Norway, in Olaus Magnus, *Carta Marina*, 1539.

effort of townspeople. A pamphlet published the following year (1669) entitled "The Flying Serpent or Strange News out of Essex" describes the events' (illus. 106).[26]

In Norwich a pageant from the 1400s, celebrating St George's Day and the slaying of 'Old Snap', continued until 1795. Samantha Riches notes that

> Many of our forebears believed that dragons were literal creatures of flesh and blood with real powers to spread pestilence, to contaminate water supplies and to threaten life and limb . . . As late as 1725, Henry Bourne, a Newcastle curate, wrote that the custom of lighting bonfires in Midsummer Eve was derived from the desire to frighten dragons away: the monsters 'being incited to lust through the heat of the season, did frequently, as they flew through the Air, Spermatise in the Wells and Fountains'.[27]

By the 1700s, however, ideas about serpentine beings were increasingly dominated by scholars of natural history and 'cryptozoology' suggesting that prehistoric beasts might have survived deep in the oceans. Fossils had previously lent verisimilitude to Greek travellers' reports; for example, Apollonius of Tyana, visiting the Himalayas in the first century, reported that the countryside was full of dragons and 'no mountain ridge was without one'.[28] In the 1800s, with the findings of the palaeontologist Mary Anning and emergent evolutionary theories, fossil 'monsters' were recognized as Jurassic remains: fearsome indeed, but rendered harmless by the passage of time.

Meanwhile technology continued to enlarge societies' material powers. The Industrial Revolution brought new ways to instrumentalize water, driving steam engines and manufacturing on a large scale. Railways cast a net of iron over the countryside, and steamships reduced the distances across oceans to a minor adventure. Understandings of the molecular structures of the world transformed water into H_2O, leaving little space between the atoms and molecules for supernatural beings.[29] New scientific knowledge highlighted material relationships between water quality and health, and through sophisticated systems of urban supplies – and bureaucratic 'devices' measuring and allocating these supplies[30] – water was integrated into techno-managerial forms of governance that brought human and non-human worlds together in highly utilitarian relationships.

As industrialization pushed rural workers into the cities, living among strangers replaced communal rural identities with more individuated bodies and selves.[31] Consequent anxieties about controlling social and physical boundaries to avoid pollution by the substances or smells of 'others' emphasized health and hygiene rather than spiritual concerns.[32] Relocation to the city therefore alienated people from each other, and from the non-human world. Thus Terje Tvedt and Eva Jakobsson suggest that 'mankind was liberated from nature or from the powers of nature . . . The separation of nature from society was one prerequisite for regarding nature instrumentally, as a set of passive objects to be exploited.'[33] They cite Marx's claim that

> Capitalism liberated man from the traditional, localised dependency on nature, and with it . . . 'nature idolatry' . . . For the first time, nature becomes purely an object for humankind, purely a matter of utility; ceases to be recognised as a power for itself, and the theoretical discovery of its autonomous laws appears merely as a ruse to subjugate it under human needs, whether as an object of consumption or as a means of production.[34]

This accords with Max Weber's assertion that Protestantism created the basis for capitalism,[35] and supports Lynn White's central argument that, despite gentler – though still patriarchal – ideas about stewardship represented by figures such as St Francis of Assisi, Christianity desanctified nature, destroyed animist beliefs and differentiated (or alienated) humankind from other species, placing

106 *Flying Serpent of Henham*, woodcut from a 1669 pamphlet titled 'The Flying Serpent; or, Strange News Out of Essex'.

many societies onto the instrumental trajectory that has led to the current ecological crisis.[36]

Ebbs and Flows

Changing human–environmental relationships coincided with the expansion of modernizing economies. Ancient trade routes had linked Europe with India, and India with Southeast Asia, carrying their water serpent beings and semi-human deities to far-flung regions.[37] Now such connections enabled the spread of monotheistic religions, Cartesian understandings of the material world and worldviews envisioning more unequal human-non-human relations. Muslim enclaves were established in Java and Sumatra, leading to the conversion of Malacca in the 1400s. By the 1500s there were sultanates in the Malay Peninsula, and Islamic beliefs were adopted across the Mughal, Safavid and Ottoman empires. As with the earlier Crusades, there was aggressive competition from Christian states. A new sea route was opened from Europe in 1492, and Malacca fell to Portuguese conquest in 1511.

In the mid-nineteenth century, naval might shifted the balance of power to European nations and enabled hegemonic expansion into colonial territories.[38] Indigenous populations were dispossessed and forced to adopt imposed modes of production and new religious beliefs and practices. Corralled into homogenizing scientific categories, colonial territories were mapped, renamed and distributed to settlers. This required legal and physical property boundaries, roads, land clearance and, above all, the zealous imposition of control over water.

European efforts to develop agriculture in Australia illustrate the instrumentality of these endeavours. Importing farming practices from a temperate, well-watered environment, colonial settlers struggled with lengthy droughts, severe floods and delicate soils easily eroded by forest clearance and hard-hooved cattle. 'Pioneers' sank water bores into the Artesian basin and built bunds to retain floodwater, but – in their terms – the landscape remained hostile and recalcitrant. In the 1800s aims to 'green the desert' were realized in the construction of major dams and irrigation schemes.

Ernestine Hill's classic text describing the transformation of the 'waterless wasteland' of the Murray–Darling basin frames 'the taming of the river' as a religious transfiguration enabled by irrigation and engineering.[39] Her chapter titles are revealing: 'Miracle of the Murray', 'Apostles of Irrigation', 'Utopia on the Murray', 'Acts of God', and 'Reining in the River' record how irrigation helped farmers to combat 'Pharaoh's plagues' and 'the fiery breath of a terrible drought'. A leading engineer, Alfred Deakin, was a 'youthful St Paul' whose vision saw 'the bare and blinding desert transmuted by industry and intelligence into orchards and fields of waving grain'.[40] All the fundamental tenets of Protestant instrumentality are there: the industrious work ethic, the imposition of patriarchal authority and infrastructure on the land and waterscape, and a determination to make the material world 'productive' in ways exclusively focused on human needs and interests.

In the nineteenth and twentieth centuries, this vision of water-driven flourishing became central to many emerging state imaginaries. Like the rulers of the ancient hydraulic societies, governments recognized that the control of water and political power were interdependent. As well as delivering water supplies to citizens and assuring their health and well-being, water infrastructures co-constructed nations and supported their growth and global influence.

There was river straightening and canalization across Europe. In 1851 the Rhine River Engineering Administration was established, and a Prussian Navigation Project sought to cut a straight path through the river's meanders, facilitating the transport of coal and iron ore through Rhineland and Westphalia.[41]

In the late 1940s, following a major drought and famine, Stalin's Great Plan for the Transformation of Nature was conceived 'to correct the mistakes of nature' by diverting Siberian rivers towards Central Asia and channelling northern European rivers to the Volga: 'We are building Communism, we are transforming life on earth.' The (unrealized) plan entailed controlling the Ob River with a 78-metre (255 ft) dam; creating a reservoir 270,000 square kilometres (104,250 sq. mi.) in size (four times larger than the fast-vanishing Aral Sea); and constructing 800 kilometres (500 mi.) of canals. 'Supplied by water, an entire agricultural-energy complex would grow up which, by itself, would exceed entire sectors of capitalist economies.' An irrigated area larger than those in Japan and Egypt would produce more cotton than the USA. Hydroelectricity generation would surpass that of the USA, France, Germany and Britain. Unlimited water transport would open up Siberia.[42]

Extreme infrastructural developments were similarly tied to notions of progress and development elsewhere. India had benefited from centuries of storage tank construction and community-based water management but, with colonial disruption and the commercial focus of the East India Company, little was invested in water infrastructures.[43] Following India's independence in 1947 the Indian government established water authorities to initiate new developments but, like the colonial leaders, they lacked local ecological expertise. Efforts were made to re-enlist village communities through irrigation cooperatives. However, after massive floods in the late 1980s, international donors promised 'mega-solutions in the form of major dams and, despite local protests, 'the initiative and management of water resources passed over totally to the government from the community and community participation was replaced by elitist technocratic institutions.'[44]

In Japan, the fortunes of the Tama River are illustrative (illus. 107).[45] During the Edo period (1600–1868), the river had supported the growth of Tokyo from a few thousand to a million people. Fish were an important food source; gravel from its banks was vital to construction; and its waters supplied the enlarging population and irrigated agriculture in the surrounding area. In the 1700s, pipes, canals and diversionary channels expanded agricultural activities and allowed the transportation of lumber, cedar bark shingles, paper, silk, tobacco, wheat, barley, cotton, thatch, soybeans, sesame oil and vegetables.

In the nineteenth century a centralized imperial government drove an industrial revolution and opened the country to international trade. This brought increased demand for construction materials. Excessive manipulation of the river led to extreme floods, one of which, in 1910, killed 1,231 people and swept away more than 500,000 houses. At the same time, with constant diversions of its

107 Katsushika Hokusai, *Tama River in Musashi Province*, from the series *Thirty-Six Views of Mount Fuji*, c. 1830–32, colour woodblock print.

flows, the river shallowed. Goods could no longer be transported, fisheries declined and seawater incursions moved further upstream.

In China, water control empowered the 'Great Leap Forward', and Florence Padovani tells us that 'in 1950 the People's Republic of China (PRC) regarded the harnessing of water as its main task.'[46] Like the earlier imperial dynasties, the nationalist government aimed to centralize power and to modernize through technology. As with other twentieth-century governments, it saw major water projects that would generate growth and development in farming and industry as a way to demonstrate its political and economic vitality.[47] But despite several decades of engineering, 20,000 people died in floods in the 1990s. Rather than raising questions about such intense instrumentality, this provided a rationale for the Three Gorges Dams on the Yangtze River, and an equally ambitious scheme for the Yellow River. Newspapers began to describe the Chinese leader Jiang Zeming as 'the new Yü the Great'.[48]

The USA had made an early start on competitive nation building. Constructed on the Colorado River in the 1930s, the Hoover Dam was one of the world's largest and most ambitious hydro-electric schemes, supplying water and power to the inhabitants of Las Vegas. At the dedication of the dam, the Interior Secretary Harold Ickes boasted, 'Pridefully, man acclaims his conquest of nature. We have taught ourselves that with our wit and with our might we have wrested from earth, sea and sky the necessities, the comforts and the luxuries of a complicated human civilization.'[49]

Downstream

The consequences of such instrumental hubris soon became visible. The infrastructural impositions on the Colorado River rapidly reduced it to a 'poisonous trickle' by the time it reached Mexico.[50] This 'liquid death' highlights a recurrent issue in arid regions. Soil salinity caused by irrigation (which draws salts to the surface), and the use of brackish water from shrinking aquifers, has rendered 20 per cent of the world's previously fertile land sterile, and 2,000 hectares (4,950 ac) of farmland is lost to salinity every day.[51]

Land drainage and the clearing of forests to expand agricultural land use continues to remove habitats vital for biodiversity. In Australia, with huge irrigation companies diverting a significant proportion of its upriver flows, the Murray–Darling basin is severely degraded: wetlands have been destroyed; downstream farmers have been bankrupted, and the river often fails to reach the sea.[52] The Brisbane River, dammed, over-used, over-dredged and polluted with heavy metals, regularly floods the city around its delta, and pours pollutants into the sea, with devastating consequences for the Barrier Reef. The Hawkesbury–Nepean River system, near Sydney, has been similarly compromised: 'From "sea grass beds and clear water" to a drain befouled by sewage effluent, agricultural pollution and dredged for sand and gravel resources, the river and its ecology has recorded a history of ignorance, greed and insensitivity.'[53]

These are the most critical freshwater issues: on the one hand there is 'water scarcity' due to a combination of rising demand for irrigation supplies; excessive abstraction from rivers and aquifers; and, with global warming, glacial retreat that removes vital water storage from the world's mountains. More than a million irrigation schemes produce over 40 per cent of the world's food, and irrigation has doubled every decade since the 1960s, now using over 70 per cent of the fresh water available. A further 15 per cent will be soon be needed to produce sufficient crops for a global population that continues to enlarge, and the World Bank predicts major shortfalls in supply.[54] On the other hand, there is sometimes too much water: exploitative land-use practices, the removal of forests and wetlands, and the brutal over-engineering of river systems have left many downstream areas vulnerable to major floods that are increasing in frequency as anthropogenically created climate change induces more volatile weather patterns.

Mining has also had major impacts on freshwater ecosystems, and Japan offers another illustrative example. In 1891, farmers alongside the Watarase River, north of Tokyo, petitioned for the closure of the Ashio copper mine because it was polluting the river and their fields. The water had turned bluish-white, fish were dying and people who ate them became sick. Flooding compounded the problem: crops shrivelled, and farm workers were covered in sores. But the copper from the mine comprised Japan's third most important export. Committed to modernizing rapidly, Japan's Meiji government was reluctant to restrict mining activities.[55]

Extractive industries are a key driver of growth in many industrialized countries, and in some, such as Australia, it is central to their economies. So too is an industrialized agricultural sector similarly committed to growth and expansion. Land clearance to extend intensive farming, logging and oil exploration are seen as a developmental necessity even in environmentally critical areas such as the Amazon. As a result, 'primary producers' are rarely required to take responsibility for the impacts of their activities, and this is exacerbated by a reality that, today, many large mines and agricultural companies are owned by transnational corporations with little local accountability.[56]

Thus, as beliefs in the moral good of growth and production flowed around the globe, societies moved further along trajectories that imposed highly directive regimes onto the material world, framing it in terms of resources, assets and 'ecosystem services'.[57] This entailed a prioritization of interests in which, the political scientist James Scott observes, 'everything that interfered with the efficient production of the key commodity was implacably eliminated.'[58] As well as cruelly widening human inequalities, this has been devastating to the non-human domain. Many of the world's lakes, rivers and aquifers have been radically compromised, as have soils, forests and wider ecosystems, air quality and the oceans. A mass extinction of non-human species has already occurred, and nearly one-third of those remaining are hovering on the brink.[59] Humans and non-human beings alike are travelling, with accelerating speed, towards a global collapse.

Enduring Serpents

There would seem to be little room in this equation for water serpent beings. Their creative non-human powers as life-makers and bringers of water have been handed over to humanized gods. Science has disenchanted water bodies and hydrological flows. Patriarchal dominion over human societies and other species has become politically and materially entrenched. And yet, even in wholly industrialized contemporary societies, water serpent beings have endured.

They have persisted, in part, because they permeate local cultural heritage so deeply and ubiquitously that there are few countries in which stories about them cannot be found. A typical example comes from the Los Picos mountains of northern Spain, where folk tales describe El Cuélebre, a giant (and sometimes multi-headed) serpent with bat-like wings, incandescent eyes and impenetrable scales, said to emerge from springs or from the fissures in the jagged mountains.[60] It is 'sea-covered' and protective of a 'nursery of diamonds', implying that its home lies deep underground, in waters under the land.[61] It appears in some images twined, in classical serpent fashion, around a cross or tree.

In traditional stories El Cuélebre is propitiated with food, but if it attacks cattle or people, it is fed bread or meat containing pins, or hot metal shards, causing it to burst. In one rendition of the narrative, it drinks torrents of water to ease the pain of the hot shards, and its vomit forms the Lake of Isaby in the High Pyrenees.[62] There is obvious inspirational material in the apocryphal story of Daniel, a prophet and advisor of Nebuchadnezzar II, who ruled Babylon from 605 to 562 BCE. Mocking rituals of propitiation venerating a local serpent being, Daniel destroyed the creature (and asserted the supremacy of his god) by feeding it pitch, fat and hair until it exploded.[63] Thus a story that probably began with

108 Celtic dragon sculpture at Dublin Castle.

a pre-Christian water being was re-visioned by Christian storytellers to detail a demonic serpent, one which must be overcome by greater (humanized) divine powers. Yet El Cuélebre remains in the mountains, illustrated in local literature, valorized as a local presence by tourist guides and celebrated in traditional Asturian costumes.

Celtic serpents have also composed a lively part of British cultural heritage, most particularly in areas determined to preserve Gaelic regional histories (illus. 108). What is the Loch Ness Monster, after all, if not an elusive water serpent being? According to the Abbot of Iona, it first appeared in the River Ness in the sixth century.[64] As was common in medieval hagiographies, the serpent was repulsed by the sign of the cross, impressing upon the local Picts the powers of Christianity. This early 'record' is taken as the starting point for the multiple purported sightings, photographs and films of the monster that followed.

109 John Tenniel, 'Jabberwocky', illustration for Lewis Carroll's *Through the Looking-Glass, and What Alice Found There* (1871).

One of Britain's most famous dragons is the Lambton Worm, said to have inhabited the River Wear in Durham at the time of the Crusades. Its story has been carried into the present, in part because it was popularized in a Geordie folk song.

> Whisht lads, haad yor gobs, [shut your
> mouths] an' aa'll tell ye all an aaful story,
> Whisht lads, haad yor gobs, an' aa'll tel
> ye 'boot the worm.[65]

Possibly based on the story of the Sockburn Worm (noted in the previous chapter), the tale of the Lambton Worm describes how, as a boy, Sir John Lambton fished 'a queer worm' from the river, and because he 'couldn't be fashed [bothered] to carry it hame' threw it down a well. Over the years it grew into a giant serpent which wrapped its tail 'ten times round Penshaw Hill'. Its first predations involved milking the local 'coos' at night, but when it began to consume sheep and 'swally little bairns [children] alive', the local villagers sent 'news ov this myest aaful worm' to Palestine, where 'the brave and bowld Sir John' was participating in the Crusades. 'So hyem [home] he cam an' catched the beast, An' cut 'im in twe haalves'.

The song provides a perennially popular topic for school drama performances in Durham, and it inspired Lewis Carroll, who spent part of his childhood in the area, to write 'Jabberwocky' (illus. 109).[66] But it is also the subject of an annual ritual involving the Bishop of Durham, one of the Church of England's most powerful leaders. Durham Cathedral was founded by monks from Lindisfarne who, fleeing Viking invaders in 793, brought the body of St Cuthbert to Durham and established a Palatine (royal) territory.[67] This semi-autonomy, necessitated by the Viking predations, and by unruly Celtic incursions from Scotland, allowed the bishop to collect taxes, establish his own army and, in effect, to run a 'parliament in the north'.

Though now performed in a light-hearted way, an annual ritual has been revived in which, before a new bishop is enthroned at Durham Cathedral, he must enter the county at its southernmost point, at Croft-on-Tees, which is the location of the Sockburn Worm story. Meeting local dignitaries on the bridge over the river, the bishop is handed a medieval sword or falchion, and has to swear to slay the dragon (illus. 110). In this ceremony, Justin Welby, who went on to become the Archbishop of Canterbury, was greeted by the local mayor, Adele Martin: '"My Lord Bishop," she said, "I here present you with the falchion wherewith the champion Conyers slew the worm, dragon or fiery flying serpent which destroyed men, women and children"'.[68]

In his enthronement speech, Welby called upon modern Christians 'to rekindle the Christian faith in the north-east and reconvert the region . . . to bring Christianity into every community'.[69] His successor, Paul Butler, described the dragon as 'all of that which we see as evil in our world'. So even today, representations of the serpent and its slaughter by a militant religious hero continue to uphold and promote monotheistic authority.[70]

St George, the epitome of this imagery, now has a more complex role in articulating conservative visions of national and religious identity. There are multiple St George Societies in the UK and its former colonial satellites. Their representations of the saint slaying the dragon, in heraldic emblems and related material culture, often include the Crusaders' red cross as well as the British Lions, not only underlining the notion of military religious evangelism but providing (ironically, given St George's geographic origins) a primary symbol of English identity.

For some 'patriots' this is an exclusive vision of uncontaminated ethnic or cultural 'purity': that is, an England without the immigration that, using the fluid terminology common to ideas about race, Margaret Thatcher claimed would result in this country being 'swamped by people with a different culture'.[71] The Society of St George was formed in 1894 'to encourage and strengthen the spirit of patriotism among all classes of the English people, and to foster and inspire our fellow-countrymen with a jealous pride in all that concerns the welfare and greatness of their native land, or the land of

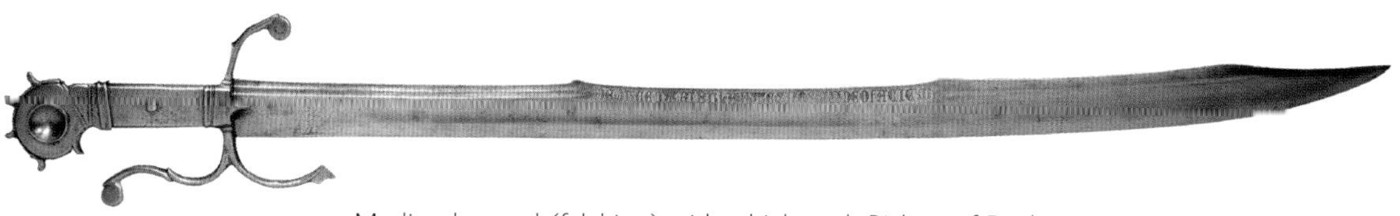

110 Medieval sword (falchion) with which each Bishop of Durham has to swear to slay the dragon, *c.* 1490, steel, gold, textile.

their fathers'. By 1920 the society had 20,000 members, including Rudyard Kipling. In 1940, a pamphlet published by the Prestatyn Guild of St George made direct reference to religious and racial supremacy:

> Englishmen!
> Do you know that: –
> Your ancestor Adam was the first Aryan king of Sumeria;
> that he founded civilisation and overthrew barbarianism;
> Introduced justice and Letters, and that security whereby men might live in Peace;
> Stamped out the blood sacrifices of the primitive barbarians and set up a pure religion based on the instinctive honesty of his race;
> Was the living original of the heroic myths of Thor, King Arthur and St George of Merrie England;
> His blood, traditions and instincts are your proud inheritance.
> Consider this, then pass it on.[72]

Founded in 1975, the League of St George, as well as promoting anti-feminism and homophobia, suggested that foreigners should be 'repatriated', and that every nation should have a 'folk community' or 'folk state' made up exclusively of people with 'a right, by reason of ancestry, to call themselves native to that place'.

In this way, narratives and images describing serpent beings continue to articulate both positive and negative ideas about cultural, religious and national identity, as well as anxieties about 'otherness' that must be overcome or excluded to maintain a perceived order. Within a neo-liberal economic system instrumentally committed to growth, this includes the 'otherness' of the non-human world and unruly nature. But many contemporary water serpent beings are not flowing in this direction: they are swimming against the tide.

Artful Beings

In Western societies, water serpent beings have often found a sympathetic home in the arts, appearing in literature, film and other media as dramatic manifestations of non-human powers. An entire book could be devoted to exploring these new representational iterations, but just a few examples must suffice to illustrate how their former roles and meanings as 'nature beings' have been carried forward into contemporary worldviews.

In the arts, water serpent beings' earlier roles personifying non-human powers remain foundational. They are still closely associated with water, emerging from lakes or rivers, inhabiting swamps and marshlands, or underground caves and mountain chasms. Their form continues to reflect the fluid characteristics of water, expressed in serpentine bodies, shining multicoloured scales and consuming, swallowing jaws, and they retain the hybrid combination of species that expresses water's elemental vitality.

There are traces of their role in representing hydro-theological flows. Films and books describe undersea dragon worlds; dragons ascending to Heaven; dragons in the 'flux' of interstellar space; and, in Keith Baker's Dungeons and Dragons campaign world of *Eberron*, there is a celestial 'Dragon Above' whose remnants form a glittering ring in the night sky.[73]

111 Poster for Ken Russell's film *The Lair of the White Worm* (1988). Based on Bram Stoker's 1911 novel of the same name, the story – like Lewis Carroll's 'Jabberwocky' – was inspired by the legend of the Lambton Worm.

Associations between water and fertility also remain strong. In Imamura's erotic film *Warm Water under a Red Bridge*, the heroine, Saeko, is 'the personification of fertility, the woman around whom flowers bloom and animals proliferate'.[74] Conflating ideas about female sexuality and notions of fluid fertility, Saeko ejaculates water, creating a river 'abundantly populated with sizeable, colourful fish'.[75] In Hidenori's *Woman of Water* (2002), downpours of rain are generated by emotional events in the life of its heroine, Ryo, who develops a relationship with a young man obsessed with fire, offering a complementary balance of male and female, fire and water.[76] In an Australian teen fantasy series, *H_2O: Just Add Water*, the female protagonists bathe in a magical pool under a volcano, become mermaids and acquire supernatural powers over water.[77]

The water serpent's role as the bringer of fertility also features in the phallic symbolism celebrated in *The Lair of the White Worm*, which similarly resuscitates ideas about consuming serpent beings requiring human sacrifices (illus. 111).[78] Primal fears about water's capacities to swallow and consume, and to impose moral judgement, come to the

112 J.R.R. Tolkien, 'Conversation with Smaug', watercolour illustration in *The Hobbit* (1937).

fore in Sarah Perry's more recent gothic novel, *The Essex Serpent* (2016), which imagines the reappearance of the 'winged serpent' sighted in the area in 1668.[79]

The arts also uphold a theme of water serpent beings as world creators and primal ancestors. In popular science fiction, there are worlds literally composed of the bones of 'progenitor' dragons'.[80] Serpent beings are described as reproducing via parthenogenesis.[81] Some coexist and mix essences with humans, creating hybrid species.[82] Ursula Le Guin's *Earthsea* series reveals the common ancestry of dragons and humankind, and the dragons speak 'the Language of Creation'.[83] In George Martin's novel series *A Song of Ice and Fire*, an affinity with dragons indicates membership of the royal 'bloodline'.[84] There are numerous tales in which dragons adopt children as kin, and an iconic animation of a Japanese folk tale describes a boy, Izumi Kotaro, riding through the clouds on his 'mother dragon ... who sacrifices herself for agricultural development and the prosperity of the boy's village'.[85]

Fluid movement between serpentine and human form is equally perennial. In Le Guin's world of Earthsea, women can transform themselves into dragons, and vice versa. The ancient Japanese folk hero Orochimaru transforms himself into a giant serpent in *The Magic Serpent*.[86] The story *Tea with the Black Dragon* contains an enigmatic Asian gentleman who is in fact a 2,000-year-old Chinese dragon,[87] and the *Dragonlord* series contains beings with both human and dragon souls, who can readily shapeshift between forms.[88]

The wisdom of serpents is similarly well-preserved and many dispense secret lore and magical knowledge. They may have magical powers, such as those in the Australian-Chinese television series *The Magic Mountain*, and they are generally clever or, to use the biblical term, 'subtil'.[89] Robert Heinlein, in *Between Worlds*, describes a Venus inhabited by dragons whose interest in scientific research is so keen that, when they find that humans cannot pronounce their names, they adopt those of leading scientists, such as Sir Isaac Newton.[90] The perspicacity of serpents is also exemplified by J.R.R. Tolkien's famously cunning Smaug, in *The Hobbit* and *The Lord of the Rings* (illus. 112).[91]

In Rudyard Kipling's novel *The Jungle Book*, the python Kaa is 'very old and very cunning' and much feared by the monkeys: 'The whisper of his name makes their wicked tails cold.' Though Mowgli also finds him frightening ('Kaa seemed to pour himself along the ground'), the snake becomes his tutelary friend and mentor.[92] Yet in the 1967 Disney film Kaa appears as an evil serpent, hoping to mesmerize and swallow Mowgli, and in the 2016 film, as well as seeking to hypnotize and consume him, Kaa is represented as a female snake, demonstrating the persistence of a narrative trope in which feminized serpent beings represent the anthropophagic chaos that threatens masculine order, culture and reason.[93]

Thus the arts also reflect societies' movements from worshipping creative and protective male and female water serpent beings, to monotheistic religions, in which they are re-formed as manifestations of unruly female 'nature'. Writers and film-makers have drawn directly on biblical ideas regarding the serpent, as well as Greek and Roman classics, *Beowulf*, the *Saga of the Volsungs*, *Melusine* and *The Golden Legend*. C.S. Lewis's *Pilgrim's Regress*, like the original seventeenth-century allegory by John Bunyan, is concerned with a religious journey to enlightenment.[94] Tolkien's landscapes are imbued with morality, and their dragons must be slain by stalwart and implicitly Christian heroes. Late nineteenth- and early twentieth-century works lean towards straightforward 'evil-serpent' slaying, such as the dispatch performed by the 'beamish boy' in Lewis Carroll's 'Jabberwocky': 'He took his vorpal sword in hand; Long time the manxome foe he sought . . .' (see illus. 109).[95]

'Chaos monster' serpents are also plentiful. The film *Q: The Winged Serpent* (1982), directed by Larry Cohen, features a secret Aztec cult in New York whose activities lead to a female Quetzalcoatl taking up residence atop the Chrysler Building and devouring local citizens. The creature and her egg are destroyed by local heroes, but the film ends ominously with a shot of an undiscovered egg containing the potential for future chaos (and future film progeny).[96] In *The Spiderwick Chronicles* by Tony DiTerlizzi and Holly Black, poisonous dragons are raised by an ogre as weapons of mass destruction, and the second series focuses on the slaying of the Wyrm King, a multicephalous serpent/hydra.[97]

113 Cover of Cressida Cowell, *How to Train Your Dragon* (2003).

Monstrous nature sometimes combines with monstrous technology: in Ray Bradbury's tale 'The Dragon' (1955), two knights set out to kill a one-eyed dragon, but the beast that kills them turns out to be a steam train;[98] and in Harry Turtledove's *Darkness* series (1999–2004), an analogue of the Second World War, the marauding dragons are implicitly fighter planes.[99] In *Song of Ice and Fire* dragons serve as terrible weapons for the protagonists, as they do in *Cry of the Winged Serpent* (2007), directed by Jim Wynorski, in which the Central American hero magically summons a serpent to punish the drug cartel that murdered his family.[100]

The use of dragons as weapons by human protagonists, or their enslavement, mirrors earlier religious representations in which humanized gods, such as Varuna, ride upon serpents, signifying the authority of humankind over nature. In Jane Yolen's *Pit Dragon* trilogy, humans train dragons to fight like giant cockerels in 'the pit',[101] and in James Cameron's *Avatar* (2009) the hero establishes himself among the humanoid Na'vi by riding the most dangerous 'banshee/*ikran*' and leading the dragon riders into battle.[102]

The domestication of dragons and serpent beings is not invariably violent. They can also be tamed in a 'soft' defeat of the monstrous. In children's stories, such as in Diana Wynne-Jones's *Charmed Life* and Cressida Cowell's *How to Train Your Dragon* (illus. 113), dragons appear as biddable pets.[103] In a twentieth-century story, Edith Nesbit's *The Last of the Dragons*, the last dragon in England is tired of being expected to fight and consume maidens, and when visited by the latest princess and her fiancé in its dark cave, sobs pitifully and confesses, 'I am tame': 'that's just it. That's what nobody but you has ever found out. I'm so tame that I'd eat out of your hands.'[104]

Such stories of rapprochement, often written by women, suggest a contemporary longing to return to more collaborative and empathetic engagements with the non-human world. The serpent beings in Anne McCaffrey's *Dragonriders of Pern* series assist humans via a telepathic link with their riders, established at their hatching (illus. 114).[105] They have a common purpose in defeating the invasive 'Thread' that – in an obvious reference to capitalism – consumes crops, animals, humans and indeed everything in its path. Le Guin's *Earthsea* dragons have a thoughtful debate about the balance between freedom and having possessions. Steven Brust's *Vlad Taltos* novels (1990–) contain serpentine beings with tentacles that can pick up psychic impressions.[106] In Elizabeth Kerner's *Song in the Silence* (1997), the Kantri dragons are telepathic, and the heroine re-establishes human contact with them.[107] A more erotic reunion with a water being is envisaged in Guillermo de Toro's *The Shape of Water*;[108] and in James Cameron's *The Abyss* (illus. 115), the alien intelligence manifested deep in the ocean, in the form of a serpentine being clearly composed of water, is sensitive and curious, changing shape to mirror the face of the film's heroine.[109]

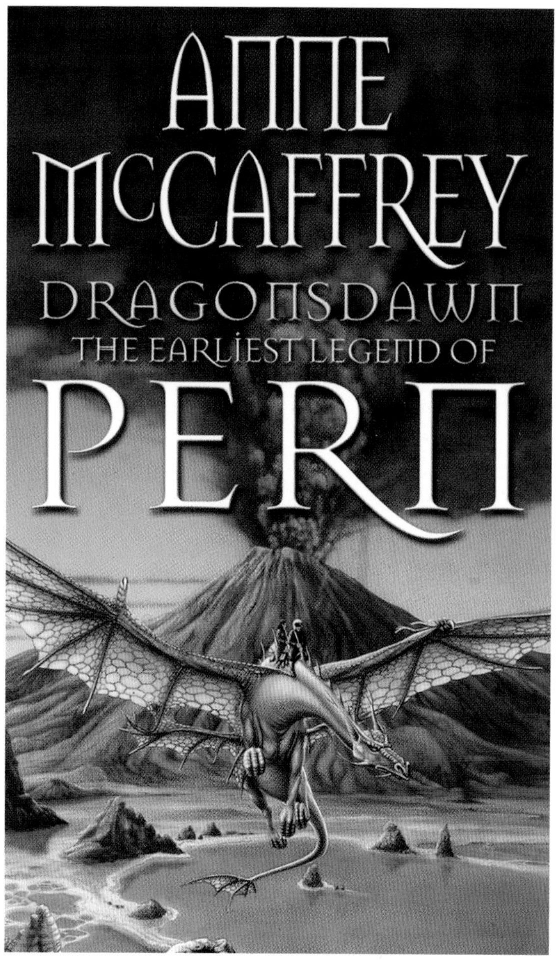

114 Cover of Anne McCaffrey, *Dragonsdawn* (1990), the ninth book in the series *The Dragonriders of Pern*.

Water serpent beings are therefore alive and well in the arts, representing old and new ways of engaging with the non-human world and its powers. They reflect the early worship of non-human beings and their co-creative agency, as well as the trajectories of change that have altered societies' lifeways and asserted human dominion over 'the other'. Since the 1960s, such representations have been influenced by environmental, feminist and civil rights movements. They have come to reflect wider concerns about social and ecological justice, and

115 The water being with Lindsey Brigman (Mary Elizabeth Mastrantonio) and Bud Brigman (Ed Harris), in *The Abyss* (1989, dir. James Cameron).

the recognition that a paradigmatic shift in human-non-human relations is dangerously overdue. The concluding section of this book therefore considers how representations of water serpent beings have regained a vital emblematic role in critiques of exploitative human–environmental relations, and in activists' efforts to create a sea change in human relations with water.

11
Transformational Beings

Water serpent beings' contemporary role as symbols of social and ecological sustainability is a logical extension of their historical capacities to represent life generation and cycles of life renewal. This has particular relevance at a time when the regeneration of all species is under threat. It is now painfully clear that, without transformational changes, human patterns of production and consumption will induce a chaotic global collapse in ecological and social order. However, although such concerns are now widely shared, societies continue to struggle to shift their trajectories in more sustainable directions.

In promoting the changes that are needed, many environmental groups have been inspired by indigenous lifeways. In the initial stages of the conservation movement this produced rather monolithic perspectives, with eighteenth-century ideas about 'noble savages' providing a convenient shorthand for imagined prelapsarian innocence and harmony with nature.[1] However, most conservationists now understand that the reality is more complex and more useful in thinking about solutions. In diverse and unique ways, place-based peoples have maintained sustainable engagements with their homelands for millennia by managing their relationships with the non-human domain carefully. Generally this has involved limiting their population growth and resource use and eschewing the intensifying patterns of instrumentality characterizing larger societies' trajectories of development. Most of all they have relied upon a deep knowledge of local ecosystems and the holistic integration of principles of sustainability into all aspects of their lives.

Contemporary indigenous communities aim to bring these principles directly into debates about human-non-human relations. In doing so they valorize their cultural traditions, but they are equally interested in shaping the future. They want this to reflect their core beliefs and values, often drawing a stark contrast between these and 'Western' ideas and practices. Dismayed by brutally exploitative uses of land, water and resources, they are often passionate in their desire to protect their homelands and the ecosystems on which they depend. But they also want protection for their rights and interests in these environments. Their goal is not to restore a romantic stereotype, but to regain – and promote – healthy and productive lifeways that assure the well-being of current and future generations.

As we have seen in earlier chapters, the cosmologies of such communities share a recurrent theme: the material environment and its non-human inhabitants are not 'other' to humankind. Human beings are located within and relationally connected to the rest of the world. Other living beings are ancestral kin and the co-creators of everyday life, and there is an ethical and practical imperative to engage with them, and with the material world, in egalitarian and mutually beneficial partnerships. The challenge for contemporary indigenous communities is to maintain these beliefs and values in a world dominated by more instrumental ways of thinking about and acting upon the world. Many seek, sometimes with the assistance of anthropologists, to communicate and promote their traditions in dialogue with larger and more powerful societies.

The indigenous communities in the Arctic and sub-Arctic territories of Alaska and northern Canada have been described as the 'original ecologists'.[2] The elders' comment to ethnographer Ann Fienup-Riordan – that 'we talk to you because we love you'[3] – illustrates their efforts to communicate a worldview in which human and non-human beings share responsibility for maintaining social and ecological order.

> Yup'ik people today continue to see themselves as living in a world of local, face-to-face relations radically different from the national and anonymous relations that characterize the non-Native world. A well-known Yup'ik oral instruction states: 'They say the world contains no others, only persons'. Often this is used as evidence that all persons – human and metahuman alike – are related and thus should be treated with respect.[4]
>
> The qualities of personhood shared by humans and animals establish the basis for a mutual and necessary respect. Respect is understood in both positive and negative terms, including love and fear. Perhaps the most often used term is *takar-* (to be shy of, respectful toward, and/or intimidated by).[5]

In the Arctic, efforts to promote more sustainable lifeways have become more urgent as, with temperatures rising at twice the rate found in other parts of the planet, the permafrost is melting. In a symbolic and literal return to formlessness, the land on which villages are located is dissolving into mud, forcing coastal communities to shift to firmer ground elsewhere. For their elders, this reflects larger societies' failure to respect the non-human world created by Sedna, the mother sea-goddess.

These issues emerge clearly in debates about hunting and fishing.[6] Indigenous activities are framed by rituals and practices aiming towards 'collaborative reciprocity', rather than conforming to Western ideas about quotas and management. This has created some tensions with incoming experts, and legal philospher Nancy Doubleday observes that Arctic worldviews 'represent a long-standing conflict within Western traditions of nature and environmental protection, in which humans are positioned apart from the environment'; hence there are 'competing visions of sustainability, development and justice'.[7]

Marshall Sahlins points to the potential of indigenous perspectives to encourage others to question their own assumptions about human dominion and create

> something like a Copernican revolution in the sciences of society and culture. I mean a shift in perspective from human society as the center of a universe onto which it projects its own forms . . . to the ethnographic realities of people's dependence on the encompassing metaperson-others who rule earthly order, welfare, and existence.[8]

In the wake of the civil rights movement, and with the connectivity permitted by modern communications technologies, many indigenous groups have been able to articulate their values in the public arena. Forging transnational networks and alliances with other counter-movements seeking social and ecological justice, they have established cultural centres and institutes and participated in international events, such as the World Water Forum, Earth Summits and Conference of the Parties (COP) meetings. The recommendations of the 1992 United Nations Conference on the Environment in Rio de Janeiro placed traditional knowledge and practice among the pillars of sustainable development, and this premise is now integral to international debates on environmental issues.

Inspirational Beings

Water serpent beings circulate through these endeavours. Even when forced underground by monotheistic religions, or suppressed by colonial regimes, they have flowed beneath the surface in imaginative undercurrents. Today they are resurgent, gaining powerful new roles in communicating alternate visions of human–environmental relations. They support critiques of exploitative practices and promote sustainable lifeways.

In some contexts, though marginalized as 'folklore' by political elites, they have remained highly visible in everyday life. This is particularly the case in many parts of Asia (illus. 116). However, that is not to say that the veneration of water serpent beings has been untroubled even when they are omnipresent. As noted previously, in China, their original role as powerful creator beings in Neolithic societies was appropriated by emperors, who sought to control the provision of water and employed images of dragons to express their own divine powers. The last century has brought particular challenges, but a nice example of water beings' resilience is provided by anthropologist Zongze Hu's account of the travails of the Ninth Dragon God in a village called Ten Mile Inn, in northern China. He describes how the longstanding status of this important deity was challenged in the village by the 'anti-superstition' (*mixin*) campaigns launched by nationalist- and communist-led governments.[9]

As the deity primarily responsible for rainwater, lakes, rivers and seas, the Ninth Dragon God appeared in the Chinese pantheon in the Tang dynasty (established in 618 CE). The worship of the Holy Mother and her Nine Dragons gained popularity in the region around the middle of the Qing dynasty (1644–1911), and the Ninth Dragon was particularly important in Ten Mile Inn because the village often struggled to gain sufficient access to water. Following the fall of the Qing Empire in 1911, the New Cultural Movement (1915–23) advocated modernity, rationality and secularity: 'Different forms of religiosity including such practices as rain-making rituals, were classified as "superstition" and

116 Chinese dragons ascending and descending in the Forbidden City, Beijing, decorative tile.

regarded as obstacles to the creation of a modern society.'[10] Religious statues across China were destroyed, and their temples were used for other purposes.

The inhabitants of Ten Mile Inn continued to perform rituals celebrating the Ninth Dragon until the late 1930s, but in the 1940s the government made more repressive efforts to discourage religious practices. Despite a severe drought, communist officials forbade rituals appealing to the Dragon God for help. Statues of the deity were smashed, and a villager, who was also a communist official, snapped off the snout of the Ninth Dragon's statue and prevented a procession from taking place. The next year his millet and corn failed, which was seen as punishment by the dragon, and other misfortunes followed 'due to the Dragon's revenge'.[11] Villagers repaired and hid the remaining statue and spent the next two decades playing hide-and-seek with communist officials to protect it. As well as enabling religious practices to continue covertly, this undermined the authority of the Maoist regime, whose officials were fooled into publicly destroying a replica of the deity. Conflicts escalated in the 1960s when the *People's Daily* called upon Chinese citizens to 'sweep away all demons and monsters'.[12] In 1971, the dragon statue was found and smashed. Severe droughts followed, only partially alleviated by the digging of a well deep enough to supply piped water to the village.

In the 1980s, the state relaxed its policies on religious activities and there was a covert resurgence of dragon worship. In Ten Mile Inn village tablets were produced to worship the Ninth Dragon and the Holy Mother goddess, and a shrine for the dragon was rebuilt, but sealed. 'In the following four years, the leaders secretly pleaded with the Dragon for rain twice, and in both cases it responded to their plea.' A third time they promised to replace the sealed shrine with a temple, and the rain poured. A temple was built. Then in 1993 some nearby villagers placed statues in a shrine without being punished; in 1994, with much excitement, the Ten Mile villagers inaugurated three new statues and resumed open veneration of the Ninth Dragon God.

In Japan, water beings have also played a role in contemporary debates. If we return to Tokyo and the Tama River, there was resistance in the early 1900s when the Japanese government proposed a programme of dam building, not just because of the costs and risks, and the displacement of villages, but because of the local temples and shrines that would be lost. Villagers protested at the Hikawa Shrine, and it was not until 1936 that a compromise was reached. Construction began on the Ogochi Dam, and Shinto rites were held 'to purify the site' of the proposed reservoir.[13] When it was completed in 1957, Tokyo's population had reached 8 million. By the late 1900s, with 10 million inhabitants in the city, there was increasing concern about the well-being of the catchment area and a drive 'to clean up and restore the "original" beauty of the river and its "natural" ecosystem'.[14] Although dam building continues, the government has shifted its infrastructural policy towards 'close-to-nature' river construction.

Debates about the Tama River reflect wider concerns regarding the impacts of Japan's rapid industrialization in the 1950s and '60s and its continued commitment to economic growth that externalizes costs to the non-human domain. Contemporary Shintoism promotes a harmonious relationship with the non-human world through rituals and practices. A divine power of growth (*musubi*) is celebrated in annual festivals, and large areas of forest, laid out in accord with the principles of *feng shui* and the related celestial dragons, have been placed under the protection of 'religious forestry standards'.

Japan's cultural landscape contains more than 80,000 Shinto shrines, and thousands of dragon springs at which water beings are venerated. Temples are guarded by dragons presiding over the water with which visitors are expected to purify themselves. The landscape ecologist Yukihiro Morimoto suggests the miniature landscapes provided by shrines and temple precincts also serve practical purposes, providing flood mitigation and concentrations of biodiversity.[15] Water serpent beings therefore retain an important role as creative 'spirits of place', and this sacred landscape of temples, parks and gardens, and an appreciation of the spiritual 'liveliness' of the non-human world, remain central in people's daily lives.[16] In this sense, Japan's water serpent beings support efforts to encourage reform in the government's environmental policies.[17]

Confluencing Beings

In other parts of Asia, the influx of new belief systems and the creation of religious states created complex negotiations between centralized authorities and local communities determined to retain their own cultural traditions. A major water serpent being in Java is the goddess of the South Seas, Ratu Lara Kidul, a pre-Hindu Buddhist figure described by environmental historian Peter Boomgaard as a multifaceted, complex being who delivers many of the functions of deities with more specialized roles elsewhere. She has a variety of names, such as Nyai

117 Unknown artist, *Nyai Blorong, Goddess of the South Sea*, Java, before 1928, watercolour on paper.

Blorong, and in Balinese traditions is described as a 'mermaid' with powers over the seas (illus. 117). Though commonly depicted in human form today, early images of this powerful marine goddess are more serpentine in nature.

Records from the ninth century present Ratu Lara Kidul as a powerful and unpredictable deity. People still say that she is able to bring epidemics, and that it is risky even to feel the sea breeze. She is 'a dangerous deity, living in a palace at the bottom of the ocean, made of the hair and bones of her victims . . . Sea deities, however, also had much to offer, as they held the key to the riches of the sea. They were supposed to assist those who were in search of these riches, provided that they knew how to deal with the goddess.'[18] In the maritime environment of the Indonesian Archipelago, many origin stories describe the ancestors of local people coming from the sea.[19] It is the primary source of both prosperity and chaos, and in the Javanese cosmos is seen as a 'wilderness beyond human control', imbued with supernatural powers.[20] Local relationships with the ocean are therefore a mix of veneration, dependence and thalassophobic fears.

However, other worldviews flowed into the region. Southeast Asia's accessibility via sea routes 'made it quite vulnerable to political control by strong outsiders'.[21] It was influenced, over many centuries, by both India and China, and when Muslim invaders established the centralized Javanese state of Mataram between the seventeenth and nineteenth centuries, Islamic beliefs were imposed upon the local population. The new government recognized the need to retain a connection with the indigenous population's powerful sea deity. A new religious practice was therefore created in which, each year, Ratu Lara Kidul was ritually wedded to the Muslim rulers of the state.

Such religious accommodations are common in Southeast Asia, enabling local populations to continue their veneration of non-human deities. In Burma, for example, a local water goddess is said to have assisted the Buddha by wringing out her hair in order to flood an invading army.[22] In Bali, activists are promoting a local version of Hinduism, Agama Tirtha – the 'religion of the holy water'. A Water Protection Programme has been initiated that invites people to adopt and protect wells and rivers, aiming 'to raise awareness about the water issue and favour sustainable behaviours from both population and businesses'. As the proponents put it, 'This is our chance to show respect to Agama Tirtha and to the gods of Bali.'[23] Similar connections between water beings and environmental activism can be seen in other parts of Asia, where religious devotion to aquatic mammals has segued into their use as symbols of nature conservation and resistance to environmental degradation.[24]

Accommodations between indigenous and imported religious beliefs can also be seen in Africa, where the major monotheisms continue to proselytize hegemonically, and many small towns contain mosques and churches facing off across dusty streets. As in other parts of the world, colonialization in Africa introduced more patriarchal structures, to the extent that women have been doubly disempowered, losing important leadership roles as queen mothers and chiefs, and economic roles as traders.[25]

Nevertheless, local beliefs remain resilient. In Malawi, for example, the teachings of the Catholic Church have been synthesized with the beliefs of the local Chewa population in the mother goddess Makewana/Mwali, and the rainbow serpent sky god Thunga. Thus in central Malawi, at the Catholic church in the Mua Mission, a rain shrine sits on the altar and a generative rainbow, containing multiple life forms, is painted on the wall behind it (illus. 118). The nearby Kongoni cultural centre celebrates Chewa deities, telling their stories through artworks and dance. As well as preserving traditional narratives, these performances present moral parables promoting Catholic ideas about behaviour, including the sexual restraint deemed necessary to tackle the devastating effects of AIDS.

There are also rainmaking ancestral beings such as Mbona, said to be able to take the form of a snake, and historical efforts to accommodate Christianity include his recasting as a Black messiah: 'It was clear that people saw Mbona as a counterpart of the biblical Christ, referring to him as their "Black Jesus". They said that god had two sons, a white one to look after Europeans and a black one for them.'[26] Like Jesus, Mbona is killed by his enemies and revives:

> His murderers cut his head off, tossing it in a forest patch . . . Miraculously, however, blood kept gushing from the body in such quantities that it formed a small lake and finally a river. A few days later . . . Mbona manifested himself in a storm wind and made it known through the mouth of a medium that he wanted a shrine dedicated to his name. The local villagers obeyed his command, buried his head and built a shrine over the place.[27]

Many people came to worship at the shrine, and to participate in its annual rainmaking ceremony. In the 1930s, Mbona was called upon to express

118 Altar at Mua Parish Church, Mua Mission, Malawi.

resistance to government policies demanding more intensive agricultural methods. Since that time, according to the anthropologist Menno Welling, 'Mbona is up to this day very much used in popular resistance.'[28]

Another important water serpent being in Malawi has been similarly reconceptualized. Like many local python deities, Napolo flows under the ground. He brings the water supplied by spirit beings in the mountains, but when they are not happy, he creates floods and landslides 'because we people have not behaved . . . people are no longer behaving as their culture demands of them. For instance nowadays we have promiscuity.'[29] In contemporary Malawi, therefore, Napolo articulates concerns about the societal chaos created by AIDS, and people's fears about their environment being destroyed for commercial purposes.[30]

The Malawian poet Zondiwe Mbano describes Napolo's role in expressing social and ecological disorder:

We have always feared this
As tobacco estates deflower
Forests ancient as the rain,
And elders instruct adolescents
To play touch-and-run in the dark
Following rules in condom packets
Did Napolo not quake mountains
And flush down rocks and water
To sweep away entire villages.[31]

In 1946 and 1992, flash floods in Zomba and Phalombe killed many people, and Mbano evokes Napolo as a non-human response to the over-engineering of the environment:

Until Lukonkobe urgently summons us
To replant the fields parents abandoned . . .
Otherwise we are here till another Napolo
Roars from the lake scooped on a volatile
Mountain by scatty planners and engineers
And sends flash floods down the Mulunguzi
To sweep away all our degrees and academic
Regalia and bury them in muddy lake Chilwa.[32]

Other water serpent beings in Africa have also taken on new roles. In Lesotho, traditional healers (*lethuela*) engage with serpent beings in the water to communicate with invisible ancestors and other supernatural deities. Rituals maintain harmonious relationships with rivers, and these are foregrounded today to highlight the social and spiritual costs of alienating local communities from their water bodies, and to oppose the sale of much of Lesotho's water to South Africa.[33]

The most widely known African water being, venerated along the western coast of the continent, is Mami Wata (illus. 119). As her name implies, the contemporary goddess reflects an exchange of ideas in African–European encounters in the fifteenth century. She is generally represented in the form of a mermaid, incorporating European images of semi-humanized water beings, and often appears, like the Malawian Mwali, with a (male) python.[34] However, her modernized name and imagery are founded upon longstanding indigenous ideas regarding water deities. As a water serpent being, she was traditionally associated with capacities to generate rain and fertility, and in a contemporary environment this translates into broader ideas about flourishing and productivity, and notions of wealth and health. According to Henry Drewal, her name refers to

119 Laura James, *Mami Wata*, 2011, painting.

both a specific African water-divinity as well as a vast 'school' of trans-cultural and trans-African Atlantic water spirits, mostly female but sometimes male (*papi wata*) . . . *Mami Wata*, like water itself, is omnipresent and mutable – only the frames of history, culture, social practice, and the interpretations of artists and audiences give it specificity, definition, identity, and meaning . . . For some, *Mami Wata* is helpful primarily in economic issues. She bestows good fortune and status . . . For others, she aids in matters of procreation – problems of infertility, impotence, or infant mortality. Some are drawn to her as an irresistible seductive presence who offers the pleasures and powers that come from a love affair with a spiritual force. *Mami Wata* literally creates '*wet* dreams' . . . Being a trans-gendered creature, *Mami Wata* helps women and men negotiate their sexual desires and preferences. *Mami Wata* also provides a spiritual (and professional) avenue for women to become powerful priestesses and healers of both psycho-spiritual and physical ailments – to assert female agency in generally male-dominated societies. Being trans-cultural, *Mami Wata* is ubiquitous and pervasive. While she has particular sets of attributes in specific places, she shares many of these with other water spirits over vast expanses of the African continent and beyond.[35]

Mami Wata was worshipped throughout the colonial and post-colonial periods, but more recently has come under fire from evangelical Pentecostal Christians and Muslim fundamentalists. 'For these people . . . *Mami Water* has come to personify immorality, sin, and damnation, for s/he is seen as one of Satan's most powerful presences whose work is to seduce both women and men away from the path of righteousness.'[36] In this context, Mami Wata is a classic embodiment of feminized, untamed and corrupting Nature: a misogynistic nightmare of disorder.

Mami Wata also enables a critique of untrammelled consumerism. In a market economy, representations of her are often employed to signify 'wealth' in commodities: in cosmetics, jewellery and food. But as an icon of seduction and danger she also has an important new role in expressing ambivalence about the importation of capitalist ideologies into Africa. She has recently been redeployed in Nigeria to articulate Ogoni cultural identity and to protest against Shell's oil exploitation and the destruction of the Niger delta. An organization named Mammy Wata has been established, in which spirit mediums work with 'warriors' to seek social and ecological justice. By making use of art and ritual venerating Mami Wata, it aims to awaken the world to the realities of climate change and the need to respect the sacred life-giving powers of water.[37]

Global tourism, while undoubtedly a double-edged sword for place-based communities,[38] has provided vital representational opportunities. Anthropologist Claus Deimel and museum ethnologist Elke Ruhnau describe how a contemporary Aztec group, the Huichol (Wixáritari) people in the Mexican Sierra Madre, having firmly resisted the proselytizing of Catholic missionaries since the Spanish Conquest, seek to express their own vision of the cosmos through art and performance:

> The festivals and ceremonies of the Huichol portray, in a ritualistic–theatrical event, the cosmos as a continual act of re-creation . . . the natural cosmos is understood as an ever-present event that is directly connected with people . . . The

120 Aztec *ehecacozcatl* (wind jewel) associated with Quetzalcoatl-Ehecatl, the creator and wind god, 14th–16th century, carved conch shell.

> cosmos of the Huichol is therefore an unusually rich world, in which everything is somehow connected to everything else.[39]

Drawing on a long history of artworks valorizing Aztec water deities (illus. 120), images of water serpent beings run through Huichol arts and material culture. Snake motifs can be found on clothing and handicraft, representing the potential metamorphosis of animals and plants. Visually serpentine objects, such as waving grass, fire or smoke, are also associated with snakes. Because of their cosmological relationship with water, snakes signify the rain on which maize crops and human well-being depend, as well as the temporal flows of days, seasons and years. Thus the large two-headed snake Tatei Ipou is believed to encircle the Earth: in the evening it swallows the sun god, and everything else, until dawn brings the sun back in the form of a 'rising eagle'.[40]

Tourism provides multiple ways to communicate these ideas to visitors from around the world, and Mexico's ancient archaeological sites also present major educational opportunities. At the equinoxes, thousands of people gather at Chichen Itza to watch the plumed serpent Kulkucán wriggle down the northern staircase of the great pyramid, into the human world. Even larger crowds of (local and international) visitors attend annual festivals at Teotihuacan, near Mexico City, climbing the Pyramid of the Sun to celebrate the spring equinox and ask the gods to give them energy and health.

In the pueblos of the southern states of the USA, ancient rock art depicting lightning-spitting plumed or horned serpents similarly attracts a stream of visitors. The ideas encoded in these images are further disseminated via material culture and performance. There is a lively trade in contemporary ceramic art featuring Avanyu and other water serpent beings, and tourists attend the rainmaking dances described in Chapter Five.

Public performances are not merely aimed at tourists. For many place-based communities they are a critical element in engagement with other groups – government agencies, NGOs, non-indigenous farmers – who want to manage and use local waterways. In the South American Andes, for example, rituals venerating the small irrigation channels that support indigenous agriculture are performed to transmit key ideas both intergenerationally, and to others. Andean communities have been managing small-scale communal irrigation schemes since these were established by their Inca ancestors, and irrigated terraces have been detected dating from before 2000 BCE at La Galgada, in Peru.[41]

Alongside imported Catholicism, Andean communities (*allyu*) have maintained their traditional cosmological view, Kay Pacha, in which nature beings inhabit a sentient land and waterscape, described as Pachamama (the mother goddess of the Earth, time and all things).[42] Water flows down from sacred mountains, linking spiritual and material worlds, and the collaborative reciprocity of water beings is expressed in a term for irrigation water: *yaku yachachisqa*, meaning 'water that has been taught' (illus. 121).[43]

Such beings must be venerated to maintain an orderly human-non-human relationships and, like water deities elsewhere, they can be punitive. Among the Huarochirí people in Peru, for example, the rainbows believed to emerge from springs are dangerous and, if pointed at disrespectfully, may

121 Moche nose ornament with serpents and long-necked birds, Peru, c. 100–300, gold alloy and silver.

harm the *in utero* children of pregnant women.[44] Wind and rain are also personified, so that in northern Chile 'the winds, people say, are mighty beings who struggle with the rain for supremacy.'[45]

Proper engagement with water beings in the Andes involves everyday ritual practices as well as seasonal cleansing of the irrigation channels.[46] Ritual exchange with the non-human world is described via the term *pago*, adopting the Spanish *pagar*, 'to pay'. Typically, such rituals entail digging a small 'mouth' in the earth alongside a reservoir, and placing in this votive offerings to Pachamama such as corn, alcohol and tobacco. An aromatic plant may be burned, so that the smoke will carry the *pago* up into the mountains.[47]

However, these 'earth rituals' are also publicly performed as part of indigenous protests, for example against mining activities and government appropriations of water. This is a form of what philosopher Isabelle Stengers calls 'cosmopolitics', in which non-human actants such as mountains, water and soil are brought into direct participation in political activity.[48] As cultural anthropologist Marisol de la Cadena points out, such inclusion 'challenges the separation of nature and culture that underpins the prevalent notion of politics and its according social contract'.[49]

South American societies have been similarly active in speaking internationally. In 1990, the Kogi indigenous community collaborated with a British television producer, Alan Ereira, to make *From the Heart of the World: Elder Brothers' Warning*.[50] Framed as a 'message to humanity', the film expressed deep concern about the destructive activities of 'Younger Brother'. The film generated much public interest but achieved little change in direction and, dismayed by further environmental exploitation, the Kogi followed up in 2012 with another film,

Aluna, aiming to communicate their concept of 'cosmic consciousness' and the interconnectedness of all living kinds (illus. 122).[51]

More recently, indigenous communities and environmental organizations in South America joined forces in the Pachamama Alliance. In 2019 they persuaded Pope Francis to host an Amazon Synod at the Vatican, in which indigenous shamans led a ceremony worshipping Pachamama and depicting the Earth Mother as an unclothed pregnant woman. This was a step too far for some of the more conservative members of the Church.

122 The late Jefe Mayor, Mama Jacinto Zarabata, working to ensure the safety of director Alan Ereira and his team in their film-making collaborations with the Kogi.

Citing the First Commandment, 'You shall have no other gods before Me,' Bishop Athanasius Schneider issued an enraged open letter from his diocese in Kazakhstan, condemning the ritual and articulating conservative Catholic opposition to nature worship:

> I cannot remain silent in the face of the blatant violation of God's holy will and the disastrous consequences it will have upon individual souls, the Church as a whole, and indeed the entire human race . . . Catholics cannot accept any pagan worship, nor any syncretism between pagan beliefs and practices and those of the Catholic Church.[52]

Recalling Athenagoras' second-century attack on religions who 'deify the elements', Bishop Schneider praised the men who seized 'idolatrous' statues from a nearby church and threw them into the Tiber, contrasting their puritanism with the 'treachery' of modern Church leaders:

> The gestures of these Christian men will be recorded in the annals of Church history as a heroic act which brought glory to the Christian name, while the acts of high-ranking churchmen, on the contrary, who defiled the Christian name in Rome, will go down in history as cowardly and treacherous acts of ambiguity and syncretism.

Since the 1950s, missionaries have brought evangelical Christianity (and devastating European diseases) into South American communities. But just as in the medieval period, when nature-worshipping societies resisted the imposition of

123 Nemonte Nenquimo and fellow activists celebrating their successful legal case against a bid for further oil exploration in the Ecuadorian Amazon, 2019.

patriarchal Christianity, contemporary indigenous tribes have upheld their own beliefs and values. In the face of political efforts to 'stampede' through environmental legislation further opening the rainforests to exploitative agribusinesses,[53] their collective efforts are focused on preventing the destruction of their homelands caused by clearance for cattle farming, logging, oil exploration and other exploitative enterprises.

As in Australia, indigenous people in South America have found it useful to employ ethnographic methods such as cultural mapping. In 2020 Nemonte Nenquimo, the first female president of the Waorani Pastaza Organization, conducted a cultural mapping exercise using drone cameras and a global positioning system to mount a successful legal case against oil exploration in the Ecuadorian Amazon (illus. 123). Nenquimo, who was awarded the 'Green Nobel' Goldman Environmental Prize, has encouraged indigenous tribes to forge active alliances with NGOs such as Greenpeace: 'Indigenous people have wisely known for thousands of years that you have to protect Mother Earth. Don't wait for indigenous people to fight on your behalf . . . we need to work together to protect the forest'.[54]

Similar efforts are being made elsewhere in South America. In the La Mojana delta in northern Colombia, where the community's agricultural and fishing livelihoods depend on both land and water, a local turtle species, the *hicotea*, is used to represent the community's 'amphibious' identity. A Red Hicotea network has been formed by local activists to develop projects focused on sustainability and cultural identity. There are also useful alliances between indigenous communities and academic experts, and their collaborative use of serpent beings to valorize and articulate indigenous thinking is exemplified in the logo of the Instituto Colombiano de Antropología e Historia (ICANH). This logo replicates an ancient petroglyph of a rattlesnake/caiman

124 Serpent logo of the Instituto Colombiano de Antropología e Historia, Bogotá.

that served as the traditional emblem of the Tairona people, who imprinted the serpentine image on their bodies using a clay seal (illus. 124).

The active presence of non-human beings in indigenous activism is similarly taken for granted by Australian Aboriginal communities.[55] Government agents, national parks staff and others meeting with indigenous leaders are 'baptized' with water by the local elders upon their arrival at sacred sites, so that they will be recognized by the ancestral beings.

> The serpent is sure to become incensed if it doesn't recognise someone's sweat, if strangers come into its midst without cautionary introduction to local waters by 'watering' of their head. Those venturing into new terrain should have their heads watered from pools or other local water bodies by locals who belong to the area . . . At the same time the local person speaks to the serpent, telling it about the person being watered, and asking them not to harm the newcomer.[56]

As well as receiving this unequivocal message regarding the authority of the ancestral beings, and thus the local community elders, visitors are usually given some information about the stories relating to particular sites, although not their deeper sacred and secret meanings. On public occasions, these stories are told through songs, dance and ritual performances similarly evoking the authority of local ancestral beings. Communities often make astute use of anthropologists, and I spent much of my doctoral fieldwork collaborating with elders in Cape York on major cultural mapping exercises, recording material about sacred sites and story lines, the results of which supported their subsequent efforts to reclaim their homelands.

In the last several decades traditional art and material culture, suffused with images of the Rainbow Serpent and other water serpent beings, has become central to Aboriginal engagement with others. Originally focused on the intergenerational transmission of 'the Law' residing in the Rainbow Serpent, the objects and images displayed in museums and galleries around the world now provide an equally sophisticated external vehicle for the dissemination of Aboriginal beliefs and values.[57] Both purposes cohere: the major intention of Aboriginal art is not only to communicate cultural knowledge but also, by emanating ancestral power (via the shimmering light and colour – *bir'yan'* – of the artwork), to 'act upon' the viewer.[58] In this sense the ancestral beings are seen to participate directly in educational processes.

Supernatural deities are also a central presence in more confrontational situations. Aboriginal images and narratives of water serpent beings have featured strongly in protests against mining and extractive activities that threaten to invade the ancestral otherworld. In the northern Australian town of Katherine, Aboriginal elders said that the mining was extracting and killing local rainbow serpents (*bolung*). A major rainbow serpent was destroyed: 'They killed that rainbow right there, the mother one, the big one, killed it, pulled it out too and took it away. I don't know what they did with it, maybe used it for oil.'[59]

The destruction of any local manifestation of the Rainbow Serpent removes the community's protection against further invasion.[60] It is therefore entirely logical that it has had a vital representational role in resisting both colonial and economic hegemony. It appears, for example, in the famous 'bark petition' to the government protesting against the mining of the Gove Peninsula in 1963. The petition is visually surrounded by depictions of the community's totemic beings, and serpent beings underline both pages, including the signatures at the conclusion of the document (illus. 126).

Since indigenous people gained Australian citizenship in the 1960s, national legislation has expanded to encompass some of the tenets of Aboriginal law.[61] The Aboriginal Rights Act (1976) recognized their inalienable connections to place, and related rights to land and resources, and in 1993 the Native Title Act dismantled the convenient calumny of 'empty' *terra nullius*, acknowledging the Aboriginal common property regimes that preceded European settlement. This led to a series of Native Title claims and Indigenous Land Use Agreements.

Re-establishing indigenous ownership and rights relating to fresh water has proved more elusive,

125 Pormpuraaw artist Syd Bruce Shortjoe with his Rainbow Serpent ghost net sculpture, rope and plastic, North Queensland, Australia.

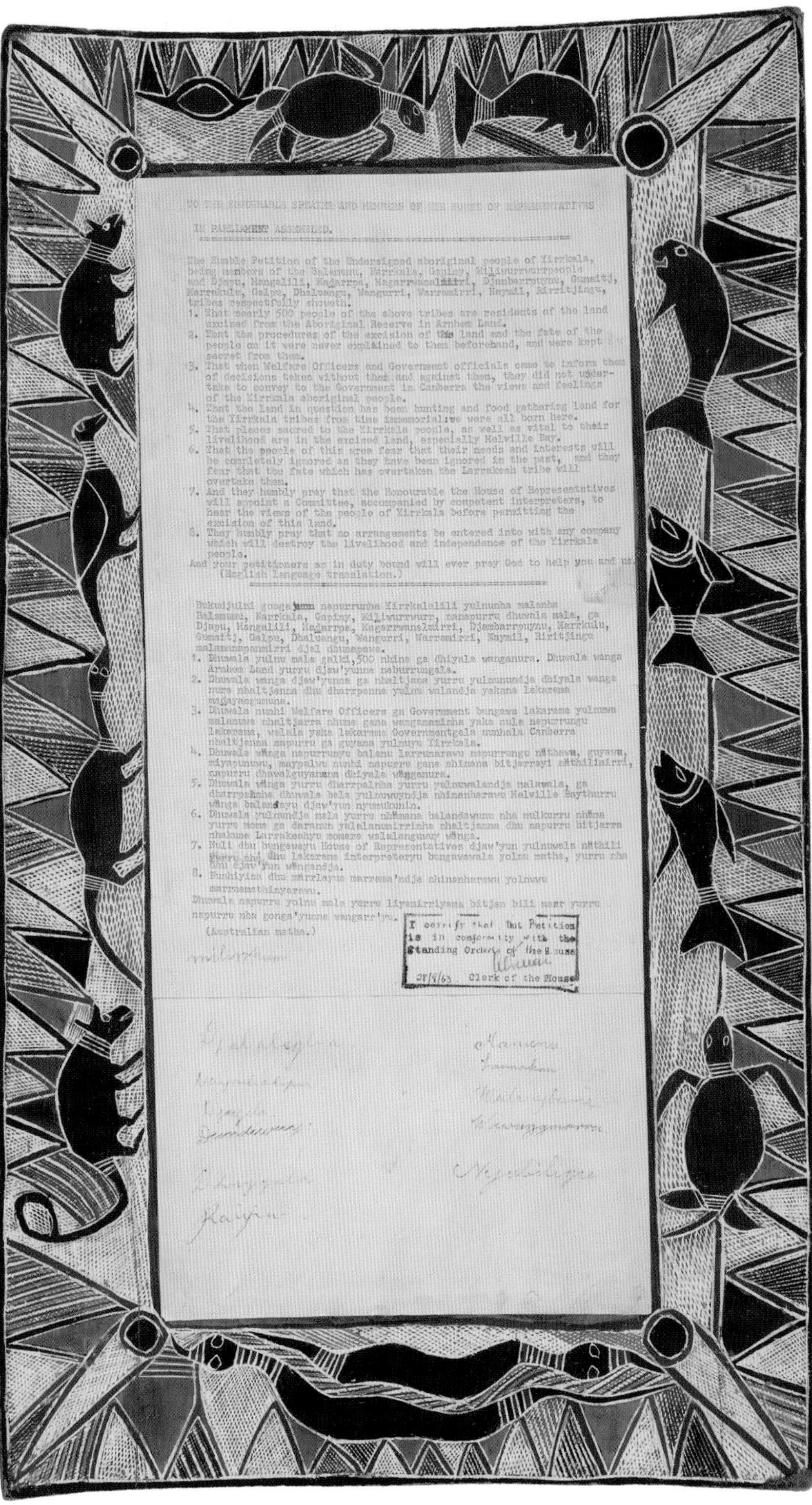

TO THE HONOURABLE SPEAKER AND MEMBERS OF THE HOUSE OF REPRESENTATIVES

IN PARLIAMENT ASSEMBLED.

The Humble Petition of the Undersigned aboriginal people of Yirrkala, being members of the Balamumu, Narrkala, Gapiny, Miliwurrwurrpeople and Djapu, Mangalili, Madarrpa, Magarrwanalmirri, Djambarrpuyngu, Gumaitj, Marrakulu, Galpu, Dhaluangu, Wangurri, Warramirri, Naymil, Riritjingu, tribes respectfully showeth.

1. That nearly 500 people of the above tribes are residents of the land excised from the Aboriginal Reserve in Arnhem Land.
2. That the procedures of the excision of this land and the fate of the people on it were never explained to them beforehand, and were kept secret from them.
3. That when Welfare Officers and Government officials came to inform them of decisions taken without them and against them, they did not undertake to convey to the Government in Canberra the views and feelings of the Yirrkala aboriginal people.
4. That the land in question has been hunting and food gathering land for the Yirrkala tribes from time immemorial: we were all born here.
5. That places sacred to the Yirrkala people, as well as vital to their livelihood are in the excised land, especially Melville Bay.
6. That the people of this area fear that their needs and interests will be completely ignored as they have been ignored in the past, and they fear that the fate which has overtaken the Larrakeah tribe will overtake them.
7. And they humbly pray that the Honourable the House of Representatives will appoint a Committee, accompanied by competent interpreters, to hear the views of the people of Yirrkala before permitting the excision of this land.
8. They humbly pray that no arrangements be entered into with any company which will destroy the livelihood and independence of the Yirrkala people.

And your petitioners as in duty bound will ever pray God to help you and us.

(English language translation.)

Bukudjulni gonga'yuwn napurrunha Yirrkalalili yulnunha malanha Balamumu, Narrkala, Gapiny, Miliwurrwurr, nanapurru dhuwala mala, ga Djapu, Mangalili, Madarrpa, Magarrwanalmirri, Djambarrpuyngu, Marrkulu, Gumaitj, Galpu, Dhaluangu, Wangurri, Warramirri, Naymil, Riritjingu malamanapanmirri djal dhumapawa.

1. Dhuwala yulnu mala galki, 500 nhina ga dhiyala wanganura. Dhuwala wanga Arnhem Land yurru djaw'yunna naburrungala.
2. Dhuwala wanga djaw'yunna ga nhaltjana yurru yulnunundja dhiyala wanga nura nhaltjanna dhu dharrpanna yulnu walandja yakana lakarama madayangumuna.
3. Dhuwala numhi Welfare Officers ga Government bungawa lakarama yulnuwa malanuwa nhaltjarra nhuma gana wanganaminha yaka nula napurrungu lakarama, walala yaka lakarama Governmentgala munhala Canberra nhaltjanna napurru ga guyana yulnuyu Yirrkala.
4. Dhuwala wänga napurrunyu balanu larrunarawu napurrungu näthawa, guyawu, miyapunuwu, maypalwu numhi napurru gana nhinana bitjarrayi näthilimirri, napurru dhawalguyanana dhiyala wänganura.
5. Dhuwala wänga yurru dharrpalnha yurru yulnuwalandja nalawala, ga dharrpalnha dhuwala bala yulnuwuyndja nhinanharawu Melville Baythurru wänga balandayu djaw'yun nyumukunin.
6. Dhuwala yulnundja mala yurru nhämana balandawunu nha mulkurru nhäma yurru moma ga daramun yalalanumirrinha nhaltjanna dhu napurru bitjarra nhakuna Larrakeahyu momara walalanguway wänga.
7. Nuli dhu bungawayu House of Representatives djaw'yun yulnuwala näthili yurru nha dhu lakarama interpreteryu bungawawala yolnu matha, yurru nha dhu djaw'yun wängandja.
8. Nunhiyina dhu märrlayun marrama'ndja nhinanharawu yolnuwu marrnamathinyarawu.

Dhuwala napurru yolnu mala yurru liyamirriyama bitjan bili marr yurru napurru nha gonga'yuna wangarr'yu.

(Australian matha.)

I certify that this Petition is in conformity with the Standing Orders of the House

28/8/63. Clerk of the House

126 Yirrkala community artists, *Bark Petition*, 1963, natural ochres on bark, ink on paper.

particularly with the de facto privatization achieved through water trading schemes. While Aboriginal representatives are included in river catchment management groups, their ability to influence decisions remains limited. However, some progress has been made in relation to sea rights. In a landmark Northern Territory case in 2008, informed by bark paintings describing ancestral stories and sites along the coast, the High Court recognized Yolngu traditional owners' rights to the intertidal waters in Blue Mud Bay.[62]

Contemporary Aboriginal art stresses the need to protect rivers and marine areas. A recent exhibition of sea beings made sculptural use of 'ghost nets', the discarded nets of fishing vessels, that are currently endangering sea life around the world (see illus. 125). Underlying the important alliances between indigenous people and arts and conservation counter-movements, Aboriginal ceremonies, songs, music and dance are regularly performed at 'Rainbow Serpent' arts festivals. Making serendipitous use of the way that 'the Rainbow' is used to valorize diversity, these events often include performances by indigenous groups from the Pacific, the USA and South America, drawing attention to the international links between people hoping to promote alternate ideas about human–environmental relationships.

Similar alliances have been forged in the USA. In 2016, thousands of people – representing Native American First Nations, other indigenous communities and environmental and social activist organizations – joined together to oppose the imposition of the Dakota Access Pipeline. This was designed to carry 500,000 barrels of oil a day alongside the Standing Rock Sioux reservation, but the activists argued that this was a violation of treaty rights and would damage the local community's water sources and sacred sites.

Noting major oil spillages on other Native American reservations, the Dakota leader Chief Arvol Looking Horse stressed the spiritual centrality of the 'water of life', and – implying that it was an inversion of ideas about creative water serpent beings – described the polluting pipeline as a chaos-making 'Black Snake':

> Our Elders foretold of a Black Snake and how the Water of Life – 'Mni Woc'oni', which is our first medicine – would be affected if we did not stop this oncoming disaster. Mni Woc'oni is part of our creation story, and the same story that exists in many creation stories around Mother Earth.
>
> When we say 'Mni Woc'oni' – Water of Life – people all over the world are now beginning to understand that it is a living spirit: it can heal when you pray with it and die if you do not respect it. We wanted the world to know there have been warnings in our prophecies . . . It was said water would be like gold. It was said that our spirit of water would begin to leave us.
>
> We are at the crossroads.
>
> Standing Rock has marked the beginning of an international movement that will continue to work peacefully, purposefully, and tirelessly for the protection of water along all areas of poisonous oil pipelines and across all of Mother Earth.
>
> . . .
>
> It is more than oil pipelines threatening the well-being and future of our water. Near the native territory of the Sisseton Wahpeton Oyate,

127 Protest against the Dakota Access Pipeline as it marches past San Francisco City Hall, November 2016.

> concentrated animal feeding operations or 'CAFOS' are draining and degrading the land and water. As a result, the air is toxic, swamps have dried up, and aquifers, to which the people are supposed to have water rights, are being drained ... In other places – in mining spills across South America and Africa and at Fukushima – man has gone too far.
>
> Water is a source of life, not a resource ... When the environment that we live in is sick and suffering, so too are the minds and decisions of our leaders.
>
> We must continue to work together for the health and well-being of our water and our Earth. In a Sacred Hoop of Life, there is no ending and no beginning.[63]

As well as promoting an alternative perspective, the Sioux tribes challenged the legality of the plans for the Dakota pipeline, assisted by a non-profit environmental law firm, Earthjustice, so named 'because the Earth needs a good lawyer' (illus. 127).[64] Barack Obama's administration refused the final permit for the pipeline, but the victory was short-lived. Donald Trump had invested in the firm behind the project, Energy Transfer Partners, and had received more than $100,000 in campaign donations from its chief executive. Four days after his election, he approved the final permit. Evicted by armed police from the Oceti Sakowin Camp at which several thousand protesters had gathered, the self-proclaimed 'water protectors' remained defiant: 'The closing of the camp is not the end of a movement or fight, it is a new beginning,' said Tom Goldtooth, director of the Indigenous Environmental Network. 'They cannot extinguish the fire that Standing Rock started. It burns within each of us.'[65]

Across the border, Native Canadians achieved some progress with the Canadian Constitution Act of 1982, which stated, 'The existing aboriginal and treaty rights of the aboriginal peoples of Canada are hereby recognized and affirmed.' It promised 'a restructuring of power and responsibility with regard to natural resources' and greater environmental protection.[66] However, as in Australia, subsequent right-wing federal governments sought to reform the legislation, and conflicts have continued. Idle No More, a campaign linking Canadian and American tribal communities, 'calls upon all people to join in a peaceful revolution to honour indigenous sovereignty and protect the land and water'.

> Our people and our mother earth can no longer afford to be economic hostages in the race to industrialise our homelands. It is time for our people to rise up and take back our role as caretakers and stewards of the land.[67]

In New Zealand, water serpent beings (*taniwha*) have long been central to indigenous campaigns (illus. 128). They aided Māori resistance to colonialism in the 1800s, when 'prophets' such as Papahurihia led visionary movements refuting the teachings of Christian missionaries, while employing images of biblical serpents to uphold Māori religious practices:

> He warned against the Protestants' heaven: it being, he said little better than their hell . . . His teachings consciously rejected the written Scriptures, but he had also absorbed some of their precepts. The *ariā* (manifestation) of his god was the biblical serpent Nākahi. Nākahi was not simply the serpent of Genesis; it was also the fiery serpent on the rod of Moses . . . Nākahi became the active intervening agent summoned up by Papahurihia in the manner of previous Māori *tohunga* [religious leaders].[68]

Māori beliefs envisage an animated non-human world composed and inhabited by sentient beings with whom they maintain a reciprocal ethic. 'Living water' has its own life force or *mauri*, and resources are seen as the gift of the river. The ritual performance of special *karakia* is necessary in anticipation of these gifts, and to thank the river when they are received. This relationship is articulated by the water serpent beings who inhabit rivers, lakes and seas:

> The *taniwha* is a generative 'life essence' . . . encapsulating ideas about shared substance and social connections between people and places. The well-being of the *taniwha* is connected to the well-being of the people . . . and harm to the *taniwha* or its home is believed to have an impact on [their] health and well-being.'[69]

The spiritual importance of Māori *taniwha* is recognized in legislation such as the Resource Managment Act (1991), which protects 'cultural well-being, including spiritual lore and customs, both specifically to Māori and on a more general basis'.[70] *Taniwha* express Māori worldviews in multiple representational forms. It is therefore unsurprising that they have a central role in political negotiations: as mediator Ian McDuff asks, 'What do you do with a *taniwha* at the table?'[71] *Taniwha* are regularly evoked to challenge projects imposing major infrastructures on environments, particularly those disrupting waterways. At various times they have surfaced to express Māori concerns about plans for an underground rail system that would disrupt a subterranean river in Auckland, the building of a new motorway, and the location of a new prison near the home of an important *taniwha*.

128 Karen Kennedy, mosaic 'dragon seat' with Ngataringa *taniwha*, Ngataringa Reserve, Devonport, New Zealand. Inscription: 'Be at peace with Nature: hear the song of Ngataringa'.

Māori communities in New Zealand/Aotearoa are better placed to promote their interests than many indigenous people. They compose approximately 15 per cent of the population, compared to indigenous percentages of about 2.5 per cent in Australia, 4.3 per cent in Canada, 2 per cent in the USA and 2 per cent in most Central and South American countries. They are also assisted by New Zealand's founding document, the Treaty of Waitangi (*te Tiriti o Waitangi*), signed in 1840, which acknowledged prior Māori ownership of land and resources.

In the early 2000s, drawing on the experience of other indigenous communities around the world, Māori *iwis* sought to regain their legal rights to freshwater and marine areas.[72] The action was driven by deepening concern about the government's attempts to privatize hydro-electricity corporations and their substantial water allocations. Much of the debate was focused on the Waikato River. Its multiple *taniwha*, linked with powerful chiefs, are celebrated in the proverb: '*Waikato taniwha rau, he piko he taniwha, he piko he taniwha*' (Waikato of a hundred *taniwha*, at every bend, a *taniwha*).

As the co-chair of the Māori Council, the Honourable Sir Edward Taihakurei Durie, put it: 'This is not a claim to the ownership of all water . . . This is a claim to proprietary interests.'[73] Nevertheless, the action generated widespread concern and sparked a lively debate about water privatization. The Māori claims were heard by the Waitangi Tribunal, the High Court and finally the Supreme Court. Like governments in Australia and Canada, the Crown distinguished 'rights' from 'ownership', but conceded that Māori people had some customary rights in relation to water: 'The Crown accepts that Māori have legitimate rights and interests in water but asserts no one owns water and therefore the best way forward is not to develop a framework for Māori proprietary rights but to strengthen the role and authority of Māori in resource management processes.'[74] The Supreme Court ruled that any process of privatization must remain subject to an obligation to act consistently with the principles of the Treaty of Waitangi, in effect upholding Māori rights to maintain their customary relationships with waterways.[75]

Thus, in diverse cultural contexts, water serpent beings give robust representational support to the promotion of indigenous and place-based communities' beliefs and values. In the form of Sedna, the Ninth Dragon God, Ratu Lara Kidul, Thunga, Napolo, Mami Wata, Tatei Ipou, Kulkucán, Quetzalcoatl, Yaku Yachachisqa, Avanyu, the Rainbow Serpent, Aluna, the Black Snake, Mni Woc'oni' and multiple *taniwha*, they are symbolically foundational to indigenous struggles to regain customary rights and protect their homelands. They offer insights into lifeways in which human and non-human beings are not alienated into separate categories of nature and culture, but are fully engaged in reciprocal partnerships that demand mutual respect. How can these insights be translated into wider action to create more sustainable lifeways for humankind?

Turning the Tide

Throughout human history, water serpent beings have had an essential role in communicating foundational ideas. Even in larger societies, where they have been demonized by dominant religions and scientifically disenchanted, they have retained a strong narrative presence in objects and images, in religious and secular architecture, and in ancient sites. They flow with imaginative verve through literature and the visual arts, folklore and popular culture and, increasingly, into political debates. They continue to express the powers of water and the co-creative agency of the non-human world, and reveal how different societies have chosen to engage with the non-human domain. Modes of engagement range from careful efforts to maintain a sustainable balance of human and non-human interests to instrumental and unsustainable interactions in which human interests override all others. Today, in a world urgently in need of a change in direction, the stories that water serpent beings tell, and their capacities to represent alternate visions of human-non-human relations, may be the most crucial role that they have ever had.

How can objects and images representing water beings promote sustainable ideas and practices? A key part of the answer lies in their capacities to reveal the historical developments that have caused many societies to embark upon unsustainable patterns of development. Comparing what has happened to water deities over time confirms Durkheim's thesis that socio-political arrangements and religious beliefs co-constitute each other, and supports my suggestion that we need to triangulate this theory by recognizing how instrumental technologies and practices also push societies along particular developmental trajectories.[1]

The revelations provided by water serpent beings are intrinsically challenging to the status quo. They require societies to question political hierarchies that normalize inequalities and position the non-human domain as a subservient 'other' which can be exploited or even destroyed to meet human goals. They raise sensitive issues about the wisdom of adhering to religious beliefs that sanctify patriarchal power and human exceptionalism, and which prioritize (male) culture over (female) nature.

Advocating sustainable lifeways similarly challenges ideological assumptions that economic growth is necessary and desirable. As Ivan Illich observed, externalizing the costs of our activities to non-human beings and destabilizing ecosystems makes the phrase 'sustainable development' an oxymoron. This intrinsic contradiction could be resolved if development meant 'doing it better rather than doing it more'.[2] Although neo-liberalism has normalized the mantra that 'growth is good', it is worth bearing in mind that, as our water serpent beings have shown, societies that have achieved long-term sustainability have done so by maintaining steady-state or circular economies, rather than embarking upon spirals of growth and expansion. And, although this is another politically charged topic, it appears that managing population numbers, providing political equality, and ensuring just distributions of resources and opportunities are similarly critical to stability.

The illustrative narratives provided by water serpent beings also draw attention to how societies conceptualize 'progress', highlighting the dangerous allure of infrastructures that confer an illusion of godlike control over water and the material world, but result in 'infrastructural violence'.[3] Though there are no easy solutions to any of these issues, there is a widening realization that radical changes to current human–environmental engagements are imperative, and that this requires new ways of thinking as well as doing. Water serpent beings offer alternate ways to imagine the world, and they connect other useful undercurrents of ideas. The challenge is to bring these into a shared stream of consciousness powerful enough to turn the tide.

Alternative Beings

The most critical message that water serpent beings convey is that all living kinds, including humans, inhabit and co-create a single indivisible world. There have been various efforts to articulate these kinds of ideas. 'Natural science' models include geochemist Volodymyr Vernadsky's notion of the 'biosphere', which holistically imagined a global living system.[4] Evolutionary biologist Lynn Margulis's vision of a 'symbiotic planet', and her collaborator James Lovelock's Gaia hypothesis, describe the collective regulation of planetary systems by all living organisms.[5] Palaeontologists Dianna and Mark McMenamin's vision of the 'hypersea' reminds us that these organisms emerged from primal oceans and that all remain dependent upon and connected by water.[6] Evolutionary biology elucidates the genetic commonalities between human and non-human kinds, and ecology highlights the material flows between them. These are all usefully connective models in physical terms but, as the designation of these sciences as 'natural' suggests, they tend to retain dualistic categories of culture and nature. By obscuring the social and political dimensions of interspecies relations, such models enable the externalization of the costs of human activities to non-human 'others'.

Recognizing that material and social relations are mutually constitutive, social scientists have been more critical of this intellectual dualism. Anthropology has brought diverse cultural worldviews into academic debates, including those perceiving all living kinds as an undifferentiated community.[7] Socio-technical systems (STS) thinking,[8] and actor-network theory (ANT) have focused usefully on the fluid relationalities between people, non-human beings and things.[9] Material-culture studies have highlighted how objects, images and material environments convey meaning and have an active social and political role in our lives.[10] New materialism has further highlighted the creative agency of all living and material participants in acting upon each other,[11] and the 'friction' that shapes these interactions.[12] All of these perspectives help us to understand how the material properties and behaviours of water act upon all living kinds and the physical environment in ways that are so essential and profound that they lead naturally to water worship.[13]

Critics of nature–culture dualism have also recognized that dividing the academic landscape into 'two cultures' and an array of boundaried specialisms is not the best way to achieve coherent responses to complex issues.[14] There is growing acceptance of the need for interdisciplinary collaboration. Similarly, at a popular level, political counter-movements are reviving an understanding that social and ecological justice are not divisible. This is not new: although disciplinary boundaries have hardened in a neo-liberal academic world, long-standing 'environmental' organizations such as Friends of the Earth have always had an explicit social agenda. With deep roots in nineteenth-century Romanticism, the conservation movement was deeply influenced by civil rights campaigns, and by a feminist movement that readily recognized the relationship between gender and race inequalities and the imposition of patriarchal dominion over nature.[15]

Another important influence on current debates is the rise of new religious movements expressing a desire to reconnect with the non-human domain. Despite widening secularization, water has never lost its association with spiritual being. As the poet Philip Larkin said, if called upon to construct a religion 'I should make use of water.'[16] Changing religious affiliations suggest a move towards more nature-oriented spiritual beliefs.[17] The UK 2011 census recorded 59.3 per cent of the population as Christian, a decline of 13 per cent since 2001.[18] A 2019 survey suggested a further drop, to 51 per cent.[19] In 2011, 25 per cent of the population declared themselves to be without a religion; by 2019 this had increased to nearly 40 per cent, and among young people to 53.4 per cent. Meanwhile, the number of Pagans doubled between 2001 and 2011, and was still increasing in 2019.

Like conservation organizations, New Age or neo-pagan groups have drawn inspiration from ideas and practices envisaging a spiritually animated non-human world. Major water festivals have continued in many cultural contexts. The Hindu Kumbh Mela festivals in India attract millions of pilgrims to bathe in holy rivers. New Year celebrations in Cambodia, Thailand and Myanmar entail the joyous sprinkling of water on participants as a blessing conferring prosperity and goodwill. In China, the Dai 'Water Splashing Festival', along with dragon boat races and the floating of lanterns down the Lancang (Mekong) River, includes a ritual bathing of the Buddha.

Celebrations of the powers of water have persisted in the global North too. In Armenia people mark the annual festival of Vardavar by splashing each other with water. This was originally an ancient pagan festival worshipping Astghik, the creator of Heaven and Earth and goddess of water and fertility, whose prehistoric presence is marked by numerous *vishaps* (serpent or dragon stones) across the country.[20] Similar water festivals, echoing pagan solstice rituals and celebrating Slavic fertility deities, can be found across Poland, Ukraine, Czechia and Slovakia.

129 National flag of Wales.

Water serpent beings are often central to the revival of 'nature religions'. For example, the Welsh Dragon has a long been a vital symbol of Celtic cultural heritage (illus. 129). Having emerged in the late 600s as the Red Dragon of the legendary leader Cadwaladr, it was adopted as an emblem by a series of Welsh kings. With such historical authority it is ideally suited to affirming contemporary Celtic identity and the alternative values that many Celts espouse.

Druid ceremonies at Stonehenge and other ancient sites continue to articulate pre-Christian ideas about the spiritual meanings of henges or sacred groves and their complementary water places and deities.[21] In numerous English villages annual well-dressings are sponsored by community organizations. Replicating a Roman ritual, *fontanalia*, which venerated the water beings inhabiting wells and springs, these events have been reformed to celebrate contemporary ideas about local *communitas*.

Votive offerings are still made at ancient holy wells throughout Europe, many of which, like Coventina's Well in Northumbria, are linked with local narratives about water beings. In Dorset, where St Augustine's Well sits beneath the lusty figure of the Cerne Abbas Giant, the trees around the holy spring are festooned with strips of cloth offered by people seeking its powers to enhance fertility. Just a few kilometres north of the well, people visit the springs that are the source of the River Stour, now contained in a Renaissance-style tufa grotto at Stour Head.

Spas all over Europe remain popular with visitors, who drink their waters to cure a variety of ills.[22] Age-old beliefs in water's revitalizing powers can also be seen in the enduring popularity of bottled mineral waters. The advertisements for these, redolent with spouting volcanic ejaculations of water, or babies gambolling beneath the waves, draw directly on ideas about water's regenerative capacities that have remained constant throughout human history.[23] Along with this return to vitalizing wells and springs, a complementary veneration of sacred groves has taken modern form in ideas about the therapeutic value of the (originally Japanese) notion of *shinrin-yoku*, or 'forest bathing'.[24]

Of particular relevance are rituals that combine ecological and religious interests in what has been described as eco-paganism. The anthropologist Jonathan Woolley describes the inauguration of a nature-worshipping ceremony called the Warriors' Call:

> Around 120 people gathered below Glastonbury Tor to conduct a ritual to protect the Red and White Springs (and the waters of Britain as a whole) from fracking and other forms of unconventional energy. The fabric and wooden construct [that they made] is a water dragon. There were four elemental dragons in the ritual – Earth, Air, Fire and Water – one at each corresponding cardinal direction, that circulated the

ritual space at the beginning and end of the ceremony.

In the ritual, a female shaman 'put herself in a trance and was possessed by the goddess Bride (the spirit of the White Spring)'. Using holy spring water collected from wells 'across the British Isles and beyond', she offered libations and 'voiced the will of the waters'.[25] Many such ceremonies are now taking place in Britain, celebrating the powers of water and hoping to prevent ecologically harmful activities with prayers, 'water blessing songs' and offerings to lakes and rivers.

There have been similar revivals of water worship in other parts of the world. An antipodean example is provided by the Splash! Festival in Queensland, Australia, which takes place on an island in the Maroochydore River. Here, a combination of New Age spirituality, environmentalism and the valorization of indigenous beliefs has produced a 'Ceremony of the Waters'. With participation from local Aboriginal groups, and inspiration from their Rainbow Serpent beings, communities in the river catchment area bring water from their particular waterways and pour it into a central vessel, affirming the fluid bonds between them. Rejecting the alienation of contemporary lifeways believed to undermine social and environmental well-being, the Splash! Festival aims to valorize waterborne connections.[26]

Also gaining popularity in recent years are burial practices involving resomation, a form of 'water cremation' that involves alkaline hydrolysis.[27] Although opposed by some elements of the Catholic Church, resomation has become an increasingly popular choice in Western countries, primarily because it is 'greener' but also, perhaps, because it enables a return to water, rather than to dust.

Various explanations have been offered for the resurgence in forms of nature worship. Art historian Megan Aldrich and archaeologist Robert Wallis argue that such ritual reinventions hope to 're-enchant' the world, and the anthropologist Jonathan Benthall maintains that even the most secular societies remain 'haunted' by a yearning for faith.[28] Neo-pagan forms of water worship therefore suggest a need to find spiritual solace outside the constraints of monotheistic religions and a desire to reconnect with the non-human domain.

Wonderful Water

Not all 'water worship' is intentionally spiritual in content. Aesthetic and sensory engagements with water also elicit affective responses and evoke wonder. 'Wonder' is a useful concept: it is historically associated with religious experience, and it is certainly the goal of religious rituals to elicit wonderment and awe, but such experiences are by no means confined to religious contexts.

A sense of wonder is readily experienced through the arts, in which landscape design, paintings, poetry and other media celebrate the multiple visual and symbolic attributes of water. It can be found in science, or in the films, documentaries and literature devoted to exploring the 'wonders of nature'. These media seek to engender respect for the beauty and complexity of all living beings, plants and the material world without assuming that they are the product of a divine plan. As many interviewees in the field have told me, feelings of wonder and joyous appreciation of water are also evoked through everyday phenomenological experiences: a walk beside a lake or river; a swim in the sea; a chance to sit beside the pond in a local park. Wherever it is encountered, water engages the senses, mesmerising the eye and freeing the mind.[29]

This is important for several reasons. Many people in secular societies balk at the notion of re-adopting religious beliefs, even when these are more orientated towards non-human powers, but they are quite open to valorizing nature as 'wonderful' in itself. There is also a well-documented relationship between the capacities of the non-human world to elicit wonder and appreciation and the levels of concern that people have about protecting other living kinds.[30]

A key part of this process involves the capacity to connect and to co-identify with places and their non-human inhabitants and to express 'biophilia', a term based on Aristotle's discussions about *philia* (friendship) as an expression of reciprocity.[31] The naturalist Edward Wilson defined it as an inherent urge to affiliate with other forms of life, and Richard Louv suggests that being alienated from other species incurs an emotional deficit.[32] Biophilia naturally includes a 'love of water' as the essence of life, and Deborah Bird Rose observes that indigenous Australian relationships with water provide an ideal philosophical model:

> Indigenous water philosophy offers a broadly life-affirming account of water . . . A first step is to situate water within a realm of biophilia, for it is surely clear that those who love life must love water. Perhaps it is finally time for non Aboriginal Australians to develop a water philosophy that will hold their lives, too, in patterns of connectivity.[33]

Personifying Beings

A desire to connect with the non-human world also reflects human cognitive processes that extend the mind outwards and encode personhood in other living kinds and the material environment.[34] A propensity to locate consciousness beyond the self means that, while rationality may rule, there is always fertile imaginative ground for visions of an animated and sentient non-human domain. Emotional connectivity is greatly assisted, of course, by personifications of the other, epitomized by serpentine water beings and their abiding capacities to manifest water's properties and powers.

Empathy with 'the other' entails some co-identification, and there have been lively debates about whether non-human species should be considered as persons. Anthropological writing about human–animal relations has shown how readily people relate to domesticated animals, and especially pets, as persons and as 'kin'.[35] More recently, in rejecting anthropocentric perspectives, multispecies ethnographers, philosophers and artists have made imaginative leaps into non-human lifeworlds.[36] Noting the relationship between connection and concern, Louv argues that a 'shared interspecies gaze' can both transform our lives and save theirs.[37]

Much depends on the extent to which a categorical distinction is drawn between human and non-human kinds. Like the Yup'ik notion that all living beings are persons, there are many cultural contexts without such divisions. For example, the anthropologist Joanna Overing describes how the South American Piaroa tribe consider jungle animals to be the 'same kind' as themselves, and see consuming them as a form of endo-cannibalism requiring shamanic rituals that transform their flesh into vegetable matter.[38] Many non-Western cultures, with millennia of beliefs in totemic beings and sentient landscapes, do not struggle with the idea that personhood can be extended to other living kinds and to land and waterscapes.

For societies in which religious trajectories have established a fiercely defended border between humans and others this is a thornier question. Considerable boundary anxieties were raised in the 1990s by the Great Ape Project, in which philosophers Peter Singer and Paola Cavalieri led protests against scientific experimentation on primates, arguing that 'non-human hominids' should enjoy the right to life and freedom from torture, and should be regarded as sentient 'persons'.[39] Since then human exceptionalism has been further challenged by the animal rights movement and its efforts to protect the rights of other species. Moral questions about human-non-human relations logically extend further, to the management of living ecosystems, and the need to ask whether societies have any right to exploit these in ways that compromise their well-being.

Water is invariably central in such debates, and there is an emerging literature on the ethics of human engagements with water.[40] Does the substantial contribution that mining provides to national economies justify polluting ecosystems? Must over-abstraction from rivers and aquifers to support industrial agriculture override the needs of non-human species and the viability of their habitats? Should desires for cheap hydro-electricity result in more giant dams? However worthy the aims, does anyone – an individual, a government or a private corporation – have the right to redirect water to meet particular needs and interests at the expense of human and non-human others? More often than not exploitative practices are driven by social and economic pressures for short-term solutions, but reliance upon such measures has led to an ecological crisis that is likely to render them futile. The designation of non-human kinds as persons with formal legal rights opens up the potential for decision-making processes in which their needs and interests have to be considered.[41]

A helpful example comes from New Zealand where Māori water serpent beings (*taniwha*) played a central role in legal debates about the extension of personhood to the Whanganui River. As well as defining the river as sacred (*taonga*), the local *iwi* use a kin term to describe it, *Tupuna Awa*, defining it as 'an important tribal ancestor'.[42] Springs (*puna wai*) have a similarly integral role in *whānau* (extended kin groups): 'The water from the *puna wai* of a *whānau* is considered a *taonga* [sacred or special thing] to that *whānau* as it carries the *Mauri* [life force] of that particular *whānau* . . . The very spiritual being of every *whānau* is part of the river . . . In this sense the river is more than a *taonga*, it is the people themselves' (illus. 130).[43]

As the descendants of the river's spiritual being, Māori *iwis* have a responsibility to protect this 'living ancestor' for future generations. In 2017, this ancestral connection provided the basis of a successful legal action that established the personhood of the Whanganui River as a 'living entity', with concomitant rights.[44] Building on an earlier case providing legal identity and rights to the homeland forest of the Ngäi Tuhoe *iwi*,[45] the legal ruling defined 'the River from the mountains to the sea, its tributaries, and all its physical and metaphysical elements, as an indivisible and living whole . . . *Te Awa Tupua* is a legal person and has all the rights, powers, duties, and liabilities of a legal person'.[46] Nominated representatives for the Crown and from the Whanganui *iwi* would have a responsibility to 'speak for' the river in relation to its management and use, and within the legal system. A new role, *To Pou Tupua*, was created by the bill 'to be the human face of *Te Awa Tupua* and act in the name of *Te Awa Tupua*'.[47]

Māori commentators expressed the hope that this successful action would provide a model for similar reforms elsewhere,[48] and there have certainly been other efforts to establish rights for rivers as persons or living entities. In 2017 the Ganges and the Yamuna River in India were both declared to be living entities/legal persons by the Uttarakhand High Court, although the Supreme Court stayed the ruling. In 2016 the Colombian constitutional court recognized the Atrato River as a legal subject.[49]

In Australia, Aboriginal groups in the Kimberley region have called for contemporary river management to respect the 'First Law' that sacred water beings embody. The Martuwarra Fitzroy River Council describes Yoongoorrookoo, an ancestral serpent being, as a living ancestor, positioning it as an actor and co-author in a public dialogue. Joe Nangan, an indigenous elder, described how the Rainbow Serpent upholds the Law and embodies the personhood of the river:

> In the Bookarrarra stories of Nyikina people, Yoongoorrookoo, the powerful and sacred Rainbow Snake, the giver of rain and life . . . can be very kind, bringing gentle rains and filling the water holes for the Nyikina and his chosen people. But when he is angry, he is capable of causing whirlwinds, floods, or even cyclones. Aboriginal people are always very careful near waterholes for fear that they should offend Yoongoorrookoo, the sacred and powerful rainbow snake.[50]

In Ecuador and Bolivia indigenous groups have persuaded the governments to enshrine in their Constitutions the broader rights of Mother Earth, *Pachamama*. This builds on a widespread vision of *buen vivir* (good living/living well) that has permeated Latin American discourses. Drawn from indigenous worldviews, *buen vivir* critiques dominant notions of sustainable development and promotes an alternative future based on collective and indivisible human and non-human well-being.[51]

Many indigenous and environmental activists maintain that acknowledging non-human beings and ecosystems as persons will promote the kind of inclusive thinking that will drive changes in practice. However, as well as outraging conservative religious groups, it has raised some secular unease about 'religious' efforts to re-enchant the

130 Māori pendant, '*koropepe*' *manaia* (water being, guardian), bowenite (nephrite jade), New Zealand.

non-human world and reintroduce ideas about animism that are at odds with scientific thinking.[52]

Earth Law

While the definition of other living kinds and ecosystems as persons usefully focuses attention on ethical questions about human-non-human relations, it is also possible simply to ask whether – as 'persons' or not – they should have legal rights to life and flourishing. A more abstract approach along these lines has been promoted since the 1970s, coalescing into a broader concept of ecological justice.[53] The Earth Law Centre aspires to be 'a global force of advocates for the rights of nature':

> Just as people have fundamental rights, so too should nature. Earth Law is the idea that ecosystems have the right to exist, thrive, and evolve – and that nature should be able to defend its rights in court. Earth law looks at the pressures on the Earth that contribute to the destruction of its ecosystems and species. It then argues that a balanced approach can provide for the entire Earth community, including humans. We envision a future in which humans and nature flourish together.[54]

In 2018, the Global Alliance for the Rights of Nature issued a Universal Declaration of the Rights of Rivers stating that 'all rivers are living entities that have legal standing in a court of law.'[55] The declaration asserts their rights to have normal patterns of flow and groundwater storage, to be free from pollution, to sustain essential habitats and native biodiversity, and to be able to regenerate and restore themselves. Much depends on the strength of these rights. As Bettina Wilk and her colleagues observe, in relation to the 'Father Rhine', establishing rights for rivers may drive longer-term changes in river basin governance, but in the immediate term the primacy of human vested interests make it 'unlikely that the river will get a decisive role in decision making over Rhine water governance issues':

> In the Rhine basin some de facto implementation of material rights is already present. The voice of the river could reinforce these trends, but granting rights to Father Rhine may also be considered an example of symbolic ('feel-good') policy making. In other basins, where ecological recovery is not yet being addressed, granting rights to the river may put new ecological ideas on the governance agenda. In such cases, granting rights to the river may really make a difference. But since rivers need to be represented by people, the question arises whether a real ecocentric approach can be achieved by granting rights to rivers. In the end, it will always be humans who must interpret what the river might want.[56]

Protecting non-human rights requires a legal framework with some teeth. In 2017, leading legal activist Polly Higgins (1968–2019) co-founded Stop Ecocide International to establish an international law that treats 'ecocide' as a crime:

> Ecocide is 'loss or damage to, or destruction of ecosystem(s) of a given territory(ies), such that peaceful enjoyment by the inhabitants has been or will be severely diminished'... Ecocide is a crime against the Earth, not just humans.

> Further, ecocide can also be climate crime: dangerous industrial activity *causes* climate ecocide. Currently there is a missing responsibility to protect. Unlike crimes against humanity, ecocide has severe impact on *inhabitants*, not just humans. Thus, what is required is the expansion of our collective duty of care to protect the natural living world and all life. International ecocide crime is a law to protect the Earth.[57]

The ecocide campaign cited the Rome Statute, 'one of the most powerful laws in the world', which governs the International Criminal Court (ICC). The ICC prioritizes – above all national laws – the four crimes of most concern to humankind. These 'crimes against peace' include genocide, crimes against humanity, war crimes and crimes of aggression. On ethical grounds, and on the basis that environmental destruction is the world's most common cause of conflict, the ecocide activists argued, 'Despite the existence of many international agreements – codes of conduct, UN Resolutions, Treaties, Conventions, Protocols etc. – the harm is escalating. Not one of these international agreements prohibits ecocide. The power of ecocide crime is that it creates a legal duty of care that holds persons of "superior responsibility" to account in a criminal court of law.'[58] Progress was made in 2021 when an international panel agreed a draft law defining ecocide as 'unlawful or wanton acts committed with knowledge that there is a substantial likelihood of severe and widespread or long-term damage to the environment caused by those acts'. If adopted by the ICC, this will become 'the first new international crime since the 1940s, when senior Nazi leaders were prosecuted at the Nuremberg trials'. As the panel's co-chair QC Philippe Sands observed:

> The four other crimes all focus exclusively on human beings. This one of course does that but it introduces a new non-anthropocentric approach, namely putting the environment at the heart of international law, and so that is original and innovative . . . For me, the single most important thing about this initiative is that it's part of that broader process of changing public consciousness recognizing that we are in a relationship with our environment, we are dependent for our wellbeing on the wellbeing of the environment and that we have to use various instruments – political, diplomatic, but also legal – to achieve the protection of the environment.[59]

By establishing rights for non-human beings, and proposing punitive action when these are transgressed, legal activists hope that the law will be effective in confronting ecologically exploitative practices. Their efforts underline a reality that laws, like ancient religious texts, distil prevailing societal beliefs and values in ways that represent some degree of consensus. Their aim, therefore, is to guide international and national laws towards more progressive ideas that will recursively transform societies' ways of thinking about and engaging with non-human beings, environments and water.[60]

Confluence

What we can see here is a confluence of counter-movements: indigenous activists, campaigners for social and ecological justice, nature-worshipping religious groups, legal activists, and scholars from across the disciplinary spectrum (illus. 131). Underlining the urgent need to respect the non-human domain and promote more convivial relationships with other living kinds, their collective efforts have succeeded in bringing environmental issues to the front and centre of contemporary debates. There is now widespread recognition that humankind is running out of time to prevent irreversible damage to the entire planet and rising fears that we are heading for a global collapse. There is little doubt regarding the practical measures that are needed. Yet governments continue to drag their feet, seeking to delay action in the knowledge that many voters are resistant to changes that threaten established norms.

This deeply inculcated commitment to a destructive direction of travel is the major impediment. It is for this reason that we need to understand how particular societal trajectories emerge and why it is so difficult to change direction. As this narrative about the changing fortunes of water serpent beings has revealed, contemporary societies have been heading towards where we are now for a long time. Political, religious and technological changes have created steeper socio-political hierarchies, more alienated social and ecological relationships, and more instrumental material practices. Achieving the vital tipping point that will alter the direction of these trajectories requires radical changes – not just in practice, but in how we think. As Greta Thunberg put it in a TED Talk in 2018: 'we can't save the world by playing by the rules, because the rules have to be changed. Everything needs to change – and it has to start today.'

A real change in direction requires a mode of thought that rejects assumptions about human exceptionalism and recognizes that all living kinds are part of a single interconnected system. How might this kind of thinking be enacted in practice? In order to have a meaningful effect it surely needs to permeate all areas of human activity, at every scale, but let us consider, as an illustrative example, how it might be employed to reframe human-non-human relations within river catchment areas.

Re-Imagined Communities

In addressing this question, I have drawn on the political scientist Benedict Anderson's well-known text *Imagined Communities: Reflections on the Origin and Spread of Nationalism*, which describes how humans visualize their extended social relationships.[61] I propose a concept of 're-imagined communities', in which the notion of community is extended to include all the living kinds that a river catchment contains. In this way, as well as thinking about the familial, professional and recreational human communities to which we belong, we would also consider the non-human communities co-inhabiting the catchment area.[62] Our understandings of the interactions between human groups within river catchment areas would therefore be imaginatively enlarged to encompass relationships with all of the non-human beings: from the smallest microbial constituents of soils, to all of the aquatic and terrestrial, wild and domesticated, plant and animal species within a shared ecosystem.

There are some resonances here with earlier ideas about integrated water resource management, but also a fundamental ontological shift away from the divided visions of culture and nature that have limited earlier approaches. This dualism persists even in recent 'eco-centric' or 'bio-centric' approaches, which – though usefully shifting the emphasis to non-human rights and interests – continue to reify a vision of nature or ecology as 'other'. Vestigial dualism remains even in progressive notions of 'ecological democracy', which considers how ecosystems might be represented in discursive fora.[63]

Recognizing an indivisible world takes us further towards a concept of 'pan-species democracy', in which both human and non-human kinds, and their needs and interests, are similarly represented in decision-making processes. Karen Barad notes that it is still difficult to maintain ontological equality between those who cannot speak and those speaking for them.[64] But pan-species democracy clearly rejects nature–culture dualism and underlines the point that non-human beings and ecosystems have a political presence whether they are explicitly enfranchised or not.[65] They are not passive subjects awaiting human voices to represent their interests: they are actively involved in material and social exchanges with human beings, and with each other,[66] and in the co-creation of shared human-non-human lifeworlds.[67] Fully acknowledging their co-production of these lifeworlds strengthens the case for non-human rights and democratic inclusion.

Once this imaginative thought-shift is accomplished, there are many possible mechanisms for

131 Neo-pagan water celebration, Port Meadow, Oxford.

representational pan-species democracy in diverse cultural contexts. These might entail appointing indigenous elders as legal guardians, such as the Māori *To Pou Tupua*, or those envisaged by the Universal Declaration of the Rights of Rivers.[68] Use could be made of interdisciplinary advisory bodies providing expertise and local knowledge about a cross-section of non-human communities in the relevant area. The central aim is to find ways to ensure that non-human needs and interests are articulated with equality in the multiple decision-making processes that constitute human-non-human relations.[69]

These ideas are readily imaginable in relation to river catchment management, but it is important to stress that it is not sufficient to apply this kind of thinking selectively, to decision-making processes putatively dealing with 'environmental issues', while 'economic' activities trample merrily on externalizing their costs via business as usual. An inclusive vision encompassing the needs and interests of all living kinds needs to be integrated into every area of governance and management. This requires structural rearrangements so that these are no longer 'departmentalized' into unrelated siloes, and joined-up thinking in all areas of legislation and regulation. Thus, housing or transport policy would also consider the needs and interests of all of the species and material environments that it might potentially affect. Economic policy could not proceed without consideration of its ecological impacts. Every infrastructural development would be considered in these terms.

Because social and ecological relationships are multi-scalar, this kind of re-imagining also needs to permeate leadership and decision making at local, regional, national and international levels. Having people 'speak for' human *and* non-human needs and interests in river catchment areas could be replicated at every scale, with grassroots local practices that bring these ideas into practice 'on the ground', as well as more visionary national and international leadership.

Re-Imagining an International Community

A sustainable way forward can only be achieved through global cooperation.[70] The United Nations was formed in 1945 to uphold 'international peace and security', which depends to a great extent on environmental stability. In the last three decades it has held annual climate change summits (COPs) and multiple ecologically oriented events seeking to inspire collective action. However, their efficacy is limited partly by the sheer complexity of achieving international agreement between multiple national participants with diverse priorities, and partly by the reality that discussions are still framed by conventional visions of nature and culture. The division of the UN's activities into separate siloes dealing with 'climate', 'development', 'environment' and 'culture' is a gift to climate change deniers keen to delay any action that might affect their interests.[71]

The UN's interests in water focused first on the provision of clean drinking water and sanitation for disadvantaged human communities. Though laudable and necessary, this gave little consideration to ecological issues beyond those affecting human access to water supplies. The Sustainable Development Goals articulated in 2015 are more comprehensive, but they replicate the contradictions inherent in an anthropocentric worldview that divides social, economic and ecological issues, sees water largely as a 'resource', and remains committed to growth-based development.

In 2016 the UN established a High-Level Panel on Water. This aimed to articulate 'cultural and spiritual values' in relation to water with a view to encouraging heads of state to give these greater priority.[72] It included consideration of diverse human–water relationships, and reflected the increasing influence of indigenous perspectives.[73] Some progress was evident in the UN's 2018 'World Water Development Report'. Though still couched in conventional managerial language, this recommended shifts towards 'nature-based solutions', implicitly acknowledging the agentive capacities of non-human systems and the need to engage with them more sympathetically.[74]

The work of the High Level Panel has continued to encourage fresh perspectives. In 2021 the UN's annual water report emphasized the need to recognize and respect the diversity of people's values and the reality that many important aspects of human-water relations – in particular water's social meanings – cannot be quantified or monetized. It underlined the need for 'inclusive planning and decision-making processes'. In 2022 the annual report focused on groundwater and the need to make the 'invisible' aspects of water visible. Though this was quite literal in its concerns, it also carried some promising metaphorical implications about the need to understand what lies under the surface of human engagements with water.

Much more could be done, however. The UN could take a lead in recognizing the need for new analytic paradigms that support reciprocal human-non-human relations. It could respond positively to demands for a UN declaration protecting the 'Rights of Nature',[75] although a more ontologically transformational goal would be to conflate this with the 1948 Declaration of Human Rights and create a joint UN declaration for the rights of all living kinds. Such a declaration would require more stringent international legislation protecting non-human rights and interests and an apparatus with the power to implement these changes, linked with the International Court and bodies such as the IPCC.

Some doubt that the UN has sufficient coherence to be effective in driving change, suggesting that global problems require a world government.[76] Drawing on historic models such as the League of Nations and the World Health Organization, international affairs specialists Richard Haass and Charles Kupchan propose a Concert of Powers: 'an informal steering group of the world's most influential countries' with a remit to maintain stability.[77] Any form of shared international governance, even on smaller scales such as in the European Union, struggles to reconcile diversity and assure democratic equality. But in a global crisis there is an urgent need for robust mechanisms to support international negotiations and to enact international laws. This may entail strengthening the UN's powers to uphold human *and* non-human rights, or developing new international arrangements that do so, but to make meaningful changes any such endeavours need to start by re-imagining the world as an indivisible community of living kinds.

In concert with local and national moves in this direction, strong international leadership could help societies to reach the imaginative and practical tipping points needed to redirect their trajectories towards more sustainable and convivial lifeways.

The world's multiple water serpent beings still have an important role to play in these endeavours. As I hope this book has illustrated, they offer an engaging narrative device for communicating complex ideas to a diverse range of audiences. Manifesting the creative powers of water, and expressing the realities of human-non-human relations, they continue to illuminate key social and ecological issues at every scale. Despite – and perhaps because of – the changes in their fortunes over time, they still have much potential to give the non-human domain a powerful presence in the debates and decisions that will determine the future of life on Earth.

REFERENCES

Introduction

1 World Wildlife Fund, *Living Planet Report – 2018: Aiming Higher* (Gland, 2018); Intergovernmental Science-Policy Platform on Biodiversity, 'Nature's Dangerous Decline "Unprecedented": Species Extinction Rates "Accelerating"', media release, 29 April 2019, https://ipbes.net; International Panel on Climate Change (IPCC), 'Global Warming of 1.5 °C' (2018), www.ipcc.ch.
2 Barry Powell, *Classical Myth*, trans. H. Howe (Upper Saddle River, NJ, 1998), p. 685.
3 Émile Durkheim, *The Elementary Forms of the Religious Life* (New York, 1961).
4 A note on terminology. I have generally made use of the term 'living kinds' to denote all living organisms, as (unlike 'creatures' or 'beings') it more readily includes plants and vegetation. I have avoided terms such as 'living things' or 'life forms' on the basis that these are rather objectifying, which runs against the central arguments in the text. 'Kinds', on the other hand, is literally more kindly, reminding us of the fundamental 'kinship' that links humans and other kinds.

1 Being Ubiquitous

1 Stephen Oppenheimer, *Out of Africa's Eden: The Peopling of the World* (Johannesburg, 2003).
2 Lauriston Sharp, 'Steel Axes for Stone Age Australians', in *Human Problems in Technological Change: A Casebook*, ed. E. Spicer (New York, 1952), pp. 69–92.
3 Bronislaw Malinowski, *Argonauts of the Western Pacific: An Account of Native Enterprise and Adventure in the Archipelagos of Melanesian New Guinea* (London, 1922).
4 Heather Sutherland, 'Geography as Destiny? The Role of Water in Southeast Asian History', in *A World of Water: Rain, Rivers and Seas in Southern Histories*, ed. P. Boomgaard (Leiden, 2007), pp. 27–70 (p. 32).
5 David Hopkins, *Across the Anatolian Plateau: Readings in the Archaeology of Ancient Turkey* (Boston, MA, 2002).
6 Wilfred Hambly, *Serpent Worship in Africa* (Chicago, IL, 1931), p. 41.
7 Edward Schafer, *The Divine Woman: Dragon Ladies and Rain Maidens in T'ang Literature* (San Francisco, CA, 1980), p. 13; Peter Boomgaard, ed., *A World of Water: Rain, Rivers and Seas in Southeast Asian Histories* (Leiden, 2007), p. 4.
8 John Day, personal communication with author, 2021; Irving Finkel, *The Ark before Noah: Decoding the Story of the Flood* (London, 2014).
9 Bernard Batto, *Slaying the Dragon: Mythmaking in the Biblical Tradition* (Louisville, KY, 1992), pp. 1–2.
10 Mary Condren, *The Serpent and the Goddess: Women, Religion, and Power in Celtic Ireland* (San Francisco, CA, 1989), p. 7.
11 Georges Dumézil, *From Myth to Fiction*, trans. Derek Coleman (Chicago, IL, and London, 1970), pp. x, vii, ix.
12 Wilfred Lambert, *Babylonian Creation Myths* (Winona Lakes, IN, 2013).
13 William Albright, *From the Stone Age to Christianity: Monotheism and the Historical Process* (Baltimore, MD, 1946), p. 98.
14 Alex Wilder, *The Serpent Symbol* (London, 1894), pp. 11, 17.
15 James Fergusson, *Tree and Serpent Worship: Illustrations of Mythology and Art in India* (London, 1868), pp. 8–9.
16 Arjun Appadurai, *The Social Life of Things: Commodities in Cultural Perspective* (Cambridge, 1986).
17 Ananda Coomaraswamy, *Yaksas* (New Delhi, 1961). Cited in Carol Bolon, *Forms of the Goddess Lajjā Gaurī in Indian Art* (University Park, PA, 1992), p. 2.
18 Andrew Clark, 'Embodied, Situated, and Distributed Cognition', in *Companion to Cognitive Science*, ed. W. Bechtel and G. Graham (Malden, MA, 1998), pp. 506–17.

19 Veronica Strang, 'Common Senses: Water, Sensory Experience and the Generation of Meaning', *Journal of Material Culture*, X/1 (2005), pp. 93–121.
20 Christopher Chippendale and Paul Taçon, eds, *The Archaeology of Rock Art* (Cambridge, 1998).
21 David Whitley, 'Finding Rain in the Desert: Landscape, Gender and Far-Western North American Rock-Art', in *The Archaeology of Rock Art*, ed. Chris Chippendale and Paul Taçon (Cambridge, 1998), pp. 11–29.
22 Paul Harvey, *The History of Topographical Maps* (London, 1980).
23 Condren, *The Serpent and the Goddess*, p. 25.
24 Howard Morphy, *Ancestral Connections: Art and an Aboriginal System of Knowledge* (Chicago, IL, 1991).
25 Claude Lévi-Strauss, *Totemism*, trans. R. Needham (London, 1964).
26 Paul Taçon, Meredith Wilson and Christopher Chippendale, 'Birth of the Rainbow Serpent in Arnhem Land Rock Art and Oral History', *Oceania*, XXXI (1996), pp. 103–24.
27 Frederik Bosch, *The Golden Germ: An Introduction to Indian Symbolism*, trans. A. Fontein ('s-Gravenhage, 1960).
28 Klaus Conrad, *Die beginnende Schizophrenie. Versuch einer Gestaltanalyse des Wahns* (The Onset of Schizophrenia: An Attempt to Form an Analysis of Delusion) (Stuttgart, 1958).
29 Hambly, *Serpent Worship*, p. 37.
30 Schafer, *The Divine Woman*, pp. 12–14.
31 Dennis Slifer, *The Serpent and the Sacred Fire: Fertility Images in Southwest Rock Art* (Santa Fe, NM, 2000), pp. 84, 112.
32 Philip Gardiner and Gary Osborn, *The Serpent Grail: The Truth behind the Holy Grail, the Philosopher's Stone and the Elixir of Life* (London, 2005), p. 15.
33 Robert Clark, *Myth and Symbol in Ancient Egypt* (London, 1959), p. 67.
34 Ibid., pp. 66–7.
35 Bolon, *Forms of the Goddess Lajjā Gaurī*, p. 52.
36 Andrew McDonald and Brian Stross, 'Water Lily and Cosmic Serpent: Equivalent Conduits of the Maya Spirit Realm', *Journal of Ethnobiology*, XXXII/1 (2012), pp. 72–106 (p. 88).
37 Grafton Elliot Smith, *The Evolution of the Dragon* (Manchester, London and New York, 1919), pp. 81–2.
38 Ivan Illich, H_2O *and the Waters of Forgetfulness* (London, 1986), p. 5.
39 Job 41:10–13, ET 18–21, in John Day, *God's Conflict with the Dragon and the Sea: Echoes of a Canaanite Myth in the Old Testament* (Cambridge, 1985), p. 71.
40 Charles Hudson, 'Utkena: A Cherokee Anomalous Monster', *Journal of Cherokee Studies*, III (1978), pp. 62–75.
41 Jean-Philippe Vogel, *Indian Serpent-Lore; or, The Nāgas in Hindu Legend and Art* (London, 1926), p. 15.
42 Scott Atran, *Cognitive Foundations of Natural History* (Cambridge and New York, 1990).
43 Georg Hegel considered dialectical engagement with the environment as an outward projection and reintegration of consciousness. In more contemporary debates, cognitive philosophers Andy Clark and David Chalmers describe a concept of 'extended mind'. Georg Hegel, *The Phenomenology of Spirit*, trans. A. Miller (Oxford 1979); Andy Clark and David Chalmers, 'The Extended Mind', *Analysis*, LVIII (1998), pp. 7–19.
44 Atran, *Cognitive Foundations*.
45 Joseph Campbell, *Creative Mythology* (New York, 1968), p. 154. See also Joseph Campbell, *The Masks of God: Creative Mythology* (London, 2001).
46 Daniel Kahneman, *Thinking Fast and Slow* (London, 2011), pp. 76–7.
47 Ron Bacon, *Parata the Taniwha: Another Legend of the Sea* (Auckland, 2004).
48 Hampden DuBose, *The Dragon, Image, and Demon; or, The Three Religions of China: Confucianism, Buddhism, and Taoism* (New York, 1887).
49 Adele Getty, *Goddess: Mother of Living Nature* (London, 1990); Jeremy Narby, *The Cosmic Serpent: DNA and the Origins of Knowledge* (London, 1998), p. 54.
50 Ian Ridpath and Wil Tirion, *Stars and Planets Guide* (Princeton, NJ, 2001).
51 Susie Green, *Tiger* (London, 2006), p. 39.
52 Bingxiang Zhu, *'Fuxi' and Chinese Culture* (Kunming, 2014), pp. 10–11.
53 Narby, *The Cosmic Serpent*, p. 54.
54 John Day, personal communication with the author 2021.
55 Colin Blakemore, personal communications with the author 2018–20.
56 Jean-Pierre Chaumiel, 'Voir, Savoir, Pouvoir: Le Chamanisme Chez les Yaguas du Nord-Est Péruvien', *Journal de la Sociétié des Américanistes*, LXX (1984), pp. 203–11; Graham Townsley, 'Song Paths: The Ways and Means of Yaminahua Shamanic Knowledge', *L'Homme, La remontée de l'Amazone*, CXXVI (1993), pp. 449–68.
57 Geraldo Reichel-Dolmatoff, 'Brain and Mind in Desana Shamanism', *Journal of Latin American Lore*, VII/1 (1981), pp. 73–113.
58 Claude Lévi-Strauss, *Histoire de Lynx* (Paris, 1991), pp. 295.
59 Schafer, *The Divine Woman*, pp. 12–14.

60 Mary Douglas, *Implicit Meanings: Essays in Anthropology* (London, 1975), p. 50.
61 Hannah Arendt, *The Human Condition* (Chicago, IL, 1998).
62 Anna Tsing, *The Mushroom at the End of the World: On the Possibility of Life in Capitalist Ruins* (Princeton, NJ, 2017).
63 Veronica Strang, 'The Hard Way: Volatility and Stability in the Brisbane River Delta', *Social Anthropology* Special Issue, ed. F. Krause and T. Hylland-Eriksen (in press).
64 Jared Diamond, *Collapse: How Societies Choose to Fail or Succeed* (New York, 2005).
65 Douglas, *Implicit Meanings*.
66 Veronica Strang, *The Meaning of Water* (Oxford and New York, 2004).
67 Matthew Edgeworth, *Fluid Pasts: Archaeology of Flow* (London, 2011), p. 25.
68 Rodney Giblett, *Landscapes of Culture and Nature* (Basingstoke and New York, 2009), p. 61.
69 Stephen Asma, *On Monsters: An Unnatural History of Our Worst Fears* (Oxford, 2009).
70 See Pliny the Elder, *Naturalis historia: The Historie of the World* [1601] (Cambridge, MA, 1949).
71 Scott Poole, *Monsters in America: Our Historial Obsession with the Hideous and Haunting* (Waco, TX, 2011).
72 Anthony Seeger, *Nature and Society in Central Brazil: The Suya Indians of Mato Grosso* (Cambridge, MA, 1981), pp. 68–70.
73 Peter Rivière, 'Ambiguous Environments', *Tipití: Journal of the Society for the Anthropology of Lowland South America*, VIII/2 (2010) pp. 1–12 (p. 4).
74 Yasmine Musharbash and Geir Presterudstuen, eds, *Monster Anthropology in Australasia and Beyond* (New York, 2014); Yasmine Musharbash and Geir Presterudstuen, eds, *Monster Anthropology: Explorations of Transforming Social Worlds through Monsters* (London and New York, 2019).
75 Peter Dendle, 'Monsters and the Twenty-First Century: The Preternatural in an Age of Scientific Consensus', in *The Ashgate Research Companion to Monsters and the Monstrous*, ed. Asa Mittman and Peter Dendle (Aldershot, 2012), pp. 437–48; David Gilmore, *Monsters: Evil Beings, Mythical Beasts, and All Manner of Imaginary Terrors* (Philadelphia, PA, 2003), pp. 18, 19.
76 Credited to Madame de Pompadour, prior to the French Revolution; Michael Mould, *Routledge Dictionary of Cultural References in Modern French* (London and New York, 2011), p. 43.
77 Richard Boer, trans., *Örvar-Odds Saga* (Leiden, 1888).
78 Robert Macfarlane, *Underland: A Deep Time Journey* (London, 2019).
79 Yasmine Musharbash and Sophie Creighton, 'The Underground Panel', Australian Anthropological Society Conference, Canberra, 2–5 December 2019.
80 Dinah Rajak and Emma Gilberthorpe, 'The Anthropology of Extraction: Critical Perspectives on the Resource Curse', *Journal of Development Studies*, LIII/2 (2016), pp. 186–204; Sabine Luning, 'The Underground', in *The Anthropology of Resource Extraction*, ed. Robert Pijpers and Lorenzo d'Angelo (London, 2022).
81 Caryl Johnston, *Consecrated Venom: The Serpent and the Tree of Knowledge* (Edinburgh, 2000), p. 31.

2 Original Beings

1 'The Book of Baruch', 3:16–19, in the Vulgate Bible, fourth century.
2 Wilfred Lambert, *Babylonian Creation Myths* (Winona Lakes, IN, 2013).
3 Ibid., pp. 273–4.
4 Robert Clark, *Myth and Symbol in Ancient Egypt* (London, 1959), p. 36.
5 British Museum, *The Babylonian Legends of the Creation and the Fight between Bel and the Dragon: As Told by Assyrian Tablets from Ninevah* (London, 1931), pp. 14, 16.
6 Geraldine Pinch, *Handbook of Egyptian Mythology* (Santa Barbara, CA, 2002), p. 111.
7 John West, *The Serpent in the Sky: The High Wisdom of Ancient Egypt* (London, 1979), pp. 70–71.
8 Book of the Dead, Chapter XL, 2–3, in Karen Joines, *Serpent Symbolism in the Old Testament: A Linguistic, Archaeological and Literary Study* (Haddonfield, NJ, 1974), p. 97.
9 Otto Kern, *Orphic Fragment* 54.36 (Berlin, 1922).
10 Cleve Barlow, *Tikanga Whakaaro: Key Concepts in Māori Culture* (Oxford and London, 1991), p. 55.
11 Ibid.
12 Ibid., p. 61.
13 Ibid., pp. 4, 11.
14 Ibid., p. 111.
15 Government of New Zealand, 'Taniwha – Taniwha of the Sea', *Te Ara – The Encyclopedia of New Zealand* (2018), www.teara.govt.nz.
16 Merle Robertson, 'The Celestial God of Number 13', PARI *Journal*, XII/1 (2011), pp. 1–6.
17 Claus Diemel and Elke Ruhnau, eds, *Jaguar and Serpent: The Cosmos of Indians in Mexico, Central and South America*, trans. Ann Davis (Berlin, 2000), p. 65.
18 Robertson, 'The Celestial God of Number 13'.
19 Clark, *Myth and Symbol*, pp. 66–7.
20 Ibid., p. 67.

21 Linda Schele and Mary Miller, *The Blood of Kings: Dynasty and Ritual in Maya Art* (New York, 1986), p. 46.
22 Eric Thompson, *Maya History and Religion* (Norman, OK, 1970), p. 202.
23 Diana Ferguson, *Tales of the Plumed Serpent: Aztec, Inca and Mayan Myths* (London, 2000), pp. 37–8.
24 Francis Huxley, *The Dragon: Nature of Spirit, Spirit of Nature* (London, 1979), p. 14.
25 Edwin Krupp, *Echoes of the Ancient Skies: The Astronomy of Lost Civilisations* (New York, 1983), pp. 315–19.
26 Pyramid Texts 1146. Cited in Rundle Clark, *Myth and Symbol in Ancient Egypt* (London, 1978), p. 51.
27 Pinch, *Egyptian Mythology*, pp. 172, 209.
28 Stephanie Dalley, *The Mystery of the Hanging Garden of Babylon: An Elusive World Wonder Traced* (Oxford, 2013), p. 154.
29 Norman Austin, *Meaning and Being in Myth* (University Park, PA, and London, 1989), p. 88.
30 Mary Condren, *The Serpent and the Goddess: Women, Religion, and Power in Celtic Ireland* (San Francisco, CA, 1989), p. 16.
31 Jean-Philippe Vogel, *Indian Serpent-Lore; or, The Nāgas in Hindu Legend and Art* (London, 1926), p. 19; Wilder, *The Serpent Symbol*, p. 8.
32 Huxley, *The Dragon*, p. 6.
33 David Anthony, *The Horse, the Wheel, and Language: How Bronze-Age Riders from the Eurasian Steppes Shaped the Modern World* (Princeton, NJ, 2007).
34 *Rigveda* (8.79:2–6), trans. W. O'Flaherty (London 1981), p. 121.
35 Wilfred Hambly, *Serpent Worship in Africa*, Anthropological Series, XXI/1 (Chicago, IL, 1931), p. 11.
36 Wade Davis, *The Serpent and the Rainbow* (London, 1986), p. 177.
37 Ferguson, *Tales of the Plumed Serpent*, p. 53.
38 Evan Vogt, *Tortillas for the Gods: A Symbolic Analysis of Zinacanteco Rituals* (New York, 1976).
39 Ibid.
40 Karl Taube, 'Where the Earth and Sky Meet: The Sea in Ancient and Contemporary Maya Cosmology', in *Fiery Pool: The Maya and the Mythic Sea*, ed. D. Finamore and S. Houston (New Haven, CT, 2010), pp. 202–22.
41 Luis Martos López, 'Objects Cast into Cenotes', in Finamore and Houston, *Fiery Pool*, pp. 223–5 (p. 225).
42 Karl Taube, 'The Iconography of Mirrors at Teotihuacan', in *Art, Ideology, and the City of Teotihuacan*, ed. Janet Berlo (Washington, DC, 1992), pp. 169–204.
43 Schele and Miller, *The Blood of Kings*.
44 David Potter, 'Prehispanic Architecture and Sculpture in Central Yucatán', *American Archaeology*, XLI (2015), pp. 430–34.
45 Jose Diaz, 'Ethnopharmacology of Sacred Psychoactive Plants Used by the Indians of Mexico', *Annual Review of Pharmacology and Toxicology*, XVII (1977), pp. 647–75.
46 Ruben Cabrera Castro, 'Human Sacrifice at the Temple of the Feathered Serpent: Recent Discoveries at Teotihuacan', in *Teotihuacan: Art from the City of the Gods*, ed. K. Berrin and E. Pasztory (San Francisco, CA, 1993), pp. 100–107.
47 George Cowgill, *Ancient Teotihuacan: Early Urbanism in Central Mexico* (Cambridge and New York, 2015).
48 John Staller and Brian Stross, *Lightning in the Andes and MesoAmerica: Pre-Colombian, Colonial and Contemporary Perspectives* (Oxford, 2013), p. 166.
49 Vogel, *Indian Serpent-Lore*, pp. 29–30.
50 Gerardo Reichel-Dolmatoff, *Desana Texts and Contexts*, Series Americana 12 (Wien, 1989), p. 19.
51 Peter Rivière, 'Ambiguous Environments', *Tipití: Journal of the Society for the Anthropology of Lowland South America*, VIII/2 (2010), pp. 1–12 (p. 5).
52 Krupp, *Echoes of the Ancient Skies*, p. 317.
53 Jesse Byock, *The Saga of the Volsungs: The Norse Epic of Sigurd the Dragon Slayer* (Berkeley, CA, 1990), p. 5.
54 Philip Gardiner and Gary Osborn, *The Serpent Grail: The Truth behind the Holy Grail, the Philosopher's Stone and the Elixir of Life* (London, 2005), p. 162. See also Anthony Mercatante and James Dow, *Encyclopedia of World Mythology and Legend*, 3rd edn (New York and Oxford, 1988).
55 Joakim Goldhahn, 'Roaring Rocks: An Audio-Visual Perspective on Hunter-Gatherer Engravings in Northern Sweden and Scandinavia', *Norwegian Archaeological Review*, XXXV/1 (2002), pp. 29–61 (p. 49).
56 Gardiner and Osborn, *The Serpent Grail*, p. 176.
57 Joshua Robertson, *The Ancient Egyptian Books of the Earth* (Atlanta, GA, 2012), p. 144.
58 Alison Roberts, *Hathor Rising: The Serpent Power of Ancient Egypt* (Totnes, 1995), p. 8.
59 Joines, *Serpent Symbolism in the Old Testament*, p. 86.
60 Wilder, *The Serpent Symbol*, p. 15.
61 Adele Berlin and Marc Brettler, *The Jewish Study Bible*, trans. Jewish Publication Society (New York, 2014), p. 779. See also Othmar Keel and Christoph Uehlinger, *Gods, Goddesses and Images of God in Ancient Israel* (Minneapolis, MN, 1988).
62 The date and authorship of this text are uncertain, but it appears to have influenced medieval thinking about the cosmos. See Andrei Orlov, *The Enoch-Metatron Tradition* (Tübingen, 2005).

63 Gustav Davidson, *A Dictionary of Angels, Including the Fallen Angels* (New York, 1967), pp. 84, 224.

64 Thomas Aquinas, *Summa Theologiae* (1225–74). Reply to Objection 5. L.108, c.6.

65 Caryl Johnston, *Consecrated Venom: The Serpent and the Tree of Knowledge* (Edinburgh, 2000).

66 Joines, *Serpent Symbolism in the Old Testament*, p. 85.

67 Wilder, *The Serpent Symbol*, p. 14.

68 Joines, *Serpent Symbolism in the Old Testament*, pp. 1, 21.

69 Gilles Deleuze and Félix Guattari, *A Thousand Plateaus* (London, 2004).

70 Veronica Strang, 'On the Matter of Time', *Interdisciplinary Science Reviews*, XL/2 (2015), pp. 101–23.

71 Ibid.

72 Marinus de Visser, *The Dragon in China and Japan* (Amsterdam, 1913), p. 36.

73 Hampden DuBose, *The Dragon, Image, and Demon; or, The Three Religions of China: Confucianism, Buddhism and Taoism* (New York, 1887), p. 315. See also Schafer, *The Divine Woman*, p. 15.

74 He Xin, cited in Bingxiang Zhu, *'Fuxi' and Chinese Culture* (Kunming, 2014), pp. 3–4.

75 Chris Gosden, *Social Being and Time* (Oxford, 1994).

76 Pinch, *Ancient Egypt*, p. 174.

77 Joann Fletcher, *Ancient Egypt: Life, Myth and Art* (London, 1999), p. 43.

78 Pyramid Texts 628–9, cited in James Breasted, *Development of Religion and Thought in Ancient Egypt* (New York, 2010), pp. 18–26.

79 Pinch, *Ancient Egypt*, p. 178.

80 Gardiner and Osborn, *The Serpent Grail*, p. 12.

81 Inscription on temple celebrating Isis, in Sais, Egypt. See also Erik Hornung, *The Ancient Egyptian Books of the Afterlife* (Ithaca, NY, 1999).

82 Joines, *Serpent Symbolism in the Old Testament*, p. 19.

83 Andrew George, trans., *The Epic of Gilgamesh: The Babylonian Epic Poem and Other Texts in Akkadian and Sumerian* (London, 2000); and Andrew George, ed., *The Babylonian Gilgamesh Epic: Introduction, Critical Edition and Cuneiform Texts* (Oxford, 2003).

84 *Prose Edda* 410, in James Fergusson, *Tree and Serpent Worship: Illustrations of Mythology and Art in India* (London, 1868), p. 24.

85 Samantha Riches, *St George: Hero, Martyr and Myth* (Stroud, 2005), p. 152.

3 Living Beings

1 John Staller and Brian Stross, *Lightning in the Andes and MesoAmerica: Pre-Colombian, Colonial and Contemporary Perspectives* (Oxford, 2013), p. 166.

2 Bingxiang Zhu, *'Fuxi' and Chinese Culture* (Kunming, 2014), p. 9.

3 Ibid., p. 6.

4 Claas Bleeker, *The Rainbow: A Collection of Studies in the Science of Religion* (Leiden, 1975), p. 214.

5 Arthur Frothingham, 'Babylonian Origin of Hermes the Snake-God, and of the Caduceus', *American Journal of Archaeology*, XX (1916), pp. 175–211. See also Stephanie Dalley, ed., *The Legacy of Mesopotamia* (Oxford, 1998).

6 Edward Schafer, *The Divine Woman: Dragon Ladies and Rain Maidens in T'ang Literature* (San Francisco, CA, 1980), pp. 14, 29.

7 Bleeker, *The Rainbow*, p. 214.

8 Schafer, *The Divine Woman*, pp. 31–2.

9 Mircea Eliade, *Myths, Dreams and Mysteries* (New York, 1961).

10 Émile Durkheim, *The Elementary Forms of the Religious Life* (New York, 1961).

11 Diana Ferguson, *Tales of the Plumed Serpent: Aztec, Inca and Mayan Myths* (London, 2000), p. 22.

12 Bernardino De Sahagún, *The Florentine Codex: An Encyclopedia of the Nahua World in Sixteenth-Century Mexico*, trans. J. Favrot Peterson and K. Terraciano (Austin, TX, 2019).

13 Ben Smith, 'Rock Art in South-Central Africa: A Study Based on the Pictographs of Dedza District, Malawi and Kasama District Zambi'a, PhD dissertation, University of Cambridge, 1995.

14 Claude Boucher and Joseph Kadzombem, museum information at Kungoni Centre of Culture and Art, Malawi, 2014. See also Claude Boucher, *When Animals Sing and Spirits Dance* (Malawi, 2012).

15 Wilfred Hambly, *Serpent Worship in Africa*, Anthropological Series, XXI/1 (Chicago, IL, 1931), pp. 9–12.

16 Gerardo Reichel-Dolmatoff, 'Brain and Mind in Desana Shamanism', *Journal of Latin American Lore*, VII/1 (1981), pp. 73–113 (p. 87).

17 Gerardo Reichel-Dolmatoff, *Desana Texts and Contexts*, Series Americana, 12 (Wien, 1989), pp. 10–11.

18 Ibid., p. 513.

19 Carol Bolon, *Forms of the Goddess Lajjā Gaurī in Indian Art* (University Park, PA, 1992), pp. 52–3.

20 *Prose Edda* 410, in James Fergusson, *Tree and Serpent Worship: Illustrations of Mythology and Art in India* (London, 1868), p. 24.

21 Ian Armit and David Reich, 'The Return of the Beaker Folk? Rethinking Migration and Population Change in British Prehistory', *Antiquity*, XCV/384 (2021), pp. 1464–77; Barry Cunliffe, *The Ancient Celts* (Oxford, 1997).

22 Edward Davies, *The Mythology and Rites of the British Druids* (London, 1809).

23 Philip Gardiner and Gary Osborn, *The Serpent Grail: The Truth behind the Holy Grail, the Philosopher's Stone and the Elixir of Life* (London, 2005), p. 176.

24 Karen Joines, *Serpent Symbolism in the Old Testament: A Linguistic, Archaeological and Literary Study* (Haddonfield, NJ, 1974), p. 71.

25 Miranda Green, ed., *The Celtic World* (London, 1995), p. 465.

26 Lindsay Allason-Jones and Bruce McKay, *Coventina's Well: A Shrine on Hadrian's Wall* (Gloucester, 1985).

27 Richard Hingley, *Hadrian's Wall: A Life* (Oxford, 2012), p. 192.

28 Mary Condren, *The Serpent and the Goddess: Women, Religion, and Power in Celtic Ireland* (San Francisco, CA, 1989), p. 58.

29 Joann Fletcher, *Ancient Egypt: Life, Myth and Art* (London, 1999), p. 40.

30 Asit Biswas, *History of Hydrology* (Amsterdam, 1970), p. 109.

31 Joseph Campbell, *Creative Mythology* (New York, 1968), p. 29.

32 Bleeker, *The Rainbow*, p. 215.

33 Alison Roberts, *Hathor Rising: The Serpent Power of Ancient Egypt* (Totnes, 1995), p. 2.

34 Ivan Illich, *H_2O and the Waters of Forgetfulness* (London, 1986), p. 5.

35 Condren, *The Serpent and the Goddess*, p. 58.

36 Geraldine Pinch, *Handbook of Egyptian Mythology* (Santa Barbara, CA, 2002), p. 179.

37 Aylward Blackman, 'The Significance of Incense and Libations in Funerary and Temple Ritual', *Zeitschrift für Ägyptische Sprache und Altertumskunde*, L/1–2 (1912), p. 69.

38 Grafton Elliot Smith, *The Evolution of the Dragon* (Manchester, London and New York, 1919), p. vii.

39 Clifford Bishop, *Sex and Spirit* (Boston, MA, 1996); Dennis Slifer, *The Serpent and the Sacred Fire: Fertility Images in Southwest Rock Art* (Santa Fe, NM, 2000), p. 9.

40 Slifer, *The Serpent and the Sacred Fire*, pp. 84–5.

41 *Enuma Elish*, Tablet 1:133, in *Babylonian Creation Myths*, trans. Wilfred Lambert (Winona Lakes, IN, 2013), p. 459. Such capacities to manifest in various forms was common among Egyptian deities: for example, the fiery serpent goddess Hathor also appears as a female hawk, as the 'Lady of the Sycamore Tree' and as a 'Cow of Gold'. Roberts, *Hathor Rising*, p. 8.

42 James Pritchard, *Archaeology and the Old Testament* (Princeton, NJ, 2012), p. 192; *Enuma Elish*, Tablet 1:96, in *Babylonian Creation Myths*, trans. Lambert, p. 55.

43 *Enuma Elish*, Tablet 5:47–51, in *Babylonian Creation Myths*, trans. Lambert, p. 101; John Day, *God's Conflict with the Dragon and the Sea: Echoes of a Canaanite Myth in the Old Testament* (Cambridge, 1985), p. 4. See also *Enuma Elish*, Tablet 5:57, 59, in *Babylonian Creation Myths*, trans. Lambert, p. 101.

44 Jianing Chen and Yang Yang, *The World of Chinese Myths* (Beijing, 1995), p. 5.

45 Diana Ferguson, *Tales of the Plumed Serpent: Aztec, Inca and Mayan Myths* (London, 2000), p. 30.

46 Ibid., p. 33.

47 Bruce Lincoln, 'The Indo-European Myth of Creation', *History of Religions*, XV/2 (1975), pp. 121–45 (p. 125).

48 Saemund Sigfusson, *The Elder Edda of Saemund Sigfusson*, trans. B. Thorpe (London, Stockholm and Copenhagen, 1866), pp. 3, 24–5.

49 Bruce Lincoln, *Myth, Cosmos and Society* (Cambridge, MA, and London, 1986), p. 2.

50 See Pierre Bourdieu, *The Logic of Practice*, trans. Richard Nice (Cambridge, 1990).

51 Lincoln, *Myth, Cosmos and Society*, p. 3.

52 Jean-Philippe Vogel, *Indian Serpent-Lore; or, The Nāgas in Hindu Legend and Art* (London, 1926), p. 4.

53 Yasmine Musharbash and Geir Presterudstuen, eds, *Monster Anthropology: Explorations of Transforming Social Worlds through Monsters* (London and New York, 2019).

54 David Gilmore, *Monsters: Evil Beings, Mythical Beasts, and All Manner of Imaginary Terrors* (Philadelphia, PA, 2003), p 149.

55 Ibid., p. 36.

56 Ernest Jones, *On the Nightmare* (New York, 1971), p. 151.

57 Gilmore, *Monsters*, p. 187.

58 Joseph Henderson and Maud Oakes, *The Wisdom of the Serpent: The Myths of Death, Rebirth, and Resurrection* (Princeton, NJ, 2020).

59 Arthur Schopenauer, *The World as Will and Idea*, trans. R. Haldane and J. Kemp (London, 1906).

60 Wes Williams, *Monsters and Their Meanings in Early Modern Culture: Mighty Magic* (Oxford, 2011), p. 1.

61 Joseph Andriano, *Immortal Monsters: The Mythological Evolution of the Fantastic Beast in Modern Fiction and Film* (Westport, CT, 1999), p. 91.

62 Schafer, *The Divine Woman*, p. 20.

63 Gilmore, *Monsters*, pp. ix, 1.

64 Gerardo Reichel-Dolmatoff, 'Cosmology as Ecological Analysis: A View from the Rain Forest', *Journal of the Royal Anthropological Institute*, XI/3 (1976), pp. 307–18. Gerardo Reichel-Dolmatoff, *The Sacred Mountain of Colombia's Kogi Indians* (Leiden, 1990).

4 Nature Beings

1 Richard Lee, *The Kung San: Men, Women and Work in a Foraging Society* (Cambridge, 1979).

2 Colin Renfrew and Iain Morley, eds, *Becoming Human: Innovation in Prehistoric Material and Spiritual Culture* (Cambridge, 2009).

3 Marshall Sahlins, 'Notes on the Original Affluent Society', in *Man the Hunter*, ed. R. Lee and L. Devore (New York, 1970), pp. 85–9.

4 Lawrence Keeley, *War before Civilisation: The Myth of the Peaceful Savage* (Oxford and New York, 1996).

5 Much of the material discussed here is drawn from my own and others' ethnographic fieldwork with the community of Kowanyama. Located near the estuary of the Mitchell River in Cape York, the community contains three language groups: the Yir Yoront, the Kunjen and the Kokobera. See also Barry Alpher, *Yir-Yoront Lexicon: Sketch and Dictionary of an Australian Language*, Trends in Linguistics Documentation, 6 (Berlin and New York, 1991); Ursula McConnel, *Myths of the Munkan* (London and New York, 1957); Walter Roth, *The Queensland Aborigines* (Sydney, 1984); and Lauriston Sharp, 'Steel Axes for Stone Age Australians', in *Human Problems in Technological Change: A Casebook*, ed. Edward Spicer (New York, 1952), pp. 69–92.

6 Paul Taçon, Meredith Wilson and Christopher Chippendale, 'Birth of the Rainbow Serpent in Arnhem Land Rock Art and Oral History', *Oceania*, XXXI (1996), pp. 103–24 (p. 120).

7 Lefty Yam and Winston Gilbert, fieldwork interviews with the author, 1992.

8 Veronica Strang, 'On the Matter of Time', *Interdisciplinary Science Reviews*, XL/2 (2015), pp. 101–23.

9 Paul Memmott, *Tangkic Orders of Time: An Anthropological Approach to Time Study* (2013), http://scan.net.au.

10 Howard Morphy, 'Australian Aboriginal Concepts of Time', in *The Story of Time*, ed. K. Lippincott (London, 1999), pp. 264–8 (p. 267).

11 Strang, 'On the Matter of Time', p. 104.

12 John Morton, 'The Effectiveness of Totemism: Increase Rituals and Resource Control in Central Australia', *Man*, XXII (1987), pp. 453–74.

13 Nancy Munn, 'The Transformation of Subjects into Objects in Walbiri and Pitjantjatjara Myth', in *Australian Aboriginal Anthropology: Modern Studies in the Social Anthropology of the Australian Aborigines*, ed. R. Berndt (Perth and Canberra, 1970), pp. 23–4.

14 Frances Morphy and Howard Morphy, 'We Think through our *Marwat* (Paintbrush): Reflections on the Yolngu Location of Thought and Knowledge', The Robert Layton Lecture, Durham University, 8 October 2014.

15 Les Hiatt, 'Swallowing and Regurgitation in Australian Myth and Ritual', in *Religion in Aboriginal Australia*, ed. M. Charlesworth, H. Morphy, D. Bell and K. Maddock (Queensland, 1984), pp. 31–56. See also Geza Roheim, *The Eternal Ones of the Dream* (New York, 1945); and Mircea Eliade, *Birth and Rebirth: The Religious Meanings of Initiation in Human Culture* (New York, 1958).

16 John Taylor, 'Of Acts and Axes: An Ethnography of Socio-Cultural Change in an Aboriginal Community, Cape York Peninsula', PhD dissertation, James Cook University, Queensland, 1984, p. 245.

17 Morphy and Morphy, 'We Think through our *Marwat* (Paintbrush)'.

18 Italicized quotes are from transcribed fieldwork interviews. Veronica Strang 1992–2019.

19 Francesca Merlan, *Dynamics of Difference in Australia: Indigenous Past and Present in a Settler Country* (Philadelphia, PA, 2018), p. 75.

20 Morton, 'The Effectiveness of Totemism', p. 457.

21 Aboriginal English refers to both genders as 'he', and gender has to be inferred from the content of a story. Similarly reflecting Aboriginal thinking, it is also primarily presentist, containing few indications about past or future, though the Dreaming or 'early days' does imply both an earlier creative era and an ongoing creative process. Narrative forms are similarly non-linear, often circling through events in non-chronological order. Here I have tried to provide some narrative structure to assist non-Aboriginal readers, while retaining their stylistic essence.

22 As well as the Olgol language term *Ewarr*, the Rainbow is also called *An-Ganb*, which is a 'deeper' name for it (that is, in the formal sacred language, Uw-Ilbmbanhdhiy).

23 This inhabitance of, or manifestation as, particular trees is symbolic rather than literal, and if a tree dies it is unproblematic for an ancestral being to inhabit a new one.

24 Nigel Dudley, Liz Higgins-Zogib and Stephanie Mansourian, 'The Links between Protected Areas, Faiths and Sacred Sites', *Conservation Biology*, XXIII/3 (2009), pp. 568–77.

25 Merlan, *Dynamics of Difference in Australia*.

26 Yirrkala Bark Petition (1963), National Archives of Australia.

27 Sandy Toussaint, ed., *Crossing Boundaries: Cultural, Legal, Historical and Practice Issues in Native Title* (Melbourne, 2004).

28 Moreau Maxwell, 'The Lake Harbour Region: Ecological Equilibrium in Sea Coast Adaptation', in *Thule Eskimo Culture: An Anthropological Retrospective*, ed. A. McCartney (Ottowa, 1979), pp. 76–87.
29 James Wright, *A History of the Native Peoples of Canada* (Quebec, 1998), p. 1047. See also Asen Baliki, *The Netsilik Eskimo* (Garden City, NY, 1970).
30 Ann Fienup-Riordan, *The Nelson Island Eskimo: Social Structure and Ritual Distribution* (Anchorage, AK, 1983), pp. 177–81.
31 Ann Fienup-Riordan, *Wise Words of the Yup'ik People: We Talk to You Because We Love You* (Lincoln, NE, 2018), p. 233.
32 Kimberley Patton, *The Sea Can Wash Away All Evils: Modern Marine Pollution and the Ancient Cathartic Ocean* (New York, 2006).
33 Lee Guemple, 'Born Again Pagans: The Inuit Cycle of Spirits', in *Amerindian Rebirth: Reincarnation Belief among North American Indians and Inuit*, ed. Antonia Mills and Richard Slobodin (Toronto, 1994), pp. 107–35 (p. 121).
34 George Sabo and Deborah Sabo, 'Belief Systems and the Ecology of Sea Mammal Hunting among the Baffinland Eskimo', *Arctic Anthropology*, XXII/2 (1985), pp. 77–86 (p. 81).
35 David Pelly, *Sacred Hunt: A Portrait of the Relationship between Seals and Inuit* (Vancouver, 2001).
36 Patton, *The Sea Can Wash Away All Evils*, p. 92.
37 Knud Rasmusen, *Intellectual Culture of the Iglulik Eskimos* (New York, 1976), p. 56.
38 Paul John, quoted in Fienup-Riordan, *Wise Words of the Yup'ik People*, p. 43.
39 Frank Andrews, quoted ibid., pp. 94–5.
40 Mark Nuttall, 'The Name Never Dies: Greenland Inuit Ideas of the Person', in *Amerindian Rebirth*, ed. Mills and Slobodin, pp. 123–35 (p. 121).
41 Wright, *A History of the Native Peoples of Canada*, p. 948.
42 Ibid., pp. 683–4.

5 Cultivating Beings

1 Alfred Gell, 'The Technology of Enchantment and the Enchantment of Technology', in *Anthropology, Art and Aesthetics*, ed. Jeremy Coote and Anthony Shelton (Oxford, 1994), pp. 40–63. See also Penny Harvey and Hannah Knox, 'The Enchantments of Infrastructure', *Mobilities*, VII (2012), pp. 520–36.
2 Jos Barlow, Toby Gardner, Alexander Lees, Luke Parry and Carlos Peres, 'How Pristine Are Tropical Forests? An Ecological Perspective on the Pre-Columbian Human Footprint in Amazonia and Implications for Contemporary Conservation', *Biological Conservation*, CL/1 (2012), pp. 45–9.
3 Fabiola Jara, 'Arawak Constellations: A Bibliographic Survey', in *Songs from the Sky: Indigenous Astronomical and Cosmological Traditions of the World*, ed. V. Chamberlain, J. Carlson and J. Young, Proceedings of the 1st International Conference on Ethnoastronomy (Bognor Regis, 2005), pp. 265–80.
4 Ibid., p. 266.
5 Ibid., p. 271.
6 Åke Hultkrantz, *Native Religions of North America: The Power of Visions and Fertility* (San Francisco, CA, 1987).
7 Robert Fletcher et al., 'Serpent Mound: A Fort Ancient Icon?', *Midcontinental Journal of Archaeology*, XXI/1 (1996), pp. 105–43.
8 Kent Reilly and James Garber, eds, *Ancient Objects and Sacred Realms: Interpretations of Mississippian Iconography* (Austin, TX, 2007), p. 132.
9 Ibid., p. 125.
10 Ibid., p. 126.
11 Polly Schaafsma, *Indian Rock Art of the Southwest* (Santa Fe, NM, 1980).
12 Polly Schaafsma and Karl Taube, 'Bringing the Rain: An Ideology of Rain-Making in the Pueblo South-West and MesoAmerica', in *A Pre-Colombian World*, ed. Jeffrey Quilter and Mary Miller (Washington, DC, 2006), pp. 231–85.
13 William Walker and Lisa Lucero, 'The Depositional History of Ritual and Power', in *Agency in Archaeology*, ed. M.-A. Dobres and J. Robb (London, 2000), pp. 130–47 (p. 132).
14 Rosemary Diaz, 'Avanyu: Spirit of Water in Pueblo Life and Art', *Bienvenidos* (2014), www.santafenewmexican.com.
15 Camille Tounouga, 'The Symbolic Function of Water in Sub-Saharan Africa', trans. Odile Brock, *Leonardo*, XXXVI/4 (2003), p. 283.
16 Luc De Heusch, *Sacrifice in Africa: A Structuralist Approach* (Bloomington, IN, 1985), pp. 38–9.
17 Ibid., p. 40.
18 Kenneth Little, 'The Mende in Sierra Leone', in *African Worlds: Studies in Cosmological Ideas and Social Values of African Peoples*, ed. Daryll Forde (Hamburg, 1999), pp. 111–37.
19 Günter Wagner, 'The Abaluyia of Kavirondo', in *African Worlds*, ed. Forde, pp. 27–54 (pp. 29, 33).
20 Colin Renfrew and Iain Morley, eds, *Becoming Human: Innovation in Prehistoric Material and Spiritual Culture* (Cambridge, 2009).
21 Amanda Mummert et al., 'Stature and Robusticity during the Agricultural Transition: Evidence from the Bioarchaeological Record', *Economics and Human Biology*, IX/3 (2011), pp. 284–301.

22 Jared Diamond, *Collapse: How Societies Choose to Fail or Succeed* (New York, 2005).
23 Joan Metge, *The Maoris of New Zealand* (London, 1967).
24 Johannes Anderson, 'Myths and Legends of the Polynesians', in *Treasury of Maori Folklore*, ed. A. Reed (Wellington, 1969), pp. 144–6.
25 Thomas Downes, 'Tutae-Poroporo', *Journal of the Polynesian Society*, XLV/177 (1936), pp. 1–4.
26 Jan Christie, 'Water and Rice in Early Java and Bali', in *A World of Water: Rain, Rivers and Seas in Southeast Asian Histories*, ed. P. Boomgaard (Leiden, 2007), pp. 235–58 (p. 235).
27 Stephen Lansing, *Priests and Programmers: Technologies of Power in the Engineered Landscape of Bali* (Princeton, NJ, and Oxford, 1991).
28 Lisa Lucero, 'A Cosmology of Conservation in the Ancient Maya World', *Journal of Anthropological Research*, LLXIV/3 (2018), pp. 327–59 (p. 327).
29 Luis Martos López, 'Objects Cast into Cenotes', in *Fiery Pool: The Maya and the Mythic Sea*, ed. Daniel Finamore and Stephen Houston (New Haven, CT, 2010), pp. 223–5 (p. 225).
30 Claus Deimel and Elke Ruhnau, *Jaguar and Serpent: The Cosmos of Indians in Mexico, Central and South America*, trans Ann Davis (Berlin, 2000), p. 14.
31 Ibid., p. 42.
32 Vernon Scarborough et al., 'Water and Sustainable Land Use at the Ancient Tropical Cty of Tikal, Guatemala', PNAS, CIX/31 (2012), pp. 12408–13; https://doi.org/10.1073/pnas.1202881109.
33 Vernon Scarborough, 'Ecology and Ritual: Water Management and the Maya', *Latin American Antiquity*, XI/2 (1998), pp. 135–59 (p. 135).
34 Lisa Lucero and Andrew Kinkella, 'Pilgrimage to the Edge of the Watery Underworld: An Ancient Maya Water Temple at Cara Blanca, Belize', *Cambridge Archaeological Journal*, XXV (2015), pp. 163–85.
35 Robert Sharer and Loa Traxler, *The Ancient Maya* (Stanford, CA, 2006); Walker and Lucero, 'The Depositional History of Ritual and Power', p. 131.
36 Scarborough, 'Ecology and Ritual', pp. 153, 155.
37 Daniel Finamore and Steven Houston, eds, *Fiery Pool: The Maya and the Mythic Sea* (Salem, MA, and New Haven, CT, 2010).
38 Lisa Lucero, 'A Cosmology of Conservation in the Ancient Maya World', *Journal of Anthropological Research*, XXIVI/3 (2018), pp. 327–59 (pp. 327–8). See also Vernon Scarborough, Lisa Lucero and Joel Gunn, 'Climate Change and Classic Maya Water Management', *Water*, Special Issue: *Managing Water Resources and Development in a Changing Climate*, 3 (2011), pp. 479–94.
39 Intergovernmental Science-Policy Platform on Biodiversity, Nature's Dangerous Decline "Unprecedented": Species Extinction Rates "Accelerating"', media release, 29 April 2019, https://ipbes.net.
40 World Bank, 'Water in Agriculture' (2020), www.worldbank.org.
41 Alfred Gell, 'The Technology of Enchantment and the Enchantment of Technology', in *Anthropology, Art and Aesthetics*, ed. J. Coote and A. Shelton (Oxford, 1992), pp. 40–66.
42 Karl Wittfogel, *Oriental Despotism: A Comparative Study of Total Power* (New Haven, CT, 1957).
43 Veronica Strang, 'Dam Nation: Cubbie Station and the Waters of the Darling', in *The Social Life of Water in a Time of Crisis*, ed. J. Wagner (Oxford and New York, 2013), pp. 36–60.
44 Stephen Lansing, 'Balinese "Water Temples" and the Management of Irrigation', *American Anthropologist*, XXXIX/2 (1987), pp. 326–41.
45 Karl Wittfogel, *The Hydraulic Civilization: Man's Role in Changing the Earth* (Chicago, IL, 1956).

6 Irrigating Beings

1 Friedrich Engels, *The Origin of the Family, Private Property and the State* [1894] (London, 1972). See also Arthur Hocart, *Kings and Councillors: An Essay in the Comparative Anatomy of Human Society* [1936] (Chicago, IL, and London, 1970).
2 Gayle Rubin, 'The Traffic in Women: Notes on the "Political Economy" of Sex', in *Toward an Anthropology of Women*, ed. R. Reiter (New York, 1975).
3 Hocart, *Kings and Councillors*; Michael Herzfeld, *The Social Production of Indifference: Exploring the Symbolic Roots of Western Bureaucracy* [1992] (London, 2021).
4 Veronica Strang, 'Infrastructural Relations: Water, Political Power and the Rise of a New "Despotic Regime"', *Water Alternatives*, Special Issue: *Water, Infrastructure and Political Rule*, XI/2 (2016), pp. 292–318.
5 Douglas Brewer, *Ancient Egypt: Foundations of a Civilization* (Harlow and New York, 2014).
6 Jonathan Sutherland and Diane Canwell, *Ancient Egypt* (Rochester, VT, 2007), p. 13.
7 Karl Butzer, *Early Hydraulic Civilisation in Egypt: A Study in Cultural Ecology* (Chicago, IL, 1976), p. 4.
8 Ian Shaw, *The Oxford History of Ancient Egypt* (Oxford, 2003).
9 Butzer, *Early Hydraulic Civilisation*, p. 41.
10 Asit Biswas, *History of Hydrology* (Amsterdam, 1970), p. 15.

11 Herodotus, *The Histories*, 2:99, trans. A. Godley (Cambridge, 1920).
12 Frederic Newhouse, M. Ionides and G. Lacey, eds, *Irrigation in Egypt, the Tigris and Euphrates Basin India and Pakistan* (London and New York, 1950), p. 11.
13 Joann Fletcher, *Ancient Egypt: Life, Myth and Art* (London, 1999), p. 131.
14 Paul Nicholson and Ian Shaw, *British Museum Dictionary of Ancient Egypt* (London, 1995), p. 45.
15 Robert Clark, *Myth and Symbol in Ancient Egypt* (London, 1959), p. 52. See also Alexander Broadie and J. Macdonald, 'The Concept of Cosmic Order in Ancient Egypt in Dynastic and Roman Times', *L'Antiquité Classique*, XLVII/1 (1978), pp. 106–28.
16 Ibid., p. 25.
17 Geraldine Pinch, *Handbook of Egyptian Mythology* (Santa Barbara, CA, 2002), p. 211.
18 Nicholson and Shaw, *British Museum Dictionary of Ancient Egypt*, p. 302.
19 William Cooper, *The Serpent Myths of Ancient Egypt* (Berwick, MW, 2005), p. 18.
20 Clark, *Myth and Symbol*, p. 28.
21 James Breasted, *Development of Religion and Thought in Ancient Egypt* (New York, 2010), p. 20.
22 Clark, *Myth and Symbol*, p. 11.
23 Ibid., p. 30.
24 Peter Clayton, *Chronicle of the Pharaohs* (London, 2006), p. 16.
25 Karen Joines, *Serpent Symbolism in the Old Testament: A Linguistic, Archaeological, and Literary Study* (Haddonfield, NJ, 1974), p. 19.
26 Nicholson and Shaw, *British Museum Dictionary of Ancient Egypt*, p. 302.
27 Robert Hannah, *Time in Antiquity* (London, 2009).
28 Newhouse, *Irrigation in Egypt*, p. 25.
29 Butzer, *Early Hydraulic Civilisation*, p. 109.
30 Code of Hammurapi, cited in Biswas, *History of Hydrology*, p. 20.
31 Marc Van de Mieroop, *King Hammurabi of Babylon: A Biography* (London, 2005), p. 126.
32 Stephanie Dalley, *The Mystery of the Hanging Garden of Babylon: An Elusive World Wonder Traced* (Oxford, 2013), p. 82.
33 Ibid., pp. 154–5.
34 Stephen Langdon, 'A Seal of Nidaba, the Goddess of Vegetation', *Proceedings of the Society of Biblical Archaeology*, XXXVI (1914), p. 281.
35 David Gilmore, *Monsters: Evil Beings, Mythical Beasts, and All Manner of Imaginary Terrors* (Philadelphia, PA, 2003).
36 Liviu Giosan et al., 'Fluvial Landscapes of the Harappan Civilization', *Proceedings of the National Academy of Sciences of the United States of America*, CIX/26 (2012), E1688–E1694.
37 Gerald Lacey, 'India and Pakistan', in *Irrigation in Egypt*, ed. Newhouse, Ionides and Lacey, pp. 32–67 (p. 39).
38 Arnold Pacey, *Technology in World Civilization: A Thousand-Year History* (Cambridge, MA, 1991).
39 Deepa Joshi and Ben Fawcett describe the contemporary relationship between water and caste in Chuni, northern India. In this well-watered village, there is an ancient jai devi (water goddess) temple that keeps the traditional irrigation channels (*guls*) flowing. The springs used by the upper castes are said to be the home of the jai devi, and are revered and worshipped in daily rituals. But water, seen as a purifying fluid, is also sprinkled on people belonging to the caste of Dalits, who are believed to be polluted and capable of polluting. Their access to springs and wells is limited, and punishment follows any transgression. Deepa Joshi and Ben Fawcett, 'Water, Hindu Mythology and an Unequal Social Order in India', in *A History of Water*, vol. III: *A World of Water*, ed. T. Tvedt and T. Oestigaard (London and New York, 2006), p. 12.
40 Emma Marris, 'Two-Hundred-Year Drought Doomed Indus Valley Civilisation', *Nature* (2014), https://doi.org/10.1038/nature.2014.14800.
41 Upinder Singh, *A History of Ancient and Early Medieval India: From the Stone Age to the 12th Century* (Delhi and London, 2008), p. 181.
42 Ahmed Kamal, 'Living with Water: Bangladesh since Ancient Times', in *A History of Water*, vol. I: *Water Control and River Biographies*, ed. T. Tvedt and E. Jakobsson, pp. 194–21 (p. 195).
43 Ibid., p. 196.
44 Ibn Battūta, *The Rehala of Ibn Battūta*, trans. M. Husain (Baroda, 1976).
45 John Marshall, ed., *Mohenjo-Daro and the Indus Civilization* (London, 1931).
46 Ankur Tewari, '5000-Year-Old Harappan Stepwell Found in Kutch, Bigger than Mohenjodaro's', *Times of India*, 8 October 2014.
47 Carol Bolon, *Forms of the Goddess Lajjā Gaurī in Indian Art* (University Park, PA, 1992), p. 3.
48 Ibid.
49 Madhu Wangu, *Images of Indian Goddesses: Myths, Meanings and Models* (New Delhi, 2003), pp. 5–86.
50 Bolon, *Forms of the Goddess Lajjā Gaurī*, p 4.
51 Jean-Philippe Vogel, 'Preface', in *Indian Serpent-Lore; or, The Nāgas in Hindu Legend and Art* (London, 1926), pp. i–ii.
52 Matthew Clark, *The Tawny One: Soma, Haoma and Ayahuasca* (London, 2017).
53 Vogel, *Indian Serpent-Lore*, p. 19.

54 David Shulman, 'The Serpent and the Sacrifice: An Anthill Myth from Tiruvārūr', *History of Religions*, XVIII/2 (1978), pp. 107–37.
55 Ravindran Nair, *Snake Worship in India* (New Delhi, 1973).
56 *Rigveda* (ix, 86, 44), trans. W. O'Flaherty (London, 1981).
57 *Tāṇḍya-Mahābrāhmaṇa* 25:15.
58 *Maitrāyani.sanhitā* ii.7.15, cited in Vogel, *Indian Serpent-Lore*, p. 7.
59 Ibid., p. 4.
60 Nair, *Snake Worship in India*.
61 Joshi and Fawcett, 'Water, Hindu Mythology', p. 121.
62 Partha Mitter, *Indian Art* (Oxford and New York, 2001).
63 Elizabeth Harding, *Kali: The Black Goddess of Dakshineswar* (Newburyport, MA, 1993).
64 Thomas Coburn, *Devī-Māhātmya: Crystallization of the Goddess Tradition* (Delhi, 1984).
65 *Bhāgavata Purāṇa*, Canto Ten.
66 Vogel, 'Preface', in *Indian Serpent-Lore*.
67 Dominik Wujastyk, '*The Path to Liberation through Yogic Mindfulness in Early Ayurveda*': *Yoga in Practice*, ed. D. White (Princeton, NJ, 2011).
68 Shulman, 'The Serpent and the Sacrifice', p. 107.
69 Norman Austin, *Meaning and Being in Myth* (London, 1989), p. 88.
70 *Bhāgavata Purāna*, Canto Ten.
71 Ibid.

7 Travelling Beings

1 Heather Sutherland, 'Geography as Destiny? The Role of Water in Southeast Asian History', in *A World of Water: Rain, Rivers and Seas in Southeast Asian Histories*, ed. P. Boomgaard (Leiden, 2007), pp. 27–70.
2 Johannes Gijsbertus De Casparis and Ian Mabbett, 'Religion and Popular Beliefs of Southeast Asia before *c.* 1500', in *The Cambridge History of Southeast Asia*, ed. Nicholas Tarling (Cambridge, 1999), pp. 276–334.
3 Monica Janowski, 'The Shape of Water: The Great Spirit Manifests as a Dragon', Borneo Research Council Conference, Kuching, Sarawak, 6–8 August 2018.
4 Korean National Folk Museum, 'From Nature to Human Beings', information panel, Gyeongbokgung Palace, Seoul, 2012.
5 Heo Gyun, *Korean Temple Motifs: Beautiful Symbols of the Buddhist Faith*, trans. Timothy Atkinson (Seoul, 2005), p. 23.
6 Ibid., p. 34.
7 Marinus de Visser, *The Dragon in China and Japan* (Amsterdam, 1913).
8 Helen Hardacre, *Shinto: A History* (Oxford, 2017).
9 Richard Bowring, *The Religious Traditions of Japan, 500–1600* (Cambridge, 2005).
10 Jan Christie, 'Water and Rice in Early Java and Bali', in *A World of Water*, ed. Boomgaard, pp. 235–58.
11 Francis Huxley, *The Dragon: Nature of Spirit, Spirit of Nature* (London, 1979), p. 15.
12 Emiko Ohnuki-Tierney, 'The Emperor of Japan as Deity (Kami)', *Ethnology*, XXX/3 (1991), pp. 199–215.
13 Bingxiang Zhu, *'Fuxi' and Chinese Culture* (Kunming, 2014), p. 2.
14 Kexin Liu et al., *Radiocarbon Dating of Oracle Bones of the Late Shang Period in Ancient China* (Cambridge 2020).
15 Zhu, *'Fuxi' and Chinese Culture*, p. 9.
16 Edward Schafer, *The Divine Woman: Dragon Ladies and Rain Maidens in T'ang Literature* (San Francisco, CA, 1980), p. 10.
17 De Visser, *The Dragon in China and Japan*, p. 38.
18 Wang Chong, *Lun heng* (first century), cited in Zhu, *'Fuxi' and Chinese Culture*, p. 2.
19 Ibid., p. 6.
20 Lu, *Lü Shi Chunqiu: Mr Lü's Spring and Autumn Annals*, *c.* 239 BCE, cited in Zhu, *'Fuxi' and Chinese Culture*, p. 9.
21 Jean-Philippe Vogel, *Indian Serpent-Lore; or, The Nāgas in Hindu Legend and Art* (London, 1926), p. 94.
22 Charles Oldham, *The Sun and the Serpent: A Contribution to the History of Serpent-Worship* (London, 2013), p. 50.
23 Zhu, *'Fuxi' and Chinese Culture*, pp. 3–4.
24 Xin He, *Dragon, Myth and Truth* (Shanghai, 1989), p. 23.
25 Zhu, *'Fuxi' and Chinese Culture*, pp. 6, 10.
26 Grafton Elliot Smith, *The Evolution of the Dragon* (Manchester, London and New York, 1919), p. 99.
27 Schafer, *The Divine Woman*, pp. 7–8.
28 Jianing Chen and Yang Yang, *The World of Chinese Myths* (Beijing, 1995), pp. 13, 26.
29 Susie Green, *Tiger* (London, 2006), pp. 39–40.
30 He, *Dragon, Myth and Truth*, pp. 2–3.
31 Florence Padovani, 'The Chinese Way of Harnessing Rivers: The Yangtze River', in *A History of Water*, vol. I: *Water Control and River Biographies*, ed. T. Tvedt and E. Jakobsson (London and New York, 2006), pp. 120–43 (p. 120).
32 David Pietz, 'Controlling the Waters in Twentieth-Century China: The Nationalist State and the Huai River', in *A History of Water*, vol. I, ed. Tvedt and Jakobsson, pp. 92–119 (pp. 92–3).
33 Padovani, 'The Chinese Way of Harnessing Rivers', p. 121.
34 Karl Wittfogel, *Oriental Despotism: A Comparative Study of Total Power* (New Haven, CT, 1957).

35 Schafer, *The Divine Woman*, p. 29.
36 Charles Gould, *Dragons, Unicorns, and Sea Serpents: A Classic Study of the Evidence for Their Existence* [1886] (Mineola, NY, 2002), p. 215.
37 Padovani, 'The Chinese Way of Harnessing Rivers', pp. 123–4.
38 Hampden DuBose, *The Dragon, Image, and Demon; or, The Three Religions of China: Confucianism, Buddhism and Taoism* (New York, 1887), p. 47.
39 Jane Harrison, *Prolegomena to the Study of Greek Religion* (Cambridge, 1908). See also Simon Price and Peter Thonemann, *The Birth of Classical Europe: A History from Troy to Augustine* (London, 2011).
40 Joseph Henderson and Maud Oakes, *The Wisdom of the Serpent: The Myths of Death, Rebirth, and Resurrection* (Princeton, NJ, 2020), p. 19. See also Marija Gimbutas, *Bronze Age Cultures in Central and Eastern Europe* (Berlin and Boston, MA, 2011).
41 Emily Bonney, 'Disarming the Snake Goddess: A Reconsideration of the Faience Figurines from the Temple Repositories at Knossos', *Journal of Mediterranean Archaeology*, XXIV/2 (2011), pp. 171–90.
42 Knowledge about the Pelasgians is fragmentary, but Homer and Herodotus suggest that they preceded or joined the people they recognized as Greek society. Homer, *Odyssey* 19.177; Herodotus, *Histories* 2.51.1.56, 7.94–5, 8.44.
43 Robert Graves, *The Greek Myths* (London, 1955), p. 27.
44 Marija Gimbutas, Shan Winn and Daniel Shimbaku, *Achilleion: A Neolithic Settlement in Thessaly, Greece, 6400–5600 BC* (Los Angeles, CA, 1989); Heide Goettner-Abendroth, ed., *Societies of Peace: Matriarchies Past, Present and Future* (Toronto, 2009). See Charlene Spretnak, *Lost Goddesses of Early Greece: A Collection of Pre-Hellenic Myths* (Boston, MA, 1992).
45 Hesiod, *Theogony* [*c.* 800–700 BCE], 116ff.
46 Plato, *Timaeus* [*c.* 360 BCE], 40e.
47 David Sacks, *Encyclopedia of the Ancient Greek World* (New York, 2005), pp. 49–50.
48 Barry Powell, *Classical Myth*, trans. H. Howe (Upper Saddle River, NJ, 1998), p. 368.
49 Mark Morford and Robert Lenardon, *Classical Mythology* (New York and Oxford, 1999).
50 Homer, *Iliad*, Book 14.
51 Hesiod, *Theogony* 133.
52 Johann Hofmann, *Etymologisches Wörterbuch des Griechischen* (Munich, 1950).
53 Robert Beekes, *Etymological Dictionary of Greek* (Leiden, 2009), pp. 1128–9. Georges Dumézil, *Ouranos-Varuna: Essai de Mythologie Comparée Indo-Européenne* (Paris, 1934).
54 Campbell, *Creative Mythology*.
55 Apollonius of Rhodes, *Argonautica* [3rd century BCE], 1.495f.
56 Ian Ridpath and Wil Tirion, *Stars and Planets Guide* (Princeton, NJ, 2001).
57 Julius Staal, *The New Patterns in the Sky* (Blacksburg, VA, 1988).
58 James Charlesworth, *The Good and Evil Serpent: How a Universal Symbol Became Christianized* (London and New Haven, CT, 2010).
59 Alex Wilder, *The Serpent Symbol* (London, 1894), p. 15.
60 Walter Burkert, *Greek Religion* (Cambridge, MA, 1985), pp. 23, 30.
61 Martin Nilsson, *Die Geschichte der Griechischen Religion* (Munich, 1967).
62 Harrison, *Prolegomena to the Study of Greek Religion*, p. 17.
63 Plutarch, *Life of Alexander* 3.2.
64 Herodotus, *Histories* 1.59.
65 Örjan Wikander, 'The Water-Mill', in *Handbook of Ancient Water Technology*, ed. Örjan Wikander (Leiden, 2000), pp 371–401.
66 Simon Price, *Rituals and Power: The Roman Imperial Cult in Asia Minor* (Cambridge, 1986).
67 Jörg Rüpke, ed., *A Companion to Roman Religion* (Oxford, 2011); Mary Beard, John North and Simon Price, *Religions of Rome*, vol. I: *A History* (Cambridge, 1998). See Arnold Jones, *Constantine and the Conversion of Europe* (London, 1948).
68 Charles Scott-Giles, *The Romance of Heraldry* (London and New York, 1957).
69 Vasile Pârvan, *Dacia: An Outline of the Early Civilization of the Carpatho-Danubian Countries* (Cambridge, 1928).
70 Aristotle, *History of Animals*, Book viii, Chap. xxvii.
71 Aëtius, *On the Opinions of the Philosophers* v.30.1. Hippocrates, *Airs, Waters, Places*: 1, 7, 8, 9; *Internal Affections*: 6, 21, 23, 26, 34, 45, 47; *Diseases* I: 24; *Epidemics* II: 2.11; *Epidemics* VI: 4.8, 4.17; *Aphorisms*: 5.26; *Humours*: 12; *Regimen* IV, *or Dreams*: 93.
72 Spretnak, *Lost Goddesses of Early Greece*, p. 18.
73 Valerius Flaccus, *Argonautica* 5.452, trans. Mozley, 1st century.
74 Pseudo-Apollodorus, *Bibliotheca* 1.146, trans. Aldrich, 1st century.
75 Apollonius of Rhodes, *Argonautica* 4.1515; Ovid, *Metamorphoses* 4.770; Lucan, *Pharsalia* 9.820.
76 Pliny the Elder, *Naturalis Historia: The Historie of the World* (Cambridge, MA, 1949).
77 Norman Austin, *Meaning and Being in Myth* (London, 1989), pp. 79–80.
78 Ibid., pp. 98–9.

8 Supreme Beings

1 Polanyi describes this process of abstraction and delocalization as a form of 'disembedding'. Karl Polanyi, *The Great Transformation* (Boston, MA, 1957).

2 Francesca Stavrakopoulou, *Land of Our Fathers: The Roles of Ancestor Veneration in Biblical Land Claims* (New York, 2010).

3 Francesca Stavrakopoulou and John Barton, eds, *Religious Diversity in Ancient Israel and Judah* (London, 2010).

4 Bernard Batto, *Slaying the Dragon: Mythmaking in the Biblical Tradition* (Louisville, KY, 1992), p. 1.

5 Arthur Hocart, 'The Origin of Monotheism', *Folklore*, XXXIII/3 (1922), pp. 282–93.

6 Pyramid Texts 1146. Cited in Rundle Clark, *Myth and Symbol in Ancient Egypt* (London, 1978), p. 51; John Day, *God's Conflict with the Dragon and the Sea: Echoes of a Canaanite Myth in the Old Testament* (Cambridge, 1985), p. 49.

7 Batto, *Slaying the Dragon*, p. 131.

8 Robert Miller, *Baal, St George, and Khidr: A Study of the Historical Geography of the Levant* (University Park, PA, 2019), p. 83.

9 Francesca Stavrakopoulou, *God: An Anatomy* (London, 2021).

10 1 Samuel 11. See also Leslie Wilson, *The Serpent Symbol in the Ancient Near East: Nahash and Asherah, Death, Life, and Healing* (Lanham, MD, 2001).

11 Wilder, *The Serpent Symbol*, p. 16.

12 Gary Varner, *Sacred Wells: A Study in the History, Meaning, and Mythology of Holy Wells and Waters* (New York, 2002), p. 14.

13 Campbell, *Creative Mythology*, p. 30.

14 Mary Condren, *The Serpent and the Goddess: Women, Religion, and Power in Celtic Ireland* (San Francisco, CA, 1989), p. 7.

15 Arvid Kapelrud in Johannes Botterweck, Heinz-Josef Fabry and Helmer Ringgren, eds, *Theological Dictionary of the Old Testament* IV (Grand Rapids, MI, 1981), pp. 257–9ff. See also Mark Lidzbarski, *Ephemeris für semitische Epigraphik* [1902] (Berlin, 2020).

16 Dennis Slifer, *The Serpent and the Sacred Fire: Fertility Images in Southwest Rock Art* (Santa Fe, NM, 2000), pp. 111–12.

17 John Day, *From Creation to Babel: Studies in Genesis 1–11* (London, 2013), pp. 54–5.

18 Arthur Basham, *The Wonder That Was India* (London, 1954).

19 William Cooper, *The Serpent Myths of Ancient Egypt* (Berwick, ME, 2005), p. 9.

20 Arthur Frothingham, 'Babylonian Origin of Hermes the Snake-God, and of the Caduceus', *American Journal of Archaeology*, XX (1916), pp. 175–211 (p. 181).

21 Mircea Eliade, *A History of Religious Ideas: From Gautama Buddha to the Triumph of Christianity*, trans. W. Trask (Chicago, IL, and London, 1982), pp. 401–2.

22 Herbert Cutner, *Jesus: God, Man, or Myth? An Examination of the Evidence* (Escondido, CA, 2000), p. 137.

23 Terence Mitchell, *The Bible in the British Museum* (London, 1988).

24 Apollonius Rhodius, *Argonautica* 2.1267ff., 3rd century BCE.

25 Martin Larson, *The Story of Christian Origins* (Washington, DC, 1977).

26 Sarah Stewart, ed., *The Everlasting Flame: Zoroastrianism in History and Imagination* (London, 2013).

27 Charles Penglase, *Greek Myths and Mesopotamia: Parallels and Influence in the Homeric Hymns and Hesiod* (New York, 1994).

28 Martin Nilsson, *Die Geschichte der Griechischen Religion* (Munich, 1967), p. 470.

29 Gordon Wasson, Carl Ruck and Albert Hofmann, *The Road to Eleusis: Unveiling the Secret of the Mysteries* (Berkeley, CA, 2008).

30 Joseph Henderson and Maud Oakes, *The Wisdom of the Serpent: The Myths of Death, Rebirth, and Resurrection* (Princeton, NJ, 2020), p. 19.

31 Barry Powell, *Classical Myth* (Upper Saddle River, NJ, 1998), pp. 105–7. See also Walter Otto, *Dionysus Myth and Cult* (Dallas, TX, 1981); and Karl Kerényi, *Dionysos: Archetypal Image of Indestructible Life* (Princeton, NJ, 1976).

32 Alain Daniélou, *Gods of Love and Ecstasy* (Rochester, VT, 1992), p. 15.

33 Michael Janda, *Die Musik nach dem Chaos* (Innsbruck, 2010).

34 Xavier Riu, *Dionysism and Comedy* (Lanham, MD, and Oxford, 1999), p. 105.

35 Kenneth Dover, ed., *Aristophanes, Frogs* (Oxford, 1993), p. 2.

36 Jonah 2:1, ET 1:17; Jonah 2:11, ET 2:10.

37 Day, *God's Conflict with the Dragon and the Sea*, p. 111.

38 Philip Gardiner and Gary Osborn, *The Serpent Grail: The Truth behind the Holy Grail, the Philosopher's Stone and the Elixir of Life* (London, 2005), p. 171.

39 Geraldine Pinch, *Handbook of Egyptian Mythology* (Santa Barbara, CA, 2002), p. 206.

40 Pope Pius XII, *Munificentissimus Deus: Defining the Dogma of the Assumption* (Rome, 1950), para. 44.

41 Stephanie Dalley, ed., *The Legacy of Mesopotamia* (Oxford, 1998), p. 65.

42 Catherine Keller, *The Face of the Deep: A Theology of Becoming* (Oxford and New York, 2003), p. xvii.
43 Ibid.
44 Morris Jastrow, *Aspects of Religious Belief and Practice in Babylonia and Assyria* (New York, 1910), pp. 71–2.
45 Psalm 29:3–6, cited ibid., p. 73.
46 Terje Oestigaard, 'The Topography of Holy Water in England after the Reformation', in *Perceptions of Water in Britain from Early Modern Times to the Present: An Introduction*, ed. K. V. Lykke Syse and T. Oestigaard (Bergen, 2010), pp. 15–34 (p. 27).
47 Adrian Armstrong and Margaret Armstrong, 'A Christian Perspective on Water and Water Rights', in *A History of Water*, vol. III: *A World of Water*, ed. T. Tvedt and T. Oestigaard (London and New York, 2006), pp. 367–84.
48 John Reeves, *Bible and Qur'ān: Essays in Scriptural Intertextuality* (Leiden, 2004).
49 Greg Fisher, ed., *Arabs and Empires Before Islam* (Oxford, London and New York, 2015), p. 118.
50 Qur'an 71:23.
51 Maulvi Ali, *The Holy Qur'an, with English Translation and Commentary* (Lahore, 1917).
52 Cyril Glassé, *The New Encyclopedia of Islam* (Walnut Creek, CA, 2001), p. 185.
53 David Leeming, *Jealous Gods and Chosen People: The Mythology of the Middle East* (Oxford and New York, 2004), p. 121.
54 Robert Morey, *The Moon-God Allah in the Archeology of the Middle East* (Newport, PA, 1994).
55 Arthur Jeffrey, *Islam: Muhammad and His Religion* (New York, 1958), p. 85; Timothy Tennent, *Theology in the Context of World Christianity: How the Global Church Is Influencing the Way We Think About and Discuss Theology* (Grand Rapids, MI, 2007), p. 7.
56 Gaston Maspero, *The Dawn of Civilization: Egypt and Chaldæa* (London, 1910).
57 Muhammad Al-Tabari, *The Last Years of the Prophet*, trans. Isma'il Qurban Husayn (New York, 1990); Gerald Hawting, *The Idea of Idolatry and the Emergence of Islam: From Polemic to History* (Cambridge, 1999).
58 John Healey, *The Religion of the Nabataeans: A Conspectus* (Leiden, 2001), p. 136.
59 John Esposito, ed., *The Oxford Encyclopedia of the Islamic World* (Oxford, 2009).
60 Al-Kisa'I, *Qisas Al-anbiya* (Tales of the Prophet) cited in Carole Hillenbrand, 'Gardens between Which Rivers Flow', in *Rivers of Paradise: Water in Islamic Art and Culture*, ed. S. Blair and J. Bloom (New Haven, CT, and London 2009), p. 27.
61 D. Fairchild Ruggles, 'From the Heavens and Hills: The Flow of Water to the Fruited Trees and Ablution Fountains in the Great Mosque of Cordoba', in Blair and Bloom, *Rivers of Paradise*, pp. 81–103 (p. 82).
62 Ahmad Ghabin, 'The Well of Zamzam: A Pilgrimage Site and Curative Water in Islam', in *Sacred Waters: A Cross-Cultural Compendium of Hallowed Springs and Holy Wells*, ed. C. Ray (London, 2020), pp. 71–9.
63 Hillenbrand, 'Gardens between Which Rivers Flow', pp. 31–2.
64 Seyyed Nasr, *An Introduction to Islamic Cosmological Doctrines: Conceptions of Nature and Methods Used for Its Study* (London, 1978), p. 78.
65 Ibid., p. 81.
66 Hillenbrand, 'Gardens between Which Rivers Flow', pp. 27–58 (p. 33).
67 Ibrham Özdemir, 'Environment', in *The Oxford Encyclopedia of Philosophy, Science, and Technology in Islam*, ed. Ibrahim Kalin (Oxford, 2014), pp. 198–202 (p. 199).

9 Demonized Beings

1 Val Plumwood, *Feminism and the Mastery of Nature* (London, 1993).
2 Joseph Campbell, *The Masks of God: Occidental Mythology* (New York, 1964), p. 17.
3 Karen Joines, *Serpent Symbolism in the Old Testament: A Linguistic, Archaeological, and Literary Study* (Haddonfield, NJ, 1974), pp. 43–4.
4 Mary Condren, *The Serpent and the Goddess: Women, Religion, and Power in Celtic Ireland* (San Francisco, CA, 1989), p. 8.
5 Joines, *Serpent Symbolism in the Old Testament*, p. 17.
6 James Fergusson, *Tree and Serpent Worship: Illustrations of Mythology and Art in India* (London, 1868), p. 9.
7 Ibid., p. 24.
8 Norman Austin, *Meaning and Being in Myth* (London, 1989), p. 7.
9 Catherine Nixey, *The Darkening Age: The Christian Destruction of the Classical World* (London, 2017).
10 Ann Ross, 'Ritual and the Druids', in *The Celtic World*, ed. M. Green (London, 1995), pp. 423–44.
11 David Rankin, 'The Celts through Classical Eyes', in *The Celtic World*, ed. Green, pp. 21–33 (p. 30).
12 Richard Bailey, *England's Earliest Sculptors* (Toronto, 1996), p. 94.
13 Janet Bord and Colin Bord, *Sacred Waters: Holy Wells and Water Lore in Britain and Ireland* (London, 1985), p. 18.
14 Jonathan Alexander, ed., *A Survey of Manuscripts Illuminated in the British Isles* (London, 1978), p. 9.
15 Terje Oestigaard, 'The Topography of Holy Water in England after the Reformation', in *Perceptions of Water*

in Britain from Early Modern Times to the Present: An Introduction, ed. K. V. Lykke Syse and T. Oestigaard (Bergen, 2010), pp. 15–34 (p. 16).

16 Peter Harrison, 'Subduing the Earth: Genesis 1, Early Modern Science, and the Exploitation of Nature', *Journal of Religion*, LXXIX/1 (1999), pp. 86–109 (p. 91).

17 Catherine Keller, *The Face of the Deep: A Theology of Becoming* (Oxford and New York, 2003), p. xvii.

18 Christine Rauer, *Beowulf and the Dragon: Parallels and Analogues* (Woodbridge, 2000), p. 69.

19 Louis Dumont, *La Tarasque: Essai de Description d'un Fait Local d'un Point du Vue Ethnographique* (Paris, 1951), cited in David Gilmore, *Monsters: Evil Beings, Mythical Beasts, and All Manner of Imaginary Terrors* (Philadelphia, PA, 2003), pp. 157–62.

20 Christina Hole, *English Folk-Heroes* (London, 1948), p. 114.

21 Silas Mallery, 'The Marriage Well at Teltown: Holy Well Ritual at Royal Cult Sites and the Rite of Temporary Marriage', *European Review of History*, XVIII/2 (2011), pp. 175–97.

22 Robert Steel, ed., *Medieval Lore: An Epitome of the Science, Geography, Animal and Plant Folk-Lore and Myth of the Middle Ages* (London, 1893), pp. 124–5, cited in Samantha Riches, *St George: Hero, Martyr and Myth* (Stroud, 2005), p. 142.

23 Paul Screeton, *Whisht Lads and Haad Your Gobs: The Lambton Worm and Other Northumbrian Dragon Legends* (Sunderland, 1998).

24 Francis Child, *The English and Scottish Popular Ballads* [1882] (New York, 1965), p. 306.

25 James Somerville, *Memorie of the Somervilles*, ed. W. Scott (Edinburgh, 1815).

26 Thomas Percy, 'Legend of Sir Guy', in *The Reliques of Ancient English Poetry* (London, 1765), pp. 103–11.

27 Screeton, *Whisht Lads and Haad Your Gobs*, n.p.

28 Frederick Hasluck, 'Dieudonné de Gozon and the Dragon of Rhodes', *Annual of the British School at Athens*, XX (1914), pp. 70–79.

29 Riches, *St George*, p. 1.

30 Jacobus De Voragine, *The Golden Legend* [*Legenda Aurea*], *c.* 1260 (London, 1878).

31 Riches, *St George*, p. 3.

32 Rauer, *Beowulf and the Dragon*, p. 13.

33 Riches, *St George*, p. 27.

34 Jesse Byock, *The Saga of the Volsungs: The Norse Epic of Sigurd the Dragon Slayer* (Berkeley, CA, 1990), p. 63.

35 Bailey, *England's Earliest Sculptors*, p. 93.

36 Rauer, *Beowulf and the Dragon*, pp. 42–3.

37 Adam Barkman, *Making Sense of Islamic Art and Architecture* (London, 2015), p. 74.

38 Charles Bright, *Sea Serpents* (Bowling Green, OH, 1991), pp. 4–5.

39 Grafton Elliot Smith, *The Evolution of the Dragon* (Manchester, 1919), p. 85.

40 Gilmore, *Monsters*, pp. 146–7.

41 Riches, *St George*, p. 33.

42 Robert Miller, *Baal, St George, and Khidr: A Study of the Historical Geography of the Levant* (University Park, PA, 2019), p. 8.

43 Ibid., p. 9.

44 Ibid., p. 2.

45 Ibid., p. 4.

46 Ibid., pp. 85–6.

47 Stefan Helmreich, 'The Genders of Waves', *Women's Studies Quarterly*, XLV/1/2 (2017), pp. 29–51.

48 Riches, *St George*, p. 156.

49 Francis Huxley, *The Dragon: Nature of Spirit, Spirit of Nature* (London, 1979), p. 15.

50 Bord and Bord, *Sacred Waters*, p. 114.

51 Jean D'Arras, *Le Livre de Mélusine* [1478], trans. A. Donald (London, 1985).

52 Riches, *St George*, pp. 169–72.

53 Condren, *The Serpent and the Goddess*, p. 5.

54 Éva Pócs, *Between the Living and the Dead: A Perspective on Witches and Seers in the Early Modern Age* (Budapest, 1999). See also Alan Macfarlane, *Witchcraft in Tudor and Stuart England* (London, 1999).

10 Reformed Beings

1 Charles Montalembert, *Les Moines d'Occident depuis Saint Benoît jusqu'à Saint Bernard* [The Monks of the West from Saint Benoit to Saint Bernard] (Paris, 1860). See also Katherine MacFarlane, 'Isidore of Seville on the Pagan Gods', *Transactions of the American Philosophical Society*, LLX/3 (1980), pp. 1–40.

2 Seyyed Nasr, *An Introduction to Islamic Cosmological Doctrines: Conceptions of Nature and Methods Used for Its Study* (London, 1978).

3 Judith Bennett and Warren Hollister, *Medieval Europe: A Short History* (New York, 2001).

4 David Whitehouse, *Renaissance Genius: Galileo Galilei and His Legacy to Modern Science* (London, 2009).

5 Katherine Park, 'Women, Gender, and Utopia: *The Death of Nature* and the Historiography of Early Modern Science', *Isis*, XCVII/3 (2006), p. 492. See also Jason Josephson-Storm, *The Myth of Disenchantment: Magic, Modernity, and the Birth of the Human Sciences* (Chicago, IL, 2017).

6 Robert Grosseteste, *Treatises. De colore, De iride*, *c.* 1220, see Amelia Sparavigna, 'On the Rainbow,

a Robert Grosseteste's Treatise on Optics', *International Journal of Sciences*, II /9 (2013), pp. 108–13.
7 Veronica Strang, *The Meaning of Water* (Oxford and New York, 2004).
8 Richard Holt, *The Mills of Medieval England* (Oxford, 1998).
9 Roberta Magnusson, 'Water and Wastes in Medieval London', in *A History of Water*, vol. II: *The Political Economy of Water*, ed. T. Tvedt and E. Jakobsson (London, 2006), pp. 299–313 (pp. 299–300).
10 Marjorie Honeybourne, 'The Fleet and Its Neighborhood in Early and Medieval Times', *Transactions of the London and Middlesex Archaeological Society*, XIX (1947), pp. 51–2.
11 Stefan Helmreich, 'Domesticating Waves in the Netherlands', BOMB *Magazine* (2019), pp. 153–8, https://bombmagazine.org.
12 Terje Oestigaard, 'The Topography of Holy Water in England after the Reformation', in *Perceptions of Water in Britain from Early Modern Times to the Present: An Introduction*, ed. K. V. Lykke Syse and T. Oestigaard (Bergen, 2010), pp. 15–34 (p. 15).
13 Arthur Gribben, *Holy Wells and Sacred Water Sources in Britain and Ireland* (London, 1992), p. 16.
14 Oestigaard, 'The Topography of Holy Water', p. 20.
15 Keith Thomas, *Religion and the Decline of Magic: Studies in Popular Beliefs in Sixteenth- and Seventeenth-Century England* (London, 1971).
16 Alain Corbin, *The Lure of the Sea: The Discovery of the Seaside in the Western World, 1750–1800* (Berkeley, CA, 1994), p. 7.
17 Yi-Fu Tuan, *The Hydrologic Cycle and the Wisdom of God: A Theme in Geoteleology* (Toronto, 1968).
18 Gilbert Lascault, *Le monstre dans l'art occidental: un problème esthétique* (Paris, 1973), p. 45.
19 David Gilmore, *Monsters: Evil Beings, Mythical Beasts, and All Manner of Imaginary Terrors* (Philadelphia, PA, 2003), p. 63.
20 Peter Harrison, 'Subduing the Earth: Genesis 1, Early Modern Science, and the Exploitation of Nature', *Journal of Religion*, LXXIX/1 (1999), pp. 86–109.
21 Veronica Strang, 'Dam Nation: Cubbie Station and the Waters of the Darling', in *The Social Life of Water in a Time of Crisis*, ed. J. Wagner (Oxford and New York, 2013), pp. 36–60.
22 Veronica Strang, *The Meaning of Water* (Oxford and New York, 2004).
23 Susan Anderson and Bruce Tabb, eds, *Water, Leisure and Culture: European Historical Perspectives* (Oxford and New York, 2002).
24 Erich Pontoppidan, *The Natural History of Norway*, trans. A. Berthelson (London, 1755).
25 Antoon Cornelis Oudemans, *The Great Sea-Serpent: An Historical and Critical Treatise* (Leiden and London, 1892).
26 Gilmore, *Monsters*, p. 66.
27 Samantha Riches, *St George: Hero, Martyr and Myth* (Stroud, 2005), pp. 131–2, 141.
28 Adrienne Mayor, *The First Fossil Hunters: Paleontology in Greek and Roman Times* (Princeton, NJ, 2000), p. 130.
29 Ivan Illich, *H_2O and the Waters of Forgetfulness* (London, 1986).
30 Andrea Ballestero, *A Future History of Water* (Durham, NC, 2019).
31 Jean-Pierre Goubert, *The Conquest of Water: The Advent of Health in the Industrial Age*, trans. A. Wilson (Princeton, NJ, 1986).
32 Matthew Gandy, 'Water, Modernity and the Demise of the Bacteriological City', in *A History of Water*, vol. I: *Water Control and River Biographies*, ed. T. Tvedt and E. Jakobsson (London, 2006), pp. 347–71 (p. 347).
33 Terje Tvedt and Eva Jakobsson, 'Introduction: Water History is World History', in *A History of Water*, vol. I, ed. Tvedt and Jakobsson, pp. ix–xxiii (p. xv).
34 Karl Marx, *Grundrisse: Foundations of the Critique of Political Economy*, trans. M. Nicolaus (New York, 1968), p. 410.
35 Max Weber, *The Protestant Ethic and the Spirit of Capitalism* [1905] (London, 2006).
36 Lynn White, 'The Historical Roots of Our Ecological Crisis', *Science*, CLV (1967), pp. 1203–7.
37 Kenneth Hall, 'Economic History of Southeast Asia', in *The Cambridge History of Southeast Asia*, ed. Nicholas Tarling (Cambridge, 1999), pp. 185–275 (p. 193).
38 Heather Sutherland, 'Geography as Destiny? The Role of Water in Southeast Asian History', in *A World of Water: Rain, Rivers and Seas in Southeast Asian Histories*, ed. P. Boomgaard (Leiden, 2007), pp. 27–70 (pp. 37, 43).
39 Ernestine Hill, *Water into Gold: The Taming of the Mighty Murray River* [1937] (London, 1958), p. v.
40 Ibid., pp. 38, 40.
41 Mark Cioc, 'Seeing Like the Prussian State: Re-Engineering the Rivers of Rhineland and Westphalia', in *A History of Water*, vol. I, ed. Tvedt and Jakobsson, pp. 239–52.
42 David Duke, 'Seizing Favours from Nature: The Rise and Fall of Siberian River Diversion', in *A History of Water*, vol. I, ed. Tvedt and Jakobsson, pp. 3–34 (p. 4).
43 Ahmed Kamal, 'Living with Water: Bangladesh since Ancient Times', in *A History of Water*, vol. I, ed. Tvedt and Jakobsson, pp. 194–213 (pp. 199–200).
44 Ibid., p. 207.

45 William Steele, 'The History of the Tama River: Social Reconstructions', in *A History of Water*, vol. I, ed. Tvedt and Jakobsson, pp. 217–38.

46 Florence Padovani, 'The Chinese Way of Harnessing Rivers: The Yangtze River', in *A History of Water*, vol. I, ed. Tvedt and Jakobsson, pp. 120–43 (p. 122).

47 David Pietz, 'Controlling the Waters in Twentieth-Century China: The Nationalist State and the Huai River', in *A History of Water*, vol. I, ed. Tvedt and Jakobsson, pp. 92–119 (pp. 92–3, 111).

48 Jiang Zemin was the general secretary of the Communist Party from 1989 to 2002, and president of the People's Republic of China from 1993 to 2003.

49 Kevin Wehr, *America's Fight over Water: The Environmental and Political Effects of Large-Scale Water Systems* (New York and London, 2004), p. 79.

50 Marc Reisner, *Cadillac Desert: The American West and Its Disappearing Water* (London, 2001).

51 UNU Institute for Water, Environment and Health, 'World Losing 2,000 Hectares of Farm Soil Daily to Salt-Induced Degradation' (2014), https://unu.edu.

52 Daniel Connell, *Water Politics in the Murray–Darling Basin* (Annandale, 2007).

53 Bruce Simmons and Jennifer Scott, 'The River Has Recorded the Story: Living with the Hawkesbury River, Sydney, NSW, Australia', in *A History of Water*, vol. I, ed. Tvedt and Jakobsson, pp. 253–76 (p. 254).

54 World Bank, 'Water in Agriculture' (2020), www.worldbank.org.

55 Patricia Sippel, 'Keeping Running Water Clean: Mining and Pollution in Pre-Industrial Japan', in *A History of Water*, vol. I, ed. Tvedt and Jakobsson, pp. 419–36 (p. 419).

56 Veronica Strang, 'Infrastructural Relations: Water, Political Power and the Rise of a New "Despotic Regime"', *Water Alternatives, Water, Infrastructure and Political Rule*, XI/2 (2016), pp. 292–318.

57 James Linton, *What Is Water? The History of a Modern Abstraction* (Vancouver and Toronto, 2010).

58 James Scott, *Seeing Like a State: How Certain Schemes to Improve the Human Condition Have Failed* (New Haven, CT, 2008).

59 International Union for the Conservation of Nature, 'The IUCN Red List of Threatened Species' (2019), www.iucnredlist.org.

60 Manuel Llano, *Mitos y Leyendas de Cantabria* (Myths and Legends of Cantabria) (Spain, 2001).

61 Alberto Álvarez Peña, *De las Formas de Matar al Cuélebre* (2008), http://fusionasturias.com.

62 Ibid.

63 Lorenzo DiTommaso, *The Book of Daniel and the Apocryphal Daniel Literature* (Leiden, 2005).

64 Adomnán of Iona, *Life of St Columba, c. 500–600*, trans. R. Sharpe (London, 1995), p. 176.

65 Clarence Leumane, composer, *The Lambton Worm* (Roud Folk Song Index #2337, 1867).

66 Lewis Carroll, *Jabberwocky: From Through the Looking Glass* [1871] (London, 1987). The original Cheshire Cat can also be found in Croft-on-Tees, as a stone carving at St Peter's Church.

67 Jean Scammell, 'The Origin and Limitations of the Liberty of Durham', *English Historical Review*, LXXXI/320 (1966), pp. 449–73.

68 Chris Lloyd, 'Bishop Crosses River for Sword That Slew Worm', *Northern Echo*, 26 November 2011, www.thenorthernecho.co.uk.

69 Mark Tallantire, 'Film of Bishop Justin's Installation' (enthronement ceremony), 26 November 2011, www.durham.anglican.org.

70 Veronica Strang, 'Reflecting Nature: Water Beings in History and Imagination', in *Waterworlds: Anthropology in Fluid Environments*, ed. K. Hastrup and F. Hastrup (Oxford and New York, 2015), pp. 248–78.

71 Stuart Jeffries, '"Swamped"and "Riddled": The Toxic Words That Wreck Public Discourse', *The Guardian*, 27 October 2014, www.theguardian.com.

72 Riches, *St George*, p. 178.

73 Laurence Michael Yep, *Dragon of the Lost Sea* (New York, 1982); Ryūnosuke Akutagawa, 'Dragon: The Old Potter's Tale', in *Rashōmon and 17 Other Stories* [1919], trans. J. Rubin (New York, 2006), pp. 3–9; Jeffrey Carver, *Dragons in the the Stars* (New York, 1992); Keith Baker, *Eberron* (Renton, WA, 2004).

74 Shōhei Imamura, dir., *Akai Hashi no Shita no Nurui Mizu/Warm Water under a Red Bridge* (2001).

75 Tom Mes, 'Review: *Warm Water under a Red Bridge*' (2001), www.midnighteye.com.

76 Hidenori Sugimori, dir, *Mizu no Onna (Woman of Water)* (2002).

77 Jonathan Schiff, dir., *H2O: Just Add Water* (2006).

78 Ken Russell, dir., *The Lair of the White Worm* (1988). See also Bram Stoker, *The Lair of the White Worm* (London, 1911).

79 Sarah Perry, *The Essex Serpent* (London, 2016).

80 Baker, *Eberron*.

81 Emily Rodda, *Deltora Quest* (Witney, Oxon, 2000–2005).

82 Robin Hobb, *Realm of the Elderlings* series (London 1995–2017).

83 Ursula Le Guin, *Earthsea* series (London and Boston, MA, 1964–2018).

84 George Martin, *A Game of Thrones* (London, 1996). Televised as the *Game of Thrones* series by HBO (New York, 2011–19)

85 Takehiro Watanabe, personal communication with the author, 2022.
86 Tetsya Yamauchi, dir, *The Magic Serpent* (1966).
87 Roberta MacAvoy, *Tea with the Black Dragon* (New York, 1983).
88 Joanne Bertin, *Dragonlord* (London, 1998–).
89 Ron Saunders, Claire Henderson and Xu Pei Xia, Xu Pei, prod., *The Magic Mountain* (Australia and China, 1997).
90 Robert Heinlein, *Between Worlds* (New York, 1951).
91 J.R.R. Tolkien, *The Hobbit* (London, 1937); J.R.R. Tolkien, *The Lord of the Rings* (London, 1954).
92 Rudyard Kipling, *The Jungle Book* (Project Gutenberg ebook, 2006 [1894]).
93 Wolfgang Reitherman, dir., *The Jungle Book* (1967); Jon Favreau, dir., *The Jungle Book* (2016).
94 John Bunyan, *The Pilgrim's Progress* (London, 1678); C. S. Lewis, *The Pilgrim's Regress* (London, 1933).
95 Lewis Carroll, *Through the Looking-Glass, and What Alice Found There* (London, 1871).
96 Larry Cohen, dir., *Q: The Winged Serpent* (1982).
97 Tony DiTerlizzi and Holly Black, *The Spiderwick Chronicles: The Wrath of Mulgarak* (New York, 2004); Tony DiTerlizzi and Holly Black, *Beyond the Spiderwick Chronicles: The Wyrm King* (New York, 2009).
98 Ray Bradbury, 'The Dragon', *Esquire* (August 1955).
99 Harry Turtledove, *Darkness/Derlavai* (New York, 1999–2004).
100 Jim Wynorski, dir., *Cry of the Winged Serpent* (2007).
101 Jane Yolen, *Pit Dragon Trilogy* [1982, 1984, 1987] (2005).
102 James Cameron, dir., *Avatar* (2009).
103 Diana Wynne-Jones, *Charmed Life* (London, 1977); Cressida Cowell, *How to Train Your Dragon* (2003–15).
104 Edith Nesbit, *The Last of the Dragons* (London, 1980).
105 Anne MacCaffrey, *Dragonriders of Pern* series (New York, 1967–2022); *Dragonsdawn: The Earliest Legend of Pern* (New York, 1988).
106 Steven Brust, *Vlad Taltos* (New York, 1990–).
107 Elizabeth Kerner, *Song in the Silence* (New York, 1997).
108 Guillermo del Toro, dir., *The Shape of Water* (2017).
109 James Cameron, dir., *The Abyss* (1989).

11 Transformational Beings

1 Roy Ellen, 'What Black Elk Left Unsaid: On the Illusory Images of Green Primitivism', *Anthropology Today*, II/6 (1986), pp. 8–13. See also Shepard Krech, *The Ecological Indian: Myth and History* (New York, 1999).
2 Ann Fienup-Riordan, *Eskimo Essays: Yup'ik Lives and How We See Them* (New Brunswick, NJ, 1990), p. 167.
3 Ann Fienup-Riordan, *Wise Words of the Yup'ik People: We Talk to You Because We Love You* (Lincoln, NE, 2018).
4 Ann Fienup-Riordan, 'Ella-gguq Allamek Yuituq/ They Say the World Contains No Others, Only Persons', *Hau: Journal of Ethnographic Theory*, VII/2 (2017), pp. 133–7.
5 Fienup-Riordan, *Eskimo Essays*, p. 168.
6 Ibid., p. 167.
7 Nancy Doubleday, 'Sustaining Arctic Visions, Values and Ecosystems: Writing Inuit Identity, Reading Inuit Art in Cape Dorset, Nunavut', in *Presenting and Representing Environments*, ed. G. Humphreys and M. Williams (Dordrecht, 2005), pp. 167–80.
8 Marshall Sahlins, 'The Original Political Society', *Hau: Journal of Ethnographic Theory*, VII/2 (2017), pp. 91–128 (p. 117).
9 Zongze Hu, 'The Travails of the Ninth Dragon God: The Struggle for Water, Worship and the Politics of Getting By in a North China Village', *Human Ecology*, XXXIX/1 (2011), pp. 81–91.
10 Ibid.
11 Ibid.
12 Ibid.
13 William Steele, 'The History of the Tama River: Social Reconstructions', in *A History of Water*, vol. I: *Water Control and River Biographies*, ed. T. Tvedt and E. Jakobsson (London, 2006), pp. 217–38 (p. 230).
14 Ibid., p. 233.
15 Yukihiro Morimoto, 'Rain Garden as Sustainable Urban Green Infrastructure Learned from Tradition', Urban Nature, Urban Culture symposium, Sophia University, Japan, 24 October 2021.
16 Lindsay Jones, *Encyclopedia of Religion* (New York, 2005), pp. 5071–4; John Breen and Mark Teeuwen, *Shinto in History* (London, 2000); Young-Sook Lee et al., 'Tracing Shintoism in Japanese Nature-Based Domestic Tourism Experiences', *Cogent Social Sciences*, IV/1 (2018).
17 Hidefumi Imura and Miranda Schreurs, eds, *Environmental Policy in Japan* (Cheltenham and Northampton, MA, 2005).
18 Peter Boomgaard, 'In a State of Flux: Water as a Deadly and a Life-Giving Force in Southeast Asia', in *A World of Water: Rain, Rivers and Seas in Southeast Asian Histories*, ed. P. Boomgaard (Leiden, 2007), pp. 1–23 (p. 5).
19 Stephen Headley, *Durga's Mosque: Cosmology, Conversion and Community in Central Javanese Islam* (Singapore, 2004).
20 Sandra Pannell, 'Of Gods and Monsters: Indigenous Sea Cosmologies, Promiscuous Geographies and the Depth of Local Sovereignty', in *A World of Water*, ed. Boomgaard, pp. 71–102.
21 Boomgaard, 'In a State of Flux', p. 1.

22 Barbara Andaya and Yoneo Ishii, 'Religious Development in Southeast Asia, *c.* 1500–1800, in *The Cambridge History of Southeast Asia*, vols I–II: *From c. 1500 to c. 1800*, ed. N. Tarling (Cambridge, 1999), pp. 508–71 (p. 509).
23 Jullen Goalabre, 'Our Duty to Agama Tirtha: The Religion of Holy Water' (2019), www.desaseni.com.
24 Paula Uimonen, 'Whales of Power' (2021), www.hf.uio.no.
25 Felix Meier zu Selhausen and Jacob Weisdorf, 'A Colonial Legacy of African Gender Inequality? Evidence from Christian Kampala, 1895–2011', *Economic History Review*, LXIX/1 (2016), pp. 229–57.
26 Matthew Schoffeleers, *River of Blood: The Genesis of a Martyr Cult in Southern Malawi, C.A.D. 1600* (Madison, WI, 1992), p. 5.
27 Ibid.
28 Menno Welling, fieldwork interview with the author, 2013.
29 David Nangoma, fieldwork interview with the author, 2013.
30 Steve Chimombo, fieldwork interview with the author, 2013. See also Steve Chimombo, *The Wrath of Napolo* (Malawi, 2000).
31 Zondiwe Mbano. 'Prayer for Rain', *Zondiwe's Water Poems*, p. 3. With permission from the author.
32 Ibid., p. 6.
33 Kefiloe Sello, 'Rivers That Become Reservoirs: An Ethnography of Water Commodification in Lesotho', PhD thesis, University of Cape Town, 2021.
34 Paula Uimonen, *Invoking Flora Nwapa: Nigerian Woman Writers, Femininity and Spirituality in World Literature* (Stockholm, 2020), https://doi.org/10.16993/bbe.
35 Henry Drewal, *Sacred Waters: Arts for Mami Wata and Other Water Divinities in Africa and the Diaspora* (Bloomington, IN, 2008), pp. 1–2.
36 Ibid., p. 2.
37 Ibid., p. 18.
38 Simon Coleman and Mike Crang, eds, *Tourism: Between Place and Performance* (Oxford, 2002). See also Xianghong Feng, 'Who Benefits? Tourism Development in Fenghuang County, China', *Human Organization*, LXVII/2 (2008), pp. 207–21; Veronica Strang, 'Sustaining Tourism in Far North Queensland', in *People and Tourism in Fragile Environments*, ed. Martin Price (London, 1996), pp. 51–67.
39 Claus Deimel and Elke Ruhnau, *Jaguar and Serpent: The Cosmos of Indians in Mexico, Central and South America*, trans. Ann Davis (Berlin, 2000), p. 153.
40 Ibid.
41 Penny Dransart, ed., *Kay Pacha: Cultivating Earth and Water in the Andes*, British Archaeological Reports, S1478 (Oxford, 2006).
42 Jeanette Sherbondy, 'Water Ideology in Inca Ethnogenesis', in *Andean Cosmologies through Time: Persistence and Emergence*, ed. R. Dover, K. Seibold and J. McDowell (Bloomington, IN, 1992), pp. 46–66.
43 Dransart, *Kay Pacha*, p. 11.
44 Sarah Bennison, 'Who Are the Children of Pariacaca? Exploring Identity through Narratives of Water and Landscape in Huarochirí, Peru', PhD thesis, Newcastle University, 2016, p. 82.
45 Penny Dransart and Marietta Ortega Perrier, 'When the Winds Run with the Earth: Cannibal Winds and Climate Disruption in Isluga, Northern Chile', *Current Anthropology*, LXII/1 (2021), pp. 101–9 (p. 101).
46 Barbara Göbel, 'Dangers, Experience and Luck: Living with Uncertainty in the Andes', in *Culture and the Changing Environment: Uncertainty, Cognition and Risk Management in Cross Cultural Perspective*, ed. M. Casimir (New York, 2008), pp. 221–50.
47 Rutgerd Boelens and Paul Gelles, 'Cultural Politics, Communal Resistance and Identity in Andean Irrigation Development', *Bulletin of Latin American Research*, XXIV/3 (2005), pp. 311–27.
48 Isabelle Stengers, 'The Cosmopolitical Proposal', in *Making Things Public: Atmospheres of Democracy*, ed. Bruno Latour and Peter Weibel (Cambridge, MA, 2005), pp. 994–1005.
49 Marisol de la Cadena, 'Indigenous Cosmopolitics in the Andes: Conceptual Reflections beyond "Politics"', *Cultural Anthropology*, XXV/2 (2010), pp. 334–70 (p. 334).
50 Alan Ereira, dir., *From the Heart of the World: Elder Brothers' Warning* (1990).
51 Alan Ereira, dir., *Aluna* (2012).
52 Bishop Athanasius Schneider, open letter, 26 October 2019 (Astana, Kazakhstan), Life Site News, https://www.lifesitenews.com.
53 Deborah Pinto, '"Stampede" of Legislation Threatens Destruction of the Amazon', trans. Maya Johnson, Unidades de Conservação no Brasil, Institutio Socioambiental, 26 July 2021, https://news.mongabay.com.
54 Anastasia Moloney, 'Amazon Ancestral Land Not Up for Sale Says "Green Nobel" Winner', Thomson Reuters Foundation News, 30 November 2020.
55 Stephen Muecke, 'The Cassowary Is Indifferent to All This', *Rhizomes: Cultural Studies in Emerging Knowledge*, XV/1 (2007).
56 Francesca Merlan, *Caging the Rainbow: Places, Politics and Aborigines in a North Australian Town* (Honolulu, HI, 1998), p. 70.
57 Howard Morphy, '"Not Just Pretty Pictures": Relative Autonomy and the Articulations of Yolngu Art in Its

Contexts', in *Ownership and Appropriation*, ed. Veronica Strang and Mark Busse (Oxford, 2011), pp. 261–86.

58 Howard Morphy, 'Art as Action: The Yolngu', in *Up Close and Personal: On Peripheral Perspectives and the Production of Anthropological Knowledge*, ed. Chris Shore and Susanna Trnka (New York, 2013), pp. 125–39.

59 Merlan, *Caging the Rainbow*, p. 70.

60 Ibid., pp. 50–51.

61 Veronica Strang, 'Not So Black and White: The Effects of Aboriginal Law on Australian Legislation', in *Mythical Lands, Legal Boundaries: Rites and Rights in Historical and Cultural Context*, ed. A. Abramson and D. Theodossopoulos (London, 2000), pp. 93–115.

62 Francis Morphy and Howard Morphy, 'The Blue Mud Bay Case: Refractions through Saltwater Country', *Dialogue*, XXVIII/1 (2009), pp. 15–25.

63 Chief Arvol Looking Horse, 'Standing Rock Is Everywhere: One Year Later', *The Guardian*, 22 February 2018, www.theguardian.com.

64 Earth Justice (2021), https://earthjustice.org.

65 Julia Wong, 'Police Remove Last Standing Rock Protesters in Military-Style Takeover', *The Guardian*, 23 February 2017, www.theguardian.com.

66 Government of Canada, The Canadian Constitution Act 1982: Section 35 (1982).

67 Eriel Deranger (Athabasca Chipewyan First Nations), www.idlenomore.ca, accessed 30 January 2019.

68 Judith Binney, 'Ancestral Voices: Maori Prophet Leaders', in *The Oxford Illustrated History of New Zealand*, ed. K. Sinclair (Oxford and Auckland, 1990), pp. 153–84 (p. 155).

69 Veronica Strang, 'The Taniwha and the Crown: Defending Water Rights in Aotearoa/New Zealand', *WIREs Water*, 1 (2014), pp. 121–31; Veronica Strang and Mark Busse, *Taniwha Springs – Indigenous Rights and Interests in Water: Comparative and International Perspectives* (Auckland, 2009), p. 5; Veronica Strang, 'Comparative International Claims to Water and Water Management by Indigenous Peoples', WAI 2358, Waitangi Tribunal, High Court, Supreme Court (New Zealand, 2012).

70 Rob Harris, 'Marking a Place for Taniwha in Culture and Law', *Resource Management Journal*, XI/1 (2003), pp. 18–22. See also David Round, 'Here Be Dragons', *Otago Law Review*, XI/1 (2005), pp. 31–51.

71 Ian McDuff, 'What Would You Do – With a *Taniwha* at the Table?', *Negotiation Journal*, XIX/3 (2003), pp. 195–8.

72 Strang and Busse, *Taniwha Springs*, p. 4.

73 Marae TVNZ, 'NZ Māori Council Co-Chair Sir Eddie Durie Says Claim Does Not Cover All NZ Water', *Marae Investigates*, 13 August 2012.

74 Jacinta Ruru, 'Māori Rights in Water: The Waitangi Tribunal's Interim Report', *Māori Law Review* (September 2012), http://māorilawreview.co.nz.

75 Supreme Court of New Zealand, Ruling SC 98/2012 [2013] NZSC 6: 'New Zealand Maori Council, Waikato River and Dams Claim Trust vs. The Attorney General, The Minister of Finance, the Minister for State Enterprises', 27 February 2013.

Turning the Tide

1 Émile Durkheim, *The Elementary Forms of the Religious Life* [1912] (New York, 1961).

2 Ivan Illich, 'The Shadow Our Future Throws', *New Perspectives Quarterly*, XVI/2 (1999), pp. 14–18.

3 Dennis Rodgers and Bruce O'Neill, 'Infrastructural Violence: Introduction to the Special Issue', *Ethnography*, XIII/4 (2012), pp. 401–12.

4 Volodymyr Vernadsky, *The Biosphere* [1920] (Santa Fe, NM, 1986).

5 Lynn Margulis, *The Symbiotic Planet: A New Look at Evolution* (London, 1998); James Lovelock, *Gaia: A New Look at Life on Earth* [1979] (Oxford, 1987).

6 Mark McMenamin and Dianna McMenamin, *Hypersea: Life on the Land* (New York, 1994).

7 Veronica Strang, 'A Happy Coincidence? Symbiosis and Synthesis in Anthropological and Indigenous Knowledges', *Current Anthropology*, XLVII/6 (2006), pp. 981–1008.

8 Penny Harvey, Christian Krohn-Hansen and Knut Nustad, *Anthropos and the Material* (Durham, NC, 2019). See also Noortje Marres, *Material Participation: Technology, the Environment and Everyday Publics* (Basingstoke, 2012); Paulo Savaget, Martin Geissdoerfer, Ali Kharrazi and Steve Evans, 'The Theoretical Foundations of Sociotechnical Systems Change for Sustainability: A Systematic Literature Review', *Journal of Cleaner Production*, CCVI (2019), pp. 878–92.

9 Bruno Latour, *Politics of Nature: How to Bring the Sciences into Democracy* (Cambridge, MA, 2004).

10 Langdon Winner, 'Do Artifacts Have Politics?', *Daedalus*, CIX/1 (1980), pp. 121–36.

11 Jane Bennett, *Vibrant Matter: A Political Ecology of Things* (Durham, NC, and London, 2009); Diana Coole and Samantha Frost, eds, *New Materialisms: Ontology, Agency and Politics* (Durham, NC, and London, 2010).

12 Anna Tsing, *Friction: An Ethnography of Global Connections* (Princeton, NJ, and Oxford, 2004).

13 Matthew Edgeworth, *Fluid Pasts: Archaeology of Flow* (London, 2011). See also Veronica Strang, 'Fluid Consistencies: Material Rationality in Human

Engagements with Water', *Archaeological Dialogues*, xxi/2 (2014), pp. 133–50.

14 Charles Percy Snow, *The Two Cultures* [1959] (London, 2001).

15 Carolyn Merchant, *The Death of Nature: Women, Ecology and the Scientific Revolution* (San Francisco, CA, 1980). See also Val Plumwood, *Feminism and the Mastery of Nature* (London, 1993); Carolyn Merchant, 'Environmentalism: From the Control of Nature to Partnership', public lecture, University of California, 2010; Susan Griffin, *Woman and Nature: The Roaring Inside Her* [1978] (New York, 2015).

16 Philip Larkin, 'Water', available at http://famouspoetsandpoems.com.

17 Bron Taylor, *Dark Green Religion: Nature Spirituality and the Planetary Future* (Berkeley and Los Angeles, CA, 2010).

18 Office for National Statistics, *Census UK: 2011* (London, 2011).

19 Office for National Statistics, *Population Estimates by Ethnic Group and Religion, England and Wales: 2019* (London, 2019).

20 Yerevan Gagik Artsruni, 'The Pantheon of Armenian Pagan Deities', in *Armenian Myths and Legends: The History of the Mythology and Folk Tales from Armenia*, ed. Charles River Editors (Boston, MA, 2003), p. 107.

21 Barbara Bender, *Stonehenge: Making Space* (Oxford, 1998).

22 Susan Anderson and Bruce Tabb, eds, *Water, Leisure and Culture: European Historical Perspectives* (Oxford and New York, 2002).

23 Veronica Strang, *The Meaning of Water* (Oxford and New York, 2004).

24 Catherine Knight, *Nature and Wellbeing in Aotearoa New Zealand* (Canterbury, NZ, 2020).

25 Jonathan Woolley, personal communication with the author (2017).

26 Veronica Strang, 'Making a Splash! Water Rituals, Subversion and Environmental Values in Queensland', Conference of the Association of Social Anthropologists and the Commonwealth (Edinburgh, 2005).

27 Reducing the body to its chemical components using lye and heat, resomation produces a small amount of ash and liquid. Requiring less energy, it is more ecologically sustainable than conventional cremation, and produces less CO_2 and other pollutants. It was originally developed in the late 1800s as a way of processing animal carcasses into plant food, and was taken up in 2007 by a Scottish biochemist, Sandy Sullivan, who began making contemporary machinery that would perform this function.

28 Megan Aldrich and Robert Wallis, eds, *Antiquaries and Archaists: The Past in the Past, the Past in the Present* (Reading, 2009); Jonathan Benthall, *Returning to Religion: Why a Secular Age Is Haunted by Faith* (London, 2009).

29 Strang, *The Meaning of Water.*

30 Kay Milton, *Loving Nature: Towards an Ecology of Emotion* (London and New York, 2002). See also Arne Naess, 'Identification as a Source of Deep Ecological Attitudes', in *Deep Ecology*, ed. M. Tobias (San Diego, CA, 1985), pp. 256–70.

31 Aristotle, *Nicomachean Ethics* (*c.* 335–322 BCE).

32 Edward Wilson, *Biophilia* (Cambridge, MA, 1984); Richard Louv, *Last Child in the Woods: Saving Our Children from Nature-Deficit Disorder* (Chapel Hill, NC, 2005).

33 Daryll Macer and Morita Masuru, 'Nature, Life and Water Ethics', *Eubios: Journal of Asian and International Bioethics*, XII (2002), pp. 82–8; Deborah Bird Rose, 'Fresh Water Rights and Biophilia: Indigenous Australian Perspectives', *Dialogue*, XXIII/3 (2004), pp. 35–43 (p. 41).

34 Andy Clark and David Chalmers, 'The Extended Mind', *Analysis*, LVIII (1998), pp. 7–19; Strang, 'Fluid Consistencies'.

35 James Serpell, *In the Company of Animals: A Study of Human–Animal Relationships* (Cambridge, 1996). See also Barbara Noske, *Beyond Boundaries: Humans and Animals* (Montreal, 1997); and Katherine Wills Perlo, *Kinship and Killing: The Animal in World Religions* (New York, 2009).

36 Eben Kirksey and Stefan Helmreich, 'The Emergence of Multispecies Ethnography', *Cultural Anthropology*, XXV/4 (2010), pp. 545–76. See also Donna Haraway, *When Species Meet* (Minneapolis, MA, 2008).

37 Louv, *Last Child in the Woods.*

38 Joanna Overing, 'Images of Cannibalism, Death and Domination in a "Non-Violent" Society', in *The Anthropology of Violence*, ed. David Riches (Oxford, 1986), pp. 86–102.

39 Peter Singer, *Animal Liberation* (London, 1975).

40 David Groenfeldt, *Water Ethics: A Values Approach to Solving the Water Crisis* (London, 2019). See also Macer and Masuru, 'Nature, Life and Water Ethics'.

41 Gabriel Eckstein et al., 'Conferring Legal Personality on the World's Rivers: A Brief Intellectual Assessment', *Water International*, I (2019), https://scholarship.law.tamu.edu. See also the International Water Law Project, www.internationalwaterlaw.org, accessed 18 March 2022.

42 Marama Muru-Lanning, 'Tupuna Awa and Te Awa Tupuna: Competing Discourses of the Wakiato River',

PhD thesis, University of Auckland (2010), p. ii. See also Marama Muru-Lanning, *Tupuna Awa: People and Politics of the Waikato River* (Auckland, 2016).

43 New Zealand Government, Waitangi Tribunal, 'Te Ika Whenua Report' (Wellington, 1998).

44 Veronica Strang, 'The Rights of the River: Water, Culture and Ecological Justice', in *People and Parks: Integrating Social and Ecological Justice*, ed. H. Kopnina and H. Washington (New York and London, 2019), pp. 105–19.

45 New Zealand Government, 'Te Urewera Act' (Wellington, 2014), www.legislation.govt.nz. See also Christopher Stone, 'Should Trees Have Standing: Toward Legal Rights for Natural Objects', *Southern California Law Review*, XLV (1972), pp. 450–501.

46 New Zealand Government, 'Te Awa Tupua (Whanganui River) Claims Settlement Bill' (Wellington, 2017), www.legislation.govt.nz. See also Liz Charpleix, 'The Whanganui River as Te Awa Tupua: Place-Based Law in a Legally Pluralistic Society', *Geography Journal*, CLXXXIV/1 (2017), https://doi.org/10.1111/geoj.12238.

47 New Zealand Government, 'Te Awa Tupua'.

48 Jacinta Ruru, 'Indigenous Restitution in Settling Water Claims: The Developing Cultural and Commercial Redress Opportunities in Aotearoa, New Zealand', *Pacific Rim Law and Policy Journal*, XXII/2 (2013), pp. 311–28, https://digital.law.washington.edu.

49 Philipp Wesche, 'Rights of Nature in Practice: A Case Study on the Impacts of the Colombian Atrato River Decision', *Journal of Environmental Law*, XXXIII/3 (2021), pp. 531–55.

50 Joe Nangan, quoted in Martuwarra RiverOfLife et al., 'Yoongoorrookoo: The Emergence of Ancestral Personhood', *Griffith Law Review*, November 2021, DOI: 10.1080/10383441.2021.1996882.

51 Juan Francisco Salazar, 'Buen Vivir: South America's Rethinking of the Future We Want', *The Conversation*, 24 July 2015, https://theconversation.com.

52 Nurit Bird-David, '"Animism" Revisited: Personhood, Environment and Relational Epistemology', *Current Anthropology*, XL Supplement (1999), pp. 67–91. See also Graham Harvey, *Animism: Respecting the Living World* (London, 2005).

53 Cormac Cullinan, *Wild Law: A Manifesto for Earth Justice* (Totnes, 2003). See also Brian Baxter, *A Theory of Ecological Justice* (London and New York, 2005); Joe Gray and Patrick Curry, 'Ecodemocracy: Helping Wildlife's Right to Survive', ECOS, XXVII/1 (2016), pp. 18–27.

54 Earth Law Centre, 'Universal Declaration of River Rights' (2018), https://therightsofnature.org.

55 Global Alliance for the Rights of Nature, 'Universal Declaration of the Rights of Rivers' (2018), p. 4, www.earthlawcenter.org.

56 Bettina Wilk et al., 'The Potential Limitations on Its Basin Decision-Making Processes of Granting Self-Defence Rights to Father Rhine', *Water International*, XLIV/6–7 (2019), pp. 684–700.

56 Polly Higgins, 'One Law to Protect the Earth' (2019), https://eradicatingecocide.com.

58 Ibid.

59 Haroon Siddique, 'Ecocide Defined to Establish New Global Crime', *The Guardian*, 23 June 2021.

60 Gray and Curry, 'Ecodemocracy'.

61 Benedict Anderson, *Imagined Communities: Reflections on the Origin and Spread of Nationalism* (London, 2006).

62 Veronica Strang, 'Re-Imagined Communities: The Transformational Potential of Interspecies Ethnography in Water Policy Development', in *The Oxford Handbook of Water Politics and Policy*, ed. K. Conca and E. Weinthal (Oxford and New York, 2017), pp. 142–64. See also Carl Knappett and Lambros Malafouris, eds, *Material Agency: Towards a Non-Anthropocentric Approach* (New York, 2008).

63 Robyn Eckersley, 'Deliberative Democracy, Ecological Representation and Risk: Towards a Democracy of the Affected', in *Democratic Innovations: Deliberation, Association and Representation*, ed. Michael Saward (London, 2000), pp. 117–45. See also Eva Meijer, *When Animals Speak: Toward an Interspecies Democracy* (New York, 2019).

64 Karen Barad, *Meeting the Universe Halfway: Quantum Physics and the Entanglement of Matter and Meaning* (Durham, NC, 2007).

65 Isabelle Stengers, 'The Cosmopolitical Proposal', in *Making Things Public: Atmospheres of Democracy*, ed. Bruno Latour and Peter Weibel (Cambridge, MA, 2005). See also Richard Grusin, ed., *The Nonhuman Turn* (Minneapolis, MN, 2015); Steve Hinchliffe, Matthew Kearnes, Monica Degen and Sarah Whatmore, 'Urban Wild Things: A Cosmopolitical Experiment', *Environment and Planning D: Society and Space*, XXIII (2005), pp. 643–58; Latour, *Politics of Nature*.

66 Stacy Alaimo, *Bodily Natures: Science, Environment, and the Material Self* (Bloomington, IN, 2010). See also Andrew Dobson, 'Democracy and Nature: Speaking and Listening', *Political Studies*, LVIII (2010), pp. 752–68.

66 Steve Hinchliffe, 'More Than One World, More Than One Health: Re-Configuring Interspecies Health', *Social Science and Medicine*, CXXIX (2015), pp. 28–35. See also Astrida Neimanis, *Bodies of Water: Posthuman Feminist Phenomenology* (London, 2017).

68 Earth Law Centre, 'Universal Declaration of River Rights'.

69 Veronica Strang, 'A Sustainable Future for Water', *Aqua: Journal of the International Water Association* (2020), https://doi.org/10.2166/aqua.2020.101.

70 Veronica Strang, 'Leadership in Principle: Uniting Nations to Recognize the Cultural Values of Water', in *Hydrohumanities: Water Discourse and Environmental Futures*, ed. R. Faletti, I. López-Calvo and K. De Wolff (Berkeley, CA, 2020), pp. 215–41.

71 Peter Stott, *Hot Air: The Inside Story of the Battle against Climate Change Denial* (London, 2021).

72 United Nations, 'Principles for Water' (2018), https://sustainabledevelopment.un.org.

73 Veronica Strang, 'Valuing the Cultural and Spiritual Dimensions of Water', Report to the United Nations High-Level Panel on Water (The Hague, 2017).

74 United Nations, 'World Water Development Report 2018: Nature-Based Solutions for Water', www.unwater.org. United Nations World Water Development Report 2021, 'Valuing Water', www.unwater.org; United Nations World Water Development Report 2022, 'Groundwater: Making the Invisible Visible', www.unwater.org.

75 Marie-Lise Schläppy, 'Rights of Nature: A Report on a Conference in Switzerland', *Ecological Citizen*, I/1 (2017), pp. 95–6.

76 Mark Mazower, *Governing the World: The History of an Idea* (London, 2013). See also Anne-Marie Slaughter, *A New World Order* (Princeton, NJ, 2005); Richard Haass, *The World: A Brief Introduction* (New York, 2020).

77 Richard Haass and Charles Kupchan, 'A Concert of Power for a Global Era', *Project Syndicate*, 25 March 2021, www.project-syndicate.org.

SELECT BIBLIOGRAPHY

Baxter, Brian, *A Theory of Ecological Justice* (London and New York, 2005)

Bolon, Carol, *Forms of the Goddess Lajjā Gaurī in Indian Art* (University Park, PA, 1992)

Campbell, Joseph, *The Masks of God: Creative Mythology* (London, 2001)

Condren, Mary, *The Serpent and the Goddess: Women, Religion, and Power in Celtic Ireland* (San Francisco, CA, 1989)

Day, John, *God's Conflict with the Dragon and the Sea: Echoes of a Canaanite Myth in the Old Testament* (Cambridge, 1985)

Diamond, Jared, *Collapse: How Societies Choose to Fail or Succeed* (New York, 2005)

Diemel, Claus, and Elke Ruhnau, eds, *Jaguar and Serpent: The Cosmos of Indians in Mexico, Central and South America*, trans. Ann Davis (Berlin, 2000)

Drewal, Henry, *Sacred Waters: Arts for Mami Wata and Other Water Divinities in Africa and the Diaspora* (Bloomington, IN, 2008)

Ferguson, Diana, *Tales of the Plumed Serpent: Aztec, Inca and Mayan Myths* (London, 2000)

Fienup-Riordan, Ann, *Wise Words of the Yup'ik People: We Talk to You Because We Love You* (Lincoln, NE, 2018)

Gilmore, David, *Monsters: Evil Beings, Mythical Beasts, and All Manner of Imaginary Terrors* (Philadelphia, PA, 2003)

Goettner-Abendroth, Heide, ed., *Societies of Peace: Matriarchies Past, Present and Future* (Toronto, 2009)

Gray, Joe, and Patrick Curry, 'Ecodemocracy: Helping Wildlife's Right to Survive', ECOS, XXVII/1 (2016), pp. 18–27

Grusin, Richard, ed., *The Nonhuman Turn* (Minneapolis, MN, 2015)

Haraway, Donna, *When Species Meet* (Minneapolis, MN, 2008)

Harvey, Penny, Christian Krohn-Hansen and Knut Nustad, *Anthropos and the Material* (Durham, NC, 2019)

Huxley, Francis, *The Dragon: Nature of Spirit, Spirit of Nature* (London, 1979)

Joines, Karen, *Serpent Symbolism in the Old Testament: A Linguistic, Archaeological, and Literary Study* (Haddonfield, NJ, 1974)

Lucero, Lisa, 'A Cosmology of Conservation in the Ancient Maya World', *Journal of Anthropological Research*, LXXIV/3 (2018), pp. 327–59

Meijer, Eva, *When Animals Speak: Toward an Interspecies Democracy* (New York, 2019)

Merchant, Carolyn, 'Environmentalism: From the Control of Nature to Partnership', public lecture, University of California, 2010

Miller, Robert, *Baal, St George, and Khidr: A Study of the Historical Geography of the Levant* (University Park, PA, 2019)

Musharbash, Yasmine, and Geir Presterudstuen, eds, *Monster Anthropology: Explorations of Transforming Social Worlds through Monsters* (London and New York, 2019)

Nasr, Seyyed, *An Introduction to Islamic Cosmological Doctrines: Conceptions of Nature and Methods Used for Its Study* (London, 1978)

Neimanis, Astrida, *Bodies of Water: Posthuman Feminist Phenomenology* (London, 2017)

Powell, Barry, *Classical Myth*, trans. Herbert Howe (Upper Saddle River, NJ, 1998)

Riches, Samantha, *St George: Hero, Martyr and Myth* (Stroud, 2005)

Slifer, Dennis, *The Serpent and the Sacred Fire: Fertility Images in Southwest Rock Art* (Santa Fe, NM, 2000)

Spretnak, Charlene, *Lost Goddesses of Early Greece: A Collection of Pre-Hellenic Myths* (Boston, MA, 1992)

Tsing, Anna, *The Mushroom at the End of the World: On the Possibility of Life in Capitalist Ruins* (Princeton, NJ, 2017)

ACKNOWLEDGEMENTS

This book is the outcome of a long and abiding fascination with water serpent beings. It has benefited from the research of many anthropologists, archaeologists and material-culture specialists who have produced the diverse accounts on which comparative analysis relies; from the generous collaboration of indigenous and other communities in Australia, New Zealand, Africa and the UK; and from museum curators around the world, who have shared with me their enthusiasm about the objects and images in their collections. I am also immensely grateful to the researchers in other disciplinary areas – the theologians, historians, classicists, philosophers, neuroscientists and cognitive specialists – on whose expertise I have drawn. Some have been impressively tolerant in welcoming my amateur forays into their disciplinary territories, and I hope they will forgive this endeavour's all-too-fleeting glimpses of their much deeper knowledge. I am especially grateful to the colleagues who reviewed the text and offered sage advice: Elizabeth Edwards, Robert Hannah, Sandy Toussaint and John Day. Any and all remaining errors are entirely my own. Last, but far from least, I must thank my family and friends for embracing my obsessive interest in this topic, to the extent that they are now similarly doomed to spotting serpentine water beings wherever they go. I am particularly indebted to my sister Helen, who kindly cast an eagle eye over the proofs of this text and who, for many years, has tolerated excursions to key water serpent sites, even though my renditions of the Lambton Worm Song, as we climbed Penshaw Hill, drove her to threaten sororicide.

PHOTO ACKNOWLEDGEMENTS

The author and publishers wish to express their thanks to the below sources of illustrative material and/or permission to reproduce it. Some locations of artworks are also given below, in the interest of brevity:

Adobe Stock: 18 (ahau1969), 19 (lunamarina), 25 (matho), 52 (sghiaseddin), 53 (Anton Ivanov Photo), 65 (ngchiyui), 69 (ABCDstock), 70 (frdric), 101 (wjarek), 104 (motorolka); Alamy Stock Photo: 33 (Heritage Image Partnership Ltd – Ashmolean Museum, University of Oxford), 37 (mauritius images GMBH/ Luis Castañeda), 55 (agefotostock/J. D. Dallet – The Egyptian Museum, Cairo), 108 (Jonny White), 115 (TCD/Prod.DB), 118 (John Warburton-Lee Photography/Nigel Pavitt); akg-images /Fototeca Gilardi: 24 (BNF MS grec 2327, fol. 279); © Árni Magnússon Institute/Bridgeman Images: 98; British Library, London: 88 (MS Or 2265, fol. 195r), 106 (1258.b.18); © British Library Board, all rights reserved/Bridgeman Images: 74 (MS Burney 169, fol. 14r), 94 (Maps CC.a.218); © Buku-Larrnggay Mulka Centre, Yirrkala, photo courtesy the House of Representatives, Australian Parliament House, Canberra, reproduced with permission: 126; from Lewis Carroll, *Through the Looking-Glass, and What Alice Found There* (London, 1871): 109; The Cleveland Museum of Art, OH: 2, 22, 58, 62, 121; Dolores Ochoa/AP/Shutterstock: 123; DeAgostini/Getty Images: 86 (photo G. Dagli Orti), 102 (photo G. Nimatallah – Kunsthistorisches Museum, Vienna); © Detroit Institute of Arts, MI/Bridgeman Images: 13; © Dorset Fine Arts, photos courtesy Canadian Museum of History, Gatineau, QC: 43 (IV-C-6001, D2007-04088), 44 (CD 2002-011 SP, IMG2011-0107-0091); Durham Cathedral Library, reproduced by kind permission of the Chapter of Durham Cathedral: 93 (MS A.II.4, fol. 87v); © Estate of the artist, licensed by Aboriginal Artists Agency Ltd, photo courtesy National Museum of Australia, Canberra: 39; Foundation for the Advancement of Mesoamerican Studies (FAMSI): 51; after Henry W. Hamilton, 'The Spiro Mound', *The Missouri Archaeologist*, XIV (October 1952): 45; Heritage Auctions, Ha.com: 111; reproduced by permission of Hodder Children's Books, an imprint of Hachette Children's Group (Carmelite House, 50 Victoria Embankment, London EC4Y 0DZ): 113; Hokusai Museum, Nagano: 66; courtesy Instituto Colombiano de Antropología e Historia (ICANH), Bogotá: 124; The J. Paul Getty Museum, Los Angeles: 77, 85 (MS 101, fol. 82v); © Laura James 2011, used with permission: 119; James Ford Bell Library, University of Minnesota, Minneapolis: 105; photo Stephen Lansing: 50; Los Angeles County Museum of Art (LACMA): 15; © Anne McCaffrey 1988, published by Bantam Press 1989, Corgi 1989, reproduced by permission of the Random House Group Limited: 114; © Mawalan Marika/Copyright Agency, licensed by DACS 2021, photo courtesy Art Gallery of Western Australia (AGWA), Perth: 7; The Metropolitan Museum of Art, New York: 3, 59, 67, 68, 71, 72, 83, 89, 90, 91, 107, 110, 120; courtesy Muzeo Nazionale Romano, Rome: 82 (Inv. Nr. 62666); Museum of Fine Arts, Boston: 79; © Museum of Fine Arts, Houston, TX/ Bridgeman Images: 47; National Museum of Asian Art, Smithsonian Institution, Washington, DC: 87; National Museum of Denmark: 28 (photo Lennart Larsen, CC BY-SA 4.0), 30 (photo Roberto Fortuna and Kira Ursem, CC BY-SA 4.0); National Museum of Korea, Seoul: 26 (Acc. no. Bongwan 4027); Nationalmuseum, Stockholm: 97 (photo Erik Cornelius, CC BY-SA 4.0); The New York Public Library: 46; © Pitt Rivers Museum, University of Oxford: 40; © Science Museum/ Science & Society Picture Library, all rights reserved: 20; photos Polly Schaafsma: 34, 48; photo Kathryn Scott Osler/ The Denver Post via Getty Images: 54; courtesy Pormpuraaw artist Syd Bruce Shortjoe: 125; Shutterstock.com: 9 (Barnes Ian), 14 (Andrea Izzotti – Museo Nacional de Antropología, Mexico City), 80 (Jacek Wojnarowski), 129 (oxameel); photos Veronica Strang: 16, 21, 27, 41, 42, 95, 96, 103, 116, 128, 131; courtesy Tairona Heritage Trust, photo Alan Ereira: 122; photo Gary Todd: 73 (National Archaeological Museum, Athens); © The Tolkien Estate Limited 1937, photo courtesy

Bodleian Libraries, University of Oxford, reproduced with kind permission of the Tolkien Estate: 112; © The Trustees of the British Museum, London: 1, 4, 5, 8, 10, 17, 23, 29, 32, 35, 64, 100, 130; The Walters Art Museum, Baltimore, MD: 63; Wellcome Collection, London: 61 (CC BY 4.0); Werner Forman Archive/Bridgeman Images: 49; Wikimedia Commons: 12 (Chaoborus, CC BY-SA 3.0), 31 (Carole Raddato, CC BY-SA 2.0), 36 (Sarah Welch, CC BY-SA 4.0), 38 (Morio60, CC BY-SA 2.0), 57 (Anandajoti Bhikkhu, CC BY-SA 3.0), 60 (Arian Zwegers, CC BY 2.0), 75 (Carole Raddato, CC BY-SA 2.0 – Museo Archeologico Nazionale di Napoli), 76 (Rufus46, CC BY-SA 3.0), 78 (Francesco Bini/sailko, CC BY 3.0 – Museu Calouste Gulbenkian, Lisbon), 81 (Daderot, public domain – Museo Gregoriano Etrusco, Vatican City), 84 (Alberto Fernandez Fernandez/Afernand74, CC BY-SA 3.0), 92 (Dennis Jarvis, CC BY-SA 2.0), 99 (Harald Groven, CC BY-SA 2.0), 117 (Nationaal Museum van Wereldculturen, CC BY-SA 3.0), 127 (Pax Ahimsa Gethen/funcrunch.org, CC BY-SA 4.0); courtesy Wofford College, Spartanburg, SC: 56 (gift of Dr John M. Bullard); photo Ron Wolf: 6.

INDEX

Illustration numbers are indicated by *italics*

The Abyss (dir. James Cameron) 204, *115*
activism 11, 79, 191, 205–9, 211–27, 230–38
  see also ecological justice; rights, non-human
affective responses to water, biophilia 14, 231, 233–4
African water beings 7, 14, 16, 29, 35, 53, 89–90, 211–15
  Baga water serpent headdress 8, *2*
  Mua Parish Church altar, Malawi *118*
  Mwali and Thunga, Malawi 53, *27*
  see also James, Laura, *Mami Wata*
Alexander the Great's conception in *Les faize d'Alexandre* 134, *74*
Alma Wason, Cape York 75, *42*
Anglo-Saxon water beings 57, 169, *33*
Anglo-Saxon brooch, *Alfred Jewel* 59, *33*
Australian water beings 40, 53, 65, 69–80, 201, 220–23, 233, 236, *7*
  rainbow serpent cave painting, Australia 64, *37*
  see also Marika, Mawalan; Marruwarr, Yuwunyuwun; Nabegeyo, Bilinyara; Shortjoe, Syd Bruce; Yirrkala community artists

Balinese rice terraces 94, *50*
Balinese water beings 94, 211
Beck, Leonhard, *St George Fighting the Dragon* 180, *102*
Blake, William, *Moses Erecting the Brazen Serpent* 145, *79*
Borneo water beings 119
Buddhism 59, 94, 109, 113–15, 119–21
Buddhist water beings 20, 35, 39, 109–11, 113, 119, 121, 123–5, 209–11, *56*
Buddha and the serpent Mucilinda 115, *62*
Burmese water being 211

caduceus 42, 50, 107, 132, *20*
  see also serpent and staff; tree of life
Cambodian water beings 25, 35, 119, 230, *62*
Canadian and Alaskan water beings 80–84, 206
  Niviaqsi, Pitseolak, *Sedna* 81, *43*
  Qinnuayuak, Lucy, *Sedna with Spotted Bird* 83, *44*
celestial water beings 7, 11, 39, 41, 48, 80, 148, 198
  Africa 35, 89
  Australia 22, 71
  China 22–3, 44–5, 125–9, 209
  Egypt 32, 41, 45, 103, 151
  Europe 55–7
  Graeco-Roman 22, 32, 45, 57, 132
  India 111–13
  Islam 156, 159
  Japan 44, 209, *44*
  Judeo-Christian 23, 40–42, 44, 144, 151–3, 163
  Maya 20, 33–4, *39*
  Mesopotamia 23, 31, 145
  New Zealand/Aotearoa 22, 32
  North America 22, 86–9, 198, *45*
  Scandinavia 40
  South America 22, 34, 39, 85–6
  Southeast Asia 23
  see also hydro-theological cycles; sky rivers/Milky Way; swallowing and regurgitation
Cellini, Benvenuto, *Perseus with the Head of Medusa* 138, *76*
Celtic water beings 16, 40, 48, 54–7, 59, 167, 181, 194–7, 231, *28*, *29*, *30*, *129*
Celtic dragon, Dublin Castle 195, *108*
  Hellenistic/La Tène-style Braganza brooch with Celtic warrior 55, *29*
  Wales, national flag 231, *129*
Central American water beings 7, 25, 65, 202
Central American water beings, Aztec 25, 35–6, 38, 53, 61–2, 202, 215–16
  bicephalous (double-headed) serpent 6, *1*
  ehecacozcatl (wind serpent) 215, *120*

xiuhcoatl (lightning serpent) Texcoco 21, 10
xiuhcoatl, Tenochtitlan 28, 14
Central American water beings, Maya 20, 33–8, 49, 53, 59, 95–7, 177, 216, 17
House of the Serpent's Mouth, Chicanná, Mexico 38, 18
Itzam Na, creator being 95, 51
Kukulkan, feathered serpent at Chichen Itza 39, 19
Lady K'ab'al Xook conjuring Maya vision serpent 37, 17
Maya cylinder vessel with water lily serpent 30, 15
Chinese water beings 19, 22–3, 25, 44–5, 47, 49–50, 61, 65, 122–9, 177, 201, 207–9, 69, 116
ascending and descending dragons, Forbidden City, Beijing 208, 116
dragon with arched (bow) back, Beijing 19, 9
dragon pendant, China 15, 5
dragon screen, China 50, 25
Fuxi and Nūwa 51, 26
see also Gakutei, Yashima
climate change 8, 13, 26, 102, 107, 193, 237, 240
see also water issues
cognition 14, 18, 23–5, 29, 44, 216, 234
collapse 26, 90, 95–7, 102, 107–8, 128, 194, 205, 238
cosmogenesis 11, 31–5, 44, 47–8, 53–4, 142, 201, 206
Aboriginal Australia 69, 71, 76–8
Buddhism 20
Canada and Alaska 80–82
Central America 61–2, 215–16
China 47, 50, 61, 127
Greece 32, 57, 129–32, 185
Hinduism 20, 45, 108–9, 113
Islam 157–62
Japan 121–2
Judeo-Christian 31, 142–4, 154, 185
Māori 32–3, 93
Maya 33–4, 37–8, 95
Mesopotamia 31, 34–5, 54, 106, 154
parthenogenesis 60–3, 82, 103, 201, 212
Scandinavia 62
South America 34, 53, 86, 216–18
Southeast Asia 210–11
Vietnam 120
see also gender
Cowell, Cressida, *How to Train Your Dragon* 202, 113
Crusades 172, 176, 190, 196–7, 97
Crusaders slaying dragons and infidels, church carving, Acre 173, 96

damned being cast into Hell, Bourges Cathedral 65, 38
demonization 11, 137–41, 43, 162–82, 201, 218
di Paolo, Giovanni, *The Creation of the World* 164, 90
dominion 121, 194, 202–4, 228, 230
Judeo-Christian 141, 151, 162–8, 182, 185, 189–90, 197–8
see also serpent slaying and subjugation
drought 89–90, 97, 102, 135, 149, 155, 185, 190–91, 208

ecocide 236–7
ecological justice 204, 207, 215, 230, 236–8
see also rights, non-human
Egyptian water beings 20, 22, 32–4, 41–2, 45, 47, 57–9, 103–5, 148, 165, 178, 35
baton with *wedjat*-eye and lotus flowers, Thebes 18, 8
Isis and Osiris in serpent form 104, 55
Ra-Horakhty 46, 23
Wadjet 103, 129, 54
enlightenment, consciousness 20–21, 33–8, 40–44, 71–3, 103, 201–2, 217–18
Australia 71, 73–4
Judeo-Christian 155, 163, 168, 185, 202
Greece 132, 137, 184
India 111–13
Islam 184
Canada, Alaska 82
New Zealand/Aotearoa 225
Scandinavia 176
South America 86, 216–18
Etruscan (Caeretan) hydria, Herakles slaying the Lernaean Hydra 139, 77
European water beings 20, 166–7, 173, 181, 184, 187–8, 194–7, 201–2, 33, 92, 93, 101, 103, 104, 105, 106, 109, 111, 112, 113
biscione (big serpent) of Visconti of Milan 171, 95
bronze serpent, Karlovy Vary, Czechia 187, 104
Draco constellation 23, 11
Flying Serpent of Henham 189, 106
Lambton Worm 172, 196, 199
see also Celtic water beings; Graeco-Roman water beings; Scandinavian water beings
Expulsion of Adam and Eve from Eden, *Falnama*, Iran 158, 87
extinction of species 8, 97, 194, 205

feminized serpent, Notre Dame Cathedral 179, 101
fertility 19, 55–6, 59–60, 86, 106, 199–210, 230–31
Africa 53–4, 213–14
Australia 73–4
Celtic 40, 48, 55–6, 59
Central America 53
China 123, 126–7
Egypt 32, 34, 41, 57, 59–60, 165, 178
Europe 40, 177, 184, 201, 230–31
Graeco-Roman 56, 59, 132–3, 148–9, 178, 185
India 54, 59, 110–15, 178
Islam 144, 178
Japan 121, 199
Judeo-Christianity 60, 143–4, 148, 165, 177–8
Maya 34, 36–7
Mesopotamia 60, 106
North America 60, 86
Scandinavia 173
South America 34, 53
see also lotus and water lily
fiery serpents 7, 20–21, 27, 32, 199
Central America 20–21
Europe 197
Egypt 103, 144
Graeco-Roman 57, 132, 135
India 21, 35, 111, 113, 116

Judeo-Christian 40–42, 144, 163, 168–9, 170, 197
Mesopotamia 61
North America 89
see also lightning serpents

floods 13, 26–9, 80, 191–3, 236
Africa 90, 213
Australia 71, 190, 193, 236
China 123, 128
Egypt 45, 102–3, 144
Europe 184
India 20, 62–3, 108, 191
Islamic 159–61
Judeo-Christian 34, 155, 164–5, 185
Mesopotamia 47, 105–6
North America 87–8
New Zealand/Aotearoa 91
Southeast Asia 94, 191–3

Gakutei, Yashima, *Chinese Sage Evoking a Dragon* 124, *68*

gender 11, 49–55, 60–61, 67, 90, 165
Africa 53, 90, 214
Australia 53
Buddhism 57
Central America 53, 59, 61–2
China 50, 123, 127–8
Egypt 57–60, 165
Europe 54–7, 59
feminization 11, 141, 168, 178–82, 201–2, 215
Greece 57, 59, 130–32, 137, 149
India 59, 108
Islam 156–7
Japan 199
Judeo-Christian 57, 60, 144, 165
Mesopotamian 50, 60–61, 132, 165
North America 60
Scandinavia 54, 62
South America 53
see also cosmogenesis, homologues

George, St 144, 172–3, 177–8, 181, 197–8
Russian icon, *The Miracle of St George* 174, *97*
St George's Day 188
St George and the Virgin and Child Enthroned, icon, Ethiopia 161, *89*
see also Beck, Leonhard; Notkes, Bernard

Graeco-Roman water beings 22, 56–7, 130–33, 178, *71*, *72*, *74*, *76*
Bacchus and Agathodaemon (serpent), Pompeii 136, *75*
see also ouroboros

Graeco-Roman water beings, Greece 32, 35, 42, 48, 56, 129–132, 137, 148–50, 166
Zeus Meilichios 133, *73*
see also Cellini, Benvenuto

Graeco-Roman water beings, Rome 56–7, 131–2, 135, 149, *95*
Ceres, Roman goddess of fertility 148, *82*
Coventina, Romano-Celtic goddess 57, *31*
dragonesque brooch, Romano-British 58, *32*

Greek (Attic)
drinking cup, Jason and Colchian dragon 147, *81*
hippocamp (horse serpent) bell-krater 130, *71*
hydria, serpent in the Garden of Hesperides 131, *72*

Gran, Daniel, *Glory of the Newborn Christ* 152, *84*

growth 97–9, 184, 191–4, 198, 209, 228–9, 241
see also population

Gundestrup Cauldron 56, *30*

hallucinogens 24, 35, 38–9, 113, 148
see also rituals

Harrowing of Hell, The, illustrated *Vita Christi* 153, *85*

Hedgeland, George Caleb, stained-glass window, Norwich Cathedral 146, *80*

Hinduism 20, 39, 59, 94, 109–19, 211, 230
see also Indian water beings

Hokusai, Katsushika
dragon painting, Higashimachi Festival 122, *66*
Tama River in Musashi Province 192, *107*

holy water 168, 184, 211
holy wells 40, 55, 168, 184–7, 231
see also living water

homologues 19, 53–4, 60, 62, 74

Hopi snake (rain) dance 88, *46*

human exceptionalism 67, 80, 91, 189–90, 228–9, 234–5, 239
see also nature-culture dualism

humanization 97, 101, 141–2, 194, 203
Buddhism 115
China 128–9
Egypt 57, 102, 104–5, 107
Graeco-Roman 129, 132–4, 137
Hinduism 59, 107, 110–11, 113–18
Islam 161–2
Japan 121–2
Judeo-Christianity 142–4, 162, 167
Maya 33, 97
New Zealand/Aotearoa 91

hybridity 18, 27, 83–4, 91, 109, 111, 198, 201
Australia 69
China 49, 123
Japan 121
Mesopotamia 61

hydro-electricity 191–2, 226, 235

hydrological cycles 11, 20, 23, 39–40, 45, 87, 96, 127–9
scientific 137, 183, 194

hydro-theological cycles 11, 32–3, 37–8, 40, 44–5, 47, 65–6, 198, 205
Aboriginal Australian 71–4
Canada, Alaska 82–3
Central America 215
Egypt 103, 145, 148, 151
Greece 148–51
India 109, 113
Islamic 159
Judeo-Christian 148–54, 185
Maya 95
Mesopotamia 148
North America 87
South America 66
Zoroastrian 148
see also cosmogenesis; swallowing and regurgitation

immortality 14, 19, 35, 47–8, 103, 105, 113, 151, 178
see also hydro-theological cycles

India and Indian water beings 18, 35, 39, 45–8, 80, 108–9, 111–18, 121, 178, *36*, *58*, *59*, *60*, *61*, *63*, *100*
Aghasura the Serpent Demon Swallows Krishna 116, *63*

Bahram Gur Killing the Dragon, Mughal India 177, 100
Indus Valley 107–11
Krishna dancing on the serpent Kaliya 117, 64
Lajjā Gaurī, fertility goddess 111, 59
Vishnu incarnated as Matsya 114, 61
Vishnu on Ananta, the Endless Serpent 110, 58
see also Hinduism; *makaras*; *nāgas*
irrigation 93–4, 97–8, 101, 118, 141, 185, 190–93
Australia 79–80, 190
Bengal 108
China 192
Egypt 59–60, 98, 101–3
Europe 191
India 107–8, 111, 191
Japan 121, 191–2
Maya 95–7
Mesopotamia 105–6
North America 192–3
Russia 191
South America 216–17
Southeast Asia 99, 121
see also water infrastructure
Islamic beings 43, 151, 155–62, 87
Al-Lāt, goddess, Temple of Ba'alshamin 156, 86
Muhammad's ascension to Heaven 160, 88
Islamic water beings
Jonah and the Whale, from *Jami al-Tavarikh* 150, 83

'Jabberwocky' 196–7, 202
see also Tenniel, John; European water beings, Lambton Worm
James, Laura, *Mami Wata* 214, 119
Japan, water beings 7, 29, 40, 44, 121–22, 201, 209
see also Hokusai, Katsushika; Kuniyoshi, Utagawa; Nichokuan, Soga
Java, Indonesia, water beings 25, 209–11, 4, 57
Nyai Blorong, Goddess of the Sea 210, 117
Judeo-Christian beings 13, 42–3, 56–7, 65, 142–3, 151, 153–5, 164–8, 178, 38, 79, 80, 84, 85, 89, 90, 91, 92, 94, 96, 97, 101, 102
bishop's crozier, Armenia 143, 78
Gnostic gem with lion-headed serpent 166, 91
Moses' serpent, Milan 43, 21
saint trampling a serpent, St Matthew's Gospel, *Bible of William of St Calais* 169, 93
see also serpent slaying; Blake, William; Gran, Daniel

Kennedy, Karen, *taniwha* 226, 128
Kogi Mama, Jacinto Zarabata 218, 122
Kuniyoshi, Utagawa, *Recovering the Stolen Jewel from the Dragon King* 123, 67

Lancaster, Lilian, St Patrick driving the snakes out of Ireland 170, 94
Laos water beings 35, 119, 12
lightning water beings 7, 20, 41–2, 89
Australia 71
Central America 96
Europe 169–70
Graeco-Roman 133
India 111
Judeo-Christian 144, 154–5
North America 89, 216
Scandinavia 173
see also fiery serpents
living water 21–2, 187, 223, 225
see also holy water
lotus 18, 20, 33, 54, 121
Buddhism 29
Egypt 20, 33, 40, 57, 103
Hinduism 20
India 18, 33, 54, 110–11, 113–15, 118
Maya 20, 33, 96
Southeast Asia 33, 54, 121
see also water lily

McCaffrey, Anne, *Dragonsdawn* 203, 114
Magnus, Olaus, sea orm (worm), *Carta Marina* 188, 105
makaras 18, 25, 54, 109–10, 121, 56
Vientiane, Laos 24, 12
Kidal Temple, East Java 109, 57
Māori/Polynesian water beings *see* New Zealand/Aotearoa
Marika, Mawalan, *The Wawilag Sisters and Yulungurr, the Rainbow Serpent* 17, 7
Marruwarr, Yuwunyuwun, *Rainbow Serpent*, Australia 68, 39
Martinez, Maria, and Julian Martinez, *Bowl with Avanyu* 88, 47
medieval sword (falchion) 197, 110
Mesopotamian water beings 23, 31, 34–5, 45, 60–61, 106, 131–2, 1 48, 154
Neo-Assyrian horned serpent, possibly Tiâmat 61, 35
monotheisms, emergence of 11, 141–2, 156, 165
monstrous water/serpent beings 26–9, 63–5, 76, 91, 140, 153–4, 185, 201–3
China 177
Europe 170–73, 176, 181, 202
Graeco-Roman 139–40
India 176
Islamic 176
Judeo-Christian 168, 176, 185
Maya 177
New Zealand/Aotearoa 93
Scandinavia 173–6
Southeast Asia 177
Mua Parish Church, Malawi 212, 118

Nabegeyo, Bilinyara, *Yingarna, the Rainbow Serpent*, Australia 70, 40
nāgas 13, 21, 35, 39, 62–3, 111–13, 116–18
Chennakeshava Temple, Karnataka, India 112, 60
nāgarāja, Badami cave temples, Karnataka, India 63, 36
nature-culture dualism 67, 99, 140–41, 163, 189, 229–30, 239–40
alternatives to 201–2, 206–7, 227–30, 234–5, 239–41
Nenquimo, Nemonte, and Ecuadorian activists 219, 123
neo-pagan water celebration, Oxford 232, 239, 131
New Zealand/Aotearoa water beings 22, 32–3, 63, 65, 91–3, 177, 225–7, 234–6

Māori house post, carved *taniwha* 92, 49
Māori *koropepe* 130
see also Kennedy, Karen
Nichokuan, Soga, *Dragon* 44, 22
North American serpent beings 16, 25, 60, 84, 86–9, 216, 223, 6, 114, 115
horned serpent, pueblo rock art 60, 34
horned serpent with maize collar, New Mexico 89, 48
winged rattlesnakes, Oklahoma 87, 45
see also Hopi snake (rain) dance; Martinez, Maria, and Julian Martinez; Price, Dick
Notkes, Bernard, *St George and the Dragon* 167, 92

Ophites 14, 165–6
order and disorder/chaos 25–9, 31–4, 44, 84, 90, 163, 201–2, 205–7
Africa 53, 213–15
Australia 67, 69–71, 73, 80
Canada and Alaska 82–3, 206
China 61, 127
Egypt 32, 34, 103
Graeco-Roman 129–32, 140
India 176
Islam 157, 161, 185
Judeo-Christian 142, 154–5, 168, 172, 176, 178, 185, 198, 201
Maya 33, 95
Mesopotamia 31, 106
New Zealand/Aotearoa 32, 93
North America 87, 223
South America 66, 86, 216
Southeast Asia 210–11
ouroboros 19, 47–8, 50, 103, 105, 167, 173, 98
see also Pelecanos, Theodoros

paradise 14, 43, 45, 157, 159, 165, 185
Pelecanos, Theodoros, *ouroboros* 47, 24
personhood 44, 206, 234–6
shape-shifting 49, 76, 80, 121, 201, 203
population 10, 68, 85, 91, 193, 205, 229
growth, irrigation 96–7, 101, 105, 107, 184, 191–3, 205
growth, technology 135, 184, 191–2, 209
movement 7, 13, 69, 102, 108
Price, Dick, *Sisiutl* 25, 13
protest against Dakota Access Pipeline 224, 127

qanat, Iran 98, 52

rainbow 16, 50, 53, 153, 183
serpents, Africa 19, 35, 53, 89–90, 211
serpents, Australia 18, 19, 40, 53, 65, 67–80, 220–23, 236
serpents, China 19, 50
serpents, India 39
serpents, South America 24–5, 216–17
serpents, Southeast Asia 25, 121
re-imagined communities 239
rights to water
indigenous 67, 79, 205, 215–27
non-human 207, 218–24, 233–42
see also ecological justice
rituals 53, 84
Africa 86–89, 211–15
Australia 16, 40, 73–6, 78, 220, 223, 232
Canada and Alaska 82, 206
Celtic/European 40, 55, 59, 230–32
Central America 25, 36–9, 95–7, 215
China 123, 207–9, 230
Egypt 14, 59–60, 102, 151
Greece 14, 19, 132–3, 148–51
India 35, 109–13, 230
Japan 209
Judeo-Christian 14, 148, 168, 184, 194, 197, 218
New Zealand/Aotearoa 32–3, 225
North America 60, 86–9, 216, 223
Ophite 14
Roman 57
Scandinavia 40, 176
South America 24, 39–40, 53–4, 86, 216–18
Southeast Asia 94, 210–11, 230
rituals, types of
baptism and mortuary 75–6, 147–8, 220
communion 14, 148, 176, 231
dragon slaying 168, 197
enlightenment/visions 25, 35, 36–8, 150
fertility 19, 53, 57, 59–60, 74, 102, 123, 149, 231
healing 78, 82, 213, 231
mortuary 73
propitiation 14, 97, 113, 195–6
rain-making 53, 74, 86, 89–90, 96–7, 207–9, 212, 216
under/otherworld entry 38–40, 73, 76–8, 95, 149
veneration 54, 75, 84, 94, 113, 133, 135, 166–8, 194, 206
veneration as political statement 213, 215–18, 220, 225, 230–33
see also hallucinogens
Russell, Ken, *The Lair of the White Worm* 199, 111

Scandinavian water beings 29, 40, 48, 62, 170, 173–6
Jörmungandr, the Midgard serpent 48, 173, 175, 98
Sigurd slaying Fafnir, Hylestad stave church 176, 99
Viking double-headed water being 54, 28
science 21–2, 27, 129, 135–7, 183–4, 188–9, 194, 229
serpent and staff 42, 103, 106–7, 132, 144–7, 149, 80
Moses 42–3, 144–7, 165, 168, 225, 20, 21, 78, 79
see also caduceus and tree of life
serpent slaying/subjugation 166, 176, 202–3
Central America 177
China 177
Europe 171–2, 188, 194–7
Egypt 107, 166
Graeco-Roman 35, 116, 132, 139–40, 166, 76, 77
India 116, 118, 176, 63, 64, 100
Islam 176–7
Japan 122

Judeo-Christian 143–4, 163–82, 187–8, 194, 202, 85, 89, 92, 93, 94, 96, 97, 102, 106, 109, 110
New Zealand/Aotearoa 91–3, 177
Maya 177
Mesopotamia 61, 106, 35
Scandinavia 173–6, 177, 98, 99
Vietnam 177
see also dominion
Shortjoe, Syd Bruce, rainbow serpent 221, 125
sky rivers/Milky Way 7, 22, 39, 45, 47–8, 71, 59, 127
Smaug (*The Hobbit*) 200, 201, 112
South American water beings 216–17, 219–20
Arawak 22, 86
Desana 24–5, 34, 39–40, 53–4
Instituto Colombiano de Antropologia e Historia, Bogota, logo 220, 124
Kogi 66, 217–18, 122
Moche nose ornament, Peru 217, 121
Muisca *tunjos* (serpent beings) 9, 3
South Korean water being, Haedong Yonggungsa Temple 120–21, 65
swallowing and regurgitation 44–8, 65–6
Australia 40, 71–3, 76–8
Central America 38–40, 216
China 47, 125–7
Egypt 45, 57
Europe 40
Greece 150–54
India 45–7, 109, 116, 63
Islam 151
Judeo-Christian 151–3, 155, 162
Mesopotamia 47
North America 87
Scandinavia 40, 48
South America 39–40, 86–7
Southeast Asia 109
see also hydro-theological cycles; *ouroboros*; underworlds

Tenniel, John, 'Jabberwocky' illustration in *Through the Looking-Glass* 109
Tibetan sea serpent horn 108, 56
totemism, ancestral beings 22, 63, 67, 69–74, 86, 91, 235–6
trajectories of development 96–7, 99, 118, 190
tree of life 14, 54, 106–7, 145–7, 149, 151, 165–6, 194, 79, 80
tree of knowledge 43, 132, 139, 145–7
worship of, 55, 121, 168, 231
see also caduceus and serpent and staff
twin, bicephalous or multicephalous serpents
Africa 53
Central America 25, 33, 53, 61–3, 1, 17, 19
China 50, 127, 26, 69, 116
Egypt 45, 57, 55
Europe 59, 202, 20, 29
Graeco-Roman 42, 76, 77, 82
India 35, 109, 58, 60, 64
Mesopotamia 50, 107, 145
New Zealand 63, 91
North America 25, 54, 13
Scandinavia 54, 28
South America 24–5, 53, 121
Southeast Asia 35, 54, 109, 120, 12, 16, 57, 62

underworlds/other worlds 29, 44, 141, 148, 153
Australian 40, 71–3
Canadian and Alaskan 80, 82
Celtic 40
China 44–5, 127
Egypt 32, 41, 45, 103, 105, 144, 148, 151
Europe 169, 181, 198, 230
Greek 132, 148–51, 153–4
Indian 39, 111–13, 115
Islam 156–7, 159–61
Judeo-Christian 23, 65, 143, 147–8, 151–4, 163–5
Maya 20, 33, 37–9, 53, 95–7
Mesopotamia 61, 148
New Zealand/Aotearoa 32–3, 225
North American 84, 87, 89
Scandinavian 40, 54, 62
South American 39–40, 53
Southeast Asia 121

Vietnamese water beings 23, 120, 70
multi-headed serpent being 36, 16

water feature, Versailles 185, 103
water infrastructure 26, 97–8, 109, 184, 188, 190–91, 209, 229, 241
aqueducts and canals 105, 106, 107–8, 127–8, 134–5, 184, 191
dams, ancient 8, 60, 79–80, 96, 101–2, 106, 128, 157
dams, modern 184, 190–93, 209, 235
waterwheels 98–9, 106–7, 135, 157
see also irrigation
water issues
land clearance and drainage 97, 102, 182, 190, 193–4, 219
mining 79, 193–4, 235
overuse/scarcity 8, 26, 97, 191–3, 235
ownership 69, 75, 85, 194, 221, 226
pollution 26, 79, 82, 116, 184, 193, 223, 225, 237
salinity 193
water quality and health 8, 26, 79, 137, 184–6, 189, 191, 193–4, 235
water, materiality 14, 18, 22, 25–6, 28–9, 44–5
waterhole, Cape York, Australia 72, 41
water wheel (*noria*), Syria 99, 53

Yirrkala community artists, *Bark Petition* 79, 126

Zoroastrianism 143, 148, 178